Harrison's Illust...

How to make a
Single Family Appraisal on the

Uniform Residential URAR Appraisal Report

FHLMC Form 70-FNMA Form 1004
Revised 6/93

Includes:

- Full Case Study and Model Appraisal
- Current Guidelines from
  Fannie Mae, Freddie Mac, and VA

- Model Comments and
  Consistency Checks
- 400 Pages
- 230 Illustrations

by Henry S. Harrison
MAI, SRPA, RM, ASA, IFAS, CSA, DREI

Published by the H Squared Company
315 Whitney Avenue
New Haven, CT 06511

Phone: (203) 561-3159 • FAX: (203) 562-5481

COPYRIGHT PAGE

How to Make a Single Family Appraisal on the Uniform Residential URAR Appraisal Report FHLMC Form 70 - FNMA Form 1004 Revised 6/93

by Henry S. Harrison
MAI, SRPA, RM, ASA, IFAS, CSA, DREI

ISBN 0-927054-33-7

©2005 by H Squared Company
All rights reserved.
Printed in the United States of America

1st	Printing	Edition 1	December	1977
11th	Printing	Edition 2	March	1987
18th	Printing	Edition 3	January	1990
25th	Printing	Edition 4	November	1993
28th	Printing	Edition 5	February	1994
29th	Printing	Edition 6	April	1998
34th	Printing		March	2002
35th	Printing		March	2003
36th	Printing	Edition 7	January	2005

No copyrighted material in this book may be reproduced in any manner, including photo-copies or slides for AV presentations or Internet or other electronic reproduction or transmission without prior written permission.

For permission, write: The H Squared Co, 315 Whitney Avenue, New Haven, CT 06511

Cover Design: Jeffrey Starkes

Printed in the United State of America

THE APPRAISER'S LEGACY

THE APPRAISERS' LEGACY: THE UNIFORM RESIDENTIAL APPRAISAL REPORT

The industry and diligence of a small dedicated, independent ad hoc committee, the Uniform Appraisal Form committee, has produced the Uniform Residential Appraisal Report. What began in late 1983 as an exploratory dialogue regarding the feasibility of having a common residential appraisal form involving the Department of Housing and Urban Development (FHA), the Veterans Administration, the Farmers Home Administration, the Federal National Mortgage Association (Fannie Mae), the Federal Home Loan Mortgage Corporation (Freddie Mac) and the appraisal profession, itself, has culminated three years later in a finished common form.

The UAF committee consisted of representatives from these six various factions, who in total accounted for 5,000,000 residential appraisals per year on several different forms. As of October, 1986, Fannie Mae and Freddie Mac made the joint public announcement that they have adopted the URAR. The government agencies followed suit as of 1987. And so it happened! What was once only an appraiser's dream, a Uniform Residential Appraisal Report, has become a reality.

In reflection, the URAR had three development stages from late 1983, through the fall of 1986: (1) Three years of dialogue, creative design and planning and development control by the Uniform Appraisal Committee; (2) the six month test and critque period, from October of 1985 through March of 1986, wherein over 40,000 appraisals were made across the country; and (3) the vendor review, which provided final software and print position counsel, once the form itself had been determined. The UAF committee sincerely believes that this development plan has resulted in a uniform appraisal report that is professional in concept and practice, has grassroots support before the fact, and is technically print position accurate.

Indoctrination regarding the URAR is of paramount importance to appraisers and mortgage loan underwiters. The new form satisfies and complements current professional appraisal standards of practice, including the new Uniform Standards of Professional Appraisal Practice. The URAR is not a standards document per se, nor is it a form dictated by regulators of financial institutions. Suffice it to say, appraisers and lenders, as well as all other real estate practitioners related to housing America should learn the nuances of this new valuation report. Ergo: "HARRISON'S ILLUSTRATED GUIDE-HOW TO FILL OUT A FREDDIE MAC-FANNIE MAE SINGLE FAMILY RESIDENTIAL APPRAISAL REPORT -- 1987."

Now that the uniform appraisal report has been created through the unprecedented communion of efforts of HUD, the VA, FmHA, Fannie Mae, Freddie Mac and the appraisal profession, the major concern of the UAF committee is that the integrity of the form should be preserved by the appraisal community-at-large, lest the benefits of the uniform report be lost forever.

The slightest URAR changes, i.e. substitute statements, moved boxes and/or lines, would serve to make obsolete the form as it relates to software programs, pre-printed forms, data retrieval programs and main frame computer programs. Accordingly, capricious or random URAR modification places in jeopardy the entire uniform appraisal concept.

If time argues that a URAR change may be warranted, the UAF committee mechanism that brought the URAR into being might be reconvened for review and update purposes. Absent the professional need for change, the appraisal community should appreciate its URAR legacy.

F. Gregory Opelka, MAI-SREA

FOREWORD

This 2005 Illustrated Guide, like its predecessors, was prepared to help appraisers make better use of the URAR (Uniform Residential Appraisal Report (Freddie Mac #70 - Fannie Mae #1004). The original URAR was the result of years of work by the Uniform Appraisal Form Committee. The driving force behind this effort was F. Gregory Opelka, SREA, MAI - appraisal consultant to the US League of Savings Institutions. Old timers will remember that he was one of the original developers of the "Green Hornet", the great-grandfather of the URAR form.

The revised June 1993 URAR has been in use for appraisal of single family properties as of January 1, 1994. The revisions resulted from a joint effort that included Fannie Mae, Freddie Mac, HUD, VA and an appraisal industry working group. Representatives of the Appraisal Standards Board of the Appraisal Foundation reviewed the revised forms to assure that they were in compliance with the Uniform Standards of Professional Appraisal Practice (USPAP).

Incorporated into this book are many Fannie Mae, Freddie Mac, and VA guidelines. Many of these guidelines are no longer in effect. They are included because they provide an insight in to how these organizations expected the URAR to be completed. The 01/01/05 USPAP revisions were also considered. Suggestions are made in the appropriate places on how to make your appraisals comply with the revised 2005 USPAP. It is important that you make yourself aware of all current USPAP requirements.

The Model Comments section of the book has been expanded in this edition. By purchasing a copy of this guide, you have obtained our permission to use them as you wish. I recommend that you customize them for each property and appraisal assignment you do. The Model Comments and other material in this book were developed and field-tested by ABC-America's Home buying Consultants, of North Haven, Connecticut.

In July 2004 Fannie Mae released a new test version of the URAR. As a result of this test a second test version was released in November 2004. This new test version is specifically designed for a mortgage appraisal. It is very rigid and is designed to be for a limited appraisal only. In its current format it is six pages. Fannie Mae announced at the sometime that they are hoping to issue a final revised URAR in the spring of 2005 that will be mandatory for their purposes in the Summer of 2005. If the final revised URAR is designed only for a limited appraisal it is likely that the current URAR will continue to be used by appraisers for non Fannie Mae appraisals

My thanks to my wife, Ruth Lambert, who helped me update this book.

I like to hear from appraisers who use this book, who have questions or suggestions or problems. Please contact me by phone at (203) 562-3159 or FAX to (203) 562-5481 or E-mail henryhsq@aol.com or write to: 315 Whitney Avenue; New Haven, CT 06511.

Henry S. Harrison
January 2005

TABLE OF CONTENTS

Title Page	i
Copyright Page	ii
Appraiser's Legacy	iii
Foreword	iv
Table of Contents	v
Special Instructions - FNMA	viii
Special Instructions - VA	ix
Uniform Standards of Appraisal Practice (USPAP)	xiii
Front of the Form	xvii

SUBJECT

Introduction	1-1
Property Address	1-2
Legal Description	1-3
Assessor's Parcel No.	1-4
Tax Year & R.E. Taxes	1-5
Special Assessments	1-6
Borrower	1-7
Owner	1-8
Occupant	1-9
Property rights appraised	1-10
HOA $/Mo.	1-12
Neighborhood or Project Name	1-13
Map Reference	1-14
Census Tract	1-15
Sale Price, Date of Sale	1-16
Loan Charges/concessions by seller $	1-18
Lender/Client & Address	1-19
Appraiser Name & Address	1-20

NEIGHBORHOOD

Introduction	2-1
Location	2-4
Built up	2-6
Growth Rate	2-7
Property Values	2-7
Demand Supply	2-8
Marketing Time	2-9
Predominant Occupancy	2-11
Single Family Housing Price & Age Range	2-12
Present Land Use %	2-14
Land Use Change	2-15
Racial Composition	2-16
Boundaries	2-17
Factors that affect the marketability of the properties	2-19
Market conditions in the subject neighborhood	2-24

PUD

Introduction	3-1
Project Information for PUDs (if applicable)	3-3
Approximate total number of units in subject project	3-4
Approximate total number of units for sale in subject project	3-5
Describe common elements and recreational facilities	3-6
Addenda	3-7
Addenda Form	3-8

SITE

Introduction	4-1
Dimensions, Site Area	4-2
Corner Lot	4-4
Specific zoning classification and description	4-5
Zoning compliance	4-6
Highest & best use as improved	4-9
Utilities	4-12
Off-site improvements	4-14
Topography, Size, Shape, Drainage	4-16
View	4-18
Landscaping	4-19
Driveway Surface	4-20
Apparent easements	4-21
FEMA Special Flood Hazard Area, FEMA Zone, Map Date, FEMA Map No.	4-23
Comments	4-26

DESCRIPTION OF THE IMPROVEMENTS

Introduction	5-1

GENERAL DESCRIPTION

No. of Units	5-4
No. of Stories	5-4
Type (Det./Att.)	5-5
Design (Style)	5-8
Existing/Proposed	5-9
Age (Yrs), Effective Age (Yrs)	5-11

EXTERIOR DESCRIPTION

Foundation	5-13
Exterior Walls	5-14
Roof Surface	5-15
Gutters & Dwnspts	5-16
Window Type	5-17
Storm/Screens	5-18
Manufactured House	5-19

TABLE OF CONTENTS

FOUNDATION
- Slab, Crawl Space, Basement — 5-20
- Sump Pump, Dampness — 5-22
- Settlement — 5-23
- Infestation — 5-24

BASEMENT
- Area Sq. Ft., % Finished — 5-25
- Ceiling, Walls, Floor — 5-26
- Outside Entry — 5-27
- Comments (Blank) — 5-27

INSULATION
- Roof/Ceiling/Walls/Floor/ — 5-28
- None/Unknown — 5-28

ROOMS
- Description — 5-30
- Gross Living Area — 5-30

INTERIOR
- Introduction — 5-35
- Floors — 5-36
- Walls — 5-36
- Trim/Finish — 5-37
- Bath Floor — 5-38
- Bath Wainscot — 5-39
- Doors — 5-40
- Comments (Blank) — 5-41

HEATING
- Type, Fuel, Condition — 5-42

COOLING
- Central, Other, Condition — 5-43

KITCHEN EQUIP.
- Refrigerator, Range/Oven, Disposal, Dishwasher, Fan/Hood, Microwave, Washer/Dryer — 5-44

ATTIC
- None/Stairs/Drop Stair/ Scuttle/Floor/Heating/Finished — 5-46

AMENITIES
- Fireplace(s)#, Patio, Deck, Porch, Fence, Pool — 5-48

CAR STORAGE — 5-49
None — 5-49

- Garage # of cars — 5-49
  - Attached/Detached/Built-in — 5-49
- Carport — 5-49
- Driveway — 5-49

COMMENTS
- Additional Features
  - energy efficient items — 6-1
  - etc. — 6-2
- Condition of improvements — 6-4
- Depreciation
  - physical — 6-5
  - functional — 6-7
  - external — 6-9
- repairs needed — 6-11
- quality of construction — 6-13
- remodeling/additions — 6-14
- etc.
  - warranty information, other — 6-16
  - room size/layout — 6-18
  - closets and storage — 6-20
  - energy efficiency — 6-21
  - plumbing - adequacy & condition — 6-22
  - electrical - adequacy & condition — 6-23
  - kitchen cabinets - adequacy & condition — 6-25
  - conformity to neighborhood — 6-27
  - appeal and marketability — 6-28
- Adverse environmental conditions — 6-29

VALUATION SECTION
Back of Form — 6-33

COST APPROACH
- Introduction — 7-1
- ESTIMATED SITE VALUE — 7-3
- ESTIMATED REPRODUCTION COST-NEW-OF THE IMPROVEMENTS — 7-4
- Total Estimated Cost New — 7-5
- Depreciation:
  - Physical/Functional/External — 7-6
- Depreciated Value of Improvements — 7-8
- "As-is" Value of Site Improvements — 7-9
- **INDICATED VALUE BY COST APPROACH** — 7-10
- Comments on Cost Approach
  - source of cost estimate — 7-11
  - site value — 7-12
  - square foot calculation — 7-14
  - for HUD, VA, FmHA, — 7-15
    - the estimated remaining economic life of the property

TABLE OF CONTENTS

SALES COMPARISON ANALYSIS
- Introduction — 8-1
- Grid — 8-3
- General Instructions — 8-4
- Address — 8-7
- Proximity to Subject — 8-8
- Sales Price — 8-9
- Price/Gross Liv. Area — 8-10
- Data and/or Verification Source — 8-11

VALUE ADJUSTMENTS
- Sales or Financing Concessions — 8-14
- Date of Sale/Time — 8-17
- Location — 8-19
- Leasehold/Fee Simple — 8-21
- Site — 8-22
- View — 8-24
- Design & Appeal — 8-25
- Quality of Construction — 8-27
- Age — 8-29
- Condition — 8-31
- Above Grade Room Count/ Gross Living Area — 8-33
- Basement & Finished Rooms Below Grade — 8-37
- Functional Utility — 8-39
- Heating/Cooling — 8-41
- Energy Efficient Items — 8-43
- Garage/Carport — 8-44
- Porches, Patio, Deck, Fireplace(s), Fence, Pool, etc. — 8-46
- Other (blank) — 8-48
- Net Adj. (total) — 8-49
- Adjusted Sale Price of Comparable — 8-50
- Comments on Sales Comparison — 8-51

SALES HISTORY
- Subject and Comparables — 8-53
- Analysis of Current Agreement of Sale/Option or Listing of Subject Property — 8-55
- Analysis of Prior Sales — 8-55

INDICATED VALUE BY SALES COMPARISON APPROACH — 8-57

INDICATED VALUE BY INCOME APPROACH — 9-1

RECONCILIATION
- Introduction — 10-1
- This appraisal is made: — 10-4
  "as is", subject to repairs, alterations, inspections, conditions, subject to completion per plans and specifications
- Conditions of Appraisal — 10-7
- Final Reconciliation — 10-8
- Purpose of the appraisal — 10-10
- Conditions — 10-12
- Certification — 10-12
- Contingent & limiting conditions — 10-12
- Market Value Definition — 10-12

MARKET VALUE — 10-12

DATE OF APPRAISAL, EFFECTIVE DATE — 10-12

APPRAISER:
- Signature/Name — 10-14
- Date Report Signed — 10-14
- Certification#/License #/State — 10-14

SUPERVISORY APPRAISER (ONLY IF REQUIRED):
- Signature/Name — 10-17
- Did/Did Not Inspect Property — 10-17
- Date Report Signed — 10-17
- Certification#/License #/State — 10-17

ATTACHMENTS — 10-19

APPRAISER'S CERTIFICATION AND LIMITING CONDITIONS (FHLMC 439-FNMA 1004B)
- front of form — 10-21
- back of form — 10-22
- Statement of Limiting Conditions and Appraiser's Certification — 10-23

ENERGY ADDENDUM — EA-1 TO EA-8

SINGLE FAMILY — RS-1 to RS-3

COMPARABLE RENT SCHEDULE (FNMA 1007)

OPERATING INCOME STATEMENT (FNMA 216) — OI-1 to OI-10

APPRAISAL CASE STUDY — CS-1 to CS-22

CASE STUDY SOLUTION — CS-23 to CS-43

FREDDIE MAC BULLETIN — FM-1 to FM-16

Advertisements

SPECIAL INSTRUCTIONS - FNMA

Fannie Mae   June 30, 2002   Part XI Chapter 2, Section 203
Appraisal (or Property Inspection Reports)

Our appraisal report forms recognize the Uniform Standards of Professional Appraisal Practice as the minimum appraisal standards for the appraisal industry. In addition, we have established our own separate appraisal requirements to supplement the Uniform Standards because we believe that this is necessary to assure that all of our specific concerns are addressed for any given appraisal. Our appraisal report forms are designed in a way that results in an appraiser's being in full compliance with our requirements if he or she provides all of the information required by the forms and presents the applicable data accurately and completely.

The appraisal report forms we use provide a concise format for presenting both the appraiser's description of the subject property and the valuation analysis that leads to the opinion of market value. The appraisal report that should be used generally, depends on the underwriting method and the type of property that is being appraised. The appraiser must complete our forms in a way that will clearly reflect the thoroughness of his or her investigation and analysis and provide the rationale for the opinion of market value. Although the scope or extent of the appraisal process is guided by our appraisal report forms, the forms do not limit or control the appraisal process. The appraiser's analysis should go beyond any limitations of the forms, with additional comments and exhibits being used if they are needed ~to adequately describe the subject property; document the analysis and valuation process, or support the appraiser's conclusions. The extent of the appraiser's data collection, analysis, and reporting must be determined by the complexity of the appraisal assignment.

An appraiser may use computer software programs that are designed to reproduce our appraisal report forms—including programs that have—"expandability" features that allow increases in areas of the forms that call for the insertion of narrative comments. However, the sequence of the Information—as well as all of the specific information (including the instructions, entries, directions, etc.)—must be exactly as it appears on the hard-copy of the forms(s).

A lender may accept an appraisal report that is transmitted electronically using facsimile (fax) machines, Internet connections, wireless transmissions, or any other types of transmissions that use public or private telephone lines-as long as the appraisal report adequately identifies the appraiser and includes a reproduced signature of the appraiser whose name appears on the report, and the lender represents and warrants to us that the appraisal report was created by the appraiser identified on the appraisal report and that the appraisal report is the complete and unaltered report submitted by the identified appraiser. The lender may store any appraisal reports it receives (whether they are originally provided as paper documents or in electronic format) by using any photographic, electronic, optical, or other storage technology that enables it to retrieve and reproduce a complete and clear copy of an appraisal report (and Its related addenda, photographs, and attachments) at any time in response to a request from us. Regardless of the transmission or storage method used, the lender will be responsible for the accuracy of the information and the integrity of the documents and for assuring that the appraisal was prepared in accordance with our appraisal guidelines.

We have five different appraisal forms that can be used for manually underwritten mortgages, depending on either the type of property being appraised or the type of mortgage that is secured by the property The appraiser must use our latest version of one of the following forms and include any other data—either as an attachment or addendum to the appraisal report form-needed to adequately support the opinion of market value:

• *Uniform Residential Appraisal Report* (Form 1004), for one-family properties and units in planned unit developments (including those that have an illegal second unit or accessory apartment that we will consider as acceptable security) that secure either first or second mortgages. Form 1004 may also be used for two-family properties, if each of the units is occupied by one of the co-borrowers as his or her principal residence or if the value of the legal second unit is relatively insignificant in relation to the total value of the property (as might be the case for a basement unit or a unit over a garage). In addition, appraisals for units in condominium projects that consist solely of detached dwellings may be documented on Form 1004, if the appraiser includes an adequate description of the project and information about the owners' association fees and the quality of the project maintenance.

Fannie Mae   June 30, 2002   Part XI   Property and Appraisal Guidelines Introduction

This Part—Property and Appraisal Guidelines—details our general requirements for analyzing the property appraisal aspects of conventional mortgages secured by one- to four-family properties. It also discusses

SPECIAL INSTRUCTIONS - FNMA

special considerations for certain types of housing—units in condominium, PUD, and cooperative projects; manufactured (and other factory-built) homes; Community Living group homes; mixed-use properties; properties affected by environmental hazards; urban properties; affordable housing program properties; properties located in special assessment or community facilities districts; properties subject to leasehold interests (including those held by community land trusts); and energy-efficient properties—that merit special consideration in the property and appraisal review. Because the evaluation of a property is such a vital part of the risk analysis, we expect a lender to place as much emphasis on underwriting the property and reviewing the appraisal as it does on underwriting the borrower's creditworthiness.

We require the appraiser to provide complete and accurate reports; to report neighborhood and property conditions in factual and specific terms; to be impartial and specific in describing favorable or unfavorable factors; and to avoid the use of subjective, racial, or stereotypical terms, phrases, or comments in the appraisal report. The opinion of market value must represent the appraiser's professional conclusion, based on market data, logical analysis, and judgment. When the information or methodology of an appraisal requires additional clarification or justification, the lender's underwriter must obtain from the appraiser any information that is necessary to make an informed decision concerning the property.

We require that the appraiser and the lender follow appropriate practices in the property valuation and underwriting processes. Our appraisal standards specifically prohibit the' development of a valuation conclusion that is based on race, color, religion, sex, handicap, familial status, or national origin. The effectiveness of our property underwriting guidelines is dependent on the ability of a lender and its appraisers to avoid the use of potentially discriminatory practices in the property appraisal and underwriting processes.

We hold the lender responsible for the accuracy of both the appraisal and its assessment of the marketability of the property; therefore, it is important for a lender's underwriters to understand their role in the appraisal process and their relationship to the appraiser.

• **The appraiser's role** is to provide the lender with an accurate, and adequately supported, opinion of value and an accurate description of the property

• **The underwriter's role** is to review the appraisal report to assure that it is of professional quality and is prepared in a way that is consistent with our appraisal standards, to analyze the property based on the appraisal, and to judge the property's acceptability as security for the mortgage requested in view of its value and marketability.

These requirements are intended to provide guidance to an underwriter and an appraiser about the type of Information that is needed to make a prudent underwriting decision. They are also designed to provide our minimum acceptable appraisal standards. We recognize that our guidelines may not address every appraisal problem; therefore, we allow the appraiser discretion to properly develop the value opinion. The appraiser must, however, provide sound reasoning in his or her appraisal report for any decisions he or she makes that are not specifically covered by our guidelines.

Fannie Mae   June 30, 2002   Part XI Section 102.02   Unacceptable Appraisal Practices
Since we hold the lender responsible for the quality of the appraisals it uses to support the value of a security property the lender should take appropriate action to assure that the appraisers it uses do not engage in unacceptable practices. The following are examples of appraisal practices that we consider as unacceptable:

• Development of and/or reporting an opinion of value that is not supportable by market data or that is misleading;

• Development of a valuation conclusion that Is based-either partially or completely- on the sex, race, color, religion, handicap, national origin, or familial status of either the prospective owners or occupants of the subject property or the present owners or occupants of the properties in the vicinity of the subject property; or that is based on any other factor that local, state, or federal law designates as being discriminatory and thus; prohibited;

• Inclusion of inaccurate factual data about the subject neighborhood, site, improvements, or comparable sales;

SPECIAL INSTRUCTIONS - FNMA

- Failure to comment on negative factors with respect to the subject neighborhood, subject property, or proximity of the subject property to adverse influences;

Failure to analyze and report any current agreement of sale, option, or listing of the subject property and the prior sales of the subject property and the comparable sales;

Selection and use of inappropriate comparable sales or the failure to use comparable sales that are locationally and physically the most similar to the subject property;

Creation of comparable sales by combining vacant land sales with the contract purchase price of a home that has been built or will be built on the land

Use of comparable sales in the valuation process even though the appraiser has not personally inspected the exterior of the comparable properties by, at least, driving by them;

Use of adjustments to the comparable sales that do not reflect the market's reaction to the differences between the subject property and the comparable sales, or the failure to make adjustments when they are clearly indicated;

Use of data—particularly comparable sales data—that was provided by parties who have a financial interest in the sale or financing of the subject property without the appraiser's verification of the information from a disinterested source. For example, it would be inappropriate for an appraiser to use comparable sale provided by the real estate broker who is handling the sale of the subject property, unless the appraiser verifies the accuracy of the data provided with another source and makes an independent investigation to determine that the comparable sales provided were the best ones available;

Development of and/or reporting an appraisal in a manner or direction that favors either the cause of the client or any related party, the amount of the opinion of value, the attainment of a specific result, or the occurrence of a subsequent event in order to receive compensation and/or employment for performing the appraisal and/or in anticipation of receiving future assignments; and

Development of and/or reporting an appraisal in a manner that is inconsistent with the requirements of the Uniform Standards of Professional Appraisal Practice that were in place as of the effective date of the appraisal

Fannie Mae   June 30, 2002   Part XI Section 102.02   Unacceptable Appraisal Practices
The lender must disclose to the appraiser any and all information about the subject property that it is aware of, if the information could affect either the marketability of the property or the appraiser's opinion of the market value of the property. Specifically, the lender must make sure that it provides the appraiser with all appropriate financing data and sales concessions for the subject property that will be, or have been, granted by anyone associated with the transaction. Generally, this can be accomplished by providing the appraiser a copy of the complete, ratified sales contract for the property that is to be appraised. If the lender is aware of additional pertinent information that is not included in the sales contract, it should inform the appraiser. Information that must be disclosed includes:

settlement charges;
loan fees or charges;
discounts to the sales price;
payment of condominium/PUD fees;
    interest rate buydowns, or other below-market-rate financing;
    credits or refunds of the borrower's expenses;
    absorption of monthly payments;
assignment of rent payments;
and non-realty items that were included in the transaction.

The lender must also disclose to the appraiser any information about an environmental hazard in or on the subject property or in the vicinity of the property that it obtains from the borrower, the real estate broker, or any other party to the transaction so the appraiser can consider any influence the hazard may have on the value and marketability of the property.

SPECIAL INSTRUCTIONS - VA

Veterans Benefits Administration, Department of Veterans Affairs
Circular 26-93-25   10/22/93

REVISED FREDDIE MAC FORM 70/FANNIE MAE FORM 1004,
AND FREDDIE MAC FORM 439/FANNIE MAE FORM 1004B

TO: All Fee Appraisers and Lenders

SUBJ: Revised Appraisal Forms

1.   Over the last year, Fannie Mae, Freddie Mac, HUD, and VA performed a review of the effectiveness of the appraisal report forms that are currently in use for single-family properties. Each agency used a test version of the forms for a number of months. Revisions resulted from the test and a joint review effort of those agencies and an industry working group (which consisted of representatives from the Appraisal Foundation Advisory Council, Appraisal Standards Advisory Council, Mortgage Bankers Association of America, Mortgage Insurance Companies of America, American Bankers Association, Savings and Community Bankers of America, Farmers Home Administration, the staff of the Appraisal Subcommittee of the Federal Financial Institutions Examination Council, and representatives of several appraisal data collection, form and software companies). Representatives of the Appraisal Standards Board of The Appraisal Foundation also reviewed the forms to assure they were in compliance with the Uniform Standards of Professional Appraisal Practice.

2.   Based on the comments received, a number of revisions were made that resulted in improvements to the test forms. The resulting June 1993 version of the URAR (Freddie Mac Form 70/Fannie Mae Form 1004, Uniform Residential Appraisal Report) and Freddie Mac Form 439/Fannie Mae Form 1004B, Statement of Limiting Conditions and Appraiser's Certification, must be used by VA fee appraisers effective January 1, 1994. Until then, the June 1993 version, the December 1992 test version, or the October 1986 current version of those forms may be used. Until the effective date, in lieu of Form 439/1004B, VA fee appraisers may provide any other certification which is considered to be consistent with USPAP.

3.   Computer-Generated Forms

   a.   Although every effort was made to expand the space for comments on the URAR form, some of the appraisers and lenders who participated in the review of the forms felt that there might not be adequate space for comments because the amount and location of any additional space that is needed varies on a case-by-case basis. To accommodate this concern, VA, HUD, Fannie Mae and Freddie Mac will accept the URAR generated by software programs that include expandability features that allow for increases in any areas of the form that call for the insertion of narrative comments when the appraiser believes this is necessary to accommodate a particular appraisal assignment. (The expansion must not, however, result in the "Sales Comparison Analysis" section being separated so that it appears on two pages.) This should give appraisers the flexibility to take advantage of such technology if they so choose.

   b.   Regardless of whether the two-page format or a computer-generated expandable format is used, the sequence of the information on the URAR, as well as all of the specific information (including the instructions, entries, directions, etc.), cannot be changed in any manner.

4.   Explanation of Proposed Changes

   a.   The changes that are reflected in the revised URAR and Freddie Mac Form 439/Fannie Mae Form 1004B recognize the USPAP (Uniform Standards of Professional Appraisal Practice) that were adopted and promulgated by the Appraisal Standards Board of The Appraisal Foundation (with the exception of the departure provision, see note below) as the minimum appraisal standards for the appraisal industry. VA will continue to have separate appraisal requirements to supplement the minimum requirements of USPAP because it is considered necessary to assure that all agency concerns are addressed for any specific appraisal. Appraisers are required to complete the URAR in compliance with outstanding VA directives and in a way that will clearly reflect the thoroughness of the investigation and analysis and provide the rationale for the estimate of market value. Appraisers will go beyond any

SPECIAL INSTRUCTIONS - VA

limitations of the form by providing additional comments and exhibits when they are needed to support their conclusions.

NOTE: The "departure provision permits limited exceptions to sections of the Uniform Standards of Professional Appraisal Practice that are classified as specific guidelines rather than binding requirements. For VA purposes, use of the departure provision will be determined by VA on a case-by-case basis; eg., liquidation appraisal updates. VA fee appraisers are not authorized to make the determination to use the departure provision.

 b. Because VA is modifying its appraisal standards to specifically acknowledge the Uniform Standards of Professional Appraisal Practice as the minimum standards of the appraisal industry, VA will require the Freddie Mac Form 439/Fannie Mae Form 1004B to be signed and submitted by the appraiser as an exhibit to the appraisal report form for each appraisal assignment. Maintaining a copy "on file" is not consistent with USPAP. As noted in paragraph 2, mandatory use of Freddie Mac Form 439/Fannie Mae Form 1004B for VA purposes is effective January 1, 1994. Appraisers will not be permitted to make additions or deletions to the certification and statement of limiting conditions form. (For VA purposes, an exception to this is allowed for those liquidation appraisal reports in which the appraiser was either denied or unable to gain access to the subject property. Certification number 8 may be altered to reflect that fact.) It is believed that the reasons appraisers felt it was necessary to modify the existing Freddie Mac Form 439/Fannie Mae Form 1004B have been addressed in the revised test form. However, the appraiser will be permitted to make additional certifications (but not limiting conditions) on a separate form or page. Among other things, acceptable additional certifications include those required by State law or those related to the appraiser's continuing education or membership in an appraisal organization(s). Any additional certifications made by an appraiser must not conflict with the standard certifications on Freddie Mac Form 439/Fannie Mae Form 1004B or with any of VA's policies. In several locations, VA field stations tested the reporting of specific competitive listings or contract offerings in all appraisal assignments. The review and analysis of this information is recognized in appraisal texts as an integral part of the basic research involved in the appraisal process and is a generally accepted industry practice. VA fee appraisers have been required for some time now to report this information in all liquidation appraisal assignments and it is our experience that it has resulted in improved appraisal quality and more accurate and reliable appraisals. Given the no money down feature of many VA loans, objective appraisal reports that accurately reflect overall market conditions and the market value of each property are especially important. As a result of VA's liquidation appraisal experience and the positive comment that we received from the industry that the analysis, review and reporting of competitive listings/contract offerings yield more accurate estimates of market value, VA is also adopting the requirement for all origination appraisal assignments. Briefly, under this new requirement appraisers will be required to certify in each case that they have considered relevant competitive listings or contract offerings in the performance of the appraisal. If time adjustments are made or a significant market transition is indicated, the appraiser must also provide an addendum reporting at least 3 relevant competitive listings or contract offerings. If a stable market is indicated and there are no time adjustments, the appraiser does not have to provide the addendum. VA staffs will be reconciling situations where appraisers in the same market area are indicating significantly divergent market conditions. See attachment 1 for specific instructions concerning this requirement.

 d. The policy in subparagraph c above is effective for all origination appraisal assignments received by VA dated 1 week or more from the date of this release. It is also effective whether the October 1986 version, the December 1992 test version, or the June 1993 version of the URAR is being used.

 e. Effective _____ appraisal fees for origination appraisals are increased as follows:
_____

 f. Attachments 1 and 2 contain explanations of the major changes and modifications made to the forms, VA guidelines, and a discussion of the more significant issues previously raised by appraisers and lenders that the working group addressed during the development and testing of the forms. Attachment 1 addresses the modifications to the URAR (Freddie Mac Form 70/Fannie Mae Form 1004) and Attachment 2 addresses the modifications to the Statement of Limiting Conditions and Appraiser's Certification (Freddie Mac Form 439/Fannie Mae Form 1004B).

Highlights of the USPAP - Items directly related to the URAR

The 3/31/99 revisions of the Uniform Standards of Professional Appraisal Practice require that certain information be included in every appraisal that were not required before.

Most of the time the URAR will be used to make a "Complete Appraisal-Summary Appraisal Report." The following is a summary of what things are now required when the URAR is determined by the appraiser to be a "Complete Appraisal-Summary Appraisal Report." There are substantial additional requirements when the URAR is used to report a "Limited Appraisal" or when the URAR is used to make a "Self Contained Report" or "Limited Use Appraisal Report." In this book we only cover how to make a Complete Appraisal using the URAR as a Summary Appraisal Report.

1. At the top of the first page of the URAR report you must add to the title of the report that it is a Complete Appraisal/Summary Appraisal Report.

USPAP STANDARDS RULE 2.2: "Each written real property appraisal report must be prepared under one of the following three options and prominently state which option is used"

2. You must identify who is the user(s) of the report. A good place for this information is on the Lender/Client line in the SUBJECT section of the URAR.

USPAP STANDARDS RULE 1-2 (a) "Identify the client and other intended users"

3. You must identify the intended use of the appraisers opinions and conclusions.

USPAP STANDARDS RULE 1-2 (b) "Identify the intended use of the appraiser's opinions and conclusions"

4. You must state your opinion as to what is "reasonable exposure time linked to the value opinion."

USPAP STANDARDS RULE 1-2 (c)) Comment: "When the purpose of an assignment is to develop an opinion of market value, the appraiser must also develop an opinion of reasonable exposure time linked to the value opinion."

5. For all types of property (including Single Family Residence) you are required to report a **three year sales history** if the information is available.

USPAP STANDARDS RULE 1-5: This rule effective 01/01/03 requires an appraiser to report and analyze all prior sales of the subject property within the past three (3) years, if such information available in the normal course of business.

The USPAP contains many requirements concerning how an appraisal is to be made. It is imperative that you are familiar with these requirements before you attempt to make any appraisal.

Appraisal Standards Board
The Appraisal Foundation

APPRAISAL STANDARDS BOARD - SUMMARY OF ACTIONS
JUNE 15, 2004

(THE FOLLOWING IS A CONDENSATIONS OF THE SUMMARY OF ACTIONS THAT APPEARS IN THE 2005 UNIFORM STANDARDS OF PROFESSIONAL PRACTICE)

On June 15, 2004, the Appraisal Standards Board (ASB) approved and adopte modifications to the 2004 edition of the Uniform Standards of Professional Appraisa Practice (USPAP). These changes to USPAP were the result of two exposure draft: issued on February 17, 2004 (First Exposure Draft) and April 26, 2004 (Secon Exposure Draft). The changes will be incorporated in the 2005 USPAP with an effectiv date of January 1, 2005. The first Exposure Draft was presented in ten sections, a follows:

- Edits to Definition of "Appraisal Review" and STANDARD 3
- "Appraising Land as Though Vacant~' Edits to Standards Rules 1 T^3 and 6-2
- "Impact on Value" Edits to STANDARDS 2, 3, 5, 6, 8, and 10, and STATEMENT ON APPRAISAL STANDARDS NO 10 (SMT-10)
- Certifications for Multi-Discipline Reports
- Reporting Requirements Regarding Reconciliation
- Reporting Requirements Regarding Exposure Time
- "Levels of Reliability" in STATEMENT ON APPRAISAL STANDARDS NO. 7 (SMT-7)
- Retirement of Advisory Opinion 6 (AO-6) - The Appraisal Review Function
- Revision of Advisory Opinion 21 (AO-21) - When Does USPAP Apply in Valuation Services?
- "Purpose," Type and Definition of Value, and Citation of Value Definition

The following is a topic-by-topic analysis of the actions taken by the Board and their rationale for some of those decisions.

1. The requirement to report exposure time was deleted from SMT – 6.

2. The Board adopted revisions to the definition of "Appraisal Review" and 'STANDARD 3 as exposed in the April 26 Exposure Draft.

Confusion existed regarding what is covered by the definition and 'by STANDARD 3. The revisions made are an attempt to clarify that STANDARD 3 only applies to the review of work performed as part of an appraisal, appraisal review or appraisal consulting assignment

3. Revisions to Standards Rules 1-3 and 6-2 were approved.

The revisions made underscore that USPAP does not dictate the use of any particular theory or technique. USPAP does not dictate the use of any particular method, only that appraisers *"employ those recognized methods and techniques that are necessary to produce a credible appraisal...."*

APPRAISAL STANDARDS BOARD - SUMMARY OF ACTIONS
JUNE 15, 2004

4. Revisions to STANDARDS 2, 3, *5, 6,* 8 and 10, and STATEMENT ON APPRAISAL STANDARDS NO. 10 were approved. The ASB decided, not to delete references to the term "limiting conditions."

The revisions made are intended to clarify an appraiser's obligations, and can be grouped into the following three categories:

5. Eliminating the requirement to "indicate the impact on value" for extraordinary assumptions hypothetical conditions, etc. found in STANDARDS 2, *5,* 6, 8 and 10.

The existing requirements have caused confusion regarding the extent of analysis necessary to properly satisfy the obligation to indicate the impact on value i.e., must the appraiser provide a second valuation as if the condition was not as described?

6. Eliminating a portion of the Comment found in STANDARDS Z, 6, 8 and 10, that addresses the location in reports for disclosures of assumptions and conditions.

7. Eliminating other requirements in STANDARDS 2, 3, *5,* 6, 8, and 10 related to the location of disclosures for assumptions and conditions, and providing edits to clarify appropriate disclosure.

Note that the terms *"assumption, extraordinary assumption, hypothetical condition,"* were edited where necessary for consistency.

8. Revisions to Standards Rules 2-3, 3-3, *5-3,* 6-8, 8-3 and 10-3 were approved.

Because some reports may combine assignment results developed by real property, personal property, and/or intangible asset appraisers, the ASB has edited the Comment language that accompanies each Standards Rule regarding certification.

The edits have been designed to clarify the responsibility of each appraiser in assignments where appraisers of different disciplines jointly prepare a report that communicates assignment results for the appraisal of multiple asset types. For example, a single report may communicate value opinions for real property, machinery and equipment, and intangible assets.

9. The Board adopted the revisions to Standards Rules 2-2, 6-7, 8-2 and 10-2.

Currently, in STANDARDS 2 and 8 the requirement to report the results of the reconciliation process is included only in reporting requirements related to sales history, offers and listings, while STANDARDS 6 and 10 do not contain any reporting requirements directly addressing reconciliation. For improved clarity, the ASB has deleted the current references to Standards Rules 1-6 and 7-6, and added separate requirements for reporting reconciliation in positions of more prominence.

XV

APPRAISAL STANDARDS BOARD - SUMMARY OF ACTIONS
JUNE 15, 2004

10. The Board adopted the revisions to STATEMENT ON APPRAISAL STANDARDS NO. 6. The requirement to report exposure time was deleted from SMT 6. This was done because disclosure of reporting time does not apply to all assignments. However, this change does not affect the requirement for the appraiser to develop an estimate of exposure time in market value assignments.

11. The Board adopted the revisions to STATEMENT ON APPRAISAL STANDARDS NO. 7.

Revisions were made to SMT-7 to separate the concept of reliability from departure. The edits correct the inaccurate statement indicating that a Complete Appraisal is always more reliable than a Limited Appraisal.

12. The Board approved -retiring Advisory Opinion 6 (AO-6).

Advisory Opinion 6 was retired because more recent guidance has been issued by the Board since first publishing AO-6 in 1992. Specifically, AO-20 and the newly revised AO-2 I offer more up-to-date guidance, as does the *Frequently Asked Questions* publication.

13. The Board adopted the proposed revisions to Advisory Opinion 21 (AO-2 1) as however, the Board elected not to change the term "Valuation Services" to "Property Services." The revisions made to Advisory Opinion 21 were not intended to modify the substance and guidance of the prior AO-21; rather, to promote the understandability of USPAP through improved clarity.

AO 21 offers guidance on when an individual should comply with~ USPAP and how an appraiser recognizes an obligation to comply with USPAP.

14. Changes in "Purpose", Type and Definition of Value, and Citation of Value Definitions. Edits were made throughout the document regarding the term "purpose." This word has been used in USPAP with different meanings. It will now be used only to mean "intent"; it will not be used as a reference to the type and definition of value.

15. Deletion of the term "Cash Flow Analysis" and deletion of references to report types in the Comment of the definition of "Report." The term "Cash Flow Analysis" was deleted because it no longer appears in USPAP.

UNIFORM RESIDENTIAL APPRAISAL REPORT

File No. _____

Property Description — SUBJECT

Property Address	City ____ State ____ Zip Code ____
Legal Description	County ____
Assessor's Parcel No.	Tax Year ____ R.E. Taxes $ ____ Special Assessments $ ____
Borrower ____	Current Owner ____ Occupant: ☐ Owner ☐ Tenant ☐ Vacant
Property rights appraised ☐ Fee Simple ☐ Leasehold	Project Type ☐ PUD ☐ Condominium (HUD/VA only) HOA $ ____ /Mo.
Neighborhood or Project Name ____	Map Reference ____ Census Tract ____
Sale Price $ ____ Date of Sale ____	Description and $ amount of loan charges/concessions to be paid by seller
Lender/Client ____	Address ____
Appraiser ____	Address ____

NEIGHBORHOOD

Location	☐ Urban ☐ Suburban ☐ Rural	Predominant occupancy	Single family housing PRICE $(000) / AGE (yrs)	Present land use %	Land use change
Built up	☐ Over 75% ☐ 25-75% ☐ Under 25%			One family ____	☐ Not likely ☐ Likely
Growth rate	☐ Rapid ☐ Stable ☐ Slow	☐ Owner	Low	2-4 family ____	☐ In process
Property values	☐ Increasing ☐ Stable ☐ Declining	☐ Tenant	High	Multi-family ____	To: ____
Demand/supply	☐ Shortage ☐ In balance ☐ Over supply	☐ Vacant (0-5%)	Predominant	Commercial ____	
Marketing time	☐ Under 3 mos. ☐ 3-6 mos. ☐ Over 6 mos.	☐ Vacant (over 5%)			

Note: Race and the racial composition of the neighborhood are not appraisal factors.

Neighborhood boundaries and characteristics: ____

Factors that affect the marketability of the properties in the neighborhood (proximity to employment and amenities, employment stability, appeal to market, etc.): ____

Market conditions in the subject neighborhood (including support for the above conclusions related to the trend of property values, demand/supply, and marketing time - - such as data on competitive properties for sale in the neighborhood, description of the prevalence of sales and financing concessions, etc.): ____

PUD

Project Information for PUDs (If applicable) - - Is the developer/builder in control of the Home Owners' Association (HOA)? ☐ Yes ☐ No

Approximate total number of units in the subject project ____ Approximate total number of units for sale in the subject project ____

Describe common elements and recreational facilities: ____

SITE

Dimensions ____			Topography ____
Site area ____		Corner Lot ☐ Yes ☐ No	Size ____
Specific zoning classification and description ____			Shape ____
Zoning compliance ☐ Legal ☐ Legal nonconforming (Grandfathered use) ☐ Illegal ☐ No zoning			Drainage ____
Highest & best use as improved: ☐ Present use ☐ Other use (explain)			View ____
Utilities	Public	Other	Off-site Improvements Type Public Private	Landscaping ____
Electricity			Street ____	Driveway Surface ____
Gas			Curb/gutter ____	Apparent easements ____
Water			Sidewalk ____	FEMA Special Flood Hazard Area ☐ Yes ☐ No
Sanitary sewer			Street lights ____	FEMA Zone ____ Map Date ____
Storm sewer			Alley ____	FEMA Map No. ____

Comments (apparent adverse easements, encroachments, special assessments, slide areas, illegal or legal nonconforming zoning use, etc.): ____

DESCRIPTION OF IMPROVEMENTS

GENERAL DESCRIPTION	EXTERIOR DESCRIPTION	FOUNDATION	BASEMENT	INSULATION
No. of Units ____	Foundation ____	Slab ____	Area Sq. Ft. ____	Roof ☐
No. of Stories ____	Exterior Walls ____	Crawl Space ____	% Finished ____	Ceiling ☐
Type (Det./Att.) ____	Roof Surface ____	Basement ____	Ceiling ____	Walls ☐
Design (Style) ____	Gutters & Dwnspts. ____	Sump Pump ____	Walls ____	Floor ☐
Existing/Proposed ____	Window Type ____	Dampness ____	Floor ____	None ☐
Age (Yrs.) ____	Storm/Screens ____	Settlement ____	Outside Entry ____	Unknown ☐
Effective Age (Yrs.) ____	Manufactured House ____	Infestation ____		

ROOMS	Foyer	Living	Dining	Kitchen	Den	Family Rm.	Rec. Rm.	Bedrooms	# Baths	Laundry	Other	Area Sq. Ft.
Basement												
Level 1												
Level 2												

Finished area **above** grade contains: ____ Rooms; ____ Bedroom(s); ____ Bath(s); ____ Square Feet of Gross Living Area

INTERIOR	Materials/Condition	HEATING		KITCHEN EQUIP.		ATTIC		AMENITIES		CAR STORAGE:	
Floors	____	Type	____	Refrigerator	☐	None	☐	Fireplace(s) # ____		None	☐
Walls	____	Fuel	____	Range/Oven	☐	Stairs	☐	Patio ____		Garage	# of cars ____
Trim/Finish	____	Condition	____	Disposal	☐	Drop Stair	☐	Deck ____		Attached	____
Bath Floor	____	COOLING		Dishwasher	☐	Scuttle	☐	Porch ____		Detached	____
Bath Wainscot	____	Central	____	Fan/Hood	☐	Floor	☐	Fence ____		Built-In	____
Doors	____	Other	____	Microwave	☐	Heated	☐	Pool ____		Carport	____
		Condition	____	Washer/Dryer	☐	Finished	☐			Driveway	____

COMMENTS

Additional features (special energy efficient items, etc.): ____

Condition of the improvements, depreciation (physical, functional, and external), repairs needed, quality of construction, remodeling/additions, etc.: ____

Adverse environmental conditions (such as, but not limited to, hazardous wastes, toxic substances, etc.) present in the improvements, on the site, or in the immediate vicinity of the subject property: ____

Freddie Mac Form 70 6-93   PAGE 1 OF 2   Fannie Mae Form 1004 6-93

FRONT OF FORM

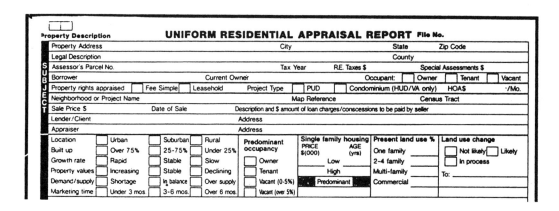

At the top of the first page of the report you usually will add to the title of the report that it is a Complete Appraisal/Summary Appraisal Report which is what Freddie Mac and Fannie Mae expect the URAR to be used for.

If the appraisal is a Limited Appraisal or the report is considered to be a Self-Contained or Limited Use Report than those words must appear as part of the title of the report.

USPAP STANDARDS RULE 2-2: "Each written real property appraisal report must be prepared under one of the following three options and prominently state which option is used"

SUBJECT

Introduction

Property Description	UNIFORM RESIDENTIAL APPRAISAL REPORT	File No.
Property Address	City	State	Zip Code
Legal Description		County	
Assessor's Parcel No.	Tax Year	R.E. Taxes $	Special Assessments $
Borrower	Current Owner	Occupant: Owner Tenant Vacant
Property rights appraised	Fee Simple Leasehold Project Type PUD	Condominium (HUD/VA only) HOA$ /Mo.
Neighborhood or Project Name	Map Reference	Census Tract
Sale Price $	Date of Sale	Description and $ amount of loan charges/conscessions to be paid by seller
Lender/Client	Address	
Appraiser	Address	

The **SUBJECT** section originally was called "To Be Completed By Lender." The revised name recognized the universal nature of the URAR form.

This section provides space for the following information:

- **File No. – Property Address**
- **Legal Description**
- **Assessor's Parcel No.**
- **Tax Year – R.E. Taxes**
- **Special Assessments $**
- **Borrower**
- **Current Owner**
- **Occupant**
- **Property rights appraised**
- **Project Type**
- **HOA $/Mo. (Homeowners Association/Monthly Charges)**
- **Neighborhood or Project Name**
- **Map Reference**
- **Census Tract**
- **Sale Price $**
- **Date of Sale**
- **Description and $ amount of loan charges/concessions to be paid by seller**
- **Lender/Client - Address**
- **Appraiser - Address**

Fannie Mae   June 30, 2002   Part XI Chapter 4, Section 401   The Subject Property
The first section of our appraisal report forms is used to identify and describe the location of the subject property; to provide information about property taxes and special assessments to indicate the occupancy status of the property; to describe the property rights to be appraised; to summarize financing data and sales concessions; and to identify the borrower, the current owner, and the client.

Veterans Benefits Administration   Circular 26-93-25   October 22, 1993
Subject Section
Include new entries for assessor's parcel number, special assessments, borrower's name, and appraiser's name and a new "occupant" entry with convenient boxes for the appraiser to indicate whether the property was owner-occupied, tenant-occupied, or vacant as of the date of inspection;

SUBJECT

File No. – Property Address

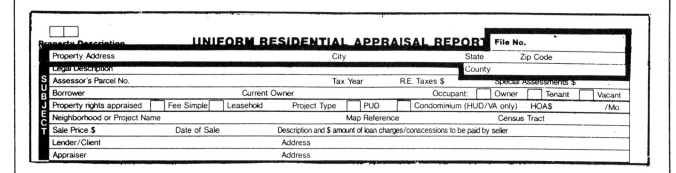

The appraisal starts with a positive identification of the subject by the **Property Address** (including the individual house number and street), **City, County, State** and the appropriate **Zip Code.** The address listed is assumed to be the mailing address for the property unless otherwise indicated.

If the above data does not completely and unambiguously identify the subject property, further information, such as additional unit letters or numbers, should be included here or in an addendum. A **Legal Description** may also be used to better identify the subject.

Fannie Mae June 30. 2002 Part XI Chapter 4. Section 401 The Subject Property

The appraiser must identify the property rights to be appraised as "fee simple" or "leasehold." In addition, the appraiser must indicate whether the subject property is located in a PUD or condominium project, if the appraisal for a PUD or condominium unit is documented on the *Uniform Residential Appraisal Report (Form 1004)* or the appraisal for a PUD unit is documented on the *Small Residential Income Property Appraisal Report* (Form 1025).

CONSISTENCY CHECK: Information in this section of the URAR relates to another section of the form as indicated below. The appraiser should check to make sure data in both places is consistent!

SUBJECT - Property Address
    also appears as
SALES COMPARISON ANALYSIS - SUBJECT: Address

SUBJECT

Legal Description

Property Description	UNIFORM RESIDENTIAL APPRAISAL REPORT		File No.	
Property Address	City	State	Zip Code	
Legal Description		County		
Assessor's Parcel No.	Tax Year	R.E. Taxes $	Special Assessments $	
Borrower	Current Owner	Occupant:	Owner / Tenant / Vacant	
Property rights appraised	Fee Simple / Leasehold / Project Type / PUD	Condominium (HUD/VA only)	HOA$	/Mo.
Neighborhood or Project Name		Map Reference	Census Tract	
Sale Price $	Date of Sale	Description and $ amount of loan charges/concessions to be paid by seller		
Lender/Client		Address		
Appraiser		Address		

Every appraisal must accurately identify the property being appraised. Often the appraiser decides that the street address number alone does not provide the required positive identification. In such cases, a **Legal Description** of the subject must be obtained from the mortgage, deed or other land record sources in the community. This information may be attached as an addendum if the space provided is insufficient.

The following gives examples of four different types of descriptions which are used to identify property.[1]

- *Lot and Block System.* This system, derived from the rectangular survey system, applies in most urban communities. It originated in the manner in which these communities grew. The early developers had their tracts surveyed and platted in rectangular blocks and lots. Each was numbered and the numbers were entered on a plat map. Copies of the plat were filed in the local government record office for permanent reference. Identification by use of lot and block numbers is usually sufficient in subdivisions where each lot is clearly distinguished from its neighbors.

- *Geodetic Survey.* A land survey that was initiated to identify tracts of land owned by the federal government gradually has been extended throughout the nation. These survey maps are prepared by the United States Geological Survey Division, Department of the Interior. They show, among other things, height contours, latitude and longitude, existing rivers and streams, buildings and railroads. They are available on various scales by named quadrangles. The skeleton of this survey is a network of "benchmarks," which cover the entire country, each of which is located by its latitude and longitude.

- *Government Survey System.* This system also developed during colonial times; it provides for a unit of land approximately 24 miles square, bounded by base lines running east and west and meridians extending north and south. Because of the curvature of the earth, the north boundary of the square is slightly shorter than the south. The 24-mile square unit is divided into areas six miles square, called townships. A "tier" is an east/west row of townships between parallels of latitude six miles apart. A "range" is a north/south row between two meridian lines also six miles apart. Ranges and tiers are assigned numbers from principal meridians and base lines. A township is divided into 36 sections, each one mile square. The sections are numbered consecutively, beginning with the northeast corner and continuing, east to west and west to east, down to Section 36 in the southeast corner. Discrepancies pertaining to the north boundary, and others due to errors in measurement or alignment, are allowed for in the most westerly half mile of the township

- *Metes and Bounds System.* Originally used in colonial America, this system identifies property by delineating its boundaries in terms of a series of directions and distances, starting at a fixed point. Typical points referred to in old deeds are large trees, rocks, streams, etc., which today in some cases have become difficult, if not impossible, to locate positively. Each boundary line is described in succession, using a compass bearing and distance, until the entire parcel has been enclosed; for example, "Starting at the old oak tree known as Grand Dad's Oak, South 63 degrees 35 minutes for a distance of 185 feet ..." (see Fig. 7-3).

FIG. 7-3: Metes and Bounds System

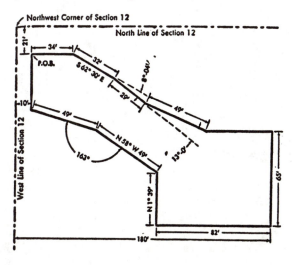

---

[1] George F. Bloom and Henry S. Harrison, Appraising the Single Family Residence, Chicago, IL: American Institute of Real Estate Appraisers, 1978.

SUBJECT

Assessor's Parcel No.

Assessor's Parcel No. is a new line which requires that the appraiser report the Assessor's parcel number when applicable. Enter "not available" if none exists.

Fannie Mae   June 30, 1993   Announcement   Subject Section
Assessors Parcel Number

"The "subject" section was modified to include new entries for ....assessor's parcel number."

SUBJECT

Tax Year – R.E. Taxes

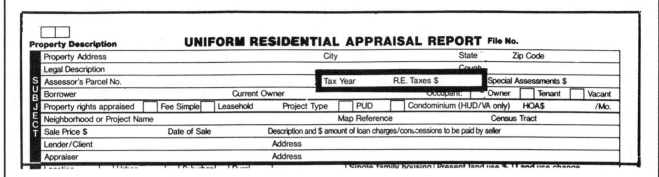

The total of all current year real estate taxes is shown in the **R.E. Taxes $** blank, whenever this information is available. When current tax data is not available, space is provided to indicate to which **Tax Year** the reported information applies. Sometimes a property is subject to more than one property tax (i.e., school district tax, fire district tax, etc.). The total of all such taxes should be indicated.

The appraiser should consider whether the taxes on the subject property are comparable to the taxes on similar properties in this market. Excessive taxes may negatively affect the value of the property.

When the subject property includes ownership of some common property, which is maintained by an association, the monthly association dues are reported in the **HOA $/Mo.** space.

SUBJECT

Special Assessments

Property Description	UNIFORM RESIDENTIAL APPRAISAL REPORT File No.
Property Address	City / State / Zip Code
Legal Description	County
Assessor's Parcel No.	Tax Year / R.E. Taxes $ / **Special Assessments $**
Borrower	Current Owner / Occupant: Owner / Tenant / Vacant
Property rights appraised	Fee Simple / Leasehold / Project Type / PUD / Condominium (HUD/VA only) / HOA$ /Mo.
Neighborhood or Project Name	Map Reference / Census Tract
Sale Price $	Date of Sale / Description and $ amount of loan charges/conscessions to be paid by seller
Lender/Client	Address
Appraiser	Address

Special Assessment is a new line for reporting special assessments such as sewer assessments. Enter "none" if there aren't any. Do not confuse association fees with special assessments. Report association fees on the **HOA $____** line.

Fannie Mae   June 30, 2002   Part XI Chapter 4, Section 401   The Subject Property

Special Assessments

The first section of our appraisal report forms is used to identify and describe the location of the subject property; to provide information about property taxes and **special assessments;** to indicate the occupancy status of the property; to describe the property rights to be appraised; to summarize financing data and sales concessions; and to identify the borrower, the current owner, the client, and the appraiser.

Fannie Mae   June 30, 2002   Part XI Section 310   Special Appraisal Considerations

Properties in Special Assessment or Community Facilities Districts

Alternative methods for raising the capital necessary to satisfy utility and infrastructure requirements are sometimes used in the development of new residential communities. Generally, this involves the creation of local districts—special assessment districts or community facilities districts—that have the authority to assess homeowners for the cost of developing utility services and various infrastructure facilities (roads, sewer services, schools, police and fire protection services, libraries, etc.). We expect the lender to know whether or not a property is located in one of these districts and to be aware of the effect that assessments levied by the district could have on property values and the marketability of the subject property. The lender's appraiser, therefore, must give special consideration to the valuation of properties located in these districts.

Fannie Mae   June 30, 2002   Part XI Section 310.01   Special Appraisal Considerations

Properties in Special Assessment Districts

Special assessment districts (which may also be called special tax districts or municipal utility districts) provide a specific service to homeowners living in a designated area. They are most often established to provide water or other utilities in areas that are not served by existing city or municipal utility services. The need for these districts arises when an existing utility service does not have sufficient capacity (or may not find it economically feasible) to provide services for newly created subdivisions that are located beyond its current operating area. State law governing the establishment of special assessment districts varies greatly, as does the financial strength of the individual districts. The districts are granted the authority to assess owners of properties within their boundaries for funds that will be used to cover their operating costs and debt service.

Special assessment districts that are established to serve newly developing subdivisions with utilities often base their financial plans (and the amount of the assessment charged to each property owner) on the expected number of properties in the area to be served. The district then depends on the continuation of development to maintain its budget expectations. If, for any reason, development stops short of the degree of development that the district anticipated in preparing its budget, the district can become financially distressed and may need to impose an additional assessment on the existing homeowners.

When the property being appraised is located in a special assessment district, the lender should request the appraiser to report on any special assessments that affect the property If the special assessment district is experiencing financial difficulty and that difficulty has an effect on the value or marketability of the subject property the appraiser must reflect that in his or her analysis and note it in the appraisal report. To assure that the reaction of the market to the potential liabilities that may arise within a financially troubled special assessment district is reflected in his or her analysis, the appraiser should consider current and expired listings of properties for sale within the district and any pending contract sales and recent closed sales within the district. There may be some instances in which the financial difficulty of a special assessment district is so severe that its actual effect on the value and marketability of a property is not measurable because there is no comparable market data available to enable the appraiser to arrive at a reliable opinion of market value. When this is the case, a mortgage secured by a property in that district will not be eligible for delivery to us—at least until such time as an active market develops that will enable the appraiser to demonstrate the value and marketability of the subject property.

Fannie Mae   June 30, 2002   Part XI Section 310.02   Community Facilities Districts
Some jurisdictions have passed legislation that creates community facilities districts and permits them to levy a special tax to fund the capital costs of a wide variety of public improvements, as well as the on-going operation and maintenance costs of a limited number of public services. Proceeds of the special tax are used to support the sale of tax-exempt bonds for the various capital improvements—roads, sewer services, schools, police and fire protection services, and libraries—that are allowed under the legislation.

The assessment that will be used to repay the tax-exempt bonds becomes an on-going responsibility of the property owner (similar to state and local property taxes). The assessment lien (and the obligation to pay the assessment) passes with the title to the property when ownership of the property is transferred. The term of the assessment obligation can be quite lengthy (up to 40 years—unless the assessment is prepaid). In some cases in California, prepayment estimates can range from $20,000 to $40,000 for a single-family property depending on the extent of the improvements that were financed, the size of the dwelling, and the year it was purchased.

Such legislation generally requires full disclosure of the special assessment to any purchaser of a property located in a community facilities district. Therefore, a lender originating mortgages in community facilities

districts should disclose to the appraiser any information that it becomes aware of regarding special assessments, on a. given property The lender also should caution its appraisers in general about the need to be aware of whether or not the subject property and the comparable sales are located within (or affected by) a community facilities district since properties subject to an assessment by one of these districts often compete against properties that are either subject to a significantly different special assessment or to no assessment at all. The appraiser must consider the reaction of the market (if any) to the assessment for the applicable community facilities district in his or her analysis by analyzing similarly affected comparable sales, and should note their effect of the assessment in the appraisal report.

SUBJECT

Borrower - Current Owner

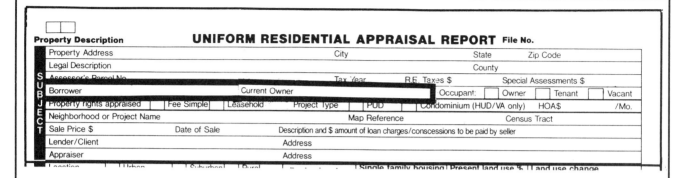

Often the Borrower is the Buyer or the current owner who is refinancing. However, there are exceptions, so to be 100% safe you should not guess. The best source of this information is your client (who is often the lender) who will make the mortgage loan.

<u>Fannie Mae   June 30, 2002   Part XI Chapter 4, Section 401   The Subject Property</u>
Borrower's Name
The first section of our appraisal report forms is used to identify and describe the location of the subject property; to provide information about property taxes and special assessments to indicate the occupancy status of the property; to describe the property rights to be appraised; to summarize financing data and sales concessions; and to **identify the borrower**, the current owner, and the client.

The **Current Owner** of the property is always named on this line. This information is on the ratified sales contract which is supplied to the appraiser if the appraisal is for a Fannie Mae loan. A simple title check at the record source will also reveal this information accurately.

<u>Fannie Mae   June 30, 2002   Part XI Chapter 4, Section 401   The Subject Property</u>
Current Owner
The first section of our appraisal report forms is used to identify and describe the location of the subject property; to provide information about property taxes and special assessments to indicate the occupancy status of the property; to describe the property rights to be appraised; to summarize financing data and sales concessions; and to identify the borrower, the **current owner**, and the client.

SUBJECT

Occupant

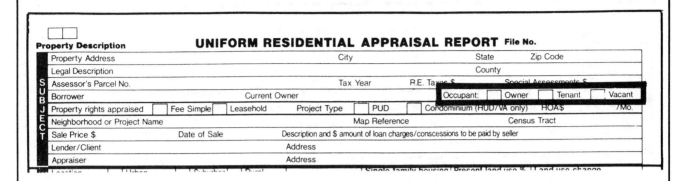

FNMA and FHLMC <u>now</u> require appraisers to indicate when a property is vacant at the time of the inspection. It is also good practice when appraising a vacant property to check the utilities and indicate whether they appear to be turned off or on. If a vacant property does not appear to be properly closed up and protected, this should also be noted.

Property Occupant (on date of inspection) is now indicated by a check in the "owner", "tenant" or "vacant" check box.

<u>Fannie Mae   June 30, 2002   Part XI Chapter 4, Section 401   The Subject Property</u>
Occupant
The first section of our appraisal report forms is used to identify and describe the location of the subject property; to provide information about property taxes and special assessments to indicate the **occupancy status** of the property; to describe the property rights to be appraised; to summarize financing data and sales concessions; and to identify the borrower, the current owner, and the client.

SUBJECT

Property rights appraised

![Form excerpt showing Property Description section of Uniform Residential Appraisal Report, with fields for Property Address, Legal Description, Assessor's Parcel No., Borrower, Property rights appraised (Fee Simple, Leasehold, Project Type, PUD, Condominium (HUD/VA only)), Neighborhood or Project Name, Sale Price, Lender/Client, Appraiser, and Location.]

Property rights appraised is divided into two parts. First, by checking the appropriate box, the appraiser indicates if the ownership is "Fee Simple" or "Leasehold". Boxes are also available to indicate if the ownership is "PUD" or "Condominium".

Fannie Mae   June 30, 2002   Part XI Section 310   Special Appraisal Considerations
Units in Condominium Projects
A condominium project is one in which individual owners hold title to units in the project along with an undivided interest in the real estate that is designated as the common area for the project.

Appraisals for condominium units that secure manually underwritten mortgages are usually documented on the *Individual Condominium Unit Appraisal Report* (Form 1073) or the *Desktop Underwriter Quantitative Analysis Appraisal Report* (Form 2055). However, we will accept appraisals of detached condominium units on the *Uniform Residential Appraisal Report* (Form 1004), if the appraiser includes an adequate description of the project and information about the owners' association fees and the quality of the project maintenance. Desktop Underwriter will specify the level of property analysis and review for Desktop Underwriter-processed mortgages that are secured by condominium units.

The appraisal of an individual unit in a condominium project requires the appraiser to analyze the condominium project as well as the individual unit. The appraiser must pay special attention to the location of the individual unit within the project, the project's amenities, and the amount and purpose of the owners' association assessment since the marketability and value of the individual units in a project depend on the marketability and appeal of the project itself.

Fannie Mae   June 30, 2002   Part XI Section 310   Special Appraisal Considerations
Units in PUD Projects
A planned unit development (PUD) is a project or subdivision that consists of common property and improvements that are owned and maintained by an owners' association for the benefit and use of the individual units within the project. For a project to qualify as a PUD, the owners' association must require automatic, nonseverable membership for each individual unit owner, and provide for mandatory assessments. Zoning should not be the basis for classifying a project as a PUD.

Appraisals for PUD units that secure manually underwritten mortgages are generally documented on the *Uniform Residential Appraisal Report* (Form 1004) or the *Desktop Underwriter Quantitative Analysis Appraisal Report* (Form *2055)*. To assure that all the specific eligibility criteria for a new PUD project are adequately addressed, it may be necessary to use an addendum to Form 1004 to provide information for appraisals related to attached units in new PUD projects (particularly when the developer is still in control of the owners' association).

The appraisal of an individual unit in a PUD requires the appraiser to analyze the PUD project as well as the individual unit. The appraiser must pay special attention to the location of the individual unit within the project, the project's amenities, and the amount and purpose of the owners association assessment since the marketability and value of the individual units in a project generally depend on the marketability and appeal of the project Itself.

A De Minimis PUD is fee simple ownership to a home with a partial interest in nearby property that is owned together with neighbors. Often the shared property is open space or recreational land. However, to be classified as 'De Minimis' (a Latin word meaning: *of little of no importance*), the joint property must contribute <u>little</u> additional value to the primary residence and any maintenance dues must be <u>insignificant</u> compared to the property value (a few hundred dollars or less per year). The homeowners' association should be <u>loosely</u> constituted and should not have the right to force an owner to pay dues by using special lien-placing rights.

In contrast, a regular PUD is usually created by formal documents filed in the land records. Common property <u>does</u> contribute additional value, because it is usually a recreational facility or a large tract of vacant land. The homeowners' association is <u>formally</u> constituted with duly elected officers and directors, charges <u>significant</u> dues and has the right to place liens or restrict the common property use of owners who do not pay the assessed dues.

<u>Fannie Mae   June 30, 1993   Announcement   Subject Section</u>
<u>Property Rights Appraised (de minimis PUD & PUD)</u>

"...delete the obsolete reference to <u>de minimis</u> PUD (Note: We eliminated the concept of <u>de minimis</u> PUD when we redefined planned unit developments in 1989.) If the appraiser indicates that the subject property is located in a PUD, we require information about the unit's owners' association fees in this section and specific information about the project in the new PUD section."

<u>Fannie Mae   June 30, 2002   Part XI Section 311   Special Appraisal Considerations</u>
<u>Properties Subject to Leasehold Interests</u>

When a mortgage is secured by a leasehold estate (or is subject to the payment of "ground rent"), the borrower has the right to use and occupy the real property under the provisions of a lease agreement (or ground lease) for a stipulated period of time, as long as the conditions of the lease are met. (When the lease holder is a community land trust, there may be significant restrictions on both the purchase and resale of the property; therefore, we provide more detailed guidance on appraising this type of leasehold estate in Section 312 below.) The valuation of a property that is subject to a leasehold interest may require a complex analysis, so an appraiser should develop (and attach as an addendum to the appraisal report form) a thorough, clear, and detailed narrative that identifies the terms, restrictions, and conditions of the lease agreement or ground lease and discusses what effect, if any, they have on the value and marketability of the subject property.

In developing the sales comparison approach to value, the appraiser generally should use as comparable sales properties that have similar leasehold interests. When there are a sufficient number of closed comparable sales of properties with similar leasehold interests available, the appraiser should use them in its analysis of the market value of the leasehold estate for the subject property and report them in the "sales comparison analysis" grid on the applicable appraisal report form. However, if not enough comparable sales with the same lease terms and restrictions are available, the appraiser may use sales of similar properties with different lease terms or, if necessary, sales of similar properties that were appraised as fee simple estates—as long as he or she explains why the use of these sales is appropriate. In such cases, the appraiser must make an appropriate adjustment on the—"sales comparison analysis" grid to reflect the market reaction to the different lease terms or property rights appraised.

<u>Veterans Benefits Administration   Circular 26-93-25   October 22, 1993</u>
<u>Subject Section - Property Rights Appraised</u>

The "property rights appraised" entry was separated into two distinct parts. One part is for the appraiser to indicate whether the property rights appraised are "fee simple" or "leasehold" (VA policy regarding the acceptability of leaseholds has not changed) and a second for the appraiser to address whether the subject property is located in a PUD or condominium project;

SUBJECT

HOA$ /Mo.

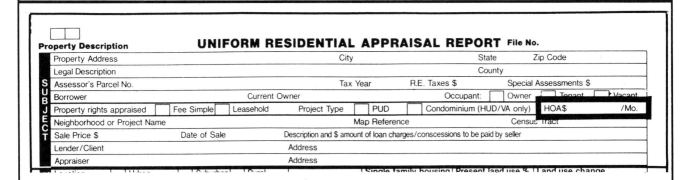

The URAR has now been approved by FNMA and FHLMC for use on some condominium and PUD appraisals.

When the subject property includes ownership of some common property, which is maintained by an association, the monthly association dues are reported in the **HOA $/Mo.** space. When the charge is annual, or for some other period except monthly, it should be converted to a monthly charge.

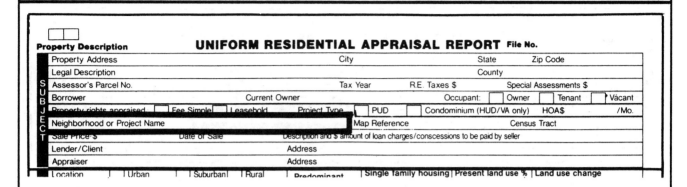

Fannie Mae and Freddie Mac have placed new emphasis on the correct identification of the neighborhood and/or project. In addition to the neighborhood name it is now also required that the appraiser either describe all the boundaries of the neighborhood and/or project or indicate them on a neighborhood/project map that is part of the addenda of the report.

Fannie Mae   January 1, 1994   Section 402   Subject Section
Neighborhood Analysis

Appraisers should use their best judgment in determining and describing neighborhood boundaries. The limits of a neighborhood can be identified by various physical characteristics – including, but not limited to, streets, bodies of water, land uses, types of dwellings, etc. The lender's underwriter should review carefully the neighborhood description to confirm that the appraiser used comparables from within the subject neighborhood in his or her analysis.

SUBJECT

Map Reference

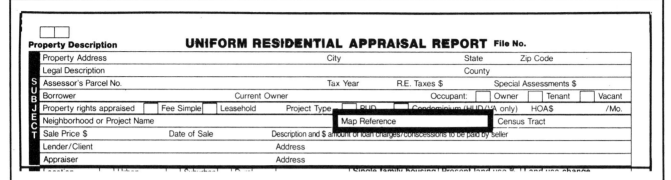

This is an optional line available to indicate an additional **Map Reference**. It is good practice to show subdivision map numbers, or any other available map number that will make a more positive identification of the property.

NOTE: Any Census Tract map numbers and SMSA numbers should <u>not</u> be included here. They are listed on the Census Tract line.

SUBJECT

Census Tract

[Form excerpt: UNIFORM RESIDENTIAL APPRAISAL REPORT — Property Description section, with the **Census Tract** field highlighted.]

The appraiser must indicate, in the applicable space, the **Census Tract** number for all properties located within an area assigned numbers. For properties located in an area without assigned tract numbers, "N/A" is entered on the **Census Tract** line to indicate there is no applicable number.

A complete census tract designation has ten digits. The first 4 are the Standard Metropolitan Statistical Area (SMSA), the next 4 indicate the Census Tract (when tract number is less than 4 digits, i.e. 22, add zeros, i.e. 0022) and the last 2, the Census Tract suffix, if any. If the property is located outside a SMSA and still has a census tract designation (most outside SMSA's do not), it is customary to enter 9999 for the first four digits.

Census tract maps may be obtained by contacting:

Superintendent of Documents   Customer Service
U.S. Government Printing Office   or   U.S. Census Bureau
Washington, DC 20402   Washington, DC 20233
(202) 783-3238   (301) 763-4100

The below map of New Haven and West Haven, CT shows SMSA 5480, Census Tract 1404 and the proper way to enter both numbers in the **Census Tract** space on the URAR. *NOTE: SMSA numbers, listed by state and city, are included in the Addenda to this Guide.*

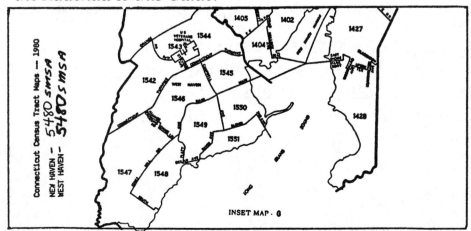

1-15

SUBJECT

Sale Price – Date of Sale

Property Description	UNIFORM RESIDENTIAL APPRAISAL REPORT File No.		
Property Address	City	State	Zip Code
Legal Description		County	
Assessor's Parcel No.	Tax Year	R.E. Taxes $	Special Assessments $
Borrower	Current Owner	Occupant: Owner Tenant	Vacant
Property rights appraised Fee Simple Leasehold	Project Type PUD	Condominium (HUD/VA only) HOA$	/Mo.
Neighborhood or Project Name	Map Reference	Census Tract	
Sale Price $ Date of Sale	Description and $ amount of loan charges/conscessions to be paid by seller		
Lender/Client	Address		
Appraiser	Address		

[Handwritten note: DATE OF MEETING OF THE MINDS. MOST RECENT WITH ALL AGREEMENTS.]

When the appraisal is for mortgage loan purposes, the **Sale Price $** and **Date of Sale** line is used to report the sale price from a pending sales contract and the date it was signed by all parties. These lines are not normally used to report a previous sale of the house, but if they are, this should be noted on the last blank line of the **SUBJECT** section.

Both Fannie Mae and Freddie Mac require that the appraiser be given all available information about a pending sale, including the sale price and date of the pending sales contract. When the appraiser does not receive this information, he or she should attempt to obtain it from the buyer, seller, broker or closing attorney. If any information is still missing, the appraiser should explain what attempts were made to obtain it in an addendum.

NOTE: If the house has been sold in the past year, the details of the sale must be reported in the COMMENTS section or an addendum.

MODEL COMMENTS: The following are examples of explanatory remarks reviewers find useful. They are especially important when data on the subject property falls outside the normal range. Usually these comments require customization to reflect the special characteristics of the specific property being appraised.

WHEN THE APPRAISAL IS FOR MORTGAGE LOAN PURPOSES AND THERE IS A SALES CONTRACT PENDING:

   Information about the pending sale was obtained from a copy of the sales contract. The sale price and date of sale _____ (were, could not be) verified by the _____ (buyer, seller, broker, closing attorney).

WHEN THE SUBJECT HAS SOLD IN THE PAST YEAR:

   The subject property sold on _____ [date] for _____ [$].

WHEN THE SUBJECT HAS NOT SOLD IN THE PAST YEAR:

   The subject property has not sold in the past year.

CONSISTENCY CHECK: Information in this section of the URAR relates to another section of the form as indicated below. The appraiser should check to make sure data in both places is consistent!

<u>**SUBJECT**</u> - **Sale Price $**
    also appears as
<u>**SALES COMPARISON ANALYSIS**</u> - SUBJECT: Sales Price.

<u>**SALES COMPARISON ANALYSIS**</u> - SUBJECT: Price/Gross Liv... Area
    is calculated by dividing the
<u>**SUBJECT**</u> - **Sale Price $**
    by the total
<u>**ROOMS**</u> - Square Feet of Gross Living Area.

<u>**SUBJECT**</u> - Date of Sale
    also appears under
<u>**SALES COMPARISON ANALYSIS**</u> - SUBJECT: Date of Sale/Time.

SUBJECT

Description and $ amount of loan charges/concessions to be paid by seller

Property Description	UNIFORM RESIDENTIAL APPRAISAL REPORT File No.		
Property Address	City	State	Zip Code
Legal Description		County	
Assessor's Parcel No.	Tax Year	R.E. Taxes $	Special Assessments $
Borrower	Current Owner	Occupant: ☐ Owner ☐ Tenant	☐ Vacant
Property rights appraised ☐ Fee Simple ☐ Leasehold Project Type ☐ PUD	Condominium (HUD/VA only)	HOA$	/Mo.
Neighborhood or Project Name	Map Reference	Census Tract	
Sale Price $ Date of Sale	**Description and $ amount of loan charges/conscessions to be paid by seller**		
Lender/Client	Address		
Appraiser	Address		

The lender must make sure that it provides the appraiser with all appropriate financing data and sales concessions for the subject property that will be, or have been, granted by anyone associated with the transaction. Generally, this can be accomplished by providing the appraiser a copy of the complete, ratified sales contract for the property that is to be appraised. If the lender is aware of additional pertinent information that is not included in the sales contract, it should inform the appraiser. Information that must be disclosed includes:

- settlement charges;
- loan fees or charges;
- discounts to the sales price;
- payment of condominium/PUD fees;
- interest rate buydowns, or other below-market rate financing;
- credits or refunds of the borrower's expenses;
- absorption of monthly payments;
- assignment of rent payments; and
- non-realty items that were included in the transaction.

MODEL COMMENTS: The following are examples of explanatory remarks reviewers find useful. They are especially important when data on the subject property falls outside the normal range. Usually these comments require customization to reflect the special characteristics of the specific property being appraised.

Fannie Mae   June 30, 2002   Part XI Chapter 4, Section 401   The Subject Property
Sales Concessions
The first section of our appraisal report forms is used to identify and describe the location of the subject property; to provide information about property taxes and special assessments to indicate the occupancy status of the property; to describe the property rights to be appraised; to summarize financing data and **sales concessions**; and to identify the borrower, the current owner, and the client.

Fannie Mae   June 30, 2002   Part XI Chapter 4, Section 401   The Subject Property
Sales Concessions
The appraiser must state the total dollar amount of the loan charges and/or concessions that will be paid by the seller (or any other party who has a financial interest in the sale or financing of the subject property) and provide a brief description of the items on the appraisal report form. If the appraiser knows that the appraisal will be used for a refinance transaction, he or she should indicate that on the form.

LOAN CHARGES/SPECIAL CONSIDERATIONS WAS OBTAINED FROM:

    Information about _____ (loan charges, special considerations) was obtained from the _____ (lender, buyer, seller, broker, closing attorney).

SUBJECT

Lender/Client & Address

Property Description	UNIFORM RESIDENTIAL APPRAISAL REPORT		File No.	
Property Address	City		State	Zip Code
Legal Description			County	
Assessor's Parcel No.	Tax Year	R.E. Taxes $	Special Assessments $	
Borrower	Current Owner	Occupant:	Owner / Tenant / Vacant	
Property rights appraised	Fee Simple / Leasehold / Project Type / PUD	Condominium (HUD/VA only)	HOA$	/Mo.
Neighborhood or Project Name		Map Reference	Census Tract	
Sale Price $	Date of Sale	Description and $ amount of loan charges/concessions to be paid by seller		
Lender/Client		**Address**		
Appraiser		Address		
Location	Urban / Suburban / Rural	Predominant	Single family housing	Present land use %	Land use change

The new 1999 USPAP requirement is that that the name of the user(s) of the report be identified. When the Lender/Client is a user (as they almost always will be) this can be indicated by changing the line title to Lender/Client/User

USPAP STANDARDS RULE 1-2 (a) "Identify the client and other intended users"

When the appraisal is for mortgage lending purposes, the **Lender's** name and address is entered on this line.

Unless otherwise indicated, it is assumed that the lender is also the client. When the client is not the lender, the client's name should also be indicated. If the client is the owner, it is now sufficient to state "Client is the Owner and User." If the Lender is also going to be a user that too must be stated somewhere.

When the **Borrower** is also a user that also be stated usually on the line that contains the name and address of the **Borrower.**

It is required that appraisers indicate the name(s) of the following somewhere in the **SUBJECT** section or in the addendum: **Owner, Occuapant, Lender, Client, Borrower** and indicate which of these are **Users** of the report.

These may be five different people, but often one person has more than one role.

Fannie Mae   June 30, 2002   Part XI Chapter 4, Section 401   The Subject Property Client

The first section of our appraisal report forms is used to identify and describe the location of the subject property; to provide information about property taxes andspecial assessments; to indicate the occupancy status of the property; to describe the property rights to be appraised; to summarize financing data and sales concessions; and to identify the borrower, the current owner, the **client**, and the appraiser.

SUBJECT

Appraiser – Address

Property Description	**UNIFORM RESIDENTIAL APPRAISAL REPORT** File No.
Property Address	City State Zip Code
Legal Description	County
Assessor's Parcel No.	Tax Year R.E. Taxes $ Special Assessments $
Borrower	Current Owner Occupant: ☐ Owner ☐ Tenant ☐ Vacant
Property rights appraised ☐ Fee Simple ☐ Leasehold	Project Type ☐ PUD ☐ Condominium (HUD/VA only) HOA$ /Mo.
Neighborhood or Project Name	Map Reference Census Tract
Sale Price $ Date of Sale	Description and $ amount of loan charges/conscessions to be paid by seller
Lender/Client	Address
Appraiser	**Address**

Appraiser's Name and Address is the place for the name and address of the appraiser who is the vendor to the client, and who will be contacted if there are problems or questions about the report.

Fannie Mae   June 30, 2002   Part XI Chapter 4, Section 401   The Subject Property

Appraiser's Name and Address

The first section of our appraisal report forms is used to identify and describe the location of the subject property; to provide information about property taxes and special assessments; to indicate the occupancy status of the property; to describe the property rights to be appraised; to summarize financing data and sales concessions; and to identify the borrower, the current owner, the client, and the **appraiser**.

MANUFACTURED HOUSING

<u>Fannie Mae</u>   June 30, 2002   Part XI Chapter 4, Section 304   <u>Factory-Built Housing</u>

Factory-built housing includes manufactured homes, modular homes, and other types of prefabricated housing. We purchase mortgages secured by factory-built housing that is designed as a one-family dwelling, assumes the characteristics of site-built housing, and is legally classified as real property. We require the factory-built home to be permanently affixed to a foundation system that is appropriate for the soil conditions of the site and designed to meet local and state codes.

The appraiser must identify the type of factory-built housing that is to be appraised since that is an important criteria in defining the appropriate market area and in selecting comparable properties.

• A *manufactured home* must be built (and installed) under the Federal Manufactured Home Construction and Safety Standards that HUD established in 1976, as they were in force at the time the home was manufactured. This can be verified by the presence of a HUD Data Plate/Compliance Certificate that is located inside the home. The appraiser must include as part of his or her appraisal report some of the information that is included on the certificate—the manufacturer's name, the trade/model name, the year of manufacture, and the serial number.

• A *modular home* must be built under the Uniform Building Code that is administered by the state agency that is responsible for adopting and administering building code requirements for the state in which the modular home is installed.

• *A facto 4-built home that is any other type of prefabricated, panelized, or sectional housing* does not have to satisfy either HUD's Federal Manufactured Home Construction and Safety Standards or the Uniform Building Codes that are adopted and administered by the state in which the home is installed. The home must conform with local building codes in the area in which it will be permanently located.

We do not have minimum requirements for width, size, roof pitch, or any other specific construction detail for manufactured homes, modular homes, or any other types of factory-built homes. Rather, each home must have sufficient square footage and room dimensions to be acceptable to typical purchasers in the subject market area. Since quality can account for large differences, in the values of factory-built homes, it is important for the appraiser to become familiar with the features that affect the quality of a factory-built home so that the information can be included in the appraisal report (if needed) to support his or her opinion of value.

The process of selecting comparable sales for factory-built housing is generally the same as that for selecting comparable sales for site-built housing. The appraiser must address both the marketability and comparability of a manufactured home by selecting comparable sales of similar manufactured homes—comparing single-width homes to single-width homes, multiwldth homes to multiwidth homes, etc. If at least three comparable sales of similar manufactured homes are not available, the appraiser may use either site-built housing or a different type of factory-built housing as one of the comparable sales. When that is the case, the appraiser must use at least two comparable sales of similar manufactured homes, explain why site-built housing or a different type of factory-built housing is being used for the one comparable sale, and make (and support) appropriate adjustments in the appraisal report. An appraiser who is unable to locate sales of manufactured homes that are truly comparable to the subject property may decide that it is appropriate to use as comparables either older sales of similar manufactured homes or sales of similar manufactured homes that are located in a competing market so that he or she can establish a baseline for the "sales comparison analysis" and determine sound adjustments to reflect the differences between the comparable sales that are available and the subject property. The appraiser should analyze and report a sufficient number of comparable sales to support his or her opinion of value (which may require the use of more than three comparable sales in some cases). The appraiser must not "create" comparable sales by combining vacant land sales with the contract purchase price of the home (although he or she may use this type of information as additional supporting documentation). If the appraiser is unable to develop a reliable appraisal based on at least two comparable sales of similar manufactured homes, the mortgage is not eligible for delivery to us.

We also require the appraiser to address both the marketability and comparability of modular homes and other types of factory-built housing. When the subject property is modular, prefabricated, panelized, or sectional housing, we do not require that one or more of the comparable sales be the same type of factory-built housing (although using comparable sales of similar types of homes generally enhance the reliability of the appraiser's opinion of value). We do expect the appraiser to include in the appraisal report the most appropriate comparable sales data to support his or her opinion of value for the subject property.

Community Living Group Homes & Mixed-Use Properties

Fannie Mae   June 30, 2002   Part XI Chapter 4, Section 305   Special Appraisal Considerations

Community Living Group Homes

The group home that secures a Community Living mortgage must maintain its residential nature and have no modifications that would make it unacceptable as a one- or two-family residence. The property appraisal for a one-family property should be documented on the *Uniform Residential Appraisal Report* (Form 1004), while the appraisal for a two-family property should be documented on the *Small Residential Income Property Appraisal Report* (Form 1025). The appraiser generally does not need to use other group home properties as comparable sales in developing the sales comparison approach to value because we expect the appraised value to reflect the value of the group home as a typical one- or two-family residence. The appraiser will not need to analyze and report comparable rental properties on the *Single-Family Comparable Rent Schedule* (Form 1007) since the room and board payments received under the contract with the state or local funding agency are not dependent on, or comparable to, market rents. However, we do expect the lender's underwriter to review the rent information that appears on our *Operating Income Statement* (Form 216) or a similar cash flow and operating income statement and to make any adjustments that are needed for any income and expense items that appear unreasonable for the market in which the group home is located.

When the loan proceeds are used to fund repairs or rehabilitation to the group home property the appraiser must have demonstrated competence and experience in evaluating properties for rehabilitation financing.

• If the rehabilitation work has already been completed, the appraiser's opinion of value must reflect the completion of the improvements—and
the borrower must provide evidence showing that the work was paid for from the borrower's own funds.

• If the rehabilitation work has not been completed, the appraiser must review the plans and specifications (and attach them to the appraisal report) and provide an opinion of the
"as completed" value of the property. The "as completed" value must be supported by market data that demonstrates the contributory value of the repairs and renovations. We will not require a second appraisal after completion of the repairs or renovations—as long as the appraiser provides a certification of completion stating that the work was completed in accordance with the plans and specifications. (If the original appraiser is not available to make the certification of completion, the lender may use a substitute appraiser provided that the appraiser reviews the original—"as completed" appraisal so that he or she can certify that the property was completed in accordance with the plans and specifications.)

Fannie Mae   June 30, 2002   Part XI Chapter 4, Section 305   Special Appraisal Considerations

Mixed-Use Properties

Although we will purchase or securitize mortgages that are secured by properties that have a business use in addition to their residential use—such as a property with space set aside for a day care facility, a beauty or barber shop, a doctor's office, a small neighborhood grocery or specialty store, etc.—we have special eligibility criteria for them. Therefore, the appraiser must provide an adequate description of the mixed-use characteristics of the subject property in the appraisal report and the lender must make sure that it considers these criteria and adequately addresses them. Specifically, for a mixed-use property to be acceptable, the following criteria must be met:
• The property must be a one-family dwelling that the borrower occupies
as a principal residence.

• The mixed use of the property must represent a legal, permissible use of the property under the local zoning requirements.

• The borrower must be both the owner and the operator of the business.

• The property must be primarily residential in nature.

• The market value of the property must be primarily a function of its residential characteristics, rather than of the business use or any special business-use modifications that were made.

NEIGHBORHOOD

Introduction

Location	Urban	Suburban	Rural	Predominant occupancy	Single family housing PRICE $(000) / AGE (yrs)	Present land use %	Land use change
Built up	Over 75%	25-75%	Under 25%			One family	Not likely / Likely
Growth rate	Rapid	Stable	Slow	Owner	Low	2-4 family	In process
Property values	Increasing	Stable	Declining	Tenant	High	Multi-family	To: _____
Demand/supply	Shortage	In balance	Over supply	Vacant (0-5%)	Predominant	Commercial	
Marketing time	Under 3 mos.	3-6 mos.	Over 6 mos.	Vacant (over 5%)		( )	

Note: Race and the racial composition of the neighborhood are not appraisal factors.

Neighborhood boundaries and characteristics: _____

Factors that affect the marketability of the properties in the neighborhood (proximity to employment and amenities, employment stability, appeal to market, etc.):

Market conditions in the subject neighborhood (including support for the above conclusions related to the trend of property values, demand/supply, and marketing time - - such as data on competitive properties for sale in the neighborhood, description of the prevalence of sales and financing concessions, etc.):

The foundation of a good appraisal is a well documented analysis of the **NEIGHBORHOOD**.

The URAR is designed to permit the appraiser to report the social and economic characteristics of the neighborhood to the extent that they are likely to affect the value of the subject property.

The reporting of detrimental neighborhood conditions is not optional. Failure to report these conditions, if they exist, is poor appraisal practice and may violate the Uniform Standards of Professional Appraisal Practice.

The following are the parts of the **NEIGHBORHOOD** section:

Location
Built up
Growth rate
Property values
Demand/supply
Marketing time
Predominant occupancy
Single family housing PRICE & AGE
Present land use %
Land use change
Race and the racial composition of the neighborhood are not appraisal factors
Neighborhood boundaries and characteristics
Factors that affect the marketability of the properties in the neighborhood
    proximity to employment and amenities
    employment stability
    appeal to market
    etc.

Convenience to Shopping
Convenience to Schools
Adequacy of Public Transportation
Recreation Facilities
Adequacy of Utilities
Property Compatibility
Protection from Detrimental Conditions
Police & Fire Protection
General Appearance of Properties

Market conditions in the subject neighborhood
   trend of property values
   demand/supply
   marketing time
   data on competitive properties for sale in the neighborhood
   description of the sales and financing concessions

Neighborhood section. The "neighborhood" section was modified to reinforce the appraiser's purpose for performing a neighborhood analysis, which is to identify the area -- based on common characteristics or trends -- that is subject to the same influences as the subject property. The sales prices of comparable properties in the identified area should reflect the positive and negative influences of the neighborhood. The results of the neighborhood analysis will enable the appraiser to define the area from which to select comparables, to understand market preferences and price patterns, to reach conclusions about the highest and best use of the subject property site, to examine the effect of different locations within the neighborhood, to determine the influence of nearby land uses, and to identify any other value influences affecting the neighborhood.

One of the more important modifications to this section was the elimination of the neighborhood analysis rating grid. This change should result in the appraiser focusing on describing the various components of a neighborhood and reporting the factors that have an impact on value in the space provided for narrative comments in the report, rather than trying to develop a "relative" rating for the neighborhood.

Fannie Mae   June 30, 2002   Part XI Chapter 4, Section 403   Neighborhood Analysis

An appraiser must perform a neighborhood analysis in order to identify the area that is subject to the same influences as the property being appraised (based on the actions of typical buyers in the market area). The results of a neighborhood analysis enable the appraiser not only to identify the factors that influence the value of properties in the market area, but also to define the area from which to select the market data needed to perform a sales comparison analysis.

To perform a neighborhood analysis, the appraiser should collect pertinent data, make a visual inspection of the market area to observe its physical characteristics and determine its boundaries, and identify land uses and any signs that the land uses are changing. The appraiser should extend the search of die subject market area as far as necessary to assure that all significant influences affecting the value of the subject property are reflected in the appraisal report, using his or her best judgment to determine and describe the neighborhood boundaries. The lender's underwriter should review carefully the neighborhood description to confirm that the appraiser used comparables from within the subject neighborhood in his or her analysis.

We expect the appraiser and the lender's underwriter to be aware of the varying conditions that characterize different types of neighborhoods or market areas. Conditions that are typical in certain neighborhoods may not be present in other neighborhoods or market areas. This does not mean that the existence of certain types of conditions or characteristics are unacceptable, rather it is an indication that they must be viewed in context with the nature of the area in which the property is located. For example, some urban neighborhoods consist of a

A neighborhood analysis should consider the influence of social, economic, government, and environmental forces on property values in the subject neighborhood. However, neither the racial composition nor the age of a neighborhood is an appraisal factor. A property located in an older neighborhood can be as sound an investment as a property located in a new neighborhood, and a property located in a neighborhood inhabited primarily by members of one race can be as sound an investment as one located in a racially mixed neighborhood or in a neighborhood inhabited primarily by a different race. The appraiser must report neighborhood conditions in factual, specific terms and be impartial and specific in describing favorable or unfavorable factors in a neighborhood. In addition, the appraiser must not use subjective terms or phrases — such as "pride of ownership," "no pride of ownership," "lack of pride of ownership," "poor neighborhood," "good neighborhood," "crime-ridden area," "desirable neighborhood or location," "undesirable neighborhood or location," etc.

Fannie Mae does not designate certain areas as being acceptable or unacceptable — in other words, Fannie Mae does not "redline." Redlining can occur when perceived property risks are based on improper locational factors — such as the arbitrary granting of unfavorable loan terms on the basis of geographic area — or when the perceptions of risk are derived from factors that do not predict risk — either reliably or not at all. An example of a factor that is not predictive of risk is race — and racial redlining is illegal under federal law. Other factors that serve as a proxy for race are equally impermissible. The appraiser, and the lender's underwriter, must be sensitive to these impermissible factors and apply Fannie Mae's guidelines in a consistent, equitable manner. None of our property guidelines is intended to foster redlining— if any provision is interpreted to do so, it has been misunderstood.

Some lenders underwrite mortgages in urban areas on a block-by-block basis. Block-by-block underwriting and appraisal analysis are acceptable in cases in which rehabilitation has started — either in the block where the subject property is located or in facing blocks visible to the property — but has not yet spread to the rest of the neighborhood. This enables the lender's underwriter to place weight on the positive influences of a neighborhood in an urban area that is being rehabilitated. The acceptability of this type of appraising or underwriting is conditioned on the appraiser demonstrating that local conditions make it appropriate and that all essential factors are considered.

The appraiser should explain any changes that have occurred that might influence the marketability of the properties within the neighborhood. For example, the appraiser must comment if there is market resistance to a neighborhood because of the known presence of an environmental hazard. The lender must be satisfied that the neighborhood will be acceptable to a sufficient number of buyers to support an active, ongoing market for the property.

Our appraisal report forms require the appraiser to address a number of important factors that are used to analyze the impact that the neighborhood has on the marketability of the property. Some of the key factors are discussed in the following subsections.

Veterans Benefits Administration   Circular 26-93-25   October 22, 1993
Neighborhood Section

The neighborhood section was modified to reinforce the appraiser's purpose for performing a neighborhood analysis, which is to identify the area (based on common characteristics or trends) that is subject to the same influences as the subject property. The sale prices of comparable properties in the identified area should reflect the positive and negative influences of the neighborhood. The results of the neighborhood analysis will enable the appraiser to define the area from which to select comparables, to understand market preferences and price patterns, to reach conclusions about the highest and best use of the subject property site, to examine the effect of different locations within the neighborhood, to determine the influence of nearby land uses, and to identify any other value influences affecting the neighborhood.

NEIGHBORHOOD

Location

Location	Urban	Suburban	Rural	Predominant	Single family housing PRICE $(000) AGE (yrs)	Present land use %	Land use change
Built up	Over 75%	25-75%	Under 25%	occupancy		One family	☐ Not likely ☐ Likely
Growth rate	☐ Rapid	☐ Stable	☐ Slow	☐ Owner	Low	2-4 family	☐ In process
Property values	☐ Increasing	☐ Stable	☐ Declining	☐ Tenant	High	Multi-family	To: _____
Demand/supply	☐ Shortage	☐ In balance	☐ Over supply	☐ Vacant (0-5%)	Predominant	Commercial	
Marketing time	☐ Under 3 mos.	☐ 3-6 mos.	☐ Over 6 mos.	☐ Vacant (over 5%)		( )	

Note: Race and the racial composition of the neighborhood are not appraisal factors.

Appraisers should think twice before classifying the **Location** of a **Rural** area as **Suburban**. The following FNMA guidelines make it clear what is necessary for an area to be classified as **Suburban**.

> The first step in the study of a neighborhood is to identify its boundaries. Sometimes they are natural, physical barriers such as lakes, rivers, streams, cliffs, swamps and valleys. They also can be highways, main traffic arteries, railroad tracks, canals and other man-made boundaries. The boundary of a residential neighborhood may also be a change of land use to commercial, industrial, institutional or public park. Some boundaries are clearly defined and others more difficult to identify precisely.... A neighborhood may be as large as an entire community, but it may be as small as a one or two block area.[1]

Fannie Mae   June 30, 2002   Part XI Chapter 4, Section 403.1   Location

We will purchase or securitize mortgages that are secured by residential properties in urban, suburban, or rural areas. An "urban" location relates to a city, a "suburban" location relates to the area adjacent to a city, and a "rural" location relates to the country or anything beyond the suburban area. We do not designate certain areas as being acceptable or unacceptable. To be eligible for purchase or securitization, a mortgage must be secured by a property that is residential in nature—based on the characteristics of the subject property, zoning, and the present land use. We do not purchase or securitize mortgages on agricultural-type properties (such as farms, orchards, or ranches), on undeveloped land, or on land development-type properties.

The appraiser and the lender's underwriter must be sensitive to the varying conditions that characterize different types of locations. The appraiser must also consider the present or anticipated use of any adjoining property that may adversely affect the value or marketability of the subject property Conditions that are typical of certain types of locations may not be present in other locale&. This does not mean that the conditions are unacceptable, rather that they must be viewed in context with the nature of the area in which the security property is located. A few examples to illustrate this are shown below:

• If the subject property is located in a rural area that is relatively undeveloped or one in which properties often have large lot sizes, the appraiser may have to go a considerable distance to find properties that can be used to develop an opinion of value for the subject property.

• If the subject property is located in a suburban or urban area, the appraiser will most likely use comparable properties in the immediate vicinity of the property since suburban and urban areas are usually more highly developed and comparable sales typically are available in the subject neighborhood. However, if the property Is located in an area in which there is a shortage of recent truly comparable sales—either because of the nature ~of the improvements of the subject property or the relatively low number' of sales transactions in the neighborhood— the appraiser might need to analyze and use' as comparable sales properties that are not truly comparable to the subject property. This is acceptable as long as the appraiser adequately documents his or her analysis in the appraisal report and explains why such comparables are being used.

---

[1] George F. Bloom and Henry S. Harrison, <u>Appraising the Single Family Residence</u>. Chicago IL: American Institute of Real Estate Appraisers, 1978. p. 86.

- If the subject property is located in an urban neighborhood that has vacant or boarded up properties, the appraiser will need to look at comparable properties in the same neighborhood to assure that any effect of the vacant or boarded up properties is taken into consideration in developing the opinion of value for the subject property.

A lender must give properties with outbuildings special consideration in the underwriting and appraisal review Properties with minimal outbuildings—such as a small barn or stable—that are of relatively insignificant value in relation to the total appraised value of the subject property are acceptable if they are typical of other residential properties in the subject area. For example, a property that has a small barn or stable is acceptable if the appraiser demonstrates through the use of comparable sales with similar improvements that the improvements are typical of properties for which an active, viable residential market exists. If the—'outbuildings do not represent typical residential improvements for the location and property type, the typical purchaser in the market would probably recognize minimal, if any, contributory value for them. A property with an atypical minimal outbuilding is acceptable to us, as long as the appraiser's analysis reflects little (or no) contributory value for it.

On the other hand, the presence of significant outbuildings—such as a large barn, a storage area or facilities for farm-type animals', or a silo-will probably indicate that the property is agricultural in nature. In such cases, the lender must review the property appraisal to determine whether the improvements are residential or agricultural in nature, regardless of whether the appraiser assigns any value to the outbuildings. All properties must be readily accessible by roads that meet local standards. Certain aspects of the location of a property will require special consideration. For example, properties in resort areas that attract people for seasonal or vacation use are acceptable only if they are suitable for year-round use. Any property that is not suitable for year-round occupancy— regardless of where it is located—is unacceptable.

MODEL COMMENTS: The following are examples of explanatory remarks reviewers find useful. They are especially important when data on the subject property falls outside the normal range. Usually these comments require customization to reflect the special characteristics of the specific property being appraised.

SUBJECT IS IN AN URBAN AREA WHERE SIGNIFICANT REHABILITATION HAS STARTED:

```
     The subject property is located in an urban area where
significant rehabilitation has started. The work is _____ (on
the same block, not on the same block as the subject property
but on blocks facing the subject property and visible to the
property).
```

SIGNIFICANT REHABILITATION IS OCCURRING IN THE NEIGHBORHOOD:

```
     In the appraisers opinion the significant rehabilitation
taking place in the neighborhood _____ (will, will not) affect
the value of the subject property because _____ [reasons the
value of subject property will or will not be affected].
```

WHEN SUBJECT PROPERTY IS IN A RURAL AREA:

```
     The property is in a rural portion of the state. A
substantial portion of the surrounding land in the area is
_____ (woodland, farms, parks, ranches, etc.).
```

NEIGHBORHOOD

Built up - Growth rate

Location	Urban	Suburban	**Rural**	Predominant occupancy	Single family housing PRICE $(000) / AGE (yrs)	Present land use %	Land use change
Built up	Over 75%	25-75%	**Under 25%**			One family	☐ Not likely ☐ Likely
Growth rate	Rapid	Stable	Slow	☐ Owner	Low	2-4 family	☐ In process
Property values	☐ Increasing	☐ Stable	☐ Declining	☐ Tenant	High	Multi-family	To: _____
Demand/supply	☐ Shortage	☐ In balance	☐ Over supply	☐ Vacant (0-5%)	**Predominant**	Commercial	
Marketing time	☐ Under 3 mos.	☐ 3-6 mos.	☐ Over 6 mos.	☐ Vacant (over 5%)		( )	

Note: Race and the racial composition of the neighborhood are not appraisal factors.

Built up refers to the percentage of available land that has been improved. For example, assume there are 10 available lots out of a total of 100 lots in a neighborhood where 50% of the land is a state park. The **Over 75%** box would be checked because 90% of the <u>available</u> land has been developed, even though substantial vacant park land still exists.

Check only one box — (arrows pointing to Growth rate row: Rapid, Stable, Slow)

Location	☐ Urban	☐ Suburban	☐ Rural	Predominant occupancy	Single family housing PRICE $(000) / AGE (yrs)	Present land use %	Land use change
Built up	Over 75%	25-75%	Under 25%			One family	☐ Not likely ☐ Likely
Growth rate	**Rapid**	**Stable**	**Slow**	☐ Owner	Low	2-4 family	☐ In process
Property values	☐ Increasing	☐ Stable	☐ Declining	☐ Tenant	High	Multi-family	To: _____
Demand/supply	☐ Shortage	☐ In balance	☐ Over supply	☐ Vacant (0-5%)	Predominant	Commercial	
Marketing time	☐ Under 3 mos.	☐ 3-6 mos.	☐ Over 6 mos.	☐ Vacant (over 5%)		( )	

When a neighborhood is fully developed, its **Growth rate**, at least for the present has ended, and the **Stable** box should be checked. A neighborhood can be fully developed even if there are vacant lots, provided they are few, scattered, and unavailable for sale at their present value. If there are many lots available, the growth rate may be **Rapid**, **Stable** or **Slow**.

<u>Fannie Mae June 30, 2002 Part XI Chapter 4, Section 403.02 Degree of Development and Growth Rate</u>

The degree of development of a neighborhood (which is referred to as "built-up" on the appraisal report forms) is the percentage of the available land in the neighborhood that has been improved. The degree of development of an area may indicate whether a particular property is residential in nature. When underwriting a mortgage secured by a property located in a rural or relatively undeveloped area, the lender should focus on the characteristics of the property, zoning, and the present land use to determine whether the property should be considered residential in nature. For example, if the typical one-family building site in a particular area (based on the zoning, the highest and best use of the land, and the present land use) is two acres in size, the mortgage will be eligible for purchase or securitization~ regardless of the percentage of the total appraised value of the property that the site represents—as long as the appraiser demonstrates through the use of comparable sales that the property is a typical residential property for that particular neighborhood.

Because we do not purchase or securitize mortgages secured by agricultural type properties undeveloped land, or land-development-type properties, the lender must review carefully the appraisal report for properties that have sites larger than those typical for residential properties in the area. Special attention must be given to the appraiser's description of the neighborhood, zoning, the highest and best use determination, and the degree of comparability between the subject property and the comparable sales. If the subject property has a significantly larger site than the comparables used in the appraiser's analysis, the subject property may not be a typical residential property for the neighborhood.

NEIGHBORHOOD

Property values

Check only one box

				Predominant occupancy	Single family housing PRICE $(000) AGE (yrs)	Present land use %	Land use change
Appraiser			Address				
Location	Urban	Suburban	Rural			One family	Not likely / Likely
Built up	Over 75%	25-75%	Under 25%	Owner	Low	2-4 family	In process
Growth rate	Rapid	Stable	Slow	Tenant	High	Multi-family	To:
Property values	Increasing	Stable	Declining	Vacant (0-5%)	Predominant	Commercial	
Demand/supply	Shortage	In balance	Over supply	Vacant (over 5%)	( )		
Marketing time	Under 3 mos.	3-6 mos.	Over 6 mos.				

The **Property values** in the neighborhood are analyzed to see if they are **Increasing**, **Stable** or **Declining**. The best method is to find houses that have sold and then resold recently and to compare the two selling prices. Adjustments should be made for any improvements to the property between sales.

<u>**Fannie Mae   June 30, 2002   Part XI Chapter 4, Section 403.03   Property Values**</u>
The appraiser must indicate whether property values in the subject neighborhood are "increasing," "stable," or "declining." Maximum financing is acceptable when property values are stable or increasing. The lender generally must not offer maximum financing in any instance in which property values are declining.

NEIGHBORHOOD

Demand/supply

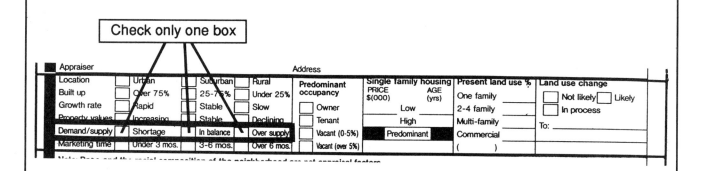

Demand/supply refers to the balance between the number of houses sold and the number of new listings available for sale. It does not refer to market activity. One market may have 20 sales and 20 new listings in a month while another may have only 2 sales and 2 listings in the same period. Both would be characterized as **In Balance**, because the number of listings equals the number of sales.

A good way to determine the **Demand/supply** balance is to check the Multiple Listing Service and compare the number of houses currently being offered to the number being offered three months ago.

<u>Fannie Mae   June 30, 2002 Part XI Chapter 4, Section 403.04   Demand, Supply, and Marketing Time</u>
An oversupply of housing is not desirable since it indicates that properties are selling slowly with a lot of competition. An oversupply of properties may be a neighborhood-wide or a city-wide problem. In either case, the appraiser must comment on the reason for the oversupply and its effect on the value of the property.

Marketing time is the average time that it takes for a reasonably priced property to sell in the subject neighborhood. When marketing time for a particular area is greater than six months, the appraiser must comment on the reason for the extended marketing period and its effect on the value of the property.

NEIGHBORHOOD

Marketing time

Appraiser					Address				
Location	☐ Urban	☐ Suburban	☐ Rural	Predominant occupancy	Single family housing PRICE $(000) / AGE (yrs)		Present land use %	Land use change	
Built up	☐ Over 75%	☐ 25-75%	☐ Under 25%				One family ___	☐ Not likely ☐ Likely	
Growth rate	☐ Rapid	☐ Stable	☐ Slow	☐ Owner	Low ___		2-4 family ___	☐ In process	
Property values	☐ Increasing	☐ Stable	☐ Declining	☐ Tenant	High ___		Multi-family ___	To: _____	
Demand/supply	☐ Shortage	☐ In balance	☐ Over supply	☐ Vacant (0-5%)	■ Predominant		Commercial ___		
Marketing time	☐ Under 3 mos.	☐ 3-6 mos.	■ Over 6 mos	☐ Vacant (over 5%)			( )		

Marketing time is the average time a similar property in the same market as the subject will take to sell when it is offered at a price close to its true market value (many appraisers use a selling price difference of 10% or less from the listing price as a guide).

The following shows a random sample of sales in the same market as the subject property, taken from an MLS Comparable sale book. The average of the number of days to sell estimates **Marketing time** for that market.

Sale #	Listing Price	Selling Price	# of Days to Sell		Remarks
1	$125,000	$120,000	85		Good sale
2	149,000	141,000	121		Good sale
3	135,000	131,000	119		Good sale
4	149,000	130,000		210	* Not Used
5	129,000	125,000	45		Good sale
6	135,000	130,000	66		Good sale
7	140,000	120,000		125	* Not Used
8	160,000	151,000	133		Good sale
9	139,000	132,000	25		Good sale
10	165,000	145,000		139	* Not Used
11	119,000	115,900	85		Good sale
12	124,000	124,000	60		Good sale
13	144,000	141,500	75		Good sale
14	160,000	160,000	85		Good sale
15	129,000	111,000		120	* Not Used
16	134,500	131,000	93		Good sale
17	144,500	132,000	135		Good sale
18	144,900	141,300	75		Good sale
19	134,000	131,250	30		Good sale
20	139,900	136,300	66		Good sale
21	143,000	143,000	65		Good sale
22	134,500	132,000	70		Good sale
23	119,000	115,500	85		Good sale
24	125,000	121,000	120		Good sale

Ave. # of days to sell = 1,638 / 20 = 79.6 Days (Mean)

* These sales were not used because of the difference between their listing price and selling price exceeded 10% of the listing price.

NOTE: A good random sample will have at least 18 good sales.

Fannie Mae   June 30, 2002 Part XI Chapter 4, Section 403.04   Demand, Supply, and Marketing Time

An oversupply of housing is not desirable since it indicates that properties are selling slowly with a lot of competition. An oversupply of properties may be a neighborhood-wide or a city-wide problem. In either case, the appraiser must comment on the reason for the oversupply and its effect on the value of the property.

Marketing time is the average time that it takes for a reasonably priced property to sell in the subject neighborhood. When marketing time for a particular area is greater than six months, the appraiser must comment on the reason for the extended marketing period and its effect on the value of the property.

MODEL COMMENTS: The following are examples of explanatory remarks reviewers find useful. They are especially important when data on the subject property falls outside the normal range. Usually these comments require customization to reflect the special characteristics of the specific property being appraised.

WHEN MARKETING TIME IS UNDER 3 MONTHS DUE TO A SHORTAGE OF HOUSES FOR SALE:

   There is a high demand for houses in this neighborhood that exceeds the supply of properties offered for sale. This _____ (does, does not) affect property values.

WHEN MARKETING TIME IS OVER 6 MONTHS DUE TO A SURPLUS OF HOUSES FOR SALE:

   There is a low demand for houses in this neighborhood, so the supply of houses for sale exceeds the demand. This has _____ (a, no) negative effect on property values.

NEIGHBORHOOD

Predominant occupancy

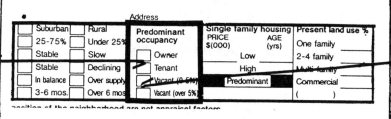

Check the appropriate box to indicate whether the neighborhood's predominant occupants are tenants or homeowners.

Check the appropriate box to indicate what percentage of the dwelling units in the neighborhood are vacant.

"If the neighborhood is of residential character, it is important to determine the percentage of homes that are **Owner** occupied. **Tenant**s, no matter how desirable, are transient in character, and frequent changes in the kind and composition of tenant families create a sense of insecurity and area instability which impairs the investment quality of a neighborhood. Tenants, too, lack a feeling of belonging, and generally their lack of pride of ownership is reflected in lax lawn and home care. Owner-occupancy status can readily be secured from public tax-record data or from tax officials, especially in states where homestead tax exemptions are accorded owner occupants.

Frequency of property turnover and percentage of home, apartment, or store vacancies provide another measure of economic rating. All else being equal, a neighborhood with well-established owner occupants of long standing poses fewer investment risks than one characterized by frequent property transfers. Excessive property sales, no matter how valid the reason, create a feeling of investment insecurity or a climate of speculation, resulting in distorted market prices that reflect transitory time-position along the ever-moving real estate business cycle. Since property values -- unless otherwise stated -- reflect the present worth of future rights to income at least over the remaining economic life of property improvements, the appraiser must take into account the influence of temporary price determinants and objectively predict future expectancy under anticipated typical market operations. **Vacant** properties, too, if in excess of normal ratios varying from 0 to 5 percent of total space supply -- depending on geographic location and kind of real property -- must be analyzed with care. Excessive vacancies may indicate a glutting of the market or a violation of the principle of balance in area development."[2]

---

[2] Alfred A. Ring, "Value Analysis of Neighborhood Characteristics", The Valuation of Real Estate. Pp. 86 - 87.

Fannie Mae   June 30, 2002   Part XI Chapter 4, Section 403.05 Predominant Occupancy

Some of our appraisal report forms provide an area for the appraiser to categorize the predominant occupancy status of the neighborhood—as "owner" or "tenant" and as "vacant (0-5%)" or "vacant (over 5%)""—as part of his or her description of the neighborhood.

The fact that the properties in a neighborhood are predominantly owner-occupied or tenant-occupied is a characteristic of the neighborhood that the appraiser needs to take into consideration when performing the neighborhood analysis and defining the neighborhood boundaries. To assure that any effects (positive or negative) of occupancy status will be reflected in the sales comparison analysis, the appraiser should select comparable sales from within the same neighborhood whenever possible. If the appraiser uses comparable sales that are outside of the subject neighborhood, he or she may need to make "neighborhood" or "location" adjustments to the sales comparison analysis for any sales that are not subject to this same neighborhood characteristic.

NEIGHBORHOOD

Single family housing PRICE and AGE range

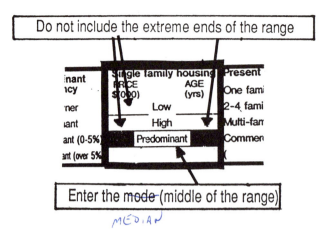

This section was designed to allow the appraiser to show a relationship between **Single family housing**'s **PRICE** and **AGE** in the subject neighborhood. If such a relationship exists, it should be indicated by appropriate comments. To avoid confusion, it is also a good idea to comment when no relationship exists.

Fannie Mae   June 30, 2002 Part XI Chapter 4, Section 403.06   Price Range and Predominant Price
The appraiser must indicate the price range and predominant price of properties in the subject neighborhood. The price range must reflect high and low prevailing prices for residential properties that are comparable to the property being appraised (one-family properties, two- to four-family properties, condominium units, or cooperative units) and, in some cases, for competing properties (one-family properties when the property being appraised is a two- to four-family property or a condominium unit, or condominium units when the property being appraised is a cooperative unit). Isolated high and low extremes should be excluded from the range, which means that the predominant price will be that which is the most common or most frequently found in the neighborhood. The appraiser may state the predominant price as a single figure or as a range (if that is more appropriate).

When the subject property has a sales price (or value) that exceeds the upper price range, the property is considered as an "over-improvement" for the neighborhood. The property is considered as an "under-improvement" if its sales price (or value) is less than the lower price range. If the subject property is an over-improvement, the mortgage terms generally should be more conservative because the property may not be acceptable to typical purchasers. The appraiser must explain why the property is an over- or under-improvement and comment on the adjustments that were made in the "sales comparison analysis" adjustment grid to reflect that condition.

The lender should consider whether a property in an urban area is among those being renovated. Since demand for this type of property can be strong, the property should not be regarded as over-improved if there is a strong market interest, which is indicated by the existence of comparable properties.

Fannie Mae   June 30, 2002   Part XI Chapter 4, Section 403.07   Age Range and Predominant Age
The appraiser must indicate the age range and predominant age of properties in the subject neighborhood. The age range should reflect the oldest and newest ages for similar types of residential properties (one-family properties, two- to four-family properties, condominium units, or cooperative units) and, in some cases, for competing properties (one-family properties when the property being appraised is a two- to four-family property or a condominium unit, or condominium units when the property being appraised is a cooperative unit.) However, isolated high and low extremes should be excluded from the range. The predominant age is the one that is the most common or most frequently found in the neighborhood. The appraiser may state the predominant age as a single figure or as a range (when that is more appropriate). The appraiser should select independently the properties that he or she uses to represent the age range and predominant age, rather than merely relying on the same properties he or she used to illustrate the price range and predominant price.

Fannie Mae   June 30, 2002   Part XI Chapter 4, Section 403.07   Age Range and Predominant Age

The age of a property should be within the general age range of the neighborhood. Normally, neighborhoods are developed over a relatively narrow span of time so that most dwelling units will fall within a particular age range. A property that has an age outside of the general age range must receive special consideration. Unless there is strong evidence of long-term neighborhood stability, a new dwelling in an old neighborhood will carry some marginal risk. Conversely, an old dwelling in a newly developed area is generally acceptable if renovation will result in its conforming to the neighborhood.

MODEL COMMENTS: The following are examples of explanatory remarks reviewers find useful. They are especially important when data on the subject property falls outside the normal range. Usually these comments require customization to reflect the special characteristics of the specific property being appraised.

WHEN A RELATIONSHIP EXISTS BETWEEN A TYPICAL HOUSE'S AGE AND ITS PRICE:

In this neighborhood there is a relationship between the age of the houses and their value. Generally newer houses sell for more per square foot of gross living area than older houses.

WHEN NO RELATIONSHIP EXISTS BETWEEN A TYPICAL HOUSE'S AGE AND ITS PRICE:

In this neighborhood there is little direct relationship between the age of houses and their value. Older houses that have been modernized sell for prices per square foot of gross living area similar to newer houses of the same size.

WHEN THERE IS MORE RELATIONSHIP BETWEEN SIZE AND VALUE THAN AGE AND VALUE:

In this neighborhood there is a direct relationship between the typical house's price and its square foot gross living area. It is the size of the house rather than the age of the house that appears to most affect its value.

WHEN THE HOUSE IS AN OVER IMPROVEMENT:

This house is excessive in _____ (cost, size) as compared to _____ (the land value, other houses in this neighborhood). The subject property's value is _____ (reduced, unaffected) by the over improvement.

WHEN THE HOUSE IS AN UNDER IMPROVEMENT:

This house is _____ (a low quality house, an under improvement, not as valuable as most) in this _____ (low, moderate, high) value neighborhood. Being an under improvement has _____ (a negative, no) effect on its value because houses in this neighborhood that do not conform seem to suffer _____ (from some functional obsolescence, no detrimental effect).

NEIGHBORHOOD

Present land use %

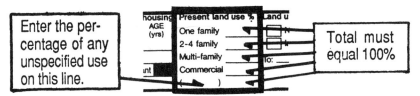

Enter the estimated percentage of each type of **Present land use** in the neighborhood. Enter a "0" or a "-" when there is no land in the neighborhood in a specified classification. When a portion of the land is parks or another unspecified classification, enter those percentages on the first line of the **NEIGHBORHOOD - COMMENTS** section.

NOTE: The total of all 6 specified plus any unspecified uses <u>must equal 100%</u>.

<u>Fannie Mae   June 30, 2002   Part XI Chapter 4, Section 403.08   Present Land Use</u>

Some of our appraisal report forms provide an area for the appraiser to report the relative percentages of the developed land in the neighborhood when discussing the present land use, rather than simply referring to the zoning classifications. The appraiser should report separately the percentage of developed one-family sites, developed two- to four-family sites, etc. Undeveloped land should be reported as vacant. In addition, if there is a significant amount of vacant or undeveloped land in the neighborhood, the appraiser should include comments to that effect to assure that he or she adequately describes the neighborhood. If the present land use in the neighborhood is not one of those listed on the appraisal report form—such as parkland—the appraiser must also indicate the type of land use and its related percentage. The total of the types of land uses must equal 100%.

Typically, dwellings best maintain their value when they are situated in neighborhoods that consist of other similar dwellings. However, some factors that are typical of a mixed-use neighborhood—such as easy access to employment centers and a high level of community activity—can actually enhance the market value of the property through increased buyer demand. Urban neighborhoods also frequently reflect a blend of residential and nonresidential land uses—including residential multifamily properties, other properties that are used to provide commercial services (such as groceries and other neighborhood stores) in support of the local neighborhood, industrial properties, etc.

When different land uses and property types are present in a neighborhood, that fact should be considered a neighborhood characteristic that the appraiser needs to take into consideration when performing the neighborhood analysis and defining the neighborhood boundaries. To assure that any positive or negative effects of the mixed land uses are reflected in the sales comparison analysis, the appraiser should select comparable sales from within the same neighborhood whenever possible. If this is not possible, the appraiser may need to make "neighborhood" or "location" adjustments to the "sales comparison analysis" grid for any sales that are not subject to this same neighborhood characteristic.

<u>Neighborhood Analysis - Present Land use</u>

Show percentage of various types of neighborhood buildings.

MODEL COMMENTS: The following are examples of explanatory remarks reviewers find useful. They are especially important when data on the subject property falls outside the normal range. Usually these comments require customization to reflect the special characteristics of the specific property being appraised.

<u>COMMERCIAL, INDUSTRIAL, OR MULTI-FAMILY LAND USE:</u>

_____ [%] percent of the present land use in the neighborhood is _____ (commercial, industrial, multi-family). The majority of this land consists of _____ (retail stores, factories,

NEIGHBORHOOD

Land use change

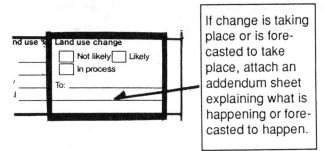

If change is taking place or is forecasted to take place, attach an addendum sheet explaining what is happening or forecasted to happen.

Indicate, by checking the appropriate box, if there is any **Land use change** currently **In process**, **Likely** to happen in the future, or **Not Likely**.

The following are typical land use changes that might take place in a residential neighborhood:
1. Conversion from single family to small income property use.
2. Introduction of high density multiple family apartments.
3. New commercial uses.
4. New industrial uses.
5. New roads and highways.
6. New recreation facilities.
7. Conversion of dwellings from fee simple to condominiums.

<u>Fannie Mae   June 30, 2002   Part XI Chapter 4, Section 403.09   Change in Land Use</u>

Some of our appraisal report forms provide an area for the appraiser to indicate whether the present land use in the neighborhood is "likely" or "not likely" to change or whether it is "in process" of changing. If the land use is likely to change or is in the process of changing, the appraiser should indicate the anticipated new land use(s). The present land use, the predominant occupancy composition, and the likelihood that either will change may be an indicator for determining whether a neighborhood is undergoing transition. However, a "neighborhood in transition" description must not be used to refer to the racial or ethnic composition—or the prospective racial or ethnic composition—of a neighborhood. If the appraiser indicates that an area is undergoing transition, he or she should describe the changes and comment about their effect on the marketability and value of the subject property.

<u>Veterans Benefits Administration   Circular 26-93-25   October 22, 1993</u>
<u>Neighborhood Section - Market Transition</u>

In any case in which information in the "neighborhood" section indicates there is a market transition, the fee appraiser must provide an addendum providing a minimum of three competitive listings or contract offerings. A market transition may be considered to include: a change to an over supply/shortage of housing stock, marketing times/listing periods which have increased/decreased significantly, change in employment stability, increase in sales and financing concessions by sellers, among other indicators.

MODEL COMMENTS: The following are examples of explanatory remarks reviewers find useful. They are especially important when data on the subject property falls outside the normal range. Usually these comments require customization to reflect the special characteristics of the specific property being appraised.

<u>WHEN CHANGES HAVE TAKEN PLACE IN THE NEIGHBORHOOD</u>:

```
    The following _____ (favorable, unfavorable) changes in the
subject neighborhood have occurred within the past year:
_____ [describe changes].
```

NEIGHBORHOOD

Race and the racial composition of the neighborhood are not appraisal factors

> Note: Race and the racial composition of the neighborhood are not appraisal factors.
>
> Neighborhood boundaries and characteristics:
>
> Factors that affect the marketability of the properties in the neighborhood (proximity to employment and amenities, employment stability, appeal to market, etc.):
>
> Market conditions in the subject neighborhood (including support for the above conclusions related to the trend of property values, demand/supply, and marketing time - - such as data on competitive properties for sale in the neighborhood, description of the prevalence of sales and financing concessions, etc.):

The URAR contains the statement, **Race or the racial composition of the neighborhood are not considered reliable appraisal factors.**

Previous editions of the form stated that the above was the policy of FHLMC and FNMA. It remains the policy of these two agencies as well as the other organizations represented on the committee that produced the URAR. The committee recognized the universal acceptance of this principle and therefore deemed it unnecessary to list the individual organizations who subscribe to it.

Fannie Mae   June 30, 2002   Part XI Chapter 4, Section 403   Neighborhood Analysis

We do not designate certain areas as being acceptable or unacceptable—in other words, we do not "red-line." Redlining can occur when perceived property risks are based on improper locational factors—such as the arbitrary granting of unfavorable loan terms on the basis of geographic area—or when the perceptions of risk are derived from factors that do not predict risk—either reliably or at all. An example of a factor that is not predictive of risk is race—and racial redlining is illegal under federal law. Other factors that serve as a proxy for race are equally impermissible. The appraiser and the lender's underwriter must be sensitive to these impermissible factors and apply our guidelines in a consistent, equitable manner. None of our property guidelines is intended to foster redlining—if any provision is interpreted to do so, it has been misunderstood.

Some lenders underwrite mortgages in urban areas on a block-by-block basis. Block-by-block underwriting and appraisal analysis is acceptable in cases in which rehabilitation has started—either in the block where the subject property is located or in facing blocks visible to the property—but has not yet spread to the rest of the neighborhood. This enables the lender's underwriter to place weight on the positive influences of a neighborhood in an urban area that is being rehabilitated. The acceptability of this type of appraising or underwriting is conditioned on the appraiser demonstrating that local conditions make it appropriate and that all essential factors are considered.

NEIGHBORHOOD

Neighborhood boundaries and characteristics

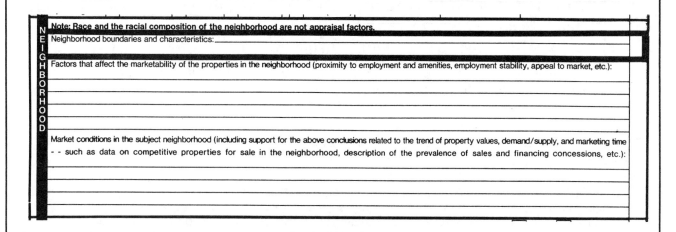

Neighborhood boundaries and characteristics is a new line which is provided for information about the neighborhood. It is now required that the neighborhood boundaries be described in the report. (As an alternative, this line can be used to refer to the neighborhood boundary map in the addenda.)

NOTE: More and more appraisers are attaching a map to their appraisals delineating the boundaries of the neighborhood.

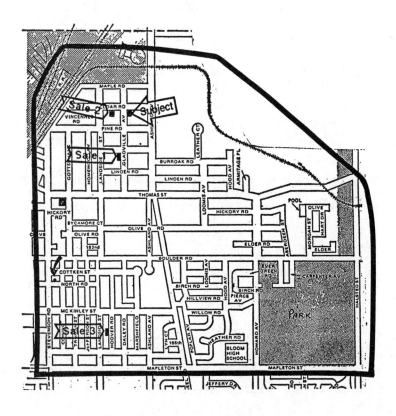

2-17

A boundary map is very helpful to reviewers. Often when a reviewer compares two appraisals of the same property, he or she finds substantially different information in the **NEIGHBORHOOD** sections. This may occur because the two appraisers have used different neighborhood boundaries to develop their information. This often is a reasonable difference of opinion rather than an error made by one of the appraisers. With a neighborhood map, the reviewer knows what area is included in each appraiser's neighborhood analysis, and is better able to determine which neighborhood boundaries are most appropriate.

Fannie Mae   June 30, 2002   Part XI Chapter 4, Section 403   Neighborhood Analysis
Neighborhood Boundries and Characteristics

Property location is a fundamental characteristic that influences the value of is residential real estate. Therefore, it is a critical factor that must be considered in the appraisal process. Neighborhood characteristics and trends also influence the value of one- to four-family residences; therefore, they are also key elements in the appraisal process. Because we purchase mortgages secured by properties in all neighborhoods and in all areas—as long as the property is acceptable as security for the mortgage based on itsvalue and marketability—property location, neighborhood characteristics, and neighborhood trends are determinants that the appraiser uses in the property valuation process, but are not factors in determining whether a particular neighborhood is acceptable or not.

Veterans Benefits Administration   Circular 26-93-25   October 22, 1993
Location Map

A location map indicating the location of the subject and comparables and a building perimeter sketch will now be required with all appraisals. Those exhibits will also be required with all assignments received 1 week or more from the date of the field station's release.

Veterans Benefits Administration   Circular 26-93-25   October 22, 1993
Neighborhood Section - Neighborhood Boundaries and Characteristics

The modifications to the neighborhood section include the creation of new entries to describe...Market conditions in the subject neighborhood (including support for the conclusions related to the trend of property values, demand/supply and marketing time).

MODEL COMMENTS: The following are examples of explanatory remarks reviewers find useful. They are especially important when data on the subject property falls outside the normal range. Usually these comments require customization to reflect the special characteristics of the specific property being appraised.

WHEN SUBJECT PROPERTY IS IN A RURAL AREA:

```
   The property is in a rural portion of the state.  A sub-
stantial portion of the surrounding land in the area is _____
(woodland, farms, parks, ranches, etc.).
```

WHEN THE NEIGHBORHOOD BOUNDARIES AND CHARACTERISTICS ARE SHOWN ON A NEIGHBORHOOD BOUNDARY MAP:

```
    The appraiser has indicated the neighborhood boundaries on a
neighborhood map that is included in the addenda of this
appraisal report.
```

NEIGHBORHOOD

Factors that affect the marketability of the properties in the neighborhood

```
Marketing time   | Under 3 mos. | 3-6 mos. | Over 6 mos. | Vacant (over 5%) |

Note: Race and the racial composition of the neighborhood are not appraisal factors.
Neighborhood boundaries and characteristics: _____

Factors that affect the marketability of the properties in the neighborhood (proximity to employment and amenities, employment stability, appeal to market, etc.):
_____
_____
_____
_____
_____

Market conditions in the subject neighborhood (including support for the above conclusions related to the trend of property values, demand/supply, and marketing time
- - such as data on competitive properties for sale in the neighborhood, description of the prevalence of sales and financing concessions, etc.):
_____
```

The old **Neighborhood rating grid** has been eliminated. In its place are five lines to report the neighborhood **Factors that affect the marketability of the properties** in the neighborhood.

The **NEIGHBORHOOD ANALYSIS** rating grid was designed to provide a summary of several important characteristics of the subject neighborhood. Details on what information to consider when rating each characteristic are provided in the following sub sections. The appraiser should consider each of these factors and when appropriate comment on them on the five provided lines or in the addenda.

Proximity to employment and amenities is a rating of the distance from the subject neighborhood to local employment sources and community amenities service in terms of mileage and travel time. The cost and convenience of public transportation for commuters should also be considered here.

Employment stability is usually indicated in an area where there is a large number and variety of employment opportunities and industries. It is also more desirable to have a variety of small employers rather than a few large employers, especially if local industry tends to be cyclical or in a state of decline.

Appeal to market is a rating by the appraiser of the overall appeal of this neighborhood as compared to competitive neighborhoods in the same market.

Rate the neighborhood's **Convenience to Shopping** facilities in terms of distance, time, and required means of transportation. Consideration should be given to convenience stores, neighborhood and community shopping centers, regional malls and downtown city shopping.

Convenience to School is determined by the distance to schools and the time it takes for a student to cover that distance. For example, when bus transportation is required, distance travel and the student's travel time on the bus are factors which should be considered.

In many areas, the market will penalize a house that is beyond safe walking distance to schools.

Veterans Benefits Administration   Circular 26-93-25   October 22, 1993
Neighborhood Section - Elimination of Rating Grid

Another significant modification to this section was the elimination of the neighborhood analysis rating grid. This change should result in the appraiser focusing on describing the various components of a neighborhood and reporting factors that have an impact on value in the space provided for narrative comments rather than trying to develop a "relative" rating for the neighborhood.

Veterans Benefits Administration   Circular 26-93-25   October 22, 1993
Neighborhood Section - Factors that Effect Marketability

The modifications to the neighborhood section include the creation of new entries to describe...Factors that affect the marketability of the properties in the neighborhood;

MODEL COMMENTS: The following are examples of explanatory remarks reviewers find useful. They are especially important when data on the subject property falls outside the normal range. Usually these comments require customization to reflect the special characteristics of the specific property being appraised.

WHEN THE HOUSE IS CONVENIENTLY LOCATED TO SCHOOLS:
    This house is within walking distance of the _____ (grammar, middle, high) school(s).

WHEN THE HOUSE IS NOT CONVENIENTLY LOCATED TO THE SCHOOLS:
    This house is beyond convenient walking distance to the _____ (grammar, middle, high) school(s). The community _____ (provides, does not provide) busing to the school(s). This has _____ (a negative, no) effect on the value of the property.

Assess the **Adequacy of Public Transportation** serving the neighborhood. The following are examples of the types of public transportation to consider: buses to employment centers, shopping areas and other communities; trains to employment centers and other communities; airports and taxi service.

Many appraisers (and FNMA) feel that in rural areas, where little public transportation is available anywhere in the competing market, "Average" is a suitable rating. Others feel that "Fair" or "Poor" is more suitable, together with a comment that the lack of public transportation has little or no effect on property values in the market.

MODEL COMMENTS: The following are examples of explanatory remarks reviewers find useful. They are especially important when data on the subject property falls outside the normal range. Usually these comments require customization to reflect the special characteristics of the specific property being appraised.

WHEN PUBLIC TRANSPORTATION IS ADEQUATE:

There is good public transportation available near the subject property. This has _____ (a positive, no) effect on value, because other properties in this market have _____ (similar, better, little, no) available public transportation.

WHEN PUBLIC TRANSPORTATION IS INADEQUATE:

There is little or no public transportation available near the subject property. There are _____ (no, few) _____ (buses, trains, taxis airports). This has _____ (a negative, no) effect on the value of the property being appraised because other properties in the market have _____ (similar, better, little, no) public transportation available.

Consider the number, type and quality of **Recreation Facilities** available to residents in the subject neighborhood as compared to competing neighborhoods. The extent to which such facilities are expected by the market for properties in the subject's price range is also a consideration.

MODEL COMMENTS: The following are examples of explanatory remarks reviewers find useful. They are especially important when data on the subject property falls outside the normal range. Usually these comments require customization to reflect the special characteristics of the specific property being appraised.

WHEN RECREATION FACILITIES ARE INADEQUATE:

There are few recreation facilities available near the subject property. They consist only of _____ (pools, courts, golf courses, stadiums, etc.). This has _____ (no, a negative) effect on the value of the subject property, because competing properties in this market have _____ (similar, better, more, poorer, fewer) recreational facilities available.

The **Adequacy of Utilities** is the extent to which the utility systems (water, sewer, electricity and gas, if the latter is available) meet residents' needs as compared to similar neighborhoods. Consideration should include public, private (community or subdivision) and individual utilities.

Factors to be considered for **Property Compatibility** include the types of land uses prevalent in a neighborhood, lot sizes, price ranges, and building ages and styles. <u>Rate the subject neighborhood</u> on the extent to which these attributes are compatible with one another <u>as compared to</u> their compatibility in similar competing neighborhoods in the same market.

Police & Fire Protection can be important factors affecting the value of houses in competing neighborhoods. When the buying public feels that a neighborhood has inadequate police or fire protection, home values are likely to be lower than those in competing neighborhoods with better protection.

Consider the **General Appearance of Properties** in the subject neighborhood, particularly the extent to which both buildings and yards are maintained. Unmaintained properties often reduce the value of all other nearby properties in the neighborhood.

Appeal to Market is essentially an overall summary rating of the market appeal of all aspects of the neighborhood -- i.e., an indication of the marketability of an average property in the subject neighborhood.

CONSISTENCY CHECK: Information in this section of the URAR relates to another section of the form as indicated below. The appraiser should check to make sure data in both places is consistent!
<u>NEIGHBORHOOD</u> - NEIGHBORHOOD ANALYSIS: Appeal to Market
    rating should be considered when rating the
<u>SALES COMPARISON ANALYSIS</u> - SUBJECT: Location.

NEIGHBORHOOD

Market conditions in the subject neighborhood

> **Note:** Race and the racial composition of the neighborhood are not appraisal factors.
>
> Neighborhood boundaries and characteristics: _____
>
> Factors that affect the marketability of the properties in the neighborhood (proximity to employment and amenities, employment stability, appeal to market, etc.):
>
> _____
>
> Market conditions in the subject neighborhood (including support for the above conclusions related to the trend of property values, demand/supply, and marketing time - - such as data on competitive properties for sale in the neighborhood, description of the prevalence of sales and financing concessions, etc.):

Another five lines are provided to report **Market conditions in the subject neighborhood**, including support for conclusions related to the trend of property values, demand/supply and marketing time.

The appraiser must be familiar with the prevailing **General market conditions**, including how houses are financed in the subject market. If sellers customarily pay loan discounts, interest buyouts or other financial concessions, these must be reported.

A comments should be made here about competitive properties for sale in the neighborhood and what effect they have on the value of the subject property.

Fannie Mae   June 30, 2002   Part XI Chapter 4, Section 403.03   Property Values
The appraiser must indicate whether property values in the subject neighborhood are "increasing," "stable," or "declining." Maximum financing is acceptable when property values are stable or increasing. The lender generally must not offer maximum financing in any instance in which property values are declining.

Fannie Mae**June 30, 2002****Part XI Chapter 4, Section 403 Neighborhood Analysis**

Factors that affect the value and marketability of properties in the neighborhood can be addressed by such things as the proximity of the property to employment and amenities, employment stability, appeal to the market, changes in land use, access to public transportation, adverse environmental influences, etc.

Generally accepted appraisal standards and our appraisal report forms require the appraiser to research, analyze, and report on the factors in the neighborhood that may affect the market value or marketability of the properties in the market area. Failing to report such factors or conditions in the appraisal report and/or making assumptions about those factors that might affect value without performing adequate market research are unacceptable appraisal practices. The appraiser must understand the value-influencing characteristics in the neighborhood and arrive at an appropriate neighborhood description and opinion of value for the property—even if this requires more extensive research for particular property types or for properties in certain geographic locations.

An appraiser must perform a neighborhood analysis in order to identify the area that is subject to the same influences as the property being appraised (based on the actions of typical buyers in the market area). The results of a neighborhood analysis enable the appraiser not only to identify the factors that influence the value of properties in the market area, but also to define the area from which to select the market data needed to perform a sales comparison analysis.

To perform a neighborhood analysis, the appraiser should collect pertinent data, make a visual inspection of the market area to observe its physical characteristics and determine its boundaries, and identify land uses and any signs that the land uses are changing. The appraiser should extend the search of die subject market area as far as necessary to assure that all significant influences affecting the value of the subject property are reflected in the appraisal report, using his or her best judgment to determine and describe the neighborhood boundaries. The lender's underwriter should review carefully the neighborhood description to confirm that the appraiser used comparables from within the subject neighborhood in his or her analysis.

```
WHEN THERE ARE NO SPECIAL SALES OR FINANCING CONCESSIONS:

    This is a good active market. No special financing, loan
discounts, interest buydowns or concessions were found for the
subject or comparable sales in this market.
    There are _____ (few, many, no, etc. competitive houses
listed for sale in the subject neighborhood. They have
_____ (little, no, a depressing) effect on the value of the
subject property.
```

This space or the addenda should be used by the appraiser for further explanation of previously described neighborhood factors, especially items described as "Fair" or "Poor" . Anything in the neighborhood that could cause external obsolescence should be described here with the appraiser's opinion as to what effect, if any, it may have on the subject's value. Failure to mention such an item may cause a reviewer to think the appraiser failed to consider the item as potential external obsolescence.

In addition, remarks should be made about any favorable or unfavorable factors which are likely to influence the long term stability of neighborhood property values, presently or in the future. Some important considerations are the quality of neighborhood schools and/or the community's school system as a whole, public parks, views common to the neighborhood and the effect of any objectionable noises or odors.

As a minimum, the appraiser should describe those factors, favorable or unfavorable, affecting the marketability of the appraisal property. This includes a statement about market area population and an analysis of the financial ability of the population (both tenants and potential new owners) to rent units or buy property.

The appraiser must be careful to avoid the use of code phrases, like "pride of ownership," that could be considered proxies for information about race.

Fannie Mae   June 30, 2002 Part XI Chapter 4, Section 403.04   Demand, Supply, and Marketing Time

An oversupply of housing is not desirable since it indicates that properties are selling slowly with a lot of competition. An oversupply of properties may be a neighborhood-wide or a city-wide problem. In either case, the appraiser must comment on the reason for the oversupply and its effect on the value of the property.

Marketing time is the average time that it takes for a reasonably priced property to sell in the subject neighborhood. When marketing time for a particular area is greater than six months, the' appraiser must comment on the reason for the extended marketing period and its effect on the value of the property.

Veterans Benefits Administration   Circular 26-93-25   October 22, 1993
Neighborhood Section - Marketing Time

Indicate to what extent the average marketing time (listing period) in subject's competing market area is expanding or contracting (e.g., in the last 3 months the listing period in the subject's market area has decreased from 180 days to 90 days); and

MODEL COMMENTS: The following are examples of explanatory remarks reviewers find useful. They are especially important when data on the subject property falls outside the normal range. Usually these comments require customization to reflect the special characteristics of the specific property being appraised.

GENERAL COMMENT TO DESCRIBE THE NEIGHBORHOOD:
    The subject neighborhood is _____ (known as _____ [name], bounded by _____ [describe neighborhood boundaries]). It provides a _____ (poor, fair, average, good) environment for the house being appraised. There are _____ (no, some, many) factors that will negatively affect the marketability of the house which are described in the addenda. The public schools, parks, view and noise level _____ (are, are not) typical for this type of neighborhood.

WHEN EXTERNAL FACTORS MAY AFFECT THE SUBJECT'S VALUE:
    The following external factors which have _____ (a negative, a positive, no) effect on the subjects appeal and marketability were noted: _____ [describe factors].

CONSISTENCY CHECK: Information in this section of the URAR relates to another section of the form as indicated below. The appraiser should check to make sure data in both places is consistent!
NEIGHBORHOOD - COMMENTS:
    Any item of external obsolescence reported here to have an effect on property values, must also be listed under "external inadequacies" in the
COMMENTS - Depreciation
    space. A consistent deduction should also be made in the
COST APPROACH - External: Depreciation
    section.

Veterans Benefits Administration   Circular 26-93-25   October 22, 1993

The neighborhood section was modified to reinforce the appraiser's purpose for performing a neighborhood analysis, which is to identify the area (based on common characteristics or trends) that is subject to the same influences as the subject property. The sale prices of comparable properties in the identified area should reflect the positive and negative influences of the neighborhood. The results of the neighborhood analysis will enable the appraiser to define the area from which to select comparables, to understand market preferences and price patterns, to reach conclusions about the highest and best use of the subject property site, to examine the effect of different locations within the neighborhood, to determine the influence of nearby land uses, and to identify any other value influences affecting the neighborhood.

Veterans Benefits Administration   Circular 26-93-25   October 22, 1993

The modifications to the neighborhood section include the creation of new entries to describe:

(a) Neighborhood boundaries and characteristics;

(b) Factors that affect the marketability of the properties in the neighborhood;

(c) Market conditions in the subject neighborhood (including support for the conclusions related to the trend of property values, demand/supply and marketing time). VA will continue to require fee appraisers to report, in each case, the existence or nonexistence of sales or financing concessions in the subject's market area and make a statement regarding their effect, if any, on the sales prices of comparable homes. That statement must be made in this section or on an addendum. In addition, fee appraisers must provide the following General Market Information in this section, or an addendum, (which was being provided in all liquidation appraisal assignments):

Veterans Benefits Administration   Circular 26-93-25   October 22, 1993
Neighborhood Section - Listing Price/Sales Price Ratio

Average listing price to sale price ratio (appraiser will use professional judgment to estimate the ratio if it cannot be determined from available data sources.)

As previously noted, the review and analysis of competitive listings and/or contract offerings is considered a basic part of the research involved in the appraisal process. It is recognized in appraisal texts, is a generally accepted industry practice and is essential in ensuring that the final value estimate is fully reflective of any trends (positive or negative) existing as of the effective date of the appraisal. This is especially important given the no money down feature of many VA loans. In all cases fee appraisers should be reviewing and analyzing this information in order to reconcile the closed sales data with current market conditions and to assist in making appropriate time adjustments. In recognition of the importance of this aspect of the appraisal process to VA, fee appraisers must make the following statement in the narrative area of the neighborhood section in all origination appraisal assignments:

"I have considered relevant competitive listings and/or contract offerings in the performance of this appraisal and in the trending information reported in this section. If a trend is indicated, I have attached an addendum providing relevant competitive listing/contract offering data."

Notes

PUD

Introduction

Project Information for PUDs (If applicable) - - Is the developer/builder in control of the Home Owners' Association (HOA)? ☐ Yes ☐ No
Approximate total number of units in the subject project_____ Approximate total number of units for sale in the subject project _____
Describe common elements and recreational facilities:

    A Planned Unit Development or **PUD** is a project (or subdivision) that includes common property and improvements that are owned and maintained by an owners' association for the use and benefit of the individual units in the project (or subdivision).

Fannie Mae classifies a project (or subdivision) as a PUD if each unit owner's **membership in the owners' association is <u>automatic and nonseverable</u>** and **<u>the owners' association has the right to impose mandatory assessments.</u>** (Fannie Mae does not consider Zoning to be a basis for classifying a project or subdivision as a PUD.)

This new **"PUD"** section was created to enable the appraiser to address the basic information about the project when the property being appraised is in a planned unit development. Information that the appraiser is asked to provide includes:

- a description of the project (including a description of the common elements and recreational facilities

- and an indication of whether the developer/builder is in control of the owner's association)

- and the approximate total number of units in the project

- and the approximate total number of units for sale in the project.

    The creation of this new section should generally eliminate the need for attaching an addendum to the form for appraisals of units in established PUD projects. However, it may still be necessary to use an addendum for appraisals related to attached units in a new PUD project for which the developer is still in control of the owners' association, in order to satisfy the specific eligibility requirements Fannie Mae has for this type of project.

Fannie Mae   June 30, 2002   Part XI Chapter 4, Section 302   Special Appraisal Considerations
Units in PUD Projects

A planned unit development (PUD) is a project or subdivision that consists of common property and improvements that are owned and maintained by an owners' association for the benefit and use of the individual units within the project. For a project to qualify as a PUD, the owners' association must require automatic, nonseverable membership for each individual unit owner, and provide for mandatory assessments. Zoning should not be the basis for classifying a project as a PUD.

Appraisals for PUD units that secure manually underwriter mortgages are generally documented on the 'Uniform Residential Appraisal Report' (Form 1004) or the Desktop Underwriter Quantitate Analysis Appraisal Report (Form 2055). To assure that all the specific eligibility criteria for a new PUD project are adequately addressed, it may be necessary to use an addendum to Form 1004 to provide information for appraisals related to attached units in new PUD projects (particularly when the developer is still in control of the owners' association). Desktop Underwriter will specify the level of property analysis and, review for Desktop Underwriter-processed mortgages that are secured by PUD units.

The appraisal of an individual unit in a PUD requires the appraiser to analyze the PUD project as well as the individual unit. The appraiser must pay special attention to the location of the individual unit within the project, the project's amenities, and the amount and purpose of the owners association assessment since the marketability and value of the individual units in a project generally depend on the marketability and appeal of the project itself.

Veterans Benefits Administration   Circular 26-93-25   October 22, 1993
Subject Section - PUD and De minimis PUD

The obsolete reference to de minimis PUD was deleted. If the appraiser indicates that the subject property is located in a PUD or a condominium, the appraiser is to provide the unit's homeowner's association fee in this part.

Veterans Benefits Administration   Circular 26-93-25   October 22, 1993
Subject Section - PUD and De minimis PUD

This section will be completed by VA fee appraisers, as appropriate. VA fee appraisers will continue to ensure that a PUD is on VA's accepted list or is otherwise acceptable to VA before proceeding with an appraisal assignment for a unit located in a PUD. In general, a PUD is a project (or subdivision) that includes common property and improvements that are owned and maintained by an owners' association for the use and benefit of the individual units in the project (or subdivision). A project (or subdivision) is classified as a PUD if each individual unit owner is automatically a mandatory member of the owners' association and is obligated to pay mandatory assessments. (Zoning is not considered to be a basis for classifying a project or subdivision as a PUD.)

PUD

Project Information for PUDs (if applicable)

Project Information for PUDs (If applicable) - - Is the developer/builder in control of the Home Owners' Association (HOA)? ☐ Yes ☐ No
Approximate total number of units in the subject project _____ Approximate total number of units for sale in the subject project _____
Describe common elements and recreational facilities:

During the time when a developer plans and builds a PUD the developer maintains control of the PUD and is responsible for the expenses incurred. When a specified percentage of the units are sold the control of the project reverts to the Association of PUD owners which is often called the "Home Owners' Association (the actual name varies from locality to locality and is often spelled out in state and local statutes). The appraiser is required to determine if control has passed from the developer to the HOA and report who controls the HOA on the URAR.

Fannie Mae   June 30, 1993 Announcement   PUD Section
Description of the Project (Control by Owner's Association)

"...the appraiser is asked to provide includes a description of the project and...an indication of whether the developer/builder is in control of the owners' association)."

PUD

Approximate total number of units in subject project

Project Information for PUDs (If applicable) - - Is the developer/builder in control of the Home Owners' Association (HOA)?	☐ Yes ☐ No
Approximate total number of units in the subject project_____ Approximate total number of units for sale in the subject project _____	
Describe common elements and recreational facilities:	
Dimensions _____ Topography	

The appraiser must report the approximate total number of units in the project.

Fannie Mae   June 30, 1993   Announcement   PUD Section
Total Number of Units in the Project

"...the appraiser is asked to provide ...the approximate total number of units in the project."

PUD

Approximate total number of units for sale in subject project

Project Information for PUDs (If applicable) - - Is the developer/builder in control of the Home Owners' Association (HOA)?	☐ Yes ☐ No
Approximate total number of units in the subject project_____	Approximate total number of units for sale in the subject project _____
Describe common elements and recreational facilities:	

    The appraiser must determine and report the approximate number of units that are for sale in the project

Fannie Mae   June 30, 1993   Announcement   PUD Section
Total Number of Units For Sale In the Project
"...the appraiser is asked to ...approximate total number of units for sale in the project."

PUD

Describe common elements and recreational facilities

Project Information for PUDs (If applicable) - - Is the developer/builder in control of the Home Owners' Association (HOA)? ☐ Yes ☐ No
Approximate total number of units in the subject project   Approximate total number of units for sale in the subject project
Describe common elements and recreational facilities:

The best place to determine what the common elements and recreational facilities are is the PUD documents. These are on file where other property records are files. Often each owner is given a copy and the officers, directors and management company (if there is one) will have copies. Note should be made of any items that appear in these documents that do not actually exist together with an explanation as to why they do not exist and if the developer is going to provide them in the future.

Fannie Mae   June 30, 1993   Announcement   PUD Section
Description of the Project (Common Elements and Recreational Facilities)

"....the appraiser is asked to provide...a description of the project...(including) a description of the common elements and recreational facilities."

PUD

Addenda

When the URAR is used to appraise a PUD, the appraiser has a choice of supplying the additional information on the form, in the addenda or on a special PUD addenda form such as the one shown on the following page. By supplying the information for which space is provided on the PUD addenda, the appraiser provides the underwriter with information needed to properly evaluate the PUD project.

PUD

Addenda Form

URAR PUD ADDENDUM
INDIVIDUAL PLANNED UNIT DEVELOPMENT (PUD) UNIT
OR DE MINIMUS PUD UNIT
SUPPLEMENTAL PROJECT INFORMATION

Borrower/Client
Property Address
City   County   State   Zip
Lender

This information is required when the appraiser uses the Uniform Residential Appraisal Report (URAR) (FHLMC #70 - FNMA #1004) to appraise a PUD Unit or a De Minimis PUD Unit.
TO BE COMPLETED FOR ALL PUD AND DE MINIMIS PUD APPRAISALS

This appraisal is of an: _____ Individual PUD Unit   _____ Individual De Minimis PUD Unit

If completed: No. Phases _____   No. Units _____   No. Sold _____

If incomplete: Planned No. Phases _____   No. Units _____   No. Sold _____

Units in Subject Phase: Total _____   Completed _____   Sold _____   Rented _____

Approx. No. Units for Sale: Subject Project _____   Subject Phase _____

Description of the common elements and recreational facilities: _____

Owners' association fees per month for the subject unit: $_____

Utilities that are included in the owners' association fees:
_____ Water   _____ Gas   _____ Heat   _____ Others _____
_____ Hot Water   _____ Telephone   _____ Electricity

Comment about whether the unit owners' association fees are reasonable in comparison to those for units in other projects of similar quality and design: _____

Comment about whether the project appears to be well-maintained: _____

The following information is a continuation of the sales comparison analysis presented in the attached URAR. The comparables used are the same as those used on the URAR. Adjustments made for the specific project information presented below are made in the same manner and are included in the total adjustments stated on the URAR.

	Subject	Comp. No. 1		Comp. No. 2		Comp. No. 3	
Project Name							
Item	Description	Description	± Adj.	Description	± Adj.	Description	± Adj.
Common Elements and Recreation Facilities							
Mo. Assessment							
Number of Units in Project							
Leasehold/Fee							
TOTAL ADJUSTMENT			$		$		$

Comments on the analysis of common property, monthly assessment, and ownership rights.

Additional Comments: _____

APPRAISER(S)   REVIEW APPRAISER
Signature   (if applicable) Signature   ☐ Did ☐ Did Not
Name   Name   Inspect Property

FW-70P   ®1989 Forms and Worms Inc.,   1(800) 243-4545   Item #117200

Notes

Notes

SITE

Introduction

[Form image showing SITE section of URAR with fields for Dimensions, Site area, Corner Lot, Specific zoning classification and description, Zoning compliance (Legal, Legal nonconforming (Grandfathered use), Illegal, No zoning), Highest & best use as improved (Present use, Other use), Utilities (Public/Other: Electricity, Gas, Water, Sanitary sewer, Storm sewer), Off-site Improvements (Type, Public, Private: Street, Curb/gutter, Sidewalk, Street lights, Alley), Topography, Size, Shape, Drainage, View, Landscaping, Driveway Surface, Apparent easements, FEMA Special Flood Hazard Area Yes/No, FEMA Zone, Map Date, FEMA Map No., and Comments.]

The **SITE** section of the URAR requires the below information. These items are described in detail on the following pages.

- **Dimensions** - **Site area**
- **Corner Lot**
- **Specific zoning classification and description**
- **Zoning compliance**
- **Highest & best use as improved**
- **Utilities**
- **Off-site improvements**

Physical Characteristics of the Site
- **Topography** - **Size** - **Shape** - **Drainage**
- **View**
- **Landscaping**
- **Driveway Surface**
- **Apparent easements**
- **FEMA Special Flood Hazard Area** - **FEMA Zone** - **Map Date** - **FEMA Map No.**
- **Comments**
    (apparent adverse easements, encroachments, special assessments, slide areas, illegal or legal nonconforming zoning use, etc.)

| Fannie Mae | June 30, 2002 | Part XI Chapter 4, Section 403.1 | Location |

Site

We will purchase or securitize mortgages that are secured by residential properties in urban, suburban, or rural areas. An "urban" location relates to a city, a "suburban" location relates to the area adjacent to a city, and a "rural" location relates to the country or anything beyond the suburban area. We do not designate certain areas as being acceptable or unacceptable. To be eligible for purchase or securitization, a mortgage must be secured by a property that is residential in nature—based on the characteristics of the subject property, zoning, and the present land use. We do not purchase or securitize mortgages on agricultural-type properties (such as farms, orchards, or ranches), on undeveloped land, or on land development-type properties.

The appraiser and the lender's underwriter must be sensitive to the varying conditions that characterize different types of locations. The appraiser must also consider the present or anticipated use of any adjoining property that may adversely affect the value or marketability of the subject property Conditions that are typical of certain types of locations may not be present in other locale&. This does not mean that the conditions are unacceptable, rather that they must be viewed in context with the nature of the area in which the security property is located. A few examples to illustrate this are shown below:

• If the subject property is located in a rural area that is relatively undeveloped or one in which properties often have large lot sizes, the appraiser may have to go a considerable distance to find properties that can be used to develop an opinion of value for the subject property.

SITE

Dimensions – Site area

```
Dimensions _____          Corner Lot [ ] Yes [ ] No      Topography _____
Site area _____                                         Size _____
Specific zoning classification and description                                      Shape _____
Zoning compliance [ ] Legal  [ ] Legal nonconforming (Grandfathered use)  [ ] Illegal  [ ] No zoning    Drainage _____
Highest & best use as improved: [ ] Present use  [ ] Other use (explain)            View _____
```

Utilities	Public	Other	Off-site Improvements	Type	Public	Private
Electricity			Street			
Gas			Curb/gutter			
Water			Sidewalk			
Sanitary sewer			Street lights			
Storm sewer			Alley			

Landscaping _____
Driveway Surface _____
Apparent easements _____
FEMA Special Flood Hazard
FEMA Zone _____
FEMA Map No. _____

Comments (apparent adverse easements, encroachments, special assessments, slide areas, illegal or legal nonconforming zoning use, e

These blanks are to contain the **Dimensions** and total **Site area.** If the lot is irregular in shape, list all the boundary dimensions in the blank (for example: 100 x 120 x 205 x 150), and attach a sketch or legal description of the site.

All measurements should be in units which are standard for the subject community or market. Some conversions between commonly used units of land measurement are shown below:

Area

Acres		Square Feet
1	=	43,560
2	=	87,120
3	=	130,680
4	=	174,240
5	=	217,800

Linear Measurements

12 inches	=	1 foot
3 feet	=	1 yard
5.5 yards (16.5 ft)	=	1 rod
40 rods	=	1 furlong
7.92 inches	=	1 link
25 links	=	1 rod
4 rods (66 feet)	=	1 chain
80 chains (8 furlong)	=	1 mile

Other Square Measurements

144 sq. ins	=	1 sq. foot	625 sq. links	=	1 pole
9 sq. feet	=	1 sq. yard	16 poles	=	1 sq. chain
30.25 sq. yd	=	1 sq. rod	10 sq. chains	=	1 acre
40 sq. rods	=	1 rood	640 acres	=	1 sq. mile
4 roods	=	1 acre	36 sq. miles	=	1 township

U.S. Dept of Housing and Urban Development Handbook 4150.1 Revision 2 Chapter 8 1994
Site Analysis - Dimensions

List all dimensions of the site. If irregular, the appraiser should show boundary dimensions, such as: 85' X 150' X 195' X 250'.

CONSISTENCY CHECK: Information in this section of the URAR relates to another section of the form as indicated below. The appraiser should check to make sure data in both places is consistent!

SITE - Site Area
  should be considered when rating
SITE - Size
  and may appear under
SALES COMPARISON ANALYSIS - SUBJECT: Site/View
  if an adjustment needs to be made for a comparable's lot area.

Fannie Mae June 30, 2002   Part XI Chapter 4, Section 404   Site Analysis

The property site should be of a size, shape, and topography that is generally conforming and acceptable in the market area. It must also have competitive utilities, street Improvements, and other amenities. Since amenities, easements, and encroachments may either detract from or enhance the marketability of a site, the appraiser must comment on them if the site has adverse conditions or is not typical for the neighborhood. If there is market resistance to a property because Its site is not compatible with the neighborhood' or with the requirements of the competitive market, the lender should underwrite the mortgage more carefully and, if appropriate, require more conservative mortgage terms.

SITE

Corner Lot

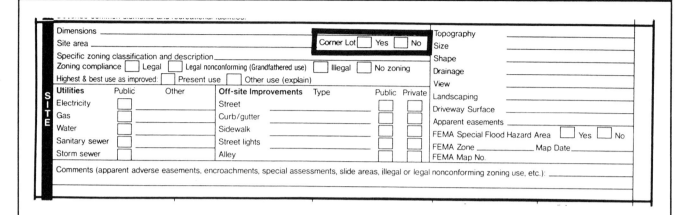

In some neighborhoods, a **Corner Lot** differs in desirability from inside lots. When a premium is paid for corner location, it should be noted in the **SITE - COMMENTS** section. Assessors and others sometimes use standard corner influence tables to estimate an adjustment to reflect this difference in value. The use of corner influence tables is appropriate only when the appraiser is satisfied that they accurately reflect the premium being paid in the subject neighborhood. In fact, some corner lots sell for less than inside lots because they are less private, exposed to more street traffic, require more care or are subject to higher taxes and special assessments.

SITE

Specific zoning classification and description

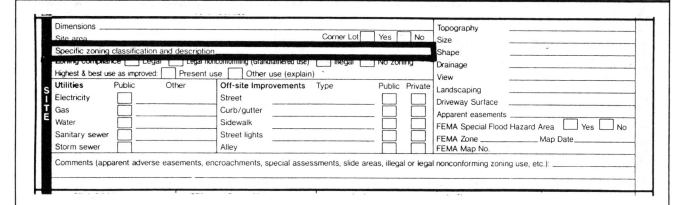

State the **Specific zoning classification and description** exactly as designated by the local zoning code and the major permitted uses.

Fannie Mae   December 31, 1994   Part VII, Chapter 4, Section 402.01   Location

To be eligible for purchase or securitization by Fannie Mae, a mortgage must be secured by a property that is residential in nature— based on the characteristics of the subject property, zoning, and the present land use.

Fannie Mae June 30, 2002 Part XI Chapter 4, Section 404.01 Zoning

The appraiser is responsible for reporting the specific zoning classification for the subject property The appraiser must include a general statement to describe what the zoning permits—"one-family," "two-family," etc.—when he or she indicates a specific zoning, such as R-l, R-2, etc. The appraiser must also include a specific statement indicating whether the improvements represent a legal use; a legal, but non-conforming (grandfathered) use; or an illegal use under the zoning regulations; or whether there is no local zoning.

SITE

Zoning compliance

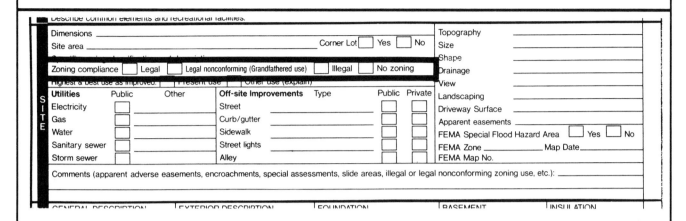

Zoning compliance is reported by checking one of four boxes to indicate whether the use of the property, on the date of inspection, was "Legal", "Legal non-conforming (Grandfathered use)", "Illegal" or in an area where there is "No zoning".

Answer the **Zoning compliance** section "legal nonconforming" when the existing property does not comply with <u>all</u> of the current zoning regulations (i.e., use, lot size, improvement size, off street parking, etc.)

When the property is nonconforming, the appraiser <u>must</u> render an opinion as to what effect, if any, being non-conforming has on the value of the property. In rendering this opinion, the appraiser should consider what will happen if the property is destroyed by fire or other causes (flood, hurricane, tornado, etc.). Rebuilding may be restricted by current zoning regulations, building codes and certain land-use regulations such as coastal tideland or wetland laws.

Several common nonconformities are described below:

<u>Nonconforming placement on site</u> - The improvements extend over the prescribed front, side or rear building lines.

<u>Grandfather clause</u> - Zoning regulations were effected after the property was constructed or the non-compliant usage began.

<u>Variance or special exception</u> - Zoning regulations are waived in reference to a specific property to permit construction of a nonconforming improvement.

<u>Illegal Use</u> - Existing improvements violate current zoning regulations, but to date the regulations have not been enforced.

Fannie Mae   January 1, 1994   Part VII, Chapter 4, Section 403.01   Zoning

The appraiser is responsible for reporting the specific zoning classification for the subject property. The appraiser must include a general statement to describe what the zoning permits — "single-family," "two-family," etc. — when he or she indicates a specific zoning such as R-1, R-2, etc. The appraiser must also include a specific statement indicating whether the improvements represent a legal use; a legal, but non-conforming (grandfathered) use; or an illegal use under the zoning regulations; or whether there is no local zoning.

Fannie Mae   June 30, 2002   Part XI Chapter 4, Section 404.01   Zoning

We generally will not purchase or securitize a mortgage on a property if the improvements do not constitute a legally permissible use of the land. We do make certain exceptions to this policy, as long as the property is appraised and underwritten in accordance with the special requirements we impose as a condition to agreeing to make the exception.

We will purchase or securitize *a—mortgage that is secured by a one- to four-family property or a unit in a PUD project* if the property represents a legal, but non-conforming, use of the land—as long as the appraiser's analysis reflects any adverse effect that the non-conforming use has on the value and marketability of the property.

- We will purchase or securitize a *condominium unit mortgage or a cooperative share loan* from a project that represents a legal, but nonconforming, use of the land only if the improvements can be rebuilt to current density in the event of their partial or full destruction. (In such cases, the mortgage file must include a copy of the applicable zoning regulations or a letter from the local zoning authority that authorizes reconstruction to current density.)

- We will purchase or securitize a *mortgage secured by a one-family property that includes an illegal additional unit or accessory apartment* (which may be referred to as a mother-in-law, mother-daughter, or granny unit) as long as the illegal use conforms to the subject neighborhood and to the market. The property must be appraised in conformity with its legal use, that of a one-family property (and the borrower must qualify for the mortgage without considering any rental income from the illegal unit). The appraiser must report that the improvements represent an illegal use and demonstrate that the improvements are typical for the market through an analysis of at least three comparable properties that have the same illegal use. The lender must also make sure that the existence of the illegal additional unit will not jeopardize any future hazard insurance claim that might need to be filed for the property. We will **not** purchase or securitize a *mortgage secured by a two- to four-family property that includes an illegal accessory apartment*.

- We will **not** purchase or securitize a *mortgage secured by a property that is subject to certain land-use regulations* (such as coastal tideland or wetland laws) that create setback lines or other provisions that prevent

Veterans Benefits Administration   Circular 26-93-25   1993
Site Section - Zoning Compliance

Modifications to the site section included both clarifications to existing entries and the addition of new entries. New entries were created for the appraiser to:

Indicate the subject property's compliance with zoning by checking one of the convenient boxes (legal use; legal, but nonconforming use; illegal use; or no zoning);

MODEL COMMENTS: The following are examples of explanatory remarks reviewers find useful. They are especially important when data on the subject property falls outside the normal range. Usually these comments require customization to reflect the special characteristics of the specific property being appraised.

WHEN THE IMPROVEMENTS CONFORM TO CURRENT ZONING REGULATIONS:

The improvements on the property are legal and conform to current zoning regulations. In the event of a loss by fire all of the improvements could be rebuilt without obtaining a zoning variance.

WHEN IMPROVEMENTS DO NOT CONFORM TO ZONING REGULATIONS:

The improvements do not conform to current zoning regulation _____ [zoning requirement the subject does not meet - e.g. R-40 which requires properties to have 40,000 sq. ft., 100 ft. frontage] because the subject's lot has _____ [subject's features which vary from zoning - e.g. 20,000 sq. ft., 75 ft. frontage]. This nonconforming use _____ (is, is not) permitted by _____ (a grandfather clause, variance, special exception, current zoning regulations {if illegal use}). In the event of a loss by fire all of the improvements _____ (could, could not) be rebuilt without obtaining a zoning variance.

WHEN NO ZONING ORDINANCE COVERS THE SUBJECT PROPERTY:

_____ [city, town, county, etc.] _____ (does, does not) have zoning ordinances. The subject property, _____ (however, therefore) is not covered by the zoning ordinances.

SITE

Highest & best use as improved

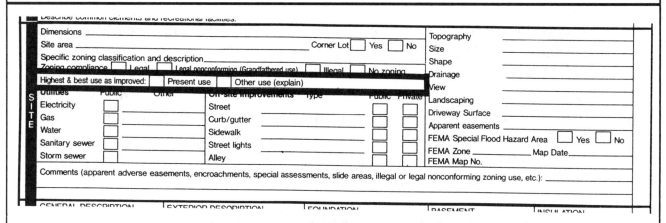

The form now calls for the **Highest & best use as improved**. When significant, the highest and best use of the property "as if vacant" should also be reported in the Addenda section of the appraisal.

Highest & best use as improved should not be interpreted too literally. Most major appraisal organizations teach that few if any properties are improved to their highest and best use, which implies the perfect improvement.

Therefore, the **Present use** line should be filled with an "X" if the property is improved reasonably close to its highest and best use as defined below.

To determine the highest and best use, the appraiser utilizes four tests. The highest and best use is the one which meets all four of these tests: (1) Legally permitted, (2) Financially feasible, (3) Physically possible, and (4) Most profitable.

The four tests are done twice. First, the site is analyzed as improved. Then the property is analyzed again, this time considering the best use for the site assuming it was vacant and ready to be built upon on the date of the appraisal.

If the proposed use fails to meet all four tests assuming the site is vacant, the process is repeated until a proper use is found. It is very possible that no improvement can be found to satisfy the criteria. In this event, the best use may be to leave the site vacant until some future date when development becomes feasible.

If building a single family home is determined to be the highest and best use of the site, the appraiser must then describe the perfect improvement. This residence would take advantage of all the previously considered factors about the neighborhood, community and region. Some of the decisions to be made about

4-9

the proposed house include its type, style, size, number of rooms, layout, special features, mechanical systems and the kind and quality of construction materials.

An analysis is then done of the existing residence to determine the highest and best use of the site and improvements. Again, as with the analysis of the site as if vacant, the appraiser must determine what the perfect utilization is. However, the appraiser must now consider existing improvements when deciding what could be done to the property to obtain maximum profit. Any new improvement which will add more value than its production cost should be analyzed. The changes to be considered can range from minor repairs to major remodeling, modernization or rehabilitation.

Finally the results of the two analyses are compared to the existing improvements. When the highest and best use of the site as if vacant describes the existing property reasonably closely, the present use is substantially the highest and best use. If this is not the case, the appraiser must enter the use that should exist in the **Other use (explain)** blank and explain in the **SITE - Comments** section or an addendum.

Fannie Mae   June 30, 2002   Part XI Chapter 4, Section 404.02   Highest and Best Use

The highest and best use of a site is the reasonable and probable use that supports the highest present value on the effective date of the appraisal. For improvements to represent the highest and .best use of a site, they must be legally permitted, financially feasible, and physically possible, and must provide more profit than any other use of the site would generate. All of these criteria must be met if the improvements are to be considered as the highest and best use of a site.

A strict theoretical 'highest and best use analysis identifies the perfect improvements for a site—assuming that the site is vacant and available to be developed. The appraiser's highest and best use analysis of the subject property should consider the property as it is improved. This treatment recognizes that the existing improvements should continue in use until it is financially feasible to remove the dwelling and build a new one, or to renovate the existing dwelling. If the use of comparable sales demonstrates that the improvements are reasonably typical and compatible with market demand for the neighborhood, and the present improvements contribute to the value of the subject property so that its value is greater than the estimated vacant site value, the appraiser should consider the existing use as reasonable and report it as the highest and best use.

On the other hand, if the current improvements clearly do not represent the highest and best use of the site as an improved site, the appraiser must so indicate on the appraisal report. In such cases, we will not purchase or securitize a mortgage that is secured by the subject property.

MODEL COMMENTS: The following are examples of explanatory remarks reviewers find useful. They are especially important when data on the subject property falls outside the normal range. Usually these comments require customization to reflect the special characteristics of the specific property being appraised.

WHEN THE PROPERTY IS IMPROVED TO SUBSTANTIALLY THE HIGHEST AND BEST USE:

```
    The improvements are substantially the highest and best use
for the subject property, except for those items of depreciation
described in the Improvements section.
```

SITE

Utilities

Dimensions		Topography	
Site area	Corner Lot ☐ Yes ☐ No	Size	
Specific zoning classification and description		Shape	
Zoning compliance ☐ Legal ☐ Legal nonconforming (Grandfathered use) ☐ Illegal ☐ No zoning		Drainage	
Highest & best use as improved: ☐ Present use ☐ Other use (explain)		View	

Utilities	Public	Other	Off-site Improvements	Type	Public	Private		
Electricity	☐		Street		☐	☐	Landscaping	
Gas	☐		Curb/gutter		☐	☐	Driveway Surface	
Water	☐		Sidewalk		☐	☐	Apparent easements	
Sanitary sewer	☐		Street lights		☐	☐	FEMA Special Flood Hazard Area ☐ Yes ☐ No	
Storm sewer	☐		Alley		☐	☐	FEMA Zone _____ Map Date _____	
							FEMA Map No.	

Comments (apparent adverse easements, encroachments, special assessments, slide areas, illegal or legal nonconforming zoning use, etc.):

| GENERAL DESCRIPTION | EXTERIOR DESCRIPTION | FOUNDATION | BASEMENT | INSULATION |

The adequacy of the **Utilities** in the neighborhood should have already been reported in the comments section of the **Neighborhood Analysis**. Here, the available utilities at the site are noted.

Public means governmentally supplied and regulated. It does not, therefore, include community systems sponsored, owned or operated by the developer or a private company not subject to government regulation or financial assistance. If such systems are found, a description thereof should be given in the **SITE - Comments** section or in an addendum to the report.

The appraiser must also report any utilities which are available to the subject, but are not connected and not being used. In resort areas, report if the utilities are available all year long.

Fannie Mae   June 30, 2002   Part XI Chapter 4, Section 404.03   Utilities

For a mortgage to be eligible for purchase or securitization, the utilities of the property must meet community standards and be adequate, in service, and accepted generally by area residents. If public sewer and/or water facilities-those that are supplied and regulated by the local government-are not available, then community-or private well and septic facilities must be available and utilized' by the subject property. If community facilities are used, the owners of the subject property must have the right to access those facilities, which must he viable on an on-going basis. Generally, private well or septic facilities must be located on the subject site, However, off-site private facilities are acceptable' if the inhabitants of the subject property have the right to access them and- if there is an adequate, legally binding agreement for their access and maintenance.

If there is market resistance to an area because of environmental hazards or any other conditions that affect well, -septic, or public water facilities, the appraiser must comment on~ the effect-of the hazards on the marketability and value of the subject property (as discussed in Section 307).

Some of our appraisal report forms provide an area for the appraiser to state the type of any off-site improvements—streets, curbs/gutters, sidewalks, street lights, and alleys—that are present and indicate whether they are publicly or privately maintained.

MODEL COMMENTS: The following are examples of explanatory remarks reviewers find useful. They are especially important when data on the subject property falls outside the normal range. Usually these comments require customization to reflect the special characteristics of the specific property being appraised.

WHEN WATER IS SUPPLIED BY A PRIVATE UTILITY COMPANY:

Water is supplied by a private utility company. This _____ (appears, does not appear) to have a negative effect on the value of the property being appraised.

WHEN SEWAGE DISPOSAL PROVIDED BY A PRIVATE PLANT:

Sewage disposal is provided by a privately owned sewerage plant. This _____ (has, does not have) a negative effect on property value.

WHEN WELL OR SEPTIC SYSTEM IS USED AND PUBLIC WATER OR SEWER IS AVAILABLE:

The subject property has access to public _____ (water, sewer lines). However, as of this appraisal, the subject is not connected to this facility and is using a _____ (well, septic system). The present set-up appears _____ (adequate, inadequate) and likely has _____ (no, an) adverse effect on marketability.

WHEN A WELL IS USED BY MORE THAN ONE PROPERTY:

The well providing water to the subject property also provides water for _____ [the number] other properties. This is _____ (common, uncommon) in this market, and _____ (will, will not) negatively affect the value of the subject property.

WHEN THE PROPERTY HAS A WELL AND/OR SEPTIC SYSTEM:

The subject property does not have access to public _____ (water, sewer lines), so there is a _____ (well, septic tank). In this market _____ (wells, septic tanks) _____ (have, do not have) a negative effect on property values. There _____ (are, are no) announced plans to provide public _____ (water, sewer lines) to the subject property. On the day of inspection there was no visible evidence of _____ (contamination, seepage).

WHEN BOTTLED GAS IS USED:

The subject property's _____ (heat, hot water, stove) is fueled by bottled gas. This is _____ (common, uncommon) for properties in this area, so there is _____ (no, an) adverse effect on marketability resulting from bottled gas use.

SITE

Off-site Improvements

```
Dimensions _____                                            Topography _____
Site area _____                    Corner Lot [ ] Yes [ ] No  Size _____
Specific zoning classification and description _____                Shape _____
Zoning compliance [ ] Legal [ ] Legal nonconforming (Grandfathered use) [ ] Illegal [ ] No zoning   Drainage _____
Highest & best use as improved: [ ] Present use [ ] Other use (explain)  View _____
Utilities     Public   Other        Off-site Improvements  Type   Public  Private   Landscaping _____
Electricity   [ ]   _____         Street     _____     [ ]    [ ]     Driveway Surface _____
Gas           [ ]   _____         Curb/gutter _____    [ ]    [ ]     Apparent easements _____
Water         [ ]   _____         Sidewalk    _____    [ ]    [ ]     FEMA Special Flood Hazard Area [ ] Yes [ ] No
Sanitary sewer [ ]  _____         Street lights _____  [ ]    [ ]     FEMA Zone _____ Map Date _____
Storm sewer   [ ]   _____         Alley       _____    [ ]    [ ]     FEMA Map No. _____
Comments (apparent adverse easements, encroachments, special assessments, slide areas, illegal or legal nonconforming zoning use, etc.): _____
```

This section was formerly called "Site Improvements". When the sidewalks are actually on the site as they are in some communities, it may be necessary to add a comment to that effect. When the property fronts on a private street it is important to determine who maintains the street and if it is effectively maintained. A property that fronts on a private street that is not properly maintained may suffer a value decrease as compared to other properties where street maintenance is not a problem

Fannie Mae   June 30, 2002   Part XI Chapter 4, Section 403.1   Location
Site
All properties must be readily accessible by roads that meet local standards. Certain aspects of the location of a property will require special consideration. For example, properties in resort areas that attract people for seasonal or vacation use are acceptable only if they are suitable for year-round use. Any property that is not suitable for year-round occupancy— regardless of where it is located—is unacceptable.

Fannie Mae   June 30, 2002   Part XI Chapter 4, Section 404.03   Off Site Improvements
Some of our appraisal report forms provide an area for the appraiser to state the type of any off-site improvements—streets, curbs/gutters, sidewalks, street lights, and alleys—that are present and indicate whether they are publicly or privately maintained.

The property should front on a publicly dedicated and maintained street that meets community standards and is accepted generally by area residents. If the property is on a community-owned or privately owned and maintained street, there should be an adequate, legally enforceable agreement for maintenance of the street. A street that does not meet city or state standards frequently requires extensive maintenance~ and property values may decline if it is not regularly maintained. If a property fronts on a street that is not typical of those found in the community, the appraiser must comment on the effect of that location on the marketability and value of the subject property.

The presence of sidewalks, curbs and gutters, street lights, and alleys depends on local custom—if they are typical in the community, they should be present on the subject site. The appraiser must comment on any adverse conditions and address their effect on the marketability and value of the subject property.

MODEL COMMENTS: The following are examples of explanatory remarks reviewers find useful. They are especially important when data on the subject property falls outside the normal range. Usually these comments require customization to reflect the special characteristics of the specific property being appraised.

WHEN THE HOUSE IS LOCATED ON A PRIVATE STREET:

This house is located on a private street, which ____ (is, is not) common in this market. Lenders _____ (are, are not) accepting houses on private streets like this one for conventional mortgages at standard interest rates and terms. Mortgage financing _____ (is, is not) more difficult to obtain. There is _____ (an, no) adequate legally enforceable agreement for community street maintenance and ____ (an, no) association of property owners to arrange for needed services. The community does not provide _____ (rubbish removal, street repairs, snow removal, etc.) for homes on this street. The estimated annual cost for all such services is ____ [$].

WHEN THE SUBJECT IS ON A DIRT ROAD:

The subject is located on a dirt road. This _____ (is, is not) typical for this area, so there is ____ (an, no) adverse effect on marketability.

WHEN THE SIDEWALK IS ON THE SITE:

The subject sidewalk is located on the site which _____ (is, is not) common in this community. There is ____ (an, no) adverse effect on value of the property because of its location.

SITE

Topography - Size - Shape - Drainage

```
Dimensions _____
Site area _____  Corner Lot [ ] Yes [ ] No
Specific zoning classification and description_____
Zoning compliance [ ] Legal  [ ] Legal nonconforming (Grandfathered use)  [ ] Illegal  [ ] No zoning
Highest & best use as improved: [ ] Present use  [ ] Other use (explain)

Utilities    Public   Other      Off-site Improvements  Type           Public  Private
Electricity  [ ]                  Street          _____          [ ]     [ ]
Gas          [ ]                  Curb/gutter     _____          [ ]     [ ]
Water        [ ]                  Sidewalk        _____          [ ]     [ ]
Sanitary sewer [ ]                Street lights   _____          [ ]     [ ]
Storm sewer  [ ]                  Alley           _____          [ ]     [ ]

Topography  _____
Size        _____
Shape       _____
Drainage    _____
View        _____
Landscaping _____
Driveway Surface _____
Apparent easements _____
FEMA Special Flood Hazard Area [ ] Yes [ ] No
FEMA Zone _____ Map Date _____
FEMA Map No. _____

Comments (apparent adverse easements, encroachments, special assessments, slide areas, illegal or legal nonconforming zoning use, etc.): _____
```

The most desirable residential lot **Topography** is a gentle slope up from the street to the house, and then a downward slope away from the house to the rear, steep enough to allow a walk-out basement door to the rear yard recreation area. However, what is true for one specific neighborhood may not be the case for another. In general, sites do tend to have lower value if they are costly to improve due to extreme topographical conditions. Sometimes, however, difficult conditions are offset by advantages recognized in the market.

If lot value were directly related only to **Size**, the unit of comparison for lot values would be value per square foot or per acre. However, frontage, width, depth and shape interplay with size to affect value. Nevertheless, the appraiser should report how the size of the site compares to the typical site size in the neighborhood.

Shape affects the value of lots differently from one neighborhood to another. Yet in most areas, an irregular shape resulting in increased construction costs decreases the value of the lot.

The site must have some type of **Drainage** for surface and storm water like a swale that channels surface water off of the lot to the street or some natural drainage. However, when the lot is level, or slopes away from the water disposal area, storm sewers are necessary.

<u>Fannie Mae</u>   <u>June 30, 2002</u>   <u>Part XI Chapter 4, Section 404.05</u>   <u>The Lot</u>
The topography, shape, size, and drainage of the lot are all important factors. Steep slopes that cause erosion, difficulty in maintaining a lawn, or difficult access to the property itself or to a garage are generally unfavorable conditions. Drainage must be away from the improvements to avoid the collection of water in or around them.

The property site should be of a size, shape, and topography that is generally conforming and acceptable in the market area. It must also have competitive utilities, street Improvements, and other amenities. Since amenities, easements, and encroachments may either detract from or enhance the marketability of a site, the appraiser must comment on them if the site has adverse conditions or is not typical for the neighborhood. If there is market resistance to a property because Its site is not compatible with the neighborhood' or with the requirements of the competitive market, the lender should underwrite the mortgage more carefully and, if appropriate, require more conservative mortgage terms.

CONSISTENCY CHECK: Information in this section of the URAR relates to another section of the form as indicated below. The appraiser should check to make sure data in both places is consistent!

SITE- Size
should consider

SITE- Site Area
and should be consistent with

SALES COMPARISON ANALYSIS- SUBJECT: Site and View

SITE

View

Dimensions					Topography	
Site area			Corner Lot ☐ Yes ☐ No		Size	
Specific zoning classification and description					Shape	
Zoning compliance ☐ Legal ☐ Legal nonconforming (Grandfathered use) ☐ Illegal ☐ No zoning					Drainage	
Highest & best use as improved: ☐ Present use ☐ Other use (explain)					View	

Utilities	Public	Other	Off-site Improvements	Type	Public	Private
Electricity			Street			
Gas			Curb/gutter			
Water			Sidewalk			
Sanitary sewer			Street lights			
Storm sewer			Alley			

Landscaping
Driveway Surface
Apparent easements
FEMA Special Flood Hazard Area ☐ Yes ☐ No
FEMA Zone _____ Map Date _____
FEMA Map No.

Comments (apparent adverse easements, encroachments, special assessments, slide areas, illegal or legal nonconforming zoning use, etc.): _____

The **View** from a property may substantially affect its value. Lots in the same neighborhood; identical in all respects except location and orientation, will often have markedly different values directly attributable to the superior view one enjoys. The most popular views are of water, mountains and valleys. Conversely, a poor view like a highway, railroad, alley or dump site will reduce value.

CONSISTENCY CHECK: Information in this section of the URAR relates to another section of the form as indicated below. The appraiser should check to make sure data in both places is consistent!

SITE - **View**
   rating also appears under
SALES COMPARISON ANALYSIS - **SUBJECT: Site and View.**

SITE

Landscaping

[Form excerpt with "Landscaping" field highlighted, showing site description fields including Dimensions, Site area, Corner Lot, Zoning compliance, Utilities (Electricity, Gas, Water, Sanitary sewer, Storm sewer), Off-site Improvements (Street, Curb/gutter, Sidewalk, Street lights, Alley), Topography, Size, Shape, Drainage, View, Landscaping, Driveway Surface, Apparent easements, FEMA Special Flood Hazard Area, FEMA Zone, FEMA Map No., and Comments.]

The amount and quality of **Landscaping** tends to vary considerably. Natural trees and shrubs are usually considered part of the site itself. Other landscaping is treated separately as a site improvement. Lawns, shrubbery, gardens and plantings in general improve the appearance and desirability of residential properties. However, special plantings are a matter of individual taste and will deteriorate in many areas without good care. In addition, typical buyers are inclined to discount the cost of any expensive custom landscaping. Thus, above average landscaping usually adds little additional value to a property.

MODEL COMMENTS: The following are examples of explanatory remarks reviewers find useful. They are especially important when data on the subject property falls outside the normal range. Usually these comments require customization to reflect the special characteristics of the specific property being appraised.

STANDARD COMMENT DESCRIBING LANDSCAPING:

     The landscaping on this site is _____ (good, average, fair, poor) which _____ (is, is not) typical of this neighborhood. The landscaping consists of _____ (seeded lawn, lawn, shrubs, hedges, small trees, etc.).

WHEN THE SUBJECT HAS NO LANDSCAPING AT INSPECTION:

     The subject property is _____ (under construction, pro-posed). All items on this appraisal regarding landscaping are from specifications provided by the _____ (buyer, seller, builder, lender, real estate agent).

SITE

Driveway Surface

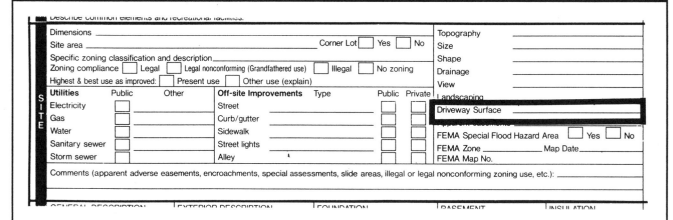

The ideal **Driveway Surface** is level or slopes gently upward from the street to provide good drainage. Downward sloping driveways may allow storm water to drain from the street onto the site. Any driveway with a slope presents a special problem in areas that freeze in the winter.

The driveway should be designed so that you can drive directly into the garage or carport without having to back up. It is also desirable to be able to back out of the garage or carport and turn around. This eliminates the dangerous need to back into the street.

Special driveways (i.e., circular or having additional paved parking areas, etc.) may or may not add extra value to the site depending on what is desirable in the neighborhood.

SITE

Apparent easements

An **Apparent easement** is a right of non-possessing interest accorded to a non-owner to use property for a specific purpose. The three broad types of easements are surface easements, sub-surface easements and overhead easements.

Typical easements found on residential sites include:

- Party driveways
- Walks & paths leading to places off the site
- Drainage easements & sewer easements
- Telephone, cable TV and electric wire easements
- Neighbor's right to place a sign, mail box, or newspaper box on the property
- High voltage power line easements
- Gas and water line easements
- Historic & view easements
- Mineral and mining easements

MODEL COMMENTS: The following are examples of explanatory remarks reviewers find useful. They are especially important when data on the subject property falls outside the normal range. Usually these comments require customization to reflect the special characteristics of the specific property being appraised.

IF THE ONLY APPARENT EASEMENTS ARE NORMAL UTILITY EASEMENTS:

This property is subject to normal utility easements, which have ____ (a, no) negative effect on the value of the property.

IF THE APPARENT EASEMENTS ARE OTHER THAN NORMAL UTILITY EASEMENTS:

There appears to be a _____ (describe easement) on the subject property. If it exists, it will have _____ (no effect, a negative effect) on the value of the property. A survey should be obtained to determine the status of the easement. The value estimated in this appraisal is based on the assumption that the described easement _____ (exists, does not exist).

CONSISTENCY CHECK: Information in this section of the URAR relates to another section of the form as indicated below. The appraiser should check to make sure data in both places is consistent!

SITE - Apparent Easements
which are adverse should be reported in detail in
SITE - COMMENTS
as "Apparent adverse easements" and in the
SALES COMPARISON ANALYSIS - SUBJECT: Site/View
box, so appropriate adjustments can be made to the comparables.

SITE

FEMA Special Flood Hazard Area - FEMA Zone - Map Date - FEMA Map No.

FEMA Special Flood Hazard Area reporting is clarified by a check box that indicates "Yes" or "No" to whether any part of the property is in a "FEMA Flood Hazard Area", which is defined as "only 100-year flood plain areas." This eliminates the confusion about whether "B" zones should be included.

The Fannie Mae Guidelines do not consider "B" zones to be in FEMA 100-year flood plain areas. However, some lenders require flood insurance when properties are in a "B" flood hazard area, so some appraisers report this, when applicable, on the URAR with an explanation in the Addenda.

Space is provided for the appraiser to indicate the "FEMA Zone," "Map Date" and "FEMA Map No." To avoid professional liability suits, appraisers must be certain to use the most current FEMA maps in their determinations. Many appraisers attach a copy of the FEMA map to their appraisal reports.

When any portion of the site is in an **FEMA Special Flood Hazard Area**, mark the **Yes** blank and list the community panel and flood zone numbers from the appropriate Flood Insurance Rate Map (FIRM) on the **FEMA Zone** line. List the map number and map date on the appropriate lines.

If part of the site is in a hazard area, but the improvements are not, report this in the **SITE - Comments**.

Fannie Mae   June 30, 2002   Part XI Chapter 4, Section 404.06   Special Flood Hazard Area
Flood Insurance Rate Maps (FIRM) can be obtained by contacting FEMA at the address, telephone number, fax number, or Web site shown below:

FEMA Map Service Center   Telephone: 1–800-358-9616
P.O. Box 1038   Fax: 1-800-358-9620
Jessup, MD 20794-1038   Web site: webi.msc.fema.gov.

If any part of the principal structure is located in a Special Flood Hazard Area—zones A, AE, AII, AO, AR, A1-30, A-99, V VE, VO, or Vi -30—flood insurance is required. If the principal structure is not located in the Special Flood Hazard Area, flood insurance is generally not required.

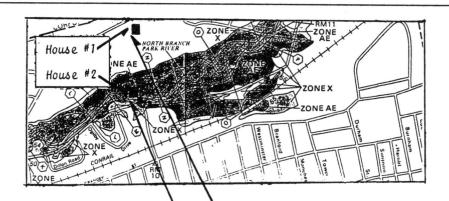

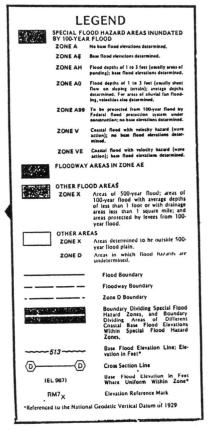

In the map shown above House #1 is located outside of the FEMA hazard area while House #2 is located in the flood hazard area.

Fannie Mae June 30, 2002   Part XI Chapter 4, Section 404.06   Special Flood Hazard Area

Some of our appraisal report forms provide an area for the appraiser to a indicate whether or not the property is located in a Special Flood Hazard Area that is identified on the Federal Emergency Management Agency's (FEMA) Flood Insurance Rate Maps (FIRM). These maps include areas that are within the 100-year flood boundary (Note: The term "100-year flood" does not mean -that a flood will occur once in every 100 years, but rather that there is a 1% or greater chance that a flood level will be equal or exceeded in any given year.) The appraiser must also indicate the specific FEMA flood zone and the map number and its effective date.

Veterans Benefits Administration   Circular 26-93-25   1993
Site Section - FEMA Flood Hazard Area

Address whether the subject community is in a FEMA (Federal Emergency Management Agency) special flood hazard area and to indicate the FEMA zone, map date and map number for all appraisals.

The clarifications to existing entries include specifying that the "FEMA Flood Hazard" entry relates only to 100-year flood areas and explaining that the appraiser's determination about the highest and best use of the property should reflect the property "as improved."

MODEL COMMENTS: The following are examples of explanatory remarks reviewers find useful. They are especially important when data on the subject property falls outside the normal range. Usually these comments require customization to reflect the special characteristics of the specific property being appraised.

WHEN IMPROVEMENTS ARE LOCATED IN A FEMA FLOOD HAZARD AREA:
```
The _____ (house, garage) is located in a FEMA identified "Flood
Hazard Area". Flood insurance is recommended. Insurance will be
required for a mortgage to be obtained from a federally insured
lender.
```

WHEN THE SITE IS IN A FEMA FLOOD HAZARD AREA BUT THE IMPROVEMENTS ARE NOT:
```
A portion of the site is located in a FEMA identified flood
area, but none of the improvements are in the hazard area. Flood
insurance will not be required for a mortgage to be obtained
from a federally insured lender.
```

SITE

Comments

Dimensions					Topography	
Site area			Corner Lot ☐ Yes ☐ No		Size	
Specific zoning classification and description					Shape	
Zoning compliance ☐ Legal ☐ Legal nonconforming (Grandfathered use) ☐ Illegal ☐ No zoning					Drainage	
Highest & best use as improved: ☐ Present use ☐ Other use (explain)					View	
Utilities	Public	Other	**Off-site Improvements** Type	Public Private	Landscaping	
Electricity	☐		Street	☐ ☐	Driveway Surface	
Gas	☐		Curb/gutter	☐ ☐	Apparent easements	
Water	☐		Sidewalk	☐ ☐	FEMA Special Flood Hazard Area ☐ Yes ☐ No	
Sanitary sewer	☐		Street lights	☐ ☐	FEMA Zone _____ Map Date _____	
Storm sewer	☐		Alley	☐ ☐	FEMA Map No.	

Comments (apparent adverse easements, encroachments, special assessments, slide areas, illegal or legal nonconforming zoning use, etc.): _____

The **SITE - Comments** lines are used to report: **apparent adverse easements, encroachments, special assessments, slide areas, illegal or legal nonconforming zoning use, etc.** It is also used for further explanation of any favorable and unfavorable factors which affect the site value.

An easement is a right of non-possessing interest accorded to a non-owner to use property for a specific purpose (for details see **apparent adverse easements** section). Typical **apparent adverse easements** are: party driveways, walks and rights of way to property owned by others, gas lines, and high voltage electric lines. Historic easements may be adverse or may add value to the property.

An **encroachment** occurs when one owner's improvements extend onto the land of an abutting owner. The encroachment can be either the improvements of the property being appraised extending onto a neighboring property, or the reverse, a neighboring improvement extending onto the property being appraised.

Special assessments may be for street improvements, sewers, electric power, etc. which are intended to add value to the property. Often they are spread over many years and become a type of lien against the property. The type, amount and remaining duration of any special assessment should be reported.

A site in or near a **slide area** presents special problems which must be reported and analyzed by the appraiser (usually in an addendum).

* An **illegal or legal nonconforming zoning use** must be carefully researched and reported if it does not comply with all of the current zoning regulations (i.e., use, lot size, improvement size, off street parking, etc.) When the property is nonconforming, the appraiser must render an opinion as to what effect, if any, being nonconforming has on the value of the property. See section on **Zoning compliance.**

Etc.: **Other adverse conditions** which should be noted if they affect site value are: unusual shape or size; drainage problems; unusual topography; substandard utility supply; poor site improvements such as sidewalks, walls, fences, driveways, landscaping, pools and courts; or poor street improvements including paving, curbing, road surfaces, lighting, width and condition.

Nearby hazards including: bodies of water; earthquake, volcano or landslide areas; ravines; unusual fire hazards; and heavy traffic and pollution also need to be discussed here.

Finally, the effect that any of the above identified items have on the value of the site should be described.

MODEL COMMENTS: The following are examples of explanatory remarks reviewers find useful. They are especially important when data on the subject property falls outside the normal range. Usually these comments require customization to reflect the special characteristics of the specific property being appraised.

STANDARD SITE COMMENT (WHEN APPLICABLE):

```
   The size, shape and landscaping of this site is typical of
sites in this neighborhood.  No apparent adverse easements,
encroachments, special assessments, slide areas, etc. negatively
affect the subject's value.
```

CONSISTENCY CHECK: Information in this section of the URAR relates to another section of the form as indicated below. The appraiser should check to make sure data in both places is consistent!

SITE - COMMENTS:
    Should any "adverse easements, encroachments, special assessments, slide areas,
    etc." have a negative effect on property value, it should be noted in the

COMMENTS - Depreciation
    section, as item of functional or external obsolescence, in the

COST APPROACH - BUILDING SKETCH
    section, as a cost approach comment, and the

SALES COMPARISON ANALYSIS - SUBJECT: Site/View
    box, so appropriate adjustments can be made to the comparables.

    The appraiser must also make an appropriate deduction in the

COST APPROACH.
    The item may have an effect on the

COST APPROACH - ESTIMATED SITE VALUE.
    and cause

COST APPROACH - Functional: Depreciation
    if it is on the site or

COST APPROACH - External: Depreciation
    if it is off the site. Care must be taken to make the proper deduction in <u>one and only
    one</u> place.

Notes

DESCRIPTION OF IMPROVEMENTS

Introduction

GENERAL DESCRIPTION	EXTERIOR DESCRIPTION	FOUNDATION	BASEMENT	INSULATION
No. of Units	Foundation	Slab	Area Sq. Ft.	Roof
No. of Stories	Exterior Walls	Crawl Space	% Finished	Ceiling
Type (Det./Att.)	Roof Surface	Basement	Ceiling	Walls
Design (Style)	Gutters & Dwnspts.	Sump Pump	Walls	Floor
Existing/Proposed	Window Type	Dampness	Floor	None
Age (Yrs.)	Storm/Screens	Settlement	Outside Entry	Unknown
Effective Age (Yrs.)	Manufactured House	Infestation		

ROOMS	Foyer	Living	Dining	Kitchen	Den	Family Rm.	Rec. Rm.	Bedrooms	# Baths	Laundry	Other	Area Sq. Ft.
Basement												
Level 1												
Level 2												

Finished area **above** grade contains: _____ Rooms; _____ Bedroom(s); _____ Bath(s); _____ Square Feet of Gross Living Area

INTERIOR	Materials/Condition	HEATING		KITCHEN EQUIP.		ATTIC		AMENITIES		CAR STORAGE:	
Floors		Type		Refrigerator		None		Fireplace(s) #		None	
Walls		Fuel		Range/Oven		Stairs		Patio		Garage	# of cars
Trim/Finish		Condition		Disposal		Drop Stair		Deck		Attached	
Bath Floor		COOLING		Dishwasher		Scuttle		Porch		Detached	
Bath Wainscot		Central		Fan/Hood		Floor		Fence		Built-In	
Doors		Other		Microwave		Heated		Pool		Carport	
		Condition		Washer/Dryer		Finished				Driveway	

Additional features (special energy efficient items, etc.):

The **Description Of Improvements** section is divided into thirteen areas. Each of the areas is broken up into smaller parts as below and described in detail on the following pages.

GENERAL DESCRIPTION
 No. of Units -- No. of Stories -- Type (Det./Att.) -- Design (Style)
 Existing/Proposed
 Age (Yrs.) -- Effective Age (Yrs.)

EXTERIOR DESCRIPTION
 Foundation -- Exterior Walls -- Roof Surface
 Gutters & Dwnspts.
 Window Type -- Storm/Screens
 Manufactured House

FOUNDATION
 Slab -- Crawl Space -- Basement
 Sump Pump -- Dampness -- Settlement
 Infestation

BASEMENT
 Area Sq. Ft., % Finished
 Ceiling -- Walls - Floors
 Outside Entry
 Blank (Other)

INSULATION
 Roof -- Ceiling -- Walls -- Floor -- None -- Unknown
 Blank (Other)

ROOMS
 Foyer -- Living -- Dining -- Kitchen -- Den -- Family Rm. -- Rec. Rm. -- Bedrooms -- # Baths -- Laundry -- Other -- Area Sq. Ft.
 Basement -- Level 1 -- Level 2

Finished area *above* grade contains: --Rooms; -- Bedroom(s); -- Bath(s);
Square Feet of Gross Living Area

INTERIOR (Materials/Condition)
Floors --Walls -- Trim/Finish
Bath Floor -- Bath Wainscot
Doors
Blank (Other)

HEATING
Type -- Fuel -- Condition

COOLING
Central -- Other -- Condition

KITCHEN EQUIP.
Refrigerator -- Range/Oven -- Disposal -- Dishwasher --
Fan/Hood -- Microwave -- Washer/Dryer

ATTIC
None -- Stairs -- Drop Stair -- Scuttle -- Floor --
Heated -- Finished

AMENITIES
Fireplace(s)# -- Patio -- Deck -- Porch -- Fence --
Pool -- Blank (Other)

CAR STORAGE
None
Garage -- # of cars
Attached/Detached/Built In-
Carport -- Driveway

The **Description of Improvements** section represents a significant streamlining of the information necessary to describe the improvements. One of the major changes was the elimination of the Improvement Analysis Rating Grid in order to emphasize that the appraiser should adequately address the condition of the improvements, needed repairs, quality of construction, etc. by providing meaningful comments, instead of marking "relative" ratings. Other modifications included the elimination of the requirement to report the estimated remaining economic and physical life, the addition of new entries for amenities, and a significantly improved format for reporting car storage.

The lines on the URAR to report the estimated remaining economic life and estimated remaining physical life have been eliminated. If the appraiser or lender believes this information should be included, it should be reported in the Addenda or **COMMENTS** section.

<u>Fannie Mae   June 30, 1993 Announcement   Description of the Improvements</u>
"The "description of improvements" section represents a significant streamlining of the information necessary to describe the improvements."

Fannie Mae   June 30, 1993 Announcement   - Description of the Improvements
Comments (Elimination of Rating Grid)

"One of the major changes was the elimination of the improvement analysis rating in order to emphasize that the appraiser should adequately address the condition of the improvements, needed repairs, quality of construction, etc. by providing meaningful comments, instead of marking "relative" ratings. Other modifications included the elimination of the requirement to report the estimated remaining economic and physical life, the addition of new entries for amenities, and a significantly improved format for reporting car storage."

Fannie Mae   June 30, 1993 Announcement   - Description of the Improvements
Estimated Remaining Economic and Physical Life

"...Other modifications included the elimination of the requirement to report the estimated remaining economic and physical life,"

Fannie Mae   June 30, 2002   Part XI Chapter 4, Section 405   Improvement Analysis

The appraiser must provide a clear, detailed, and accurate description of the site improvements that is consistent with the level of fieldwork we require in connection with 'the appraisal assignment. The appraiser should be as specific as possible ~commenting on such things as needed repairs, additional features, modernization, etc.) and should provide supporting addenda, if necessary.

Some of our- appraisal report forms require the appraiser to provide a comprehensive description of the improvements, which should include a general overall description and specific descriptions of the exterior, foundation, basement, insulation, interior surfaces, heating and cooling systems, kitchen equipment, attic, amenities, and car storage. If the property that is being appraised includes an accessory apartment, the appraiser should describe it in the "comments" section of the "improvements analysis" portion of the appraisal report form.

Fannie Mae   June 30, 2002   Part XI Chapter 4, Section 405.01   Conformity To Neighborhood

The improvements should generally conform to the neighborhood in terms of age, type, design, and materials used for their construction. If there is market resistance to a property because its improvements are not compatible with the neighborhood or with the requirements of the competitive market—because of adequacy of plumbing, heating, or electrical services; design; quality; size; condition; or any other reason directly related to market demand—the lender should underwrite the mortgage more carefully and, if appropriate, require more conservative mortgage terms. However, the lender should be aware that many older neighborhoods have favorable heterogeneity in architectural styles, land use, and age of housing. For example, older neighborhoods are especially likely to have been developed through custom building; this variety may be a positive marketing factor.

In the appraisal and underwriting process, special consideration must be given to properties that represent special or unique housing for the subject neighborhood. Mortgages secured by nontraditional types of housing—such as earth houses, geodesic domes, log houses, etc.—are eligible for delivery to us, provided the appraiser has adequate information to develop a reliable opinion of market value. It is not necessary for one or more of the comparable sales to be of the same design and appeal as the property that is being appraised (although appraisal accuracy is enhanced by using comparable sales that are the most similar to the subject property) on a case-by-case basis, both the appraiser and the underwriter must independently determine whether there is sufficient information available to develop a reliable opinion of market value. This will depend on the extent of the difference between the special or unique property and the more traditional types of houses in the market and the number of such properties that have already been sold in the market area.

• If the appraiser cannot locate recent comparable sales of the same design and appeal, but is able to determine sound adjustments for the differences between the comparables that are available and the subject property and to demonstrate the marketability of the property—based on older comparable sales, comparable sales in competing neighborhoods, the existence of similar properties in the market area, and any other reliable market data—the property is acceptable as security for a mortgage delivered to us.

• If the appraiser is not able to find any evidence of market acceptance and the characteristics of the property are so significantly different that he or she cannot establish a reliable opinion of market value, the property is not acceptable as security for a mortgage delivered to us.

We do not specify minimum size or living area requirements for properties. However, dwelling units of any type should have sufficient living area to be acceptable to typical purchasers or tenants in the subject market area. There should be comparables of similar size to the subject property to support the general acceptability of a particular property type.

DESCRIPTION OF IMPROVEMENTS

GENERAL DESCRIPTION | No. of Units - No. of Stories

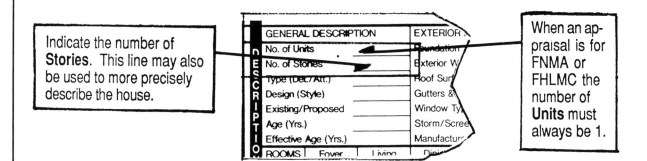

Indicate the number of dwelling **Units** contained in the subject property. Freddie Mac and Fannie Mae require the URAR be used only for properties containing a single (1) unit. However the URAR is a "Universal" form so others may accept appraisals using the URAR for properties containing more than one unit.

The Stories line is used to more precisely describe the house. The following pages show most of the common house types together with their number codes and standard abbreviations using the "CTS System" of the Realtors National Marketing Institute, a "uniform method for describing houses." [1]

---

[1] The tables and figures from the CTS system are taken from:
Henry S. Harrison, "House Types", Houses - The Illustrated Guide to Construction, Design and Systems (2nd Edition). Chicago, IL: Residential Sales Council of the National Association of Realtors, 1992.

DESCRIPTION OF IMPROVEMENTS

GENERAL DESCRIPTION	Type (Det./Att.)

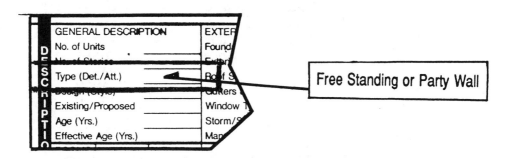

Fill in **Type** line, as indicated, with either **Det.** (Detached) when the house has free standing walls or Att. (Attached) when there is a "party wall" shared by neighboring structures. The FHA requires "R" for row houses.

CONSISTENCY CHECK: Information in this section of the URAR relates to another section of the form as indicated below. The appraiser should check to make sure data in both places is consistent!

<u>**IMPROVEMENTS**</u> - **GENERAL DESCRIPTION: Design "Type" and "Style"**
    should be considered when rating
<u>**SALES COMPARISON ANALYSIS**</u> - **SUBJECT: Design and Appeal.**

<u>Fannie Mae June 30, 2002</u>   **Part XI Chapter 4, Section 405.04**   <u>Layout and Floor Plans</u>

Dwellings with unusual layouts, peculiar floor plans, or inadequate equipment Or amenities generally have limited market appeal. A review of the room list and floor plan for the dwelling unit may indicate an unusual layout—such as bedrooms on a level with no bath, or a kitchen on a different level from the dining room. If the appraiser indicates that such inadequacies will result in market resistance to the subject property, he or she should make appropriate adjustments to reflect this in the overall analysis. On the other hand, if market acceptance can be demonstrated through the use of comparable sales with the same inadequacies, no adjustments are required.

THE CTS SYSTEM
(CLASS, TYPE, STYLE)
A UNIFORM METHOD FOR DESCRIBING HOUSES

# CODE	DESCRIPTION	ABBREVIATION
1	One-story	1 STORY
2	One-and-a-half story	1½ STORY
3	Two-story	2 STORY
4	Two-and-a-half story	2½ STORY
5	Three-or-more stories	3 STORY
6	Bi-level	BI-LEVEL
6	Raised ranch	R RANCH
6	Split entry	SPLT ENT
7	Split-level	SPLT LEV
8	Mansion	MANSION
9	Other	OTHER

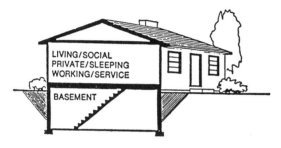

One-Story, Ranch, Rambler (1 Story - 1)

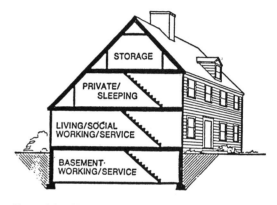

Two and One-Half Story (2½ Story - 4)

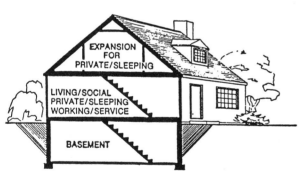

One and One-Half Story (1½ Story - 2)

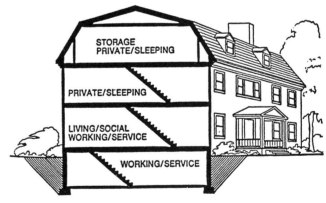

Three or More Stories (3 Story - 5)

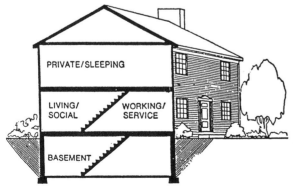

Two-Story (2 Story - 3)

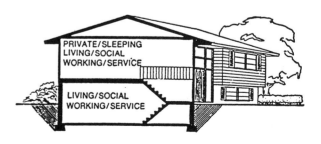

Bi-Level, Raised Ranch, Split Entry, Split Foyer
(Bi Lev or R Ranch or Splt Ent or Splt Foy-6)

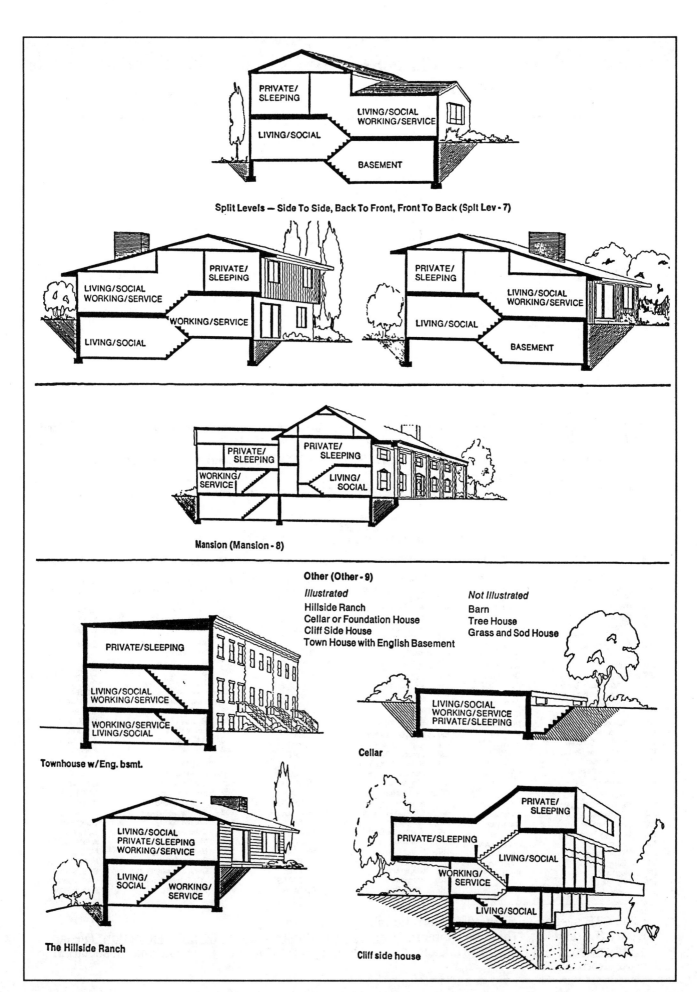
5-7

DESCRIPTION OF IMPROVEMENTS

GENERAL DESCRIPTION | Design (Style)

Design (Style) is used to describe the exterior appearance of a house based on historical or contemporary fashion. The CTS System's abbreviations for most commonly found styles are outlined below.[2]

CONSISTENCY CHECK: Information in this section of the URAR relates to another section of the form as indicated below. The appraiser should check to make sure data in both places is consistent!

DESCRIPTION OF IMPROVEMENTS - GENERAL DESCRIPTION: Design "Type" and "Style" should be considered when rating
SALES COMPARISON ANALYSIS - SUBJECT: Design and Appeal.

THE CTS SYSTEM
(CLASS, TYPE, STYLE)
A UNIFORM METHOD FOR DESCRIBING HOUSES

CODE	DESCRIPTION	ABBREVIATION	CODE	DESCRIPTION	ABBREVIATION	CODE	DESCRIPTION	ABBREVIATION
100	**COLONIAL AMERICAN**	**COL AMER**	**300**	**FRENCH**	**FRENCH**	713	EasternTownHouse	E TOWN
101	Federal	FEDERAL	301	French Farmhouse	FR FARM	714	Western Row House	WEST ROW
102	New England Farmhouse	N E FARM	302	French Provincial	FR PROV	714	Western Town House	W TOWN
103	Adams	ADAMS CO	303	French Normandy	FR NORM	715	Monterey	MONTEREY
104	Cape Cod	CAPE COD	304	Creole	CREOLE	716	Western Stick	W STICK
105	CapeAnn	CAPE ANN	304	Louisiana	LOUISIA	717	Mission Style	MISSION
106	Garrison Colonial	GARR CO	304	New Orleans	NEW OR	**800**	**EARLY-20th CENTURY**	**EARLY-20C**
107	New England	N E COL	**400**	**SWISS**	**SWISS**		**AMERICAN**	
108	Dutch	DUTCH CO	401	Swiss Chalet	SWISS CH	801	Prairie House	PRAIRIE
109	Saltbox	SALTBOX				802	Bungalow	BUNGALOW
109	Catslide	CATSLIDE	**500**	**LATIN**	**LATIN**	803	Pueblo	PUEBLO
110	Pennsylvania Dutch	PENN DUT	501	Spanish Villa	SP VILLA	803	Adobe	ADOBE
110	Pennsylvania German Farmhouse	GER FARM	502	Italian Villa	IT VILLA	804	International Style	INTERNAT
111	Classic	CLASSIC	**600**	**ORIENTAL**	**ORIENT**	805	California Bungalow	CAL BUNG
111	Neoclassical	NEO CLAS	601	Japanese	JAPAN	806	Shotgun	SHOTGUN
112	Greek Revival	GREEK				807	Foursquare	F SQUARE
113	Southern Colonial	SOUTH CO	**700**	**19th-CENTURY AMERICAN**	**19th CTY**	808	Art Deco	A DECO
114	Front Gable New England	F GAB NE	701	Early Gothic Revival	E GOTH	808	Art Moderne	A MOD
114	Charleston	CHARLES	702	Egyptian Revival	EGYPT	**900**	**POST-WORLD WAR II**	**POST WW2**
114	English Colonial	ENG COL	703	Roman Tuscan Mode	RO TU5C		**AMERICAN**	
115	Log Cabin	LOG CAB	704	Octagon House	OCTAGON	901	California Ranch	C RANCH
200	**ENGLISH**	**ENGLISH**	705	High Victorian Gothic	HI GOTH	902	Northwestern	NORTH W
201	Cotswold Cottage	COTSCOT	706	High Victorian Italianate	VIC ITAL	902	Puget Sound	P SOUND
202	Elizabethan	ELIZ	707	American Mansard	MANSARD	903	Functional Modern	FUN MOD
202	Half Timber	HALFTIM	707	Second Empire	2nd EMP	903	Contemporary	CONTEMP
203	Masonry Tudor	M TUDOR	708	Stick Style	STICK	904	Solar House	SOLAR
203	Jacobean	JACOBEAN	708	Carpenter Gothic	C GOTH	905	"A" Frame	A FRAME
204	Williamsburg	WILLIAMS	709	Eastlake	EAST L	906	Mobile Home	MOBILE
204	Early Georgian	E GEORG	710	Shingle Style	SHINGLE	907	Plastic House	PLASTIC
205	Regency	REGENCY	711	Romanesque	ROMAN	909	Contemporary Rustic	C RUSTIC
206	Georgian	GEORGE	712	QueenAnne	Q ANNE	909	California Contemporary	CAL CONTEMP
207	Tudor	TUDOR	713	Brownstone	BROWN S	910	Postmodern	P MODERN
			713	Brick Row House	BR ROW			

[2]The CTS system is outlined in, and the table taken from:
Henry S. Harrison, "The CTS System", <u>Houses - The Illustrated Guide to Construction, Design and Systems (2nd Edition)</u>. Chicago, IL: Residential Sales Council of the National Association of Realtors, 1992.

DESCRIPTION OF IMPROVEMENTS

| GENERAL DESCRIPTION | Existing/Proposed |

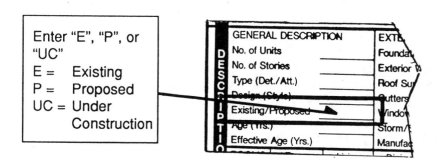

The URAR can be used for **Proposed** construction and residences **Under Construction**, as well as **Existing** improvements.

When the subject is **Proposed** or **Under Construction**, the appraiser must clearly indicate, in the **COMMENTS** section or an addendum, what plans or specifications he or she used to make the appraisal. To comply with FNMA guidelines, the appraiser must also file a certification of completion and value before the mortgage is delivered.

When the subject house is new, the appraiser should determine if a 'Certificate of Occupancy' has been issued, and if so, he or she should ascertain that it is not contingent upon any construction being completed. If the 'Certificate' requires work to be done, the appraiser should note what that work is and whether or not it has been completed, in the **COMMENTS** or Addenda.

MODEL COMMENTS: The following are examples of explanatory remarks reviewers find useful. They are especially important when data on the subject property falls outside the normal range. Usually these comments require customization to reflect the special characteristics of the specific property being appraised.

PROPOSED OR UNDER CONSTRUCTION:

   The subject improvements are _____ (proposed, under construction). All items reported in this appraisal regarding the subjects improvements are from plans or specifications provided by the _____ (bank, builder, Realtor, borrower, seller, etc.).

NEW HOUSE:

   The subject improvements are new. A certificate of occupancy _____ (has, has not) been issued as of the date of this appraisal

<u>NEW HOUSE WITH A CERTIFICATE OF OCCUPANCY THAT HAS CONDITIONS IN IT:</u>

A certificate of occupancy has been issued for this new home. However, the certificate contains the following conditions: _____ [list conditions], which _____ (have, have not) been complied with as of the date of this appraisal.

CONSISTENCY CHECK: Information in this section of the URAR relates to another section of the form as indicated below. The appraiser should check to make sure data in both places is consistent!

IMPROVEMENTS - **GENERAL DESCRIPTION: Existing /Proposed**
    should be consistent with the box marked in the

RECONCILIATION - **This appraisal is made:**
    section.

DESCRIPTION OF IMPROVEMENTS

| GENERAL DESCRIPTION | Age (Yrs.) - Effective Age (Yrs.) |

Often actual [or chronological] Age (Yrs.) differs from Effective Age (Yrs.).

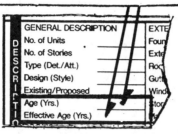

When there has been remodeling, renovation or rehabilitation, the effective age is usually reduced and may be less than the actual age.

Age (Yrs.) is the acutal age of the subject. **Effective Age (Yrs.)** is the age an improvement appears to be considering its design, condition, other houses in the market, and any economic forces affecting its value.

> To paraphrase an old saying, "If it has the physical condition and appearance of a 13-year-old house and market conditions affect it as if it were a 13-year-old house, then for appraisal purposes it should be treated as a 13-year-old house (effective age: 13 years), even if it is 10 or 20 years old."[3]

Generally, a house of average design and condition in a neighborhood that is not subject to unusual economic forces will have the <u>same</u> actual and effective age. However, when a house is modernized, its effective age is reduced. It is, therefore, unusual for a renovated, remodeled or modernized house to have an effective age as old as its actual age, unless its condition has again lapsed since the renovation. In fact, the purpose of renovation, remodeling and modernization is to reduce effective age.

Fannie Mae   June 30, 2002   Part XI Chapter 4, Section 405.02   Actual Age and Effective Age

We do not place a restriction on the actual age of the dwellings. Consequently, a mortgage secured by an older dwelling that meets our general requirements- Is acceptable~ The improvements for all properties must be of the quality and condition that will be acceptable to typical purchasers in the subject market area.

The relationship between the actual and effective ages of the property is a good indication of its condition. A property that has been well maintained will generally have an effective age somewhat lower than its actual age. On the other hand, a property that has an effective age higher than its actual age probably has not been well maintained or may have a particular physical problem. In such cases, the lender should pay particular attention to the condition of the subject property in its review of any appraisal report that requires the appraiser to address the actual and effective ages of a property.

---

[3]George F. Bloom and Henry S. Harrison, <u>Appraising the Single Family Residence</u>. Chicago, IL: American Institute of Real Estate Appraisers, 1978. P. 223.

MODEL COMMENTS: The following are examples of explanatory remarks reviewers find useful. They are especially important when data on the subject property falls outside the normal range. Usually these comments require customization to reflect the special characteristics of the specific property being appraised.

WHEN ACTUAL AGE AND EFFECTIVE AGE ARE THE SAME:

This house is in average condition for a house of this age in this neighborhood. Its actual age and effective age are the same.

WHEN ACTUAL AGE IS LESS THAN EFFECTIVE AGE:

The effective age of this house is greater than its actual age due to _____ (poor design, poor condition, poor construction, external obsolescence). These factors negatively affect the value of the property.

WHEN EFFECTIVE AGE IS LESS THAN ACTUAL AGE:

The effective age of this house is less than its actual age because the _____ (quality of construction is superior to other, design is above average for, house has been _____ {modernized, remodeled, renovated} better than, condition is superior to other) houses of the same age in this market.

WHEN ACTUAL AGE IS NOT ON FIELD CARD:

An exact age of the subject improvements is not indicated in the public records. The actual age given in this report is an estimate based on _____ (a physical inspection of the subject, a discussion with the homeowner, etc.).

CONSISTENCY CHECK: Information in this section of the URAR relates to another section of the form as indicated below. The appraiser should check to make sure data in both places is consistent!

IMPROVEMENTS - GENERAL DESCRIPTION: Age (Yrs.) or Effective Age (Yrs.)
    may also appear as
SALES COMPARISON ANALYSIS - SUBJECT: Age.
    The appraiser should make it clear which age is being entered. Also, if there is a significant difference between
IMPROVEMENTS - GENERAL DESCRIPTION: Age (Yrs.)
    and
IMPROVEMENTS - GENERAL DESCRIPTION: Effective Age (Yrs.),
    the
SALES COMPARISON ANALYSIS - SUBJECT: Condition
    rating will be affected.

DESCRIPTION OF IMPROVEMENTS

EXTERIOR DESCRIPTION | Foundation

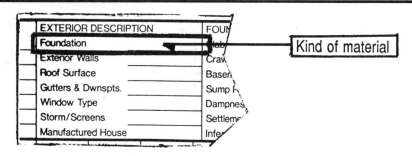

Specify the type of material used for the **Foundation** (e.g., poured concrete, cinder or concrete block, brick, field stone or treated wood).

MODEL COMMENTS: The following are examples of explanatory remarks reviewers find useful. They are especially important when data on the subject property falls outside the normal range. Usually these comments require customization to reflect the special characteristics of the specific property being appraised.

WHEN THE FOUNDATION MATERIAL IS TREATED WOOD:

```
    The foundation is made of treated wood.  I _____ (have,
have not) examined the manufacturer's guarantee.  In this market
it _____ (is, is not) necessary to make an adjustment for
treated wood foundations.
```

DESCRIPTION OF IMPROVEMENTS

EXTERIOR DESCRIPTION | Exterior Walls

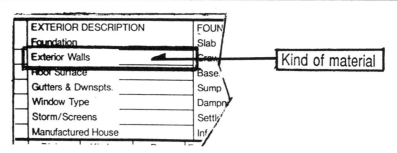

Specify the material used for the **Exterior Walls** covering such as clapboard, log, board and batten, wood or asbestos shingles, aluminum, vinyl, stucco or brick. If brick, specify whether veneer (brick on some form of masonry block) or solid masonry.

Nine out of ten houses are frame construction covered with a variety of materials. Some common types of wood siding materials are bevel, bungalow, colonial, rustic, shiplap and drop. Aluminum and vinyl siding also are very popular in some areas.

Shingles and shakes are also common siding materials. Wood shingles can be split or sawed. The most popular shingle material is cedar while other types are made of asbestos and asphalt. Shingles come in four grades, with the best being No. 1, blue label. Stucco used to be more common around the country but is still a popular siding in dry climates. It can be applied to wood framing or directly over solid masonry walls.

There are a variety of other common masonry products which can be applied over wood framing and used as siding. These include clay bricks, concrete bricks, and split blocks and stone. In houses with masonry veneer walls, all of the structural support is from the wood framing and not the one-unit thick masonry.

Exterior walls can also be made of solid masonry. The most common types are - 8" thick cement block, two layers of brick and a combination of brick and block. Masonry walls can either be solid masonry, or hollow walls known as cavity masonry walls.

DESCRIPTION OF IMPROVEMENTS

EXTERIOR DESCRIPTION | **Roof Surface**

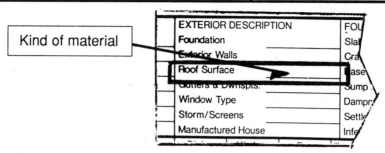

State the material used for the **Roof Surface** (e.g., wood shingles or shakes, asphalt or asbestos shingles, tile, etc.). The majority of houses have roofs covered with shingles and shakes made of wood, asphalt, asbestos, cement slate or tile. Other less frequently used materials are metal, clay tile and built-up or membrane roofs.

Most roofs start with a layer of sheathing material that is nailed to the roof framing members. (When the roof is quite steep and covered with wood shingles, the sheathing is not always required.) Asphalt felt underlayment is fastened to the sheathing. The roofing is laid on top of the underlayment.

When shingles are used, a double layer known as a starter course is attached at the bottom of the roof. Each succeeding course or row of shingles is then nailed to the sheathing so that it covers the top of the row below leaving part of the lower row exposed to the weather.

Slate is nailed over the sheathing covered with special impregnated slater's felt. Shingle tile is applied in the same manner.

Interlocking tiles known as French, Spanish, Mission, Roman or Greek tile are designed to provide maximum coverage with minimum material. These tiles have interlocking ridges on each side to reduce the overlap needed to maintain water tightness and hold tiles together.

Roll roofing is applied by nailing it down in strips that lap and then sealing the laps with roofer's cement.

DESCRIPTION OF IMPROVEMENTS

EXTERIOR DESCRIPTION | Gutters & Dwnspts

When there are no gutters or leaders, state the width of the roof overhang, note the site grading around the foundation wall and look for any evidence of dampness in the basement.

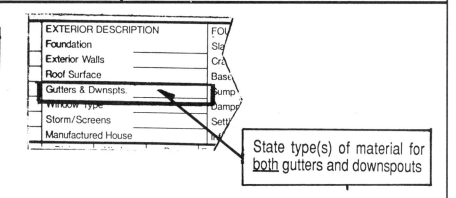

State type(s) of material for both gutters and downspouts

Gutters and Downspouts prevent damage or unsightly stains on walls where roof overhangs are not provided.

Metal **Gutters**, which are attached to the house with various types of metal hangers, are the most common type of gutter now in use. Aluminum, copper, galvanized iron and other materials are used. Wood gutters should be attached to the house with non-corroding screws bedded in elastic roofer's cement to prevent leakage. Built-up gutters are made of metal and set into the deeply notched rafter a short distance up the roof from the eaves. Pole gutters consist of a wooden strip nailed perpendicularly to the roof and covered with sheet metal.

Downspouts (or leaders) are vertical pipes that carry water from gutters to the ground and into sewers, dry wells, drain tiles, splash pans, or simply off the property. Downspouts must be large enough to carry water away as fast as they receive it from the roof. The junction of the gutter and downspout should be covered with a basket strainer to hold back leaves and twigs, especially if the gutter connects to a storm or sanitary sewer, which is difficult to clean out if clogged.

MODEL COMMENTS: The following are examples of explanatory remarks reviewers find useful. They are especially important when data on the subject property falls outside the normal range. Usually these comments require customization to reflect the special characteristics of the specific property being appraised.

WHEN THERE ARE NO GUTTERS OR DOWNSPOUTS:
   There are no _____ (gutters, downspouts). I examined the foundation wall and the basement, and I _____ (saw, did not see) evidence of dampness which may have been caused by the lack of _____ (gutters, downspouts). The roof overhang is _____ [# of inches or feet]. The site _____ (is, is not) graded to divert the water away from the foundation wall.

DESCRIPTION OF IMPROVEMENTS

EXTERIOR DESCRIPTION		Window Type

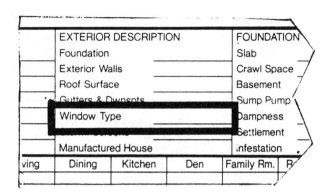

Describe the **Window Type**(s) (e.g. casement, sliding, double hung, etc.). Also identify the window frame material (e.g. wood, aluminum, steel, etc.).[4]

SLIDING WINDOWS

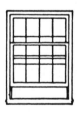

Double-hung windows open and close vertically, and are held in intermediate positions by various devices. This traditional window design remains very popular.

Gliding doors operate the same as horizontal sliding windows. Sliding windows are not as suitable as vertical swinging windows for obtaining maximum air movement. Only half of the window can be open at a time, and they cannot scoop in or direct summer breezes. Screens on sliding windows are mounted outside so that the windows can be operated year 'round.

Horizontal sliding windows glide on tracks at top and bottom.

Single-hung windows operate the same as double-hung windows except that the top half of the window remains in a fixed position permanently.

SWINGING WINDOWS

Casement windows swing outward from the side. They provide good top to bottom ventilation, and can scoop in air currents moving parallel to wall surfaces. Screens are mounted inside, and the window is operated by crank or push bar.

Awning windows open from the bottom, with an inside mounted screen. They direct airflow up, and allow ventilation in light rain. Outswinging windows, especially casements, should not be used near walkways and play areas where people can bump into the open sash.

Jalousie windows open outward with your screens mounted inside. The louvre design provides the best air ventilation while giving protection from rain and inclement weather. Window is operated by a crank.

Pivoted windows are made in types and sizes to meet all design and construction requirements in both commercial and residential buildings. They are easy to operate and provide a tight fit by means of secure locking vents.

Hopper windows open inward from the top. They direct airflow up and are very easy to clean. But they may possibly interfere with draperies and the floor space near them.

Projected windows are different from pivoted windows only in the method of hanging the ventilators. They are used particularly where economical screening or shading is desired.

---

[4]The pictures and descriptions were supplied by:
Blaine Window Hardware Inc, 1919 Blaine Drive, Route 4, Hagerstown, MD 21740
A prime supplier of replacement hardware.

DESCRIPTION OF IMPROVEMENTS

EXTERIOR DESCRIPTION | Storm/Screens

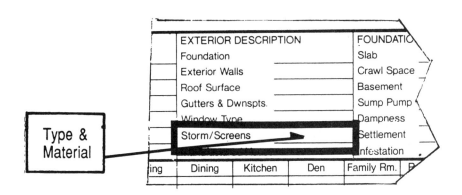

State if there are **Screens** and/or **Storm Sash**(es) and their materials. Previous page shows pictures and descriptions of the most common types of windows, with an explanation of corresponding screens.

DESCRIPTION OF IMPROVEMENTS

EXTERIOR DESCRIPTION | Manufactured House

TION	EXTERIOR DESCRIPTION		FOUNDA
	Foundation		Slab
	Exterior Walls		Crawl Sp
	Roof Surface		Basemen
	Gutters & Dwnspts.		Sump Pu
	Window Type		Dampnes
	Storm/Screens		Settleme
	Manufactured House		Infestatio
Living	Dining	Kitchen	Den	Family Rm.

Manufactured Houses are now a significant part of the housing market. They are usually partially constructed off-site in a factory and then transported to the site for installation and final assembly, although some units are totally assembled off-site. There is little difference between a small modular house and a large mobile home. Larger modular houses consist of several segments, which are shipped separately by rail and/or truck and joined together on the site. Prefabricated houses are shells that are factory-built and then shipped to the site for assembly. They usually have less mechanical equipment as part of the package than modular homes.

Modular houses and prefabs are chosen for a variety of reasons. Although the construction of single family houses has changed less than almost any other major item manufactured in this country, theoretically, the efficiency of assembly line and mass production methods should be applicable to housing. Manufacturers of modular and prefabricated homes are trying to do this. Speed of construction is another advantage to manufactured housing units, since the on-site assembly is often as little as a few days. Furthermore, lot owners can see complete model houses before they buy. This is impossible when a house is to be constructed from plans unless the builder has already completed a similar house nearby.

Manufactured houses can be appraised in the same manner as conventionally built homes. In most markets, there is little, if any, value difference between manufactured and conventional houses of the same size, design and quality. The speed of construction, cost differential and other advantages -- if they exist -- are enjoyed by the original owner, and usually do not affect the resale value.[5]

---

[5] George F. Bloom and Henry S. Harrison, <u>Appraising the Single Family Residence,</u> Chicago, IL: American Institute of Real Estate Appraisers, 1978. pp. 306-307.

DESCRIPTION OF IMPROVEMENTS

FOUNDATION | **Slab - Crawl Space - Basement**

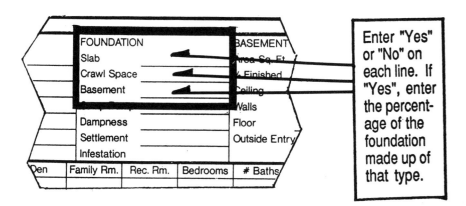

Often the **FOUNDATION** is some combination of **Basement**, **Crawl Space** and **Slab**. Mark "Yes" in the blank next to all appropriate descriptions and then indicate the percentage of the total foundation made of each. For example, if the foundation is 1/2 crawl space and 1/2 slab write "Yes - 50%" on both the **Crawl Space** and **Slab** lines.

> With the exception of those being constructed in the northern portions of the country, fewer and fewer houses are being built with **Basements**. And, where basements are built, there is an increasing trend to gain additional living space by finishing portions into family rooms, utility areas, baths and lavatories, workrooms, kitchens and even bedrooms. In the event that the house has a basement, the height between the basement floor, which is constructed similarly to a slab, and the bottom of the joists is usually 7.5 to 8 feet.
>
> For basementless houses, the finish grade is a major factor in the choice between slab or crawl space as a foundation. For **Slab** construction, it is important that the finished ground grade fall sharply away from the house...to prevent flooding. Slabs are constructed by first building footings for support, although some...known as "floating slabs," are built without them. The excavation is then covered with gravel and a vapor barrier and insulation is installed around the edge.
>
> **Crawl Spaces**, which provide flooding protection and...a convenient place to run heating ducts, plumbing pipes and wires that must be accessible for repairs, are constructed similarly to basements except that the distance from the floor to the joists is 3 to 4 feet. The floor can be concrete, as in a basement, or it can be dirt, often covered with a vapor barrier. In northern regions, crawl spaces must be insulated or heated to prevent pipe freezing and cold floors.[5]

---

[5] Henry S. Harrison, <u>Houses - The Illustrated Guide to Construction, Design and Systems (2nd Edition)</u>. Chicago, IL: Residential Sales Council of the National Association of Realtors, 1992.

Houses built over crawl spaces are subject to some special problems. The appraiser should check for the following:

1) Excessive moisture causing mildew, mold, fungus or rot;
2) Poor structural support;
3) Accumulation of water;
4) Trash and debris; and
5) Undermined footings.

If found, these problems should be reported and an adjustment made where applicable.

DESCRIPTION OF IMPROVEMENTS

| FOUNDATION | Sump Pump - Dampness |

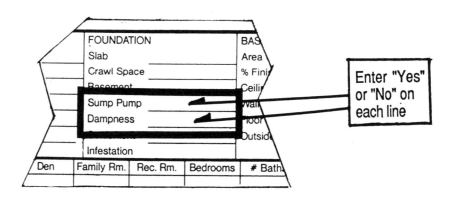

The main problem with basements is **Dampness**. The most likely causes of dampness include: poor foundation construction; excess ground water due to improper drainage; leaky windows, hatches, or clothes dryer vents; gutters or downspouts spilling water too near the foundation; or a raising ground water table. A basement that is wet only part of the year can be detected even when dry by a white mineral deposit on the walls, usually a few inches off the floor. Stains along the lower edge of columns, the furnace or hot water heater are also indications of dampness as is mild odor. [8]

MODEL COMMENTS: The following are examples of explanatory remarks reviewers find useful. They are especially important when data on the subject property falls outside the normal range. Usually these comments require customization to reflect the special characteristics of the specific property being appraised.

EVIDENCE OF DAMPNESS:
```
There is evidence of dampness in the basement. Its source _____
(could not be determines, was determined too be _____ (source).
A deduction from value _____ (is, is not) being made.
```

---

[8] George F. Bloom and Henry S. Harrison, Appraising the Single Family Residence, Chicago, IL; American Institute of Real Estate Appraisers, 1978.

DESCRIPTION OF IMPROVEMENTS

| FOUNDATION | Settlement |

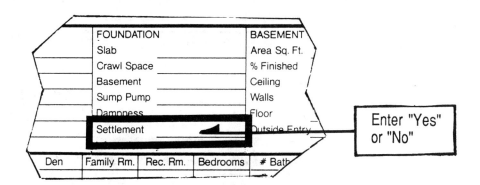

Cracks in the basement walls or floor indicate **Settlement**. Whenever the appraiser observes cracks in the basement walls or floors, they should be noted in the appraisal report. Hairline cracks normally are no problem. Medium size cracks (up to 1/4" wide) are dangerous about 50% of the time, and as the cracks get larger the possibility of serious structural damage increases. If there is any question about a crack, it is best to recommend an inspection by a structural engineer.

MODEL COMMENTS: The following are examples of explanatory remarks reviewers find useful. They are especially important when data on the subject property falls outside the normal range. Usually these comments require customization to reflect the special characteristics of the specific property being appraised.

EVIDENCE OF SETTLEMENT:

```
    There is evidence that the foundation has settled.  There are
_____ (a few, many) cracks.  A deduction from value _____
(is, is not) being made for the evidence of settlement, because
it has _____ (no, a negative) effect on marketability.  I
_____ (recommend that, do not believe it is necessary to
have) a qualified structural engineer inspect the foundation.
```

5-23

DESCRIPTION OF IMPROVEMENTS

| FOUNDATION | Infestation |

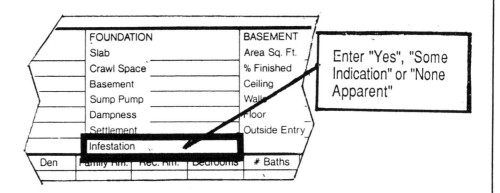

Use this space to describe any type of **Infestation** that is observed or suspected. The blank lines may also be used to recommend a professional inspection for termites and other infestations.

Fannie Mae   June 30, 2002   Part XI Chapter 4, Section 405.08   Improvement Analysis
Infestation, Dampness or Settlement
If the appraiser indicates that there is evidence of wood-boring insects, dampness, or settlement, he or she must comment on its effect on the marketability and value of the subject property. The lender must provide either satisfactory evidence that the condition was corrected or submit a professionally prepared report, which indicates that— based on an inspection of the property—the condition does not pose any threat of structural damage to the improvements.

MODEL COMMENTS: The following are examples of explanatory remarks reviewers find useful. They are especially important when data on the subject property falls outside the normal range. Usually these comments require customization to reflect the special characteristics of the specific property being appraised.

NO EVIDENCE OF TERMITE OR OTHER INFESTATION:
    There is no apparent evidence of termite or other infestation as of the date of this appraisal.

EVIDENCE OF TERMITE OR OTHER INFESTATION:
    There is evidence of _____ (termite, [other]) infestation damage. A more thorough inspection by a professional is recommended.

DESCRIPTION OF IMPROVEMENTS

| BASEMENT | Area Sq. Ft. - % Finished |

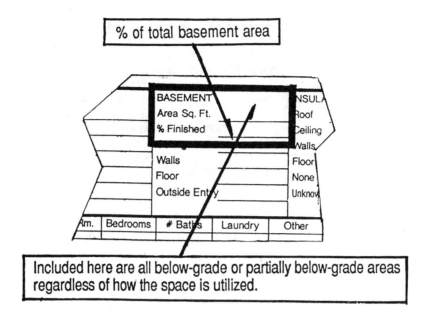

Included here are all below-grade or partially below-grade areas regardless of how the space is utilized.

Some appraisers measure **BASEMENT Area Sq. Ft.** inside the foundation walls. On a one-story ranch with a full basement, this produces an area smaller than the GLA. To eliminate this problem, other appraisers measure around the outside of the foundation wall.

% Finished is the percent of total basement area which is finished, <u>not</u> a percent of the ground floor area. A basement that is 50% of the first floor area and completely finished is indicated as 100% finished.

CONSISTENCY CHECK: Information in this section of the URAR relates to another section of the form as indicated below. The appraiser should check to make sure data in both places is consistent!
IMPROVEMENTS - BASEMENT: Area Sq. Ft. and % Finished
also appear under

SALES COMPARISON ANALYSIS - SUBJECT: Basement & Finished Rooms Below Grade.
IMPROVEMENTS - BASEMENT: Area Sq. Ft.
multiplied by

IMPROVEMENTS - BASEMENT: % Finished
also appears in

ROOMS - Basement: Area Sq. Ft.
but is <u>not</u> included in any GLA calculations.

DESCRIPTION OF IMPROVEMENTS

| BASEMENT | Ceiling - Walls - Floor |

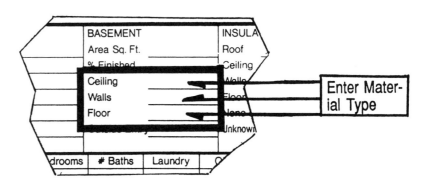

The **Ceiling**, **Walls** and **Floor** lines are used to describe how the basement is finished.

DESCRIPTION OF IMPROVEMENTS

BASEMENT	Outside Entry

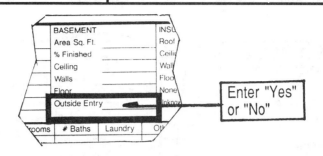

In many parts of the country an **Outside Entry** to the basement is an unknown item. In other areas (New England, for example), a house without a basement and an outside entry (usually a wood or steel hatch leading to the rear yard) probably suffers from significant functional obsolescence. Enter "Yes" or "No" as appropriate on this line and, if "Yes", use the blank line below to tell what type of entry exists.

DESCRIPTION OF IMPROVEMENTS

BASEMENT	Blank

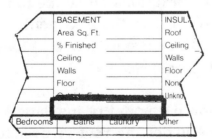

A **BASEMENT** is expected in many areas and unheard of in others. It is useful to a reviewer, who may be unfamiliar with the subject area, to know what is expected in the local market, and a good place to provide this information is on this blank line or in the addenda. This space should also be used for any other comments about the basement that the appraiser wishes to make. When there are additional comments about the basement in the addenda, put "see addenda" here.

DESCRIPTION OF IMPROVEMENTS

| INSULATION | Roof - Ceiling - Walls - Floor - None - Unknown |

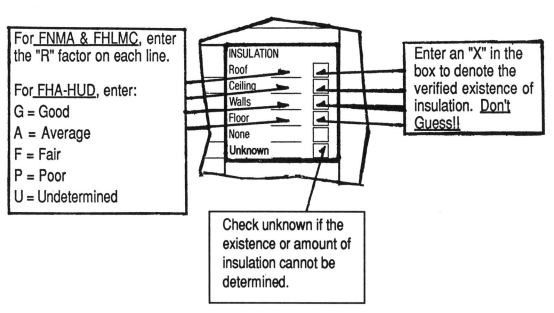

INSULATION, as important as it is now, will likely continue to increase in importance in the future. Many houses built prior to World War II, and unfortunately many postwar houses too, contain no or insufficient insulation.

There is no shortcut to determining whether a house has insulation, what kind of insulation exists and if the "R" value is high enough. First, look for insulation under the **Roof** or over the **Ceiling** of the top floor. If there is none, or if it was installed after the initial house construction, there is a good possibility the walls and floor are not insulated. Next, look along the top and bottom of the exterior **Walls** at the edge of the attic and in the basement (or crawl space). Often wall insulation can be seen from these two locations. **Floor** insulation can be seen by looking up at the floor joists from below.

Find out what the standard amount of insulation is in the subject area. In much of the country, R-24 under the roof or over the ceiling is the minimum standard, as is R-11 to R-13 in the exterior walls and under the floor.

Check the **None** box when the house is uninsulated.

REMEMBER!: If there is any question whether the residence is insulated or not, don't guess! Check the **Unknown** box.

Fannie Mae   June 30, 2002   Part XI Chapter 4, Section 405.03   **Improvement Analysis**

Insulation and Energy Efficiency

Some of our appraisal report forms provide an area for the appraiser to state the "R" value for insulation (if he or she is aware of it) and to comment on the adequacy of the insulation. The appraiser should list the additional energy-efficient features in the "comments" area. The appraiser should also compare the energy-efficient features of the subject property to those of the comparable properties in the "sales comparison analysis" grid to assure that the overall contribution of these Items is reflected in his or her opinion of the market value of the subject property.

An energy-efficient property is one that uses cost-effective design, materials, equipment, and site orientation to conserve nonrenewable fuels. Special energy saving items should be recognized in the appraisal process. The nature of these items and their contribution to value will vary throughout the country because of climactic conditions and differences in utility costs.

DESCRIPTION OF IMPROVEMENTS

| ROOMS | Description - Gross Living Area |

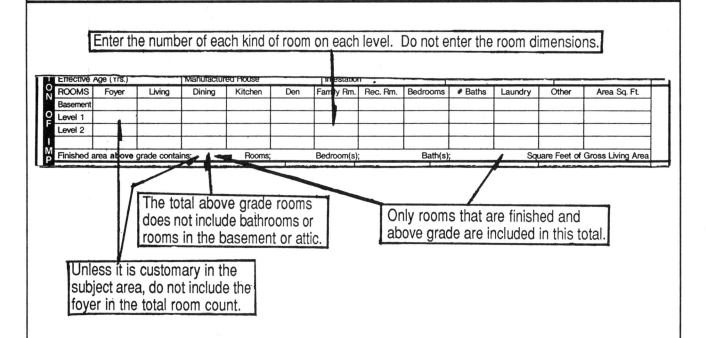

Each box in the **ROOMS** section is to be filled in with the number of each type of room (listed across the top) on each level (listed in the left-hand column). Do not enter room dimensions unless they are specifically required by the client (NOTE: FNMA, FHLMC, VA and HUD do <u>not</u> require appraisers to enter dimensions).

The **Finished area <u>above</u> grade contains:** (followed by four blanks)

The total of all <u>above grade</u> finished **Rooms** is entered in the first blank. Any rooms listed in the **Foyer** (a room just inside an entrance to the house from outdoors), **# Baths** or **Laundry** columns are <u>not</u> usually included in the **Rooms** count. If such a room is included, an explanation should appear in the **COMMENTS** section or an addendum.

The next two spaces are filled with the total number of <u>above grade</u> **Bedroom(s)** and **Bath(s)** respectively.

The last blank is for the total <u>above grade</u> **Square Feet of Gross Living Area**.

The following guidelines will help you correctly calculate the **Gross Living Area** of the house you are appraising:

1. Measure around the outside of the house above the foundation.
2. In multi-floor houses count each floor above grade.
3. Include all of the above grade habitable living area.
4. Do not include the basement (even when it is finished and heated).
5. Garages are never included in the GLA.
6. Porches are included only when they are heated and finished in a way similar in quality to the rest of the house.
7. Upper stories are divided into two areas.

a. Attic is the unfinished part or that part with low ceilings (below 5ft.).

b. Habitable area finished and heated substantially like the rest of the house with normal ceiling heights (5ft. is the most common height used by appraisers as normal ceiling height in attics).

DO NOT INCLUDE IN THE GLA THAT PORTION OF THE UPPER STORY THAT IS CLASSIFIED AS ATTIC.

COMMON PROBLEMS: Raised Ranches (a/k/a Bi-Levels and Split Foyers), hillside ranches and split level house types present special GLA measuring problems.

The problem is how to classify the lower level when it is heated and finished substantially like the rest of the house.

The appraiser has the option to include (or not include) that portion of the lower level in the GLA measurement which is 100% above grade and has normal size windows (windows size should be at least 10% of the floor area).

When this option to include the area in the GLA measurement is elected special care must be taken to be consistent throughout the form.

Do not classify or describe this space as a basement space on the room list.

When lower level space is included in the GLA measurement should be level 1 on the room list. Do not include it in the measurement of "Basement Area _____ sq. ft.". Do not include it in the Basement Section" ____% Basement" calculation.

NOTE: FNMA requires all partially-below grade areas to be excluded from GLA calculations. Any **Basement** or other area that is not fully above grade should be reported separately and adjusted for accordingly in the **SALES COMPARISON ANALYSIS**. Also see **INTERIOR - ATTIC** for a better definition of what space on the upper levels of a house is included in GLA.

 # Baths should be counted as follows:

Full bath (1)	4 fixtures - toilet, sink, tub <u>and</u> shower;
Three quarter (3/4 or .75)	3 fixtures - toilet, sink and tub <u>or</u> shower*;
Half bath (1/2 or .5)	2 fixtures - toilet and sink; and
Quarter bath (1/4 or .25)	1 fixture - a toilet only.

*In some areas, a 3 fixture bath is counted as a full (or 1) bath.

Rooms with sinks alone or showers alone are Washrooms and Shower rooms respectively and are listed under **Other** in the **ROOM LIST**.

A **Dining** area counts as a separate room when: 1) It is as large as a typical dining room in the market; or 2) If the addition of a hypothetical wall converts it into a dining room with equal or greater utility than the space has without the wall.

Fannie Mae   June 30, 2002   Part XI Chapter 4, Section 405.05   Improvement Analysis

Unit/Room List

The *Uniform Residential Appraisal Report* (Form 1004) and the *Individual Condominium Unit Appraisal Report* (Form 1073) include a "room list" section to describe the subject property and provide a column for the square footage per level, as well as space for a summary of the above-grade room count(s) and the above-grade gross living area for the finished area.

The *Small Residential Income Property Appraisal Report* (Form 1025) includes a "unit/room" list section to describe the subject property and requires the appraiser to indicate the square feet per each unit. The unit/room list section gives the appraiser the flexibility to report the units individually or to report them as a single line entry if they are all equal in size. The total square footage reported in the unit/room list section of Form 1025 should reflect the net rentable area of the property (and, as such, will not necessarily equal the gross building area).

The *Individual Cooperative Interest Appraisal Report (Form* 1075) and the *Desktop Underwriter Individual Cooperative Interest Appraisal Report* (Form 2095) do not include a "room list" section. Form 1075 provides space for the appraiser to indicate a summary of both the finished area "above grade" and the finished area "below grade"—breaking- it down by total rooms, bedrooms, baths, and square feet of gross living area. Form 2095 provides space for the appraiser to indicate a summary of the finished area—breaking it down by total rooms, bedrooms, baths, and square feet of gross living area.

Fannie Mae   June 30, 2002   Part XI Chapter 4, Section 405.06   Improvement Analysis

Gross Living Area

The most common comparison for one-family properties (including units in PUD, condominium, or cooperative projects) is above-grade gross living area. The appraiser must be consistent when he or she calculates and reports the finished above-grade room count and the square feet of gross living area that is above-grade. For units in condominium or cooperative projects, the appraiser should use interior perimeter unit dimensions to calculate the gross living area. In all other instances, the appraiser should use 'the exterior building dimensions per floor to calculate the above-grade gross living area of a property -Only finished above-grade areas should be used—garages and basements (including those that are partially above-grade) should not be included. We consider a level to be below-grade if any portion of it is below grade—regardless of the quality of its—"finish" or the window area of any room. Therefore, a walkout basement with finished rooms would not be included in the above-grade room count.

Rooms that are not included in the above-grade room count may add substantially to the value of a property— particularly when the quality of the—"finish" is high. For that reason, the appraiser should report the basement or other partially below-grade areas separately and make appropriate adjustments for them on the "basement and finished areas below-grade" line in the "sales comparison analysis" grid. To assure consistency in the sales comparison analysis, the appraiser generally should compare above-grade areas to above-grade areas and below-grade areas to below-grade areas. The appraiser may deviate from this approach if the style of the subject property or any of the comparables does not lend Itself to such comparisons. However, in such instances, he or she must explain the reason for the deviation and clearly describe the comparisons that Were made.

MODEL COMMENTS: The following are examples of explanatory remarks reviewers find useful. They are especially important when data on the subject property falls outside the normal range. Usually these comments require customization to reflect the special characteristics of the specific property being appraised

WHEN THE NUMBER OF ROOMS IS TYPICAL:
```
    The number of rooms, bedrooms, baths and lavatories is
typical of houses in this neighborhood. Foyers, laundry rooms
and all rooms below grade are excluded from the total room
count.
```

TOO FEW BEDROOMS:
```
    The number of bedrooms is less than what is typical in this
market. This has _____ (no, a) negative effect on the value of
the property.
```

<u>DISSIMILAR NUMBER OF BATHROOMS OR BEDROOMS</u>:

    The number of _____ (baths, bedrooms) is _____ (less, more) than what is typical in this market. A deduction for value _____ (is, is not) being made since there is _____ (a negative, no) effect on marketability.

CONSISTENCY CHECK: Information in this section of the URAR relates to another section of the form as indicated below. The appraiser should check to make sure data in both places is consistent!

ROOM LIST:
>The <u>total</u> of all rooms <u>above grade</u>, excepting

ROOM LIST - ROOMS: Foyer, # Baths and Laundry
>also appears as:

ROOM LIST - Rooms
>on the "Finished area **above** grade contains:" line; and

SALES COMPARISON ANALYSIS - SUBJECT: Above Grade Room Count Gross Living Area; Total.

ROOM LIST - Bedrooms:
>The <u>total</u> number of <u>above grade</u> bedrooms also appears as:

ROOM LIST - Bedroom(s)
>on the "Finished area **above** grade contains:" line; and

SALES COMPARISON ANALYSIS - SUBJECT: Above Grade Room Count Gross Living Area; Bdrms.

ROOM LIST - # Baths:
>The <u>total</u> number of <u>above grade</u> bathrooms also appears as:

ROOM LIST - Bath(s)
>on the "Finished area **above** grade contains:" line; and

SALES COMPARISON ANALYSIS - SUBJECT: Above Grade Room Count Gross Living Area; Baths.

ROOM LIST - Area Sq. Ft.:
>The <u>total above grade</u> area in sq. ft. (GLA) appears in four other places on the URAR*:

ROOM LIST - Square Feet of Gross Living Area
>on the "Finished area **above** grade contains:" line;

SALES COMPARISON ANALYSIS - SUBJECT: Above Grade Room Count Gross Living Area; Sq. Ft.;
>on the

COST APPROACH - Dwelling ___ Sq. Ft.
>line**; and in the

COST APPROACH - BUILDING SKETCH
>block either as a sketch with dimensions for HUD or as GLA calculations for FNMA and FHLMC.

> *Also note that GLA is used to calculate

SALES COMPARISON ANALYSIS - SUBJECT: Price/Gross Liv. Area.
>**An exception is when a cost service is used that does not base its square foot calculations on GLA.

INTERIOR

Introduction

Finished area above grade contains:		Rooms,		Bedroom(s),		Bath(s),		Square Feet of Gross Living Area
INTERIOR Materials/Condition	**HEATING**		**KITCHEN EQUIP.**		**ATTIC**		**AMENITIES**	**CAR STORAGE:**
Floors	Type		Refrigerator ☐		None ☐		Fireplace(s) # ☐	None ☐
Walls	Fuel		Range/Oven ☐		Stairs ☐		Patio ☐	Garage # of cars
Trim/Finish	Condition		Disposal ☐		Drop Stair ☐		Deck ☐	Attached
Bath Floor	**COOLING**		Dishwasher ☐		Scuttle ☐		Porch ☐	Detached
Bath Wainscot	Central		Fan/Hood ☐		Floor ☐		Fence ☐	Built-In
Doors	Other		Microwave ☐		Heated ☐		Pool ☐	Carport
	Condition		Washer/Dryer ☐		Finished ☐			Driveway

The **INTERIOR** section is divided into areas. Each of the major areas is broken up into smaller parts as below and described in detail on the following pages.

INTERIOR

INTERIOR	Floors

Any unusual bathroom, kitchen, recreation room and other special floors should be described in detail in the **COMMENTS- Additional features** section.

The **Floors** space is used to describe the floor finish in the major portion of the house. If wall-to-wall carpeting, indicate the material over which the carpet is installed. Otherwise state the type of floor cover under **Material**. Floor covering in the kitchen or other areas such as the foyer may be described under **COMMENTS - Additional Features**.

The **Condition** of the floors should be rated "Good," "Average," "Fair" or "Poor."

INTERIOR

INTERIOR	Walls

Indicate the type of **Walls** in the main section of the house. Most modern houses use "Drywall" construction, consisting of 2" by 4" studs (16 inches apart) covered with 3/8 inch thick gypsum board. If the studs are 24" apart they should be covered with 1/2 inch gypsum board.

Older houses and some modern custom homes have plaster walls. Other less common interior walls are made of plywood, hardboard, fiberboard, ceramic wall tile and wood paneling.

The **Condition** of walls should be rated "Good," "Average," "Fair" or "Poor."

INTERIOR

INTERIOR	Trim/Finish

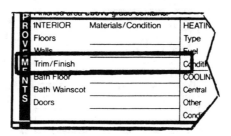

The use of various items of **Trim** in a house enhances its beauty. In lower priced houses, trim may be limited to simple casings around doors, windows, baseboards ceilings. In more elaborate houses and houses in the architectural style of certain periods, extensive or elaborate moldings may be used.

Molding is made of a variety of hardwoods and softwoods for interior and exterior use. It is milled by special machines that cut, plane and sand the lumber surfaces into desired shapes. Elaborate moldings are thicker, more intricate and often consist of two or three pieces of wood together. Most molding used today, however, is "stock" molding in one of several standard sizes and shapes.

The use of elaborate moldings, cornices, ornamental molding around the fireplaces, wainscot, chair rails, and picture moldings are signs of above-average **Trim/Finish**.

The type of **Trim/Finish** should be indicated by 1) material (wood, plastic, metal, etc.) and 2) quality of workmanship and condition (Good, Average, Fair or Poor, i.e., "Wood/Avg." or "Metal/Fair").

INTERIOR

INTERIOR	Bath Floor

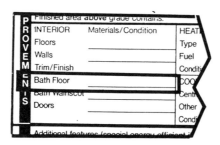

Often the **Bath Floor** has a different covering than other floors in the house. The type of bathroom floor covering should be indicated on this line. If the other bathrooms have different floor coverings, they should be described either in the **COMMENTS** section or an addendum. Until recently, the preferred material for bathroom floors was ceramic tile. This is still an excellent material, but some others are also now equally acceptable.

Ceramic tile can be installed in two basic ways. One is to set the tile into a bed of plaster at least 1.25 inches thick, known as a "mud job." Grout is then compressed between the tiles and tooled to make it smooth. Ceramic tile can also be attached to the subflooring with special waterproof adhesives. Again, grout is compressed into the spaces between tiles and tooled smooth.

There are now many attractive vinyl, rubber and asphalt tiles that make satisfactory bathroom floors when properly installed over solid subflooring. Rolled goods of the same materials, when properly installed, are excellent, especially for rental units. Recently, carpeting the bathroom has increased in popularity, but this is often expensive as the carpet must be specially made to be waterproof and easily cleaned.

The condition of the **Bath Floors** should be rated "Good," "Average," "Fair" or "Poor."

INTERIOR

| INTERIOR | Bath Wainscot |

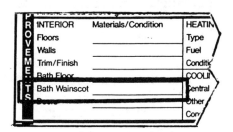

When the lower portion of a wall is finished with a different material from the upper portion, the lower portion is referred to as "wainscot" and the material with which the wainscot is finished is called "wainscoting." Many people still feel that the best material for **Bath Wainscot** is ceramic tile. Tile is now available in many colors and designs and can be glued to gypsum board wall with special adhesive or set into a plaster wall.

There is a variety of plastic wall covering products available that are suitable for bathroom wall coverings too. New waterproof wall-papers are being used successfully. It is also quite common to leave substantial portions of the walls uncovered except for a coating of waterproof paint.

When bathrooms are of the new fiber glass prefabricated type, they should be described in the **COMMENTS - Additional features**.

The condition of the **Bath Wainscot** should be rated "Good," "Average," "Fair" or "Poor," and presented in the "Materials/Condition" format.

INTERIOR

INTERIOR	Doors

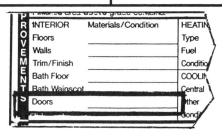

There are eight basic types of **Doors** as described below.

Batten doors consist of boards nailed together in various ways and are used where appearance is not important, like cellar and shed doors.

Sliding glass doors contain at least one fixed pane plus one or more panes that slide in a frame of wood or metal. The most common type has two panes providing a maximum of 50% ventilation.

Folding doors are usually made of wood slats connected by tape or cord forming flexible, drape-like doors. They usually fold to about the width of the jamb and are hung from ceiling tracks on nylon rollers or glides. There are also solid wood accordion doors consisting of thin slats connected by continuous metal, vinyl or nylon fabric hinges. The woven type has vertical wood strips 3/8 to 1 inch wide, interwoven basketweave style with tape. The corded type is made with wood slats similar to the woven type, but the slats are connected with cotton cord. Folding doors provide a visual screen rather than a sound barrier in such places as closets or laundry enclosures.

Flush solid doors are flat on both sides and made of planking. This type of door is rare in houses. Flush solid core doors are made of smooth face panels glued to a core of composition material or glued-together wood pieces. These are often used as exterior doors. Flush hollow core doors are also flat, but have a core consisting of a grid, usually of crossed wooden slats. These doors are light interior doors.

Stile and rail doors consist of a framework of vertical (stiles) and horizontal (rails) boards. Stiles and rails are usually softwood and give the door its strength. They are connected by dowels or mortise and tendon joints and are glued together. This type of door is good for laundry areas, furnace rooms, closets and other places where air circulation is needed, but privacy and sound insulation are not.

Storm doors, screen doors and combination storm and screen doors are often hung outside regular exterior doors to provide additional insulation in the winter and ventilation in the summer. These doors usually are lightweight wood or aluminum, and have removable glass or screen sections that can be interchanged from season to season.

Doors should be described on these lines and rated as "Good," "Average," "Fair" or "Poor."

DESCRIPTION OF IMPROVEMENTS

INTERIOR | Blank

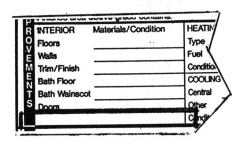

There are a variety of other interior items that can be listed here or in the addenda as needed. When there are additional comments about the interior in the addenda, put "see addenda" here.

INTERIOR

HEATING	Type - Fuel - Condition

```
HEATING          KITCH
Type             Refrig
Fuel             Range
Condition        Dispo
COOLING          Dishw
Central          Fan/H
Other            Micro
Condition        Washe
```

Type of heat means the heat distribution system, such as gravity, hot air, forced hot air, hot water (hydronic), steam, electric or radiant.

Fuels are oil, gas, liquid petroleum gas, coal and wood. Electricity is both a type of heat and a fuel. Fuel costs may be checked by asking for a year's bills from the homeowner or fuel supplier. Be aware that fuel costs can vary considerably according to residents' habits.

Condition should be described as "Good", "Average", "Fair" or "Poor". If "Fair" or "Poor" is indicated, an explanation is needed in the **COMMENTS** section or on an addendum sheet. The condition of the furnace is often reflected by its appearance. An old furnace encased in asbestos probably is obsolete, whereas an adequate-sized, clean furnace without rust usually has plenty of good life left, although it may require minor repairs. The performance of many furnaces can be improved simply by a good cleaning and adjustment including replacement of clogged air filters.

The major causes of inadequate heating are: 1) insufficient insulation; and 2) an inadequate or poorly functioning heating system. To remedy this, insulation may be added, as may storm windows and weatherstripping. Adequacy should be reported in **COMMENTS.**

A free or nominally-priced heating system inspection is often available from fuel suppliers in the area.

CONSISTENCY CHECK: Information in this section of the URAR relates to another section of the form as indicated below. The appraiser should check to make sure data in both places is consistent!

INTERIOR - HEATING: Type or Fuel
  (if different from standard for the market) should be noted under
SALES COMPARISON ANALYSIS - SUBJECT: Heating/Cooling,
  so appropriate adjustments can be made to the comparables.

INTERIOR	
COOLING	Central - Other - Condition

HEATING		KITC
Type		Refr
Fuel		Ranɡ
Condition		Disp
COOLING		Dish
Central		Fan/
Other		Micrᴏ
Condition		Wash

Central air conditioning is indicated by an "X" in the **Central** box when a single unit (or in some cases, several units) supply the house with air conditioning. The type of fuel may be shown (which may be either electricity or gas) instead.

The **Other** line is used to indicate window units or through-the-wall units that are part of the real estate based upon the custom in the area. If an air conditioning unit is <u>not</u> part of the real estate, it must be clear in the report that its value is <u>not</u> part of the appraised value (even if the units are included as part of the pending sale).

The **Condition** of the air conditioning units included as part of the real estate should be reported as "Good," "Average," "Fair" or "Poor."

The Adequacy of air conditioning is based on the competitive market standards in the area and should be reported in **COMMENTS**.

CONSISTENCY CHECK: Information in this section of the URAR relates to another section of the form as indicated below. The appraiser should check to make sure data in both places is consistent!

<u>**INTERIOR - COOLING:**</u> **Central**
    air conditioning) or an abbreviated description of the system (like "2 Wndw.", if the

<u>**INTERIOR - COOLING:**</u> **Other**
    space is filled) should be noted under

<u>**SALES COMPARISON ANALYSIS**</u> **- SUBJECT: Heating/Cooling,**
    so appropriate adjustments can be made to the comparables.

INTERIOR

KITCHEN EQUIPMENT
Refrigerator - Range/Oven - Disposal - Dishwasher - Fan - Microwave - Washer/Dryer

KITCHEN EQUIP.	
Refrigerator	☐
Range/Oven	☐
Disposal	☐
Dishwasher	☐
Fan/Hood	☐
Microwave	☐
Washer/Dryer	☐

As a result of Federal banking regulations, appraisals are now being rejected, or the final value adjusted, because the value of **KITCHEN EQUIPMENT**, which is not part of the real estate, is included. The value of kitchen appliances which are not classified as real estate in the subject area (or any other non-real estate equipment or appliances), should never be included in the appraised value of the real estate.

In many areas it is customary to include some kitchen equipment as part of the sale without any division of the sales price into real estate and included equipment. Such sales prices often are recorded and reported including a substantial amount of personal property. The best way to avoid the personal property problem is to verify the sale with the Buyer, Seller, Broker or closing Attorney. The verification process also helps the appraiser learn about any other special conditions surrounding a sale.

Some lenders instruct appraisers to indicate on the URAR any personal property observed on the premises that will be included in the sale. Items of personal property may be indicated by a letter "P" instead of an "X". To be safe, items of personal property shown in the **KITCHEN EQUIP.** block should also be listed in the **COMMENTS** section or an addendum.

MODEL COMMENTS: The following are examples of explanatory remarks reviewers find useful. They are especially important when data on the subject property falls outside the normal range. Usually these comments require customization to reflect the special characteristics of the specific property being appraised.

```
WHEN PERSONAL PROPERTY IS DESCRIBED IN THE APPRAISAL:
Items observed to be personal property and not part of the real
estate are indicated with a "P", and are not included in the
appraisal value.
```

CONSISTENCY CHECK: Information in this section of the URAR relates to another section of the form as indicated below. The appraiser should check to make sure data in both places is consistent!

INTERIOR - KITCHEN EQUIP.
    which is considered real estate, should be noted under
SALES COMPARISON ANALYSIS - **SUBJECT:** Blank or Comments
    so appropriate adjustments can be made to the comparables.

INTERIOR - KITCHEN EQUIP.
    which is personal property, should be noted in the
COMMENTS
    section.

INTERIOR	
ATTIC	None - Stairs - Drop Stair - Scuttle - Floor - Heated - Finished

ATTIC
- None
- Stairs
- Drop Stair
- Scuttle
- Floor
- Heated
- Finished

An **ATTIC** is that part of the upper levels of a house which is <u>not</u> counted as Gross Living Area (GLA) for one or more of the following reasons:

1) Finished differently from the main portion of the house.

2) Unheated.

3) Low ceiling height (many appraisers feel that ceilings less than 5 feet are below normal.

4) Inadequate window area (window area should be at least 10% of the floor area).

NOTE: When an area fits <u>one</u> of the above criteria and is described as **ATTIC**, it <u>must not be included in GLA calculations</u>.

Check the **None** box if there is no attic. Check the appropriate box describing attic access: **Stairs**, **Drop Stair**, or **Scuttle** (a hole in the ceiling leading into the attic, usually covered by an opening panel). Check the **Floor** box when the attic has a floor, the **Heated** box when the attic is heated and the **Finished** box when the attic is finished.

Use the **COMMENTS** section to describe how the attic is finished and how it is used.

MODEL COMMENTS: The following are examples of explanatory remarks reviewers find useful. They are especially important when data on the subject property falls outside the normal range. Usually these comments require customization to reflect the special characteristics of the specific property being appraised.

UNFINISHED SECOND LEVEL:

The subject is a _____ [style, usually cape or colonial] with an unfinished second level. The unfinished area is not included in the GLA. Such properties are _____ (common, uncommon) in this area and buyers _____ (are, are not) willing to pay for the potential of finishing the second level. Therefore, the subject's marketability ____ (is, is not) adversely affected.

INTERIOR

AMENITIES	Fireplace(s) # - Patio - Deck - Porch - Fence - Pool

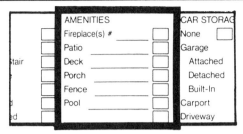

Amenities are now grouped together with check boxes for **Fireplace(s) #**, **Patio**, **Deck**, **Porch**, **Fence**, **Pool** and a blank line.

<u>Fannie Mae   June 30, 1993   Announcement   -   Description of the Improvements</u>
Amenities

"...The addition of new entries for ....amenities."

<u>Veterans Benefits Administration   Circular 26-93-25   1993</u>
Description of Improvements Section - Amenities

Other modifications included the addition of new entries for amenities;

CONSISTENCY CHECK: Information in this section of the URAR relates to another section of the form as indicated below. The appraiser should check to make sure data in both places is consistent!

INTERIOR - # Fireplace(s)
    also appears under
SALES COMPARISON ANALYSIS - SUBJECT: Fireplace(s).

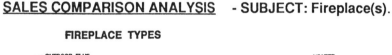

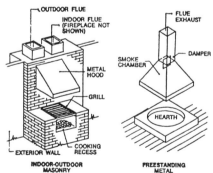
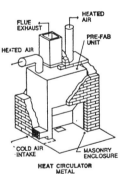
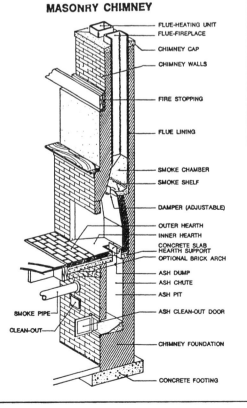

The above figures are taken from: Henry S. Harrison, <u>Houses - The Illustrated Guide to Construction, Design and Systems</u>. Chicago, IL: National Association of Realtors, 1992.

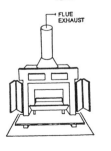

5-48

INTERIOR

CAR STORAGE	None; Garage – # of Cars – Attached, Detached, Built-In; Carport; Driveway

Car Storage reporting has been reorganized.

Each market has a **CAR STORAGE** standard and houses that fail to meet or exceed this standard suffer from functional obsolescence. For example, a house with a garage in a neighborhood with only carports has a superadequacy. Similarly, a house with a carport in an area where most homes have garages has a deficiency.

Detached garages have decreased in popularity in some areas of the country.

<u>Fannie Mae June 30, 1993 Announcement</u> - **Description of the Improvements**
<u>Car Storage</u>
"....and a significantly improved format for reporting car storage."

Notes

COMMENTS

| Additional features | special energy efficient items |

```
Additional features (special energy efficient items, etc.): _____

Condition of the improvements, depreciation (physical, functional, and external), repairs needed, quality of construction, remodeling/additions, etc.: _____

Adverse environmental conditions (such as, but not limited to, hazardous wastes, toxic substances, etc.) present in the improvements, on the site, or in the immediate vicinity of the subject property.: _____

Freddie Mac Form 70   6-93     10 CH.              PAGE 1 OF 2                    Fannie Mae Form 1004 (6-93)
```

These lines and the addenda should be used to describe any **special energy efficient items** that exist in the subject property.

Normal insulation <u>is not</u> considered to be a special energy efficient item, but super insulation <u>is</u>. Super insulation is usually found in the walls and ceilings. Typical wall insulation is 3 1/2" thick and fits between a 2" x 4" wall stud. Super wall insulation is usually about 5 1/2" thick and fits between special 2" x 6" wall studs. Typical ceiling or attic insulation is 5 1/2" to 6" thick and is installed over the ceiling. Super ceiling insulation is 10" to 12" thick. Insulation around the hot water tank and hot water pipes is also considered special insulation.

Items that are considered special energy efficient items include:

1. **Super insulation (as described above)**
2. **Special caulking and weatherstripping**
3. **Double or triple pane window(s)**
4. **Window shades and blinds used for solar control**
5. **Window quilt(s)**
6. **Landscaping used for solar control**
7. **Roof overhang designed for solar control**
8. **Storm fittings**
9. **Automatic setback thermostat(s)**
10. **Heating, cooling, lighting systems and built-in appliances designed specifically to be energy efficient**
11. **Solar systems (passive and active) for water heating, space heating and cooling**
12. **Wood-fired heating systems**
13. **Houses with other special design features which minimize energy use, such as smaller window areas and earth shelters**

CONSISTENCY CHECK: Information in this section of the URAR relates to another section of the form as indicated below. The appraiser should check to make sure data in both places is consistent!

<u>IMPROVEMENTS</u> - INSULATION: Energy Efficient Items
     should be considered when listing
<u>SALES COMPARISON ANALYSIS</u> - SUBJECT: Special Energy Efficient Items
     and
<u>COST APPROACH</u> - Special Energy Efficient Items.
     The above information should also be consistent with the
<u>INTERIOR</u> - IMPROVEMENT ANALYSIS; Energy Efficiency
     rating.

COMMENTS

Additional features	etc.

```
              Condition        Washer/Dryer   Finished                    Driveway
Additional features (special energy efficient items, etc.):
Condition of the improvements, depreciation (physical, functional, and external), repairs needed, quality of construction, remodeling/additions, etc.:
```

The **Additional features** lines may be used to provide details about special features of the house which are not fully described elsewhere on the Property Description side of the form. The appraiser should ask himself or herself whether a person reading the Property Description & Analysis will get a complete picture of the subject property. If the answer is "no", additional comments are needed here and/or on addendum sheets to complete the picture for the reader.

MODEL COMMENTS: The following are examples of explanatory remarks reviewers find useful. They are especially important when data on the subject property falls outside the normal range. Usually these comments require customization to reflect the special characteristics of the specific property being appraised.

WHEN AN ADDENDUM IS USED TO DESCRIBE ADDITIONAL FEATURES:
    See addendum for additional features.

WHEN THERE IS AN "IN-LAW" APARTMENT:
    The subject property has an additional kitchen _____ (in the basement, in the attic, over the garage, etc.). This is not _____ (uncommon, typical) for properties in this area. The extra kitchen _____ (does, does not) conform to current zoning regulations _____ (as long as it is not rented, because there are 2 kitchens, etc.). The market views such properties as single family houses with _____ (inferior, superior, average) utility. For these reasons, the additional kitchen has _____ (a negative, a positive, no) effect on marketability.

WHEN THE EQUIPMENT OR INTERIOR FINISH IS BETTER THAN THAT OF COMPETING HOUSES IN THE MARKET:
    The _____ (equipment, interior finish) is better than that usually found in houses in this market. These are the additional items that add extra value to this house: _____ [list items].

ADDITIONAL FEATURES THAT DO NOT REQUIRE ADJUSTMENTS:
    The following items mentioned as Additional Features do not warrant individual adjustments in the Cost Approach or Sales Comparison Analysis: _____ [list items]. These items were worthy of mention as they contribute to the overall _____ (cost of reproduction, appeal, quality of construction, marketability, utility, etc.), so any adjustments required will be made in the above categories.

CONSISTENCY CHECK: Information in this section of the URAR relates to another section of the form as indicated below. The appraiser should check to make sure data in both places is consistent!

COMMENTS - **Additional features:**
    When the property has a pool, porch or patio, this information also appears under
SALES COMPARISON ANALYSIS - **SUBJECT: Porches, Patio, Pools, etc.**
    and either
COST APPROACH - **Extras** or **Porches, Patios, etc.**
    Any of the above items or any courts, hobby rooms, expensive wallpaper and decorating, top-grade fixtures, etc., which contribute less value to the property than their reproduction cost minus their physical depreciation are superadequacies, and therefore constitute functional obsolescence. Such items should be listed under
COMMENTS - **Depreciation,**
    and a deduction should be made in the
COST APPROACH - **Functional: Depreciation**
    section.

COMMENTS

Condition of the improvements

```
Additional features (special energy efficient items, etc.): _____

C
O
M   Condition of the improvements, depreciation (physical, functional, and external), repairs needed, quality of construction, remodeling/additions, etc.: _____
M   _____
E   _____
N
T   Adverse environmental conditions (such as, but not limited to, hazardous wastes, toxic substances, etc.) present in the improvements, on the site, or in the
S   immediate vicinity of the subject property.: _____

Freddie Mac Form 70   6-93     10 CH.              PAGE 1 OF 2                              Fannie Mae Form 1004 (6-93)
```

In this section, the **Condition of improvements**, all significant items of **Depreciation, quality of construction, remodeling/additions, etc.** found in the subject property are itemized. The following pages give details on what information is to be considered for each type of depreciation. The appraiser should give this section careful attention so as not to omit any necessary items or include any inappropriate ones.

<u>**Fannie Mae   June 30, 2002   Part XI Chapter 4, Section 405.09   Improvement Analysis**</u>
Property Condition
Based on the factual data of the improvement analysis, the appraiser must express an opinion about the condition of the improvements. The appraiser must report the condition of the improvements in factual, specific terms. Any condition that may affect the value or marketability of the subject property must be reported to assure that the appraiser adequately describes the property. The appraiser must report a detrimental condition of the improvements even if that condition is also typical for competing properties. For instance, the appraiser should note if a property is characterized by deferred maintenance or a lack of updating even if the same condition applies to competing properties in the neighborhood.

<u>**Fannie Mae   June 30, 2002   Part XI Chapter 4, Section 405.09   Improvement Analysis**</u>
Appraiser's Comments
The appraiser must address any needed repairs or any physical, functional, or external inadequacies in the— "comments" section. In addition, the appraiser must address adverse environmental conditions (such as, but not limited to, hazardous wastes, toxic substances, etc.) that are present in the improvements, on the site, or in the immediate vicinity of the subject property in the space provided for that purpose.

CONSISTENCY CHECK: Information in this section of the URAR relates to another section of the form as indicated below. The appraiser should check to make sure data in both places is consistent!

<u>COMMENTS</u> - Depreciation:
    Items listed in this space will form the basis of the depreciation adjustments in the
<u>COST APPROACH</u>.
    Many appraisers show their dollar or percentage estimates here; these must be
    consistent with deductions in the
<u>COST APPROACH</u>.
    Conversely, any item of depreciation in the
<u>COST APPROACH</u>
    must be described here or on an addendum sheet.

COMMENTS

| depreciation | physical |

```
Additional features (special energy efficient items, etc.): _____
Condition of the improvements, depreciation (physical, functional, and external), repairs needed, quality of construction, remodeling/additions, etc.: _____
Adverse environmental conditions (such as, but not limited to, hazardous wastes, toxic substances, etc.) present in the improvements, on the site, or in the immediate vicinity of the subject property.: _____
Freddie Mac Form 70  6-93     10 CH.           PAGE 1 OF 2              Fannie Mae Form 1004 (6-93)
```

Depreciation - physical refers to the physical deterioration which is caused by wear and tear on the improvements.

Physical deterioration-<u>curable</u> describes items requiring repair, as of the appraisal date, which would cost less to repair than the increase in value that would occur after repair. Typical items falling into this category are paint touchups, minor carpentry, plumbing and electrical repairs such as leaky faucets, squeaking or tight doors and windows, etc. The appraiser should list all the repairs a prudent owner should make when the house is listed for sale or a prudent buyer should make as soon as he or she buys the house.

Physical deterioration-<u>incurable</u> refers to worn out parts of the house. However, as of the date of appraisal, the cost to fix these items is greater than the potential value increase after repair.

<u>Veterans Benefits Administration Circular 26-93-25 1993</u>
<u>Description of Improvements Section - Condition of Improvements</u>

VA has eliminated the requirement that appraisers indicate in the exterior description area the observed condition notations (i.e., good, fair, average or poor.) VA fee appraisers must provide an itemized list in the condition of the improvements narrative area of the comments section, of those recommended repairs considered necessary for the property to comply with VA's MPRs (minimum property requirements).

MODEL COMMENTS: The following are examples of explanatory remarks reviewers find useful. They are especially important when data on the subject property falls outside the normal range. Usually these comments require customization to reflect the special characteristics of the specific property being appraised.

<u>WHEN NO PHYSICAL DETERIORATION IS OBSERVED:</u>

The house is _____ (adequately, well) maintained. No significant items were observed that require immediate repair.

<u>PERCENT OF PHYSICAL DETERIORATION:</u>

The subject's physical deterioration is estimated as _____ [%]. An appropriate deduction from value is being made.

PHYSICAL (INCURABLE AND/OR DEFERRED) MAINTENANCE:

The following items were observed in the property which will require work in the foreseeable future: _____ (roof, paint, mechanical systems, decorations, etc.). The appraisal is being made "as is" which assumes these items will not be fixed now. A deduction is being made for their effect on the property value.

CONSISTENCY CHECK: Information in this section of the URAR relates to another section of the form as indicated below. The appraiser should check to make sure data in both places is consistent!

COMMENTS - **Depreciation {Physical}:**

Any physical deterioration noted should be consistent with data in the **IMPROVEMENTS** and **INTERIOR**

sections above, and appropriate deductions made under

COST APPROACH - **Physical: Depreciation.**

COMMENTS	
depreciation	**functional**

```
Additional features (special energy efficient items, etc.): _____
Condition of the improvements, depreciation (physical, functional, and external), repairs needed, quality of construction, remodeling/additions, etc.: _____
_____
Adverse environmental conditions (such as, but not limited to, hazardous wastes, toxic substances, etc.) present in the improvements, on the site, or in the immediate vicinity of the subject property.: _____

Freddie Mac Form 70   6-93      10 CH.                    PAGE 1 OF 2                         Fannie Mae Form 1004 (6-93)
```

Depreciation - functional refers to functional obsolescence due to those items which do not meet current design or material standards. They can be either deficiencies or superadequacies. Some can be cured and others are incurable; to be "curable", the cost to effect the cure must be less than the value added by curing the deficiency.

Some items of functional obsolescence which are often <u>curable</u> are: kitchens that need modernization with new counters, cabinets, fixtures and floor covering; inadequate heating, cooling, electric and domestic hot water systems; or insufficient bathrooms with old-fashioned plumbing fixtures.

Functional obsolescence caused by an excess or <u>superadequacy</u> is rarely curable. Often swimming pools, tennis courts, top grade fixtures, elaborately finished basements, hobby rooms, expensive wallpaper or decorating, wall-to-wall carpeting, over-improved kitchens, etc., contribute less value than their reproduction cost less physical deterioration. Unusual "home improvements" installed by owners for their own convenience and pleasure also fall into this category.

<u>Fannie Mae   June 30, 2002   Part XI Chapter 4, Section 405.04   Layout and Floor Plans</u>
Dwellings with unusual layouts, peculiar floor plans, or inadequate equipment Or amenities generally-have limited market appeal. A review of the room list and floor plan for the dwelling unit may indicate an unusual layout—such as bedrooms on a level with no bath, or a kitchen on a different level-from the dining room. If the appraiser-indicates that such inadequacies will result in market resistance to the subject property, he or she should make appropriate adjustments to reflect this in the overall analysis. On the other hand, if market acceptance can be demonstrated through the use of comparable sales with the same inadequacies, no adjustments are required.

MODEL COMMENTS: The following are examples of explanatory remarks reviewers find useful. They are especially important when data on the subject property falls outside the normal range. Usually these comments require customization to reflect the special characteristics of the specific property being appraised.

<u>NO FUNCTIONAL OBSOLESCENCE OR EXTERNAL INADEQUACY</u>:

   No unusual functional obsolescence or external inadequacies were observed.

<u>WHEN ITEMS OF FUNCTIONAL OBSOLESCENCE ARE OBSERVED</u>:

   The following items of functional obsolescence have been observed in this house: _____ [list items]. The appraisal is being made "as is" which assumes these items will not be cured now. A deduction is being made for their effect on the house's value.

<u>SUPERADEQUACY</u>:

   The subject has _____ (an inground pool, excess GLA, etc.) which is a superadequacy for this area. The full depreciated reproduction cost of _____ (this item, these items) cannot be recovered with resale. Therefore, a penalty for functional obsolescence is given in the Cost Approach. However, super-adequacies do contribute some value to property, so appropriate adjustments are made in the Sales Comparison Analysis.

CONSISTENCY CHECK: Information in this section of the URAR relates to another section of the form as indicated below. The appraiser should check to make sure data in both places is consistent!

<u>COMMENTS</u> - Depreciation {functional}:
   Any functional obsolescence noted should be consistent with data in the
<u>SITE</u>, <u>IMPROVEMENTS</u>, <u>ROOM LIST</u>, <u>INTERIOR</u>, <u>AUTOS</u>
   and
<u>COMMENTS</u> - Additional features
   sections above, and appropriate deductions made under
<u>COST APPROACH</u> - Functional: Depreciation.
   These items should also be considered when rating
<u>SALES COMPARISON ANALYSIS</u> - SUBJECT: Functional Utility.

COMMENTS	
depreciation	external

Additional features (special energy efficient items, etc.): _____

Condition of the improvements, depreciation (physical, functional, and external), repairs needed, quality of construction, remodeling/additions, etc.: _____

Adverse environmental conditions (such as, but not limited to, hazardous wastes, toxic substances, etc.) present in the improvements, on the site, or in the immediate vicinity of the subject property.: _____

Freddie Mac Form 70 6-93   10 CH.   PAGE 1 OF 2   Fannie Mae Form 1004 (6-93)

Depreciation - external refers to external obsolescence which describes factors causing a decrease in a property's desirability or value resulting from happenings <u>off</u> the property such as a change in zoning, traffic patterns, or supply/demand relationships. Value loss from external obsolescence can be distinguished from functional obsolescence or physical deterioration, which are due to things <u>on</u> the property. In other words, external inadequacies are factors in the subject neighborhood or community which cause property value losses, and are unique to real estate due to its fixed location.

In analyzing the location and environment of the property, the appraiser must consider governmental actions, economic forces, employment, transportation, recreation, education, services, taxes, etc. Consideration must also be given to factors in the immediate vicinity that detract from value. Unattractive natural features such as swamps, polluted waterways, and obstructed views are examples of such items. Poorly maintained nonconforming houses, numerous houses for sale, increasing ratio of rented houses, and uncollected junk in yards are all indications of possible external obsolescence. Although facilities such as fire stations, schools, stores, restaurants, hospitals, and gas stations are advantageous nearby, if they are too close to the house, they may detract from value. Nearby industry, highways and airports may be external obsolescence, especially if they are unattractive, noisy, smoky or odor emitting.

MODEL COMMENTS: The following are examples of explanatory remarks reviewers find useful. They are especially important when data on the subject property falls outside the normal range. Usually these comments require customization to reflect the special characteristics of the specific property being appraised.

<u>NO EXTERNAL OBSOLESCENCE OBSERVED:</u>
   The appraiser observed nothing in this neighborhood that might reduce the value of this property.

EXTERNAL OBSOLESCENCE OBSERVED:

    The value of the subject property is reduced by the negative influence of _____ (excessive street traffic, the rundown neighborhood, commercial properties, high taxes, poor local schools, radioactive waste, high density residential developments, utility easements, etc.). A deduction for external obsolescence is being made in the Cost Approach.

CONSISTENCY CHECK: Information in this section of the URAR relates to another section of the form as indicated below. The appraiser should check to make sure data in both places is consistent!

COMMENTS - Depreciation {external}:

    Any external obsolescence noted should be consistent with data in the
NEIGHBORHOOD
    or
SITE
    sections, and appropriate deductions made under
COST APPROACH - External: Depreciation.

COMMENTS

repairs needed

Additional features (special energy efficient items, etc.): _____

Condition of the improvements, depreciation (physical, functional, and external), repairs needed, quality of construction, remodeling/additions, etc.: _____

Adverse environmental conditions (such as, but not limited to, hazardous wastes, toxic substances, etc.) present in the improvements, on the site, or in the immediate vicinity of the subject property.: _____

Freddie Mac Form 70 6-93   10 CH.   PAGE 1 OF 2   Fannie Mae Form 1004 (6-93)

The following is a list of common **repairs needed**, especially as a house gets older. The appraiser must use good judgment and observation skills to recognize all the needed significant repairs.

- Floors
- Termite damage
- Walks and driveways
- Interior and exterior paint
- Roof, gutters and downspouts
- Stuck windows, broken glass
- Basement: walls and floors
- Kitchen: cabinets, counters and equipment
- Plumbing: septic system, pipes and fixtures
- Electrical: damaged, inadequate or substandard wiring
- Heating/Cooling: furnace, hot water heater, air conditioning

Veterans Benefits Administration   Circular 26-93-2   1993
Description of Improvements Section - Condition of Improvements

VA has eliminated the requirement that appraisers indicate in the exterior description area the observed condition notations (i.e., good, fair, average or poor). VA fee appraisers must provide an itemized list in the condition of the improvements narrative area in the comments section of those recommended repairs considered necessary for the property to comply with VA's MPRs (minimum property requirements).

Veterans Benefits Administration   Circular 26-93-2   1993
Description of Improvements Section - MPRs - Recommended Repairs

The VA/HUD statement on property standards (MPRs) has been removed from the form. However, VA fee appraisers must continue, in all origination appraisals (liquidation appraisal instructions remain unchanged), to recommend repairs considered necessary for the property to conform to the VA MPRs. (See instructions under comments and reconciliation sections regarding MPRs.)

MODEL COMMENTS: The following are examples of explanatory remarks reviewers find useful. They are especially important when data on the subject property falls outside the normal range. Usually these comments require customization to reflect the special characteristics of the specific property being appraised.

WHEN NO REPAIRS OR MODERNIZATION ARE NEEDED:

    This house needs no repairs or modernization.

WHEN REPAIRS ARE NEEDED:

    In order to make the house livable and saleable the following repairs should be made:_____ [list needed repairs]. It is estimated that these repairs will cost _____ [itemize costs or provide a lump sum estimate].

WHEN REPAIRS ARE NEEDED FOR MORTGAGE SECURITY:

    The following is a list of items that should be immediately repaired to make the house acceptable mortgage security: _____ [list repairs]. The estimated cost to make these repairs is ____ [$].

CONSISTENCY CHECK: Information in this section of the URAR relates to another section of the form as indicated below. The appraiser should check to make sure data in both places is consistent!

COMMENTS - Depreciation {repairs needed}:
    If repairs are needed, the appraiser must either: 1) Make the appraisal "subject to the repairs, alterations,...." by √'ing the appropriate box in the
RECONCILIATION
    section; or 2) √ the "as is" box in the
RECONCILIATION
    section and take an appropriate deduction from value in the
COST APPROACH - **Physical** or **Functional: Depreciation.**

COMMENTS

quality of construction

> Additional features (special energy efficient items, etc.): ___
>
> **COMMENTS**
>
> Condition of the improvements, depreciation (physical, functional, and external), repairs needed, quality of construction, remodeling/additions, etc.: ___
>
> Adverse environmental conditions (such as, but not limited to, hazardous wastes, toxic substances, etc.) present in the improvements, on the site, or in the immediate vicinity of the subject property.: ___
>
> Freddie Mac Form 70   6-93   10 CH.   PAGE 1 OF 2   Fannie Mae Form 1004 (6-93)

The former **IMPROVEMENT ANALYSIS** rating grid gave the appraiser an opportunity to indicate how the subject property's **quality of construction** compared to competing properties. Ratings are sub-jective judgments, so two appraisers might rate the same property differently. Because of problems with underwriters who automatically rejected loans whenever they saw a poor or fair rating, the rating grid has been eliminated. The items formerly covered in the rating grid should now be covered in the **COMMENTS** section.

A **quality of construction** rating should consider the workmanship throughout and the quality and durability of materials used in all components of the building.

In many areas, the FHA Minimum Standards are considered to be "Average" construction. However, a higher or lower standard may be used in the subject market, so the appraiser should determine what the standard is.

Fannie Mae   January 1, 1994   Section 405.01   Comments Section
Improvements Analysis Rating

The *Uniform Residential Appraisal Report* (Form 1004) no longer includes improvement analysis ratings for different features of the improvements. The ratings were eliminated to emphasize that the appraiser should adequately address the condition of the improvements, needed repairs, the quality of construction, etc. by providing meaningful narrative comments instead of marking "relative" ratings.

Veterans Benefits Administration   Circular 26-93-25   1993
Description of Improvements Section - Elimination of Rating Grid

Description of Improvements Section. The description of the improvements section represents a significant streamlining of the information necessary to describe the improvements. One of the major changes was the elimination of the improvement analysis rating grid in order to emphasize that the appraiser should adequately address the condition of the improvements, needed repairs, quality of construction, etc., by providing meaningful comments, instead of making "relative" ratings.

CONSISTENCY CHECK: Information in this section of the URAR relates to another section of the form as indicated below. The appraiser should check to make sure data in both places is consistent!

INTERIOR - IMPROVEMENT ANALYSIS: Quality of Construction
    comments must be consistent with the
SALES COMPARISON ANALYSIS - SUBJECT: Quality of Construction
    rating.

COMMENTS

remodeling/additions

```
                    Condition        Washer/Dryer      Finished                              Driveway
Additional features (special energy efficient items, etc.): _____

Condition of the improvements, depreciation (physical, functional, and external), repairs needed, quality of construction, remodeling/additions, etc..
_____
_____
_____
Adverse environmental conditions (such as, but not limited to, hazardous wastes, toxic substances, etc.) present in the improvements, on the site, or in the
immediate vicinity of the subject property.: _____

Freddie Mac Form 70  6-93    10 CH.              PAGE 1 OF 2                        Fannie Mae Form 1004 (6-93)
```

Remodeling/additions refers to significant changes in the form, design or style of a house to correct physical functional or economic obsolescence. These measures may be exterior, interior or additions necessary to meet standards of current demand.

MODEL COMMENTS: The following are examples of explanatory remarks reviewers find useful. They are especially important when data on the subject property falls outside the normal range. Usually these comments require customization to reflect the special characteristics of the specific property being appraised.

AN OLDER HOUSE WHICH DOES NOT REQUIRE REMODELING:

   Although this house is ____ [actual age] years old, it does not need any remodeling. The bathrooms, kitchen, mechanical equipment and other features meet current standards for houses of this age in this market.

AN OLDER HOUSE WHICH REQUIRES REMODELING:

   This is an older house requiring remodeling to be competitive in this market. The _____ (bathrooms, kitchen, mechanical equipment, etc.) are below current standards for houses of this age in this market. The estimated cost to remodel this house is ____ [$].

WHEN REMODELING IS REQUIRED:

   This is an older house needing remodeling to be competitive in this market. It requires the following work: ____ [give details], which is estimated to cost ____ [$$].

WHEN THE HOUSE NEEDS AN ADDITION:

   In order to make this house competitive in this market, it should have the following addition: _____
I estimate it will cost _____ [$] to accomplish this addition to the house.

CONSISTENCY CHECK: Information in this section of the URAR relates to another section of the form as indicated below. The appraiser should check to make sure data in both places is consistent!

COMMENTS - Remodeling/addition:
If remodeling or an addition is needed, the appraiser must either: 1) Base the appraisal on completion of the remodeling or addition by √'ing the "subject to the repairs, alterations,...." box in the

RECONCILIATION
section; or 2) √ the "as is" box in the

RECONCILIATION
section and take an appropriate deduction from value in the

COST APPROACH - **Physical** or **Functional: Depreciation**.

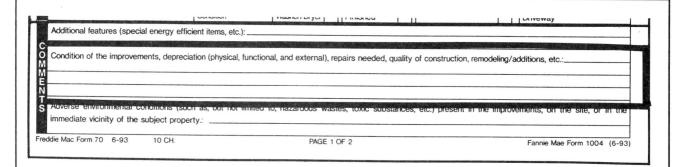

The former **IMPROVEMENT ANALYSIS** rating grid gave the appraiser an opportunity to indicate how the subject property's **condition of improvements** compared to competing properties. Ratings are subjective judgments, so two appraisers might rate the same property differently. Because of problems with underwriters who automatically rejected loans whenever they saw a poor or fair rating, the rating grid has been eliminated. The items formerly covered in the rating grid should now be covered in the **COMMENTS** section.

The **Condition of the improvements** is a rating of the subject's condition as compared to competing properties. If the appraiser finds any evidence of physical deterioration, it should be explained here in this **COMMENTS** section or in an addendum so the appropriate deduction and adjustments can be made in the **COST APPROACH** and **SALES COMPARISON ANALYSIS**.

If the improvements are newly constructed, a comment on whether the property is covered by a **Warranty program** is appropriate here. In addition, indicate this in the **COST APPROACH** on the Valuation side of the form.

If there is a significant difference between the **Actual Age (Yrs.)** of the unit and the **Effective Age (Yrs.)** in the Description of Improvements, the appraiser should note this in the **COMMENTS** section. An effective age less than actual age may indicate **Good** condition, while an effective age significantly greater than actual age may indicate that the property is in **Fair** or **Poor** condition.

CONSISTENCY CHECK: Information in this section of the URAR relates to another section of the form as indicated below. The appraiser should check to make sure data in both places is consistent!

<u>**INTERIOR**</u> **- IMPROVEMENT ANALYSIS: Condition of Improvements**
comments must also be consistent with the
<u>**SALES COMPARISON ANALYSIS**</u> **- SUBJECT: Condition**
rating. Both these ratings will also be affected if there is a significant difference between
<u>**IMPROVEMENTS**</u> **- GENERAL DESCRIPTION: Age (Yrs.) and Effective Age (Yrs.).**

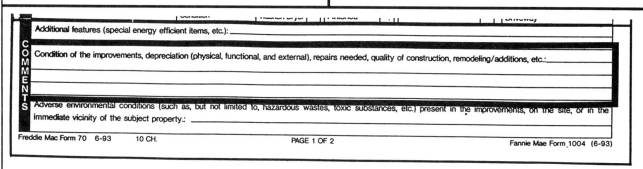

The former **IMPROVEMENT ANALYSIS** rating grid gave the appraiser an opportunity to indicate how the subject property's **Room Size/Layout** compared to competing properties. Ratings are subjective judgments, so two appraisers might rate the same property differently. Because of problems with underwriters who automatically rejected loans whenever they saw a poor or fair rating the rating grid has been eliminated. The items formerly covered in the rating grid should now be covered in the comments section.

This item includes consideration of what effect the interior design and layout will have on a typical tenant and potential buyer. The appraiser should consider the adequacy of **Room Sizes** and proportioning. Rooms should have sufficient wall area to permit appropriate furniture groupings. The **Layout** should facilitate flow of traffic, privacy of sleeping areas, and easy access to all rooms without interfering with any room's intended use. Stairways, halls, and doors must also have adequate width. Further information on design and layout can be found in my book *Houses*.[1]

Below is a list of some of the most common floor plan deficiencies:

1. Front door enters directly into living room.
2. No front hall closet.
3. No direct access from an outside door to kitchen, bathroom and bedrooms without passing through other rooms.
4. No convenient door to kitchen from street, driveway, garage or outdoor living areas (patio, deck, barbecue area, etc.).
5. No comfortable eating area in or near kitchen.
6. Separate dining area not easily reached from kitchen.
7. Stairway off a room rather than a hall or foyer.

---

[1] Henry S. Harrison, <u>Houses - The Illustrated Guide to Construction, Design and Systems (2nd Edition)</u>. Chicago, IL: Residential Sales Council of the National Association of Realtors, 1992.

8. Bedrooms and bathrooms visible from living room or foyer.
9. Walls between bedrooms not soundproof (best accomplished by separating them with a bathroom or closet).
10. Recreation room or family room poorly located.
11. No access to the basement from outside the house.
12. Walls cut up by doors and windows.

The FHA Minimum Standards provide a starting benchmark which must be adjusted for each particular market, as the minimums are often unacceptable in more expensive markets. Below is a table of the FHA Minimum Standards as well as recommended room sizes that are usually acceptable for medium-to-large residences.

Recommended Room Sizes

Name of Room	FHA Minimum Standards	Recommended Sizes
Living Room	11' x 15'6" (170 sq. ft.)	14' x 18' (252 sq. ft.)
Kitchen (galley)	10' x 8' (80 sq. ft.)	6' x 16' (96 sq. ft.)
Kitchen (standard)	10' x 10' (100 sq. ft.)	10' x 12' (120 sq. ft.)
Dining Room	8'4" x 12' (100 sq. ft.)	10' x 12' (120 sq. ft.)
Master Bedroom	9'4" x 13' (120 sq. ft.)	11' x 13' (143 sq. ft.)
Bedroom (sngl bed)	8' x 10' (80 sq. ft.)	10' x 11'6" (115 sq. ft.)
Bedroom (twin bed)	11'6" x 12' (138 sq. ft.)	11'6" x 14' (161 sq. ft.)
Bedroom (dble bed)	10' x 11'6" (115 sq. ft.)	11' x 11'6" (126.5 sq. ft.)
Bathroom	5' x 7' (35 sq. ft.)	7' x 8' (56 sq. ft.)
Lavatory	4' x 5' (20 sq. ft.)	5' x 6' (30 sq. ft.)

NOTE: Poor layout and/or inadequate room sizes are indications of functional obsolescence, which should be noted in the **COMMENTS** section and considered in the approaches to value on the back of the form.

CONSISTENCY CHECK: Information in this section of the URAR relates to another section of the form as indicated below. The appraiser should check to make sure data in both places is consistent!

INTERIOR - IMPROVEMENT ANALYSIS: Room Sizes/Layout
comment should be consistent with the
SALES COMPARISON ANALYSIS - SUBJECT: Functional Utility
rating. When a "Fair" or "Poor" rating is given, an item of functional obsolescence should be noted in the
COMMENTS - Depreciation
section, and a deduction should be made in the
COST APPROACH - Functional: Depreciation
section.

COMMENTS	
etc.	**Closets and Storage**

```
Additional features (special energy efficient items, etc.): _____
Condition of the improvements, depreciation (physical, functional, and external), repairs needed, quality of construction, remodeling/additions, etc.: ____
_____
_____
Adverse environmental conditions (such as, but not limited to, hazardous substances, toxic substances, etc.) present in the improvements, on the site, or in the
immediate vicinity of the subject property.: _____

Freddie Mac Form 70  6-93      10 CH.           PAGE 1 OF 2                    Fannie Mae Form 1004 (6-93)
```

The former **IMPROVEMENT ANALYSIS** rating grid gave the appraiser an opportunity to indicate how the subject property's **Closets and Storage** compared to competing properties. Ratings are subjective judgments, so two appraisers might rate the same property differently. Because of problems with underwriters who automatically rejected loans whenever they saw a poor or fair rating the rating grid has been eliminated. The items formerly covered in the rating grid should now be covered in the **COMMENTS** section.

Rate the adequacy and convenience of general **Storage** as compared with competing properties. Inadequate storage is a major complaint of homeowners and many buyers look carefully for storage space when shopping for a house.

Basements, when they exist, are one of the best and most popular storage places. In multiple story houses, attics provide excellent storage. To be most usable, these spaces should be accessible, dry and adequately ventilated.

Many houses have extra room in the garage for storage. When no such space is available, the garage may be converted from car parking to general storage. Carports too, are often used for general storage and may contain enclosed storage areas.

Closets provide needed everyday storage. Good shelves help increase the utility. Cedar closets used to be essential, but now fall into the luxury category.

Free standing storage sheds are common ancillary storage areas.

CONSISTENCY CHECK: Information in this section of the URAR relates to another section of the form as indicated below. The appraiser should check to make sure data in both places is consistent!

<u>**INTERIOR**</u> - **IMPROVEMENT ANALYSIS: Closets and Storage:**
    A "Fair" or "Poor" comment is made about the closets and/or storage which indicates an item of functional obsolescence. It must be noted in the
<u>**COMMENTS**</u> - **Depreciation**
    section, and a deduction should be made in the
<u>**COST APPROACH**</u> - **Functional: Depreciation**
    section.

COMMENTS

| etc. | Energy Efficiency |

```
Additional features (special energy efficient items, etc.): _____
Condition of the improvements, depreciation (physical, functional, and external), repairs needed, quality of construction, remodeling/additions, etc.: _____
Adverse environmental conditions (such as, but not limited to, hazardous wastes, toxic substances, etc.) present in the improvements, on the site, or in the immediate vicinity of the subject property.: _____
Freddie Mac Form 70  6-93   10 CH.          PAGE 1 OF 2                    Fannie Mae Form 1004 (6-93)
```

The **IMPROVEMENT ANALYSIS** rating grid used to give the appraiser an opportunity to indicate how the subject property's **Energy Efficiency** compared to competing properties. Ratings are subjective judgments, so two appraisers might rate the same property differently. Because of problems with underwriters who automatically rejected loans whenever they saw a poor or fair rating the rating grid has been eliminated. The items formerly covered in the rating grid should now be covered in the comments section.

When rating **Energy Efficiency**, the appraiser should consider the following:

1. **Heating and cooling systems**
2. **Insulation**
3. **Caulking and weatherstripping**
4. **Storm windows and doors**
5. **Orientation of the house on the site**
6. **Shade trees**
7. **Fireplaces and fireplace heat saving devices**
8. **Automatic setback thermostats**
9. **Domestic hot water heating systems**
10. **Washing machines and dryers**
11. **Kitchen appliances**
12. **Active and passive solar systems**
13. **Special window glass**
14. **Window blankets**

CONSISTENCY CHECK: Information in this section of the URAR relates to another section of the form as indicated below. The appraiser should check to make sure data in both places is consistent!

The
<u>INTERIOR</u> - IMPROVEMENT ANALYSIS: Energy Efficiency
rating should consider information listed under
<u>IMPROVEMENTS</u> - INSULATION: Energy Efficient Items.
This information should also be consistent with
<u>SALES COMPARISON ANALYSIS</u> - SUBJECT: Special Energy Efficient Items
and the
<u>COST APPROACH</u> - Special Energy Efficient Items.

COMMENTS

etc.	Plumbing—Adequacy and Condition

Additional features (special energy efficient items, etc.): _____

Condition of the improvements, depreciation (physical, functional, and external), repairs needed, quality of construction, remodeling/additions, etc.: _____

Adverse environmental conditions (such as, but not limited to, hazardous wastes, toxic substances, etc.) present in the improvements, on the site, or in the immediate vicinity of the subject property.: _____

Freddie Mac Form 70 6-93   10 CH.   PAGE 1 OF 2   Fannie Mae Form 1004 (6-93)

The former **IMPROVEMENT ANALYSIS** rating grid used to give the appraiser an opportunity to indicate how the subject property's **Plumbing - Adequacy and Condition** compared to competing properties. Ratings are subjective judgments, so two appraisers might rate the same property differently. Because of problems with underwriters who automatically rejected loans whenever they saw a poor or fair rating, the rating grid has been eliminated. **Plumbing - Adequacy and Condition** formerly covered in the rating grid should now be covered in the **COMMENTS** section.

Considerations of **Plumbing** should include the number, style and condition of plumbing fixtures, the materials used for piping and the condition thereof, and the proper operation of any on-site water or septic systems. If the evaluation of plumbing does not permit a single rating, the appraiser should indicate a rating for each plumbing system component.

Over 50% of septic systems malfunction at least once a year, dumping untreated sewage into the yard. Odors and extra green grass are signs of trouble.

NOTE: A house may be ineligible for many federally insured mortgages if an available sewer system is not connected to the house.

CONSISTENCY CHECK: Information in this section of the URAR relates to another section of the form as indicated below. The appraiser should check to make sure data in both places is consistent!

<u>INTERIOR</u> - IMPROVEMENT ANALYSIS: Plumbing-Adequacy & Condition
   comments of "Fair" or "Poor" indicates an item of physical deterioration or functional obsolescence that must be noted in the
<u>COMMENTS</u> - Depreciation
   section, and a deduction should be made in the
<u>COST APPROACH</u> - Physical or Functional: Depreciation
   section. Also, any special plumbing features or deficiencies should be itemized   under
<u>SALES COMPARISON ANALYSIS</u> - SUBJECT: Other (e.g. kitchen equip., remodeling),
   so appropriate adjustments can be made to the comparables.

COMMENTS

| etc. | Electrical—Adequacy and Condition |

```
Additional features (special energy efficient items, etc.): _____
Condition of the improvements, depreciation (physical, functional, and external), repairs needed, quality of construction, remodeling/additions, etc.:
_____
Adverse environmental conditions (such as, but not limited to, hazardous wastes, toxic substances, etc.) present in the improvements, on the site, or in the
immediate vicinity of the subject property.: _____

Freddie Mac Form 70  6-93    10 CH.         PAGE 1 OF 2              Fannie Mae Form 1004 (6-93)
```

The former **IMPROVEMENT ANALYSIS** rating grid gave the appraiser an opportunity to indicate how the subject property's **Electrical - Adequacy and Condition** compared to competing properties. Ratings are subjective judgments, so two appraisers might rate the same property differently. Because of problems with underwriters who automatically rejected loans whenever they saw a poor or fair rating, the rating grid has been eliminated. **Electrical - Adequacy and Condition** formerly covered in the rating grid should now be covered in the **COMMENTS** section.

Rating **Electrical-Adequacy & Condition** requires the appraiser to evaluate the adequacy of the building's electrical service, the number and location of outlets and switches, the quality and condition of wiring, and the adequacy and style of lighting fixtures.

Service less than 100 amperes is substandard in most markets now, and will be almost everywhere soon. When this is the case, the service size should be re-ported in the **COMMENTS** section, with an opinion as to whether it creates some functional obsolescence. The appraiser should learn how to obtain amperage ratings from either an electrician or the utility supplier.

The appraiser should also keep in mind the following:

1. Every system should have a single main shutoff switch for safety.

2. There should be at least one electrical outlet on each wall in every room.

3. Knob and tube wiring is substandard almost everywhere.

MODEL COMMENTS: The following are examples of explanatory remarks reviewers find useful. They are especially important when data on the subject property falls outside the normal range. Usually these comments require customization to reflect the special characteristics of the specific property being appraised.

WHEN LESS THAN 100 AMP ELECTRICAL:

```
    The subject has _____ (30, 60, etc.) ampere electrical
service, which _____ (is, is not) typical in this area.
Houses with _____ (30, 60) ampere electrical _____ (are, are
not) penalized in this market.
```

CONSISTENCY CHECK: Information in this section of the URAR relates to another section of the form as indicated below. The appraiser should check to make sure data in both places is consistent!

INTERIOR - IMPROVEMENT ANALYSIS: Kitchen Cabinets-Adequacy & Cond.

comments of "Fair" or "Poor" indicates an item of physical deterioration or functional obsolescence that must be noted in the

COMMENTS - Depreciation

section, and a deduction should be made in the

COST APPROACH - Physical or Functional: Depreciation

section. This also should be noted under

SALES COMPARISON ANALYSIS - SUBJECT: Other (e.g. kitchen equip., remodeling),

so appropriate adjustments can be made to the comparables.

COMMENTS

| etc. | Kitchen Cabinets—Adequacy and Condition |

```
Additional features (special energy efficient items, etc.): _____
Condition of the improvements, depreciation (physical, functional, and external), repairs needed, quality of construction, remodeling/additions, etc.: _____

Adverse environmental conditions (such as, but not limited to, hazardous wastes, toxic substances, etc.) present in the improvements, on the site, or in the
immediate vicinity of the subject property.: _____

Freddie Mac Form 70  6-93    10 CH.              PAGE 1 OF 2                     Fannie Mae Form 1004 (6-93)
```

The former **IMPROVEMENT ANALYSIS** rating grid used to give the appraiser an opportunity to indicate how the subject property's **Kitchen Cabinets - Adequacy and Condition** compared to competing properties. Ratings are subjective judgments, so two appraisers might rate the same property differently. Because of problems with underwriters who automatically rejected loans whenever they saw a poor or fair rating, the rating grid has been eliminated. The adequacy and condition of the kitchen cabinets formerly covered in the rating grid should now be covered in the **COMMENTS** section.

Although typically about 10 percent of the total cost of a new house is spent on the kitchen, a large national survey of homeowners confirms that the major complaint people have about their home is insufficient **Kitchen Cabinets** and counters.

There should be a minimum of 6 feet of wall cabinets in a small kitchen with an equal amount of counters over base cabinets. Eight or ten feet is far more satisfactory. A well designed kitchen can be as small as 8 ft. by 10 ft. in a small house or 10 ft. by 12 ft. even in a large house and still provide adequate cabinet and counter space.

Many kitchens suffer from one or more of the following inadequacies (listed in order of most common occurrence):

1. Insufficient base cabinet storage.
2. Insufficient wall cabinet storage.
3. Insufficient counter space.
4. No counter beside refrigerator.
5. Insufficient window area (less than 10% of floor area).
6. Poorly placed doors that waste wall space.
7. Traffic through work area.
8. Too little counter on either right or left of sink.
9. No counter beside range.

10. Insufficient space in front of cabinets.
11. Distance between sink, range and refrigerator too great.
12. Range under window (unsafe).

CONSISTENCY CHECK: Information in this section of the URAR relates to another section of the form as indicated below. The appraiser should check to make sure data in both places is consistent!

INTERIOR - IMPROVEMENT ANALYSIS: Kitchen Cabinets-Adequacy & Condition
comments of "Fair" or "Poor" indicates an item of physical deterioration or functional obsolescence that must be noted in the
COMMENTS - Depreciation
section, and a deduction should be made in the
COST APPROACH - Physical or Functional: Depreciation
section. This also should be noted under
SALES COMPARISON ANALYSIS - SUBJECT: Other (e.g. kitchen equip., remodeling),
so appropriate adjustments can be made to the comparables.

COMMENTS

| etc. | Conformity to Neighborhood |

Additional features (special energy efficient items, etc.): _____

Condition of the improvements, depreciation (physical, functional, and external), repairs needed, quality of construction, remodeling/additions, etc.: _____

Adverse environmental conditions (such as, but not limited to, hazardous wastes, toxic substances, etc.) present in the improvements, on the site, or in the immediate vicinity of the subject property.: _____

Freddie Mac Form 70 6-93   10 CH.   PAGE 1 OF 2   Fannie Mae Form 1004 (6-93)

The former **IMPROVEMENT ANALYSIS** rating grid used to give the appraiser an opportunity to indicate how the subject property's **Compatibility to Neighborhood** compared to competing properties. Ratings are subjective judgments, so two appraisers might rate the same property differently. Because of problems with underwriters who automatically rejected loans whenever they saw a poor or fair rating, the rating grid has been eliminated. The conformity of the subject property to the neighborhood, formerly covered in the rating grid, should now be covered in the **COMMENTS** section.

Compatibility to neighborhood indicates the extent to which the size, age, price, architectural design and construction of the subject property conform to the subject neighborhood.

Tastes and standards have changed in recent years, and it is now a mistake to assume that maximum value is achieved by **Conformity**. Nonconforming properties often suffer little or no depreciation.

Fannie Mae   **June 30, 2002**   **Part XI Chapter 4, Section 405.01**   **Improvement Analysis**

Conformity To Neighborhood

The improvements should generally conform to the neighborhood in terms of age, type, design, and materials used for their construction. If there is market resistance to a property because its improvements are not compatible with the neighborhood or with the requirements of the competitive market—because of adequacy of plumbing, heating, or electrical services; design; quality; size; condition; or any other reason directly related to market demand—the lender should underwrite the mortgage more carefully and, if appropriate, require more conservative mortgage terms. However, the lender should be aware that many older neighborhoods have favorable heterogeneity in architectural styles, land use, and age of housing. For example, older neighborhoods are especially likely to have been developed through custom building; this variety may be a positive marketing factor.

COMMENTS	
etc.	**Appeal and Marketability**

```
Additional features (special energy efficient items, etc.): _____
Condition of the improvements, depreciation (physical, functional, and external), repairs needed, quality of construction, remodeling/additions, etc.: _____
_____
_____
Adverse environmental conditions (such as, but not limited to, hazardous wastes, toxic substances, etc.) present in the improvements, on the site, or in the immediate vicinity of the subject property.: _____
Freddie Mac Form 70  6-93     10 CH.                    PAGE 1 OF 2                    Fannie Mae Form 1004 (6-93)
```

The former **IMPROVEMENT ANALYSIS** rating grid gave the appraiser an opportunity to indicate how the subject property's **Appeal and Marketability** compared to competing properties. Ratings are subjective judgments, so two appraisers might rate the same property differently. Because of problems with underwriters who automatically rejected loans whenever they saw a poor or fair rating, the rating grid has been eliminated. The appeal and marketability of the subject property formerly covered in the rating grid should now be covered in the **COMMENTS** section.

One reason computers are unlikely to replace appraisers is that good appraisals require subjective judgment based on training and experience. Considering the appeal and marketability of a property is a good example of where this judgment is needed.

The architectural attractiveness of a property (i.e., the appeal of its design) is one of the subjective ratings made by the appraiser, but it is not simply what appeals to the appraiser's individual taste. Good architecture is not an accident either; it is usually the result of careful planning by professionals (an architect, designer, contractor, developer or owner with good design taste developed by experience and training). Well-designed buildings tend to use only one or two exterior wall materials and are either good copies of older styles or carefully planned contemporary styles. As a result, houses with good design (traditional or contemporary style) tend to depreciate more slowly than poorly designed houses.

The same principles are applied to interior design and layout. The appraiser should consider what effect the interior design and layout will have on a typical tenant and potential buyer.

CONSISTENCY CHECK: Information in this section of the URAR relates to another section of the form as indicated below. The appraiser should check to make sure data in both places is consistent!

<u>INTERIOR</u> - IMPROVEMENT ANALYSIS: Appeal & Marketability
    should be considered when making the
<u>SALES COMPARISON ANALYSIS</u> - SUBJECT: Design and Appeal
    rating.

COMMENTS

Adverse environmental conditions

```
Additional features (special energy efficient items, etc.): _____

Condition of the improvements, depreciation (physical, functional, and external), repairs needed, quality of construction, remodeling/additions, etc.: _____

Adverse environmental conditions (such as, but not limited to, hazardous wastes, toxic substances, etc.) present in the improvements, on the site, or in the immediate vicinity of the subject property.: _____
```

The **COMMENTS** portion of this section includes a new entry in which the appraiser must address **Adverse environmental conditions** (such as, but not limited to, hazardous wastes, toxic substances, etc.) that are present in the improvements, on the site, or in the immediate vicinity of the subject property. This addition clarifies the appraiser's responsibility to report what he or she became aware of through the inspection of the property and the normal research involved in performing the appraisal.

Be sure to read the new appraiser's Certification and Statement of Limiting Conditions, FNMA 1004B-FHLMC 439 for the significant modifications that were made to this form regarding reporting requirements.

<u>Fannie Mae   June 30, 1993 Announcement   Description of the Improvements</u>
<u>Comments Section - Adverse Environmental Conditions</u>

"The "comments" portion of this section includes a new entry in which the appraiser must address adverse environmental conditions (such as, but not limited to, hazardous wastes, toxic substances, etc.) that are present in the improvements, on the site, or in the immediate vicinity of the subject property."

"This addition clarifies the appraiser's responsibility to report what he or she became aware of through the inspection of the property and the normal research involved in performing the appraisal. (Note: See Attachment 2 for related significant modifications that were made to the certification and statement of limiting conditions regarding the appraiser's inspection and the acknowledgment of adverse conditions.)"

<u>Fannie Mae   June 30, 2002   Part XI Chapter 3, Section 307   Special Appraisal Considerations</u>
<u>Properties Affected by Environmental Hazards</u>

If the real estate broker, the property seller, the property purchaser, or any other party to the mortgage transaction informs the lender that an environmental hazard exists in or on the property or in the vicinity of the property the lender must disclose that information to the appraiser and note the individual mortgage file accordingly. (We also require the lender to disclose such information to the borrower, and to comply with any state or local environmental laws regarding disclosure.) <u>**When the appraiser has knowledge of any hazardous condition (whether it exists in or on the subject property or on any site within the vicinity of the property)-such as the presence of hazardous wastes, toxic substances, asbestos-containing materials, urea-formaldehyde insulation, radon gas, etc., he or she must note the hazardous condition in the appraisal report and comment on any influence that the hazard has on the property's value and marketability (if it is measurable through an analysis of comparable market data as of the effective date of the appraisal) and make appropriate adjustments in the overall analysis of the property's value.**</u>

Fannie Mae   June 30, 2002   Part XI Chapter 3, Section 307   Special Appraisal Considerations
Properties Affected by Environmental Hazards

We do not consider the appraiser to be an expert in the field of environmental hazards. The typical residential real estate appraiser is neither expected nor required to be an expert in this specialized field. However, the appraiser has a responsibility to note in the appraisal report any adverse conditions that were observed during the inspection of the subject property or information that he or she became aware of through the normal research involved in performing an appraisal.

In rare situations, a particular environmental hazard may have a significant effect on the value of the subject property; although the actual effect is not measurable because the hazard is so serious or so recently discovered that an appraiser cannot arrive at a reliable opinion of market value because there is no comparable market data (such as sales, contract sales, or active listings) available to reflect the effect of the hazard. In such cases, the motgage will not be eligible for delivery to us.

We will purchase or securitize a mortgage secured by a property that is affected by an environmental hazard if the effect of the hazard is measurable through an analysis of comparable market data as of the effective date of the appraisal and the appraiser reflects in the appraisal report any adverse effect—that the hazard has on the value and marketability of the subject property or indicates that the comparable market data reveals no buyer resistance to the hazard. To illustrate: We are frequently asked to address the eligibility of mortgages secured by properties that are located in neighborhoods affected by radon gas or the presence of hazardous wastes. In such situations, we expect the appraiser to reflect any adverse effect or buyer resistance that is demonstrated and measurable through the available comparable market data, Therefore, when a property is located in a neighborhood that has a relatively high level of radon gas or is near a hazardous waste site, we expect the appraiser to consider and use comparable market data from the same affected area because the sales prices of settled sales, the contract sales prices of pending sales, and the current asking prices for active listings will reflect any negative effect on the value and marketability of the subject property.

Although our guidelines expressly require the appraiser to include in the appraisal report comments about any influence that an environmental hazard has on the value and marketability of the property and to make appropriate adjustments to the overall analysis of the value of the property, we expect the lender to oversee the performance of the appraisers it employs. The lender must make the final decision about the need for inspections and the adequacy of the property as security for the mortgage requested. We expect the lender to exercise sound judgment in determining the acceptability of the property. For example, since we require the appraiser to comment on the effect of a hazard on the marketability and value of the subject property; the appraiser would have to note when there is market resistance to an area because of environmental hazards or any other conditions that affect well, septic, or public water facilities. When the lender has reason to believe that private well water that is on or available to a property might be contaminated as the result of the proximity of the well to hazardous waste sites, the lender is exercising sound judgment if it obtains a "well certification" to determine whether the water meets community standards.

Fannie Mae   June 30, 2002   Part XI Chapter 4, Section 405.09   Improvement Analysis
Appraiser's Comments

The appraiser must address any needed repairs or any physical, functional, or external inadequacies in the— "comments" section. In addition, the appraiser must address adverse environmental conditions (such as, but not limited to, hazardous wastes, toxic substances, etc.) that are present in the improvements, on the site, or in the Immediate vicinity of the subject property in the space provided for that purpose.

U.S. Dept of Housing and Urban Development Handbook 4150.1 Revision 2 Chapter 8
Subject Unit - Comments - Condition of Improvements , Etc.)

Explain as necessary.

Veterans Benefits Administration   Circular 26-93-25   1993
Description of Improvements Section - Comments
Adverse environmental conditions

The "comments" portion of this section includes a new entry in which the appraiser must address adverse environmental conditions (such as, but not limited to, hazardous wastes, toxic substances, etc.) that are present in the improvements, on the site, or in the immediate vicinity of the subject property. This addition clarifies the appraiser's responsibility to report what he or she became aware of through the inspection of the property and the normal research involved in performing the appraisal. (Note: See Attachment 2 for related significant modifications that were made to the certification and statement of limiting conditions regarding the appraiser's inspection and the acknowledgment of adverse conditions.)

COMMENTS

Environmental Addenda

Many appraisers attach an Environmental Addenda to their appraisal report on which they indicate the extent of their environmental inspection and what inquiries they made about the subject property and its surrounding area.

By checking the appropriate lines, they report their environmental observations. The Environmental Addenda also tells the reader exactly what environmental assumptions were made by the appraiser as part of the value being estimated. It emphasizes that if any of these assumptions are not correct because of non-apparent or hidden environmental problems, then the value estimated may be invalid.

The clear disclosure of what the appraiser did and did not do and what assumptions the appraiser made are helpful to the client and reviewer. They also reduce the possibility of professional liability lawsuits caused by misunderstandings.

ENVIRONMENTAL ADDENDUM

Front of Form

ENVIRONMENTAL ADDENDUM
APPARENT* HAZARDOUS SUBSTANCES AND/OR DETRIMENTAL ENVIRONMENTAL CONDITIONS

Borrower/Client _____
Address _____
City _____ County _____ State _____ Zip code _____
Lender _____

*Apparent is defined as that which is visible, obvious, evident or manifest to the appraiser.

This universal Environmental Addendum is for use with any real estate appraisal. Only the statements which have been checked by the appraiser apply to the property being appraised.

This addendum reports the results of the appraiser's routine inspection of and inquiries about the subject property and its surrounding area. It also states what assumptions were made about the existence (or nonexistence) of any hazardous substances and/or detrimental environmental conditions. **The appraiser is not an expert environmental inspector** and therefore might be unaware of existing hazardous substances and/or detrimental environmental conditions which may have a negative effect on the safety and value of the property. It is possible that tests and inspections made by a qualified environmental inspector would reveal the existence of hazardous materials and/or detrimental environmental conditions on or around the property that would negatively affect its safety and value.

DRINKING WATER

____ Drinking Water is supplied to the subject from a municipal water supply which is considered safe. However the only way to be absolutely certain that the water meets published standards is to have it tested at all discharge points.

____ Drinking Water is supplied by a well or other non-municipal source. It is recommended that tests be made to be certain that the property is supplied with adequate pure water.

____ Lead can get into drinking water from its source, the pipes, at all discharge points, plumbing fixtures and/or appliances. The only way to be certain that water does not contain an unacceptable lead level is to have it tested at all discharge points.

____ The value estimated in this appraisal is based on the assumption that there is an adequate supply of safe, lead-free Drinking Water.

Comments _____

SANITARY WASTE DISPOSAL

____ Sanitary Waste is removed from the property by a municipal sewer system.

____ Sanitary Waste is disposed of by a septic system or other sanitary on site waste disposal system. The only way to determine that the disposal system is adequate and in good working condition is to have it inspected by a qualified inspector.

____ The value estimated in this appraisal is based on the assumption that the Sanitary Waste is disposed of by a municipal sewer or an adequate properly permitted alternate treatment system in good condition.

Comments _____

SOIL CONTAMINANTS

____ There are no *apparent* signs of Soil Contaminants on or near the subject property (except as reported in Comments below). It is possible that research, inspection and testing by a qualified environmental inspector would reveal existing and/or potential hazardous substances and/or detrimental environmental conditions on or around the property that would negatively affect its safety and value.

____ The value estimated in this appraisal is based on the assumption that the subject property is free of Soil Contaminants.

Comments _____

ASBESTOS

____ All or part of the improvements were constructed before 1979 when Asbestos was a common building material. The only way to be certain that the property is free of friable and non-friable Asbestos is to have it inspected and tested by a qualified asbestos inspector.

____ The improvements were constructed after 1979. No *apparent* friable Asbestos was observed (except as reported in Comments below).

____ The value estimated in this appraisal is based on the assumption that there is no uncontained friable Asbestos or other hazardous Asbestos material on the property.

Comments _____

PCBs (POLYCHLORINATED BIPHENYLS)

____ There were no *apparent* leaking flourescent light ballasts, capacitors or transformers anywhere on or nearby the property (except as reported in Comments below).

____ There was no *apparent* visible or documented evidence known to the appraiser of soil or groundwater contamination from PCBs anywhere on the property (except as reported in Comments below).

____ The value estimated in this appraisal is based on the assumption that there are no uncontained PCBs on or nearby the property.

Comments _____

RADON

____ The appraiser is not aware of any Radon tests made on the subject property within the past 12 months (except as reported in Comments below).

____ The appraiser is not aware of any indication that the local water supplies have been found to have elevated levels of Radon or Radium.

____ The appraiser is not aware of any nearby properties (except as reported in Comments below) that were or currently are used for uranium, thorium or radium extraction or phosphate processing.

____ The value estimated in this appraisal is based on the assumption that the Radon level is at or below EPA recommended levels.

Comments _____

Test Version 2c FW-70EZ
JANUARY 1991

Item #115050

ENVIRONMENTAL ADDENDUM

Back of Form

USTs (UNDERGROUND STORAGE TANKS)

____ There is no *apparent* visible or documented evidence known to the appraiser of any USTs on the property nor any known historical use of the property that would likely have had USTs.

____ There are no *apparent* petroleum storage and/or delivery facilities (including gasoline stations or chemical manufacturing plants) located on adjacent properties (except as reported in Comments below).

____ There are *apparent* signs of USTs existing now or in the past on the subject property. It is recommended that an inspection by a qualified UST inspector be obtained to determine the location of any USTs together with their condition and proper registration if they are active; and if they are inactive, to determine whether they were deactivated in accordance with sound industry practices.

____ The value estimated in this appraisal is based on the assumption that any functioning USTs are not leaking and are properly registered and that any abandoned USTs are free from contamination and were properly drained, filled and sealed.

Comments _____

NEARBY HAZARDOUS WASTE SITES

____ There are no *apparent* Hazardous Waste Sites on the subject property or nearby the subject property (except as reported in Comments below). Hazardous Waste Site search by a trained environmental engineer may determine that there is one or more Hazardous Waste Sites on or in the area of the subject property.

____ The value estimated in this appraisal is based on the assumption that there are no Hazardous Waste Sites on or nearby the subject property that negatively affect the value or safety of the property.

Comments _____

UREA FORMALDEHYDE (UFFI) INSULATION

____ All or part of the improvements were constructed before 1982 when UREA foam insulation was a common building material. The only way to be certain that the property is free of UREA formaldehyde is to have it inspected by a qualified UREA formaldehyde inspector.

____ The improvements were constructed after 1982. No *apparent* UREA formaldehyde materials were observed (except as reported in Comments below).

____ The value estimated in this appraisal is based on the assumption that there is no significant UFFI insulation or other UREA formaldehyde material on the property.

Comments _____

LEAD PAINT

____ All or part of the improvements were constructed before 1980 when Lead Paint was a common building material. There is no *apparent* visible or known documented evidence of peeling or flaking Lead Paint on the floors, walls or ceilings (except as reported in Comments below). The only way to be certain that the property is free of surface or subsurface Lead Paint is to have it inspected by a qualified inspector.

____ The improvements were constructed after 1980. No *apparent* Lead Paint was observed (except as reported in Comments below).

____ The value estimated in this appraisal is based on the assumption that there is no flaking or peeling Lead Paint on the property.

Comments _____

AIR POLLUTION

____ There are no *apparent* signs of Air Pollution at the time of the inspection nor were any reported (except as reported in Comments below). The only way to be certain that the air is free of pollution is to have it tested.

____ The value estimated in this appraisal is based on the assumption that the property is free of Air Pollution.

Comments _____

WETLANDS/FLOOD PLAINS

____ The site does not contain any *apparent* Wetlands/Flood Plains (except as reported in Comments below). The only way to be certain that the site is free of Wetlands/Flood Plains is to have it inspected by a qualified environmental professional.

____ The value estimated in this appraisal is based on the assumption that there are no Wetlands/Flood Plains on the property (except as reported in Comments below).

Comments _____

MISCELLANEOUS ENVIRONMENTAL HAZARDS

____ There are no other *apparent* miscellaneous hazardous substances and/or detrimental environmental conditions on or in the area of the site except as indicated below:

    ____ Excess Noise _____
    ____ Radiation + Electromagnetic Radiation _____
    ____ Light Pollution _____
    ____ Waste Heat _____
    ____ Acid Mine Drainage _____
    ____ Agricultural Pollution _____
    ____ Geological Hazards _____
    ____ Nearby Hazardous Property _____
    ____ Infectious Medical Wastes _____
    ____ Pesticides _____
    ____ Others (Chemical Storage + Storage Drums, Pipelines, etc.) _____

____ The value estimated in this appraisal is based on the assumption that there are no Miscellaneous environmental Hazards (except those reported above) that would negatively affect the value of the property.

When any of the environmental assumptions made in this addendum are not correct, the estimated value in this appraisal may not be valid.

Test Version 2c FW-70EZ
JANUARY 1991

Item #115050

COMMENTS

Environmental Disclaimer

Borrower/Client
Property Address
City   County   State   Zip Code
Lender

Environmental Disclaimer

"Unless otherwise stated in this report, the existence of hazardous materials, which may or may not be present on the property, was not observed by the appraiser. The appraiser has no knowledge of the existence of such materials on or in the property. The appraiser, however, is not qualified to detect such substances. The presence of substances such as asbestos, urea-formaldehyde foam insulation, and other potentially hazardous materials may affect the value of the property. The value estimated is predicated on the assumption that there is no such material on or in the property that would cause a loss in value. No responsibility is assumed for such conditions or for any expertise or engineering knowledge required to discover them. The client is urged to retain an expert in this field, if desired."

The Appraisal of Real Estate, 10th Edition, The Appraisal Institute, Chicago, IL; 1992, page 574.

Additional Comments

FW 70ED Rev. 11/92   1(800) 243-4545 Item #115040

VALUATION SECTION — Back of the Form

Valuation Section — UNIFORM RESIDENTIAL APPRAISAL REPORT   File No. _____

COST APPROACH

ESTIMATED SITE VALUE . . . . = $ _____	Comments on Cost Approach (such as, source of cost estimate, site value, square foot calculation and for HUD, VA and FmHA, the estimated remaining economic life of the property): _____
ESTIMATED REPRODUCTION COST-NEW-OF IMPROVEMENTS:	
Dwelling _____ Sq. Ft @ $ _____ = $ _____	
_____ Sq. Ft @ $ _____ = _____	
= _____	
Garage/Carport _____ Sq. Ft @ $ _____ = _____	
Total Estimated Cost New . . . . = $ _____	
Less Physical Functional External	
Depreciation _____ = $ _____	
Depreciated Value of Improvements . . . . = $ _____	
"As-is" Value of Site Improvements . . . . = $ _____	
INDICATED VALUE BY COST APPROACH . . . . = $ _____	

SALES COMPARISON ANALYSIS

ITEM	SUBJECT	COMPARABLE NO. 1		COMPARABLE NO. 2		COMPARABLE NO. 3	
Address							
Proximity to Subject							
Sales Price	$		$		$		$
Price/Gross Liv. Area	$	$		$		$	
Data and/or Verification Source							
VALUE ADJUSTMENTS	DESCRIPTION	DESCRIPTION	+ (-) $ Adjustment	DESCRIPTION	+ (-) $ Adjustment	DESCRIPTION	+ (-) $ Adjustment
Sales or Financing Concessions							
Date of Sale/Time							
Location							
Leasehold/Fee Simple							
Site							
View							
Design and Appeal							
Quality of Construction							
Age							
Condition							
Above Grade Room Count	Total : Bdrms : Baths	Total : Bdrms : Baths		Total : Bdrms : Baths		Total : Bdrms : Baths	
Gross Living Area	Sq. Ft.	Sq. Ft.		Sq. Ft.		Sq. Ft.	
Basement & Finished Rooms Below Grade							
Functional Utility							
Heating/Cooling							
Energy Efficient Items							
Garage/Carport							
Porch, Patio, Deck, Fireplace(s), etc.							
Fence, Pool, etc.							
Net Adj. (total)		+ □ - □	$	+ □ - □	$	+ □ - □	$
Adjusted Sales Price of Comparable			$		$		$

Comments on Sales Comparison (including the subject property's compatibility to the neighborhood, etc.): _____

ITEM	SUBJECT	COMPARABLE NO. 1	COMPARABLE NO. 2	COMPARABLE NO. 3
Date, Price and Data Source, for prior sales within year of appraisal				

Analysis of any current agreement of sale, option, or listing of the subject property and analysis of any prior sales of subject and comparables within one year of the date of appraisal: _____

INDICATED VALUE BY SALES COMPARISON APPROACH . . . . $ _____
INDICATED VALUE BY INCOME APPROACH (If Applicable) Estimated Market Rent $ _____ /Mo. x Gross Rent Multiplier _____ = $ _____

This appraisal is made □ "as is" □ subject to the repairs, alterations, inspections or conditions listed below □ subject to completion per plans and specifications.
Conditions of Appraisal: _____

RECONCILIATION

Final Reconciliation: _____

The purpose of this appraisal is to estimate the market value of the real property that is the subject of this report, based on the above conditions and the certification, contingent and limiting conditions, and market value definition that are stated in the attached Freddie Mac Form 439/Fannie Mae Form 1004B (Revised _____).
I (WE) ESTIMATE THE MARKET VALUE, AS DEFINED, OF THE REAL PROPERTY THAT IS THE SUBJECT OF THIS REPORT, AS OF _____ (WHICH IS THE DATE OF INSPECTION AND THE EFFECTIVE DATE OF THIS REPORT) TO BE $ _____
APPRAISER: SUPERVISORY APPRAISER (ONLY IF REQUIRED):
Signature _____   Signature _____   □ Did □ Did Not
Name _____   Name _____   Inspect Property
Date Report Signed _____   Date Report Signed _____
State Certification # _____   State _____   State Certification # _____   State _____
Or State License # _____   State _____   Or State License # _____   State _____

Freddie Mac Form 70 6-93   10 CH.   PAGE 2 OF 2   Fannie Mae Form 1004 (6-93)
                                                   (800) 243-4545   Item #112660

Fannie Mae   **June 30, 2002**   **Part XI Chapter 4, Section 409**   **Valuation Analysis**

The valuation sections of our appraisal report forms enable an appraiser to develop and report in concise format an adequately supported opinion of market value—based on the cost, sales comparison, and income approaches to value (as applicable), and, in the case of-small residential income properties, on comparable rental data. If the appraiser believes that additional information needs to—be provided because of the uniqueness of the property or some other condition he or she should provide additional supporting data in an addendum to the appraisal report form.

COST APPROACH

INTRODUCTION

```
Valuation Section        UNIFORM RESIDENTIAL APPRAISAL REPORT    File No.

ESTIMATED SITE VALUE ..................... = $ _____       Comments on Cost Approach (such as, source of cost estimate,
ESTIMATED REPRODUCTION COST-NEW-OF IMPROVEMENTS:              site value, square foot calculation and for HUD, VA and FmHA, the
Dwelling _____ Sq. Ft @ $ _____ = $ _____               estimated remaining economic life of the property): _____
                 Sq. Ft @ $ _____ = _____
                                   = _____
Garage/Carport _____ Sq. Ft @ $ _____ = _____
Total Estimated Cost New ............. = $ _____
Less       Physical    Functional    External
Depreciation |         |            |       = $ _____
Depreciated Value of Improvements ............. = $ _____
"As-is" Value of Site Improvements ............. = $ _____
INDICATED VALUE BY COST APPROACH ........... = $ _____
```

There are five basic steps to the **COST APPROACH**. Essentially they provide for an estimate of site value, to which is added the depreciated reproduction cost or replacement cost (new) of the improvements as of the date of the appraisal.

1. Estimate the value of the site as if vacant.
2. Estimate the reproduction cost or replacement cost (new) of all the improvements (excluding any included as part of the site value).
3. Estimate accrued **Depreciation** from all causes (**Physical** deterioration, **Functional** obsolescence and **External** obsolescence).
4. Deduct accrued depreciation from the cost (new) of the improvements to arrive at a **Depreciated Value of Improvements**.
5. Add the site value to the depreciated value of the improvements to obtain the **INDICATED VALUE BY COST APPROACH**.

The following are the subsections of the **COST APPROACH**:

ESTIMATED SITE VALUE *AT HIGHEST & BEST USE*
ESTIMATED REPRODUCTION COST-NEW-OF-IMPROVEMENTS
    Dwelling, Sq. Ft.
    Garage/Carport Sq. Ft.
    Total Estimated Cost New
Depreciation: Physical -- Functional -- External
Depreciated Value of Improvements
"As-is" Value of Site Improvements
INDICATED VALUE BY COST APPROACH
Comments on Cost Approach

Fannie Mae   June 30, 2002   Part XI Chapter 4, Section 407   Cost Approach to Value

The cost approach to value assumes that a potential purchaser will consider building a substitute residence the has the same use as the property that is being appraised. This approach, then, measures value as a cost of production. The reliability of the cost approach depends on valid reproduction cost estimates, proper depreciation estimates, and accurate site values. We will not accept appraisals that rely solely on the cost approach as an' indicator of market value.

We do not require the appraiser to consider the cost approach to value for any appraisal that is documented on the *Desktop Underwriter Quantitative Analysis Appraisal Report* (Form *2055*), the *Desktop Underwriter Qualitative Analysis Appraisal Report* (Form 2065), or the *Desktop Underwriter Individual Cooperative Interest Appraisal Report* (Form 2095).

Furthermore, the appraiser does not need to consider the cost approach to value when appraising a unit in a condominium' or cooperative project since this approach may be impractical for estimating the value of an individual unit because each unit is an integrate part of the project development.

The cost approach to value may be a good indicator of value for newer or renovated properties that are one- to four-family residences, or detached, semi-detached, or townhouse units in PUD projects. However, as the effective age of a property increases, the reliability of the cost approach may decrease because the depreciation estimates may be subjective. An appraiser should use his or her best judgment regarding the applicability of the cost approach to value when the property being appraised is an older property; however, if the appraiser does not use the cost approach, he or she must explain why it was not used and provide an opinion of value for the site,

Fannie Mae   February 15, 1994   Site Value – Rural Properties

We have recently become aware that there is some uncertainty about our property guideline that discusses the percentage of the total appraised value of a rural property that the site itself may represent. We have also received reports that this guideline is often misapplied to properties in more highly developed locations where it is not uncommon for sites to represent a relatively high percentage of the total value of a property. These misunderstandings or misapplications of policy may have the unfortunate effect of unnecessarily restricting mortgage finance opportunities for residents of rural locations. Therefore, we are eliminating our guideline about the relative percentage of value that should be applied to the site value of a property.

Determining the Residential Nature of a Property

…Our current policy for properties located in rural areas (or any other area that is less than 25% developed) states that a mortgage on that property is not eligible for delivery to us if the value of the site exceeds 30% of the total appraised value of the property, unless the property is a typical residential property for the market area. We define the degree of development -- which is referred to as "built-up" on our appraisal report forms -- as the percentage of the available land in the neighborhood or market area that has been improved. Some underwriters view the 30% guideline as a "rule" that is to be narrowly applied, rather than as a flexible guideline that should be considered in relation to what is typical of residential properties in the area in which the rural property being underwritten is located. The intent and focus of our guideline is to help determine whether a property is residential in nature. We clearly state that we will purchase a mortgage secured by a property that has a higher percentage of its total value attributed to the site if higher site values are typical in the area (and market acceptance can be demonstrated through the use of comparable properties).To ensure that our standards are properly applied, we are eliminating all reference to the 30% site value guideline effective immediately.

Veterans Benefits Administration   Circular 26-93-2   1993
Cost Approach - When Applicable

VA believes that in most situations, whether the subject is existing or proposed construction, buyers and sellers do not use the cost approach as a determinant of value, and that the cost approach does not render a highly reliable estimate of the market value for single family residential properties. The cost approach is considered most relevant in those cases involving unique properties. VA fee appraisers may choose not to report the cost approach. The Uniform Standards provide that the appraiser must explain and support the exclusion of any of the usual valuation approaches and it is VA's belief that this may be accomplished in a succinct statement in the comment area of the cost approach section.

COST APPROACH

ESTIMATED SITE VALUE

Valuation Section	UNIFORM RESIDENTIAL APPRAISAL REPORT	File No.

ESTIMATED SITE VALUE .... = $ _____

ESTIMATED REPRODUCTION COST-NEW-OF IMPROVEMENTS:
Dwelling _____ Sq. Ft @ $ _____ = $ _____
_____ Sq. Ft @ $ _____ = _____
= _____
Garage/Carport _____ Sq. Ft @ $ _____ = _____
Total Estimated Cost New .... = $ _____
Less   Physical   Functional   External
Depreciation |_____|_____|_____ = $ _____
Depreciated Value of Improvements .... = $ _____
"As-is" Value of Site Improvements .... = $ _____
INDICATED VALUE BY COST APPROACH .... = $ _____

Comments on Cost Approach (such as, source of cost estimate, site value, square foot calculation and for HUD, VA and FmHA, the estimated remaining economic life of the property): _____

The entry for the property's **ESTIMATED SITE VALUE** is now located above the ESTIMATED REPRODUCTION COST-NEW-OF IMPROVEMENTS.

<u>Fannie Mae   December 31, 1994   Part VII, Chapter 4, Section 406.01</u>

Site Value

If the appraiser's estimate of the value for the site is one that is not typical for a comparable residential property in the subject neighborhood, he or she must comment on how the variance affects the marketability of the subject property.

<u>**Veterans Benefit Administration**   **Circular 26-93-25**   **October 22, 1993**</u>

This section was modified to include a new area for comments on the cost approach (by eliminating the space dedicated to the building sketch). For VA purposes, the required economic life estimate is to be provided in this section. The entry for the appraiser's estimate of the site value is now located above the estimated reproduction cost-of-new improvements. As a new VA requirement, VA fee appraisers must now show their square foot (size) calculation for the property in this area or may indicate it on the perimeter building sketch (footprint) of the improvements which now must be provided as an exhibit to the appraisal report.

MODEL COMMENTS: The following are examples of explanatory remarks reviewers find useful. They are especially important when data on the subject property falls outside the normal range. Usually these comments require customization to reflect the special characteristics of the specific property being appraised.

<u>WHEN APPRAISER ELECTS NOT TO ANSWER WHETHER THE PROPERTY CONFORMS TO HUD/VA STANDARDS:</u>
```
No determination was made about this property's compliance with
special HUD/VA standards. The property does appear to comply to
local building codes.
```

COST APPROACH

ESTIMATED REPRODUCTION COST–NEW–OF IMPROVEMENTS

```
Valuation Section          UNIFORM RESIDENTIAL APPRAISAL REPORT    File No.
ESTIMATED SITE VALUE ................... = $            Comments on Cost Approach (such as, source of cost estimate,
ESTIMATED REPRODUCTION COST-NEW-OF IMPROVEMENTS:         site value, square foot calculation and for HUD, VA and FmHA, the
Dwelling _____ Sq. Ft @ $ _____ = $ _____         estimated remaining economic life of the property): _____
                _____ Sq. Ft @ $ _____ =   _____
                                         =   _____
Garage/Carport _____ Sq. Ft @ $ _____ =  _____
Total Estimated Cost New .............. = $ _____
Less        Physical      Functional       External
Depreciation _____ | _____ | _____ = $ _____
Depreciated Value of Improvements ............ = $ _____
"As-is" Value of Site Improvements............ = $ _____
INDICATED VALUE BY COST APPROACH ........... = $ _____
```

The **ESTIMATED REPRODUCTION COST-NEW-OF IMPROVEMENTS**, i.e., the cost of reproducing the subject structures using the same floor plan, materials and workmanship, is reproduced here. However, it is recognized that in some cases involving older buildings containing obsolete materials or unusual functional features, it is difficult, if not impossible, to estimate reproduction cost new with any reasonable degree of accuracy. Therefore, in such cases, the Replacement Cost may be used, but this should be specifically stated, with a description of the materials used for the estimate included. When using Replacement Cost, also state the functional deficiencies that have been eliminated.

If the building is too old to estimate reproduction cost, it probably is too old for the **COST APPROACH** to be meaningful.

CONSISTENCY CHECK: Information in this section of the URAR relates to another section of the form as indicated below. The appraiser should check to make sure data in both places is consistent!

COST APPROACH - Dwelling _____ Sq. Ft.:
    The GLA data here is found in three other places on the URAR*:
ROOM LIST - Square Feet of Gross Living Area
    on the "Finished area above grade contains:" line;
SALES COMPARISON ANALYSIS - SUBJECT: Above Grade Room Count; Gross Living Area; Sq. Ft.;
    and
COST APPROACH - BUILDING SKETCH; Gross Living Area Above Grade
    as either sketch dimensions (HUD) or GLA calculations (FNMA and FHLMC).
COST APPROACH - Special Energy Efficient Items
    costs should be for items listed in the

SALES COMPARISON ANALYSIS - SUBJECT: Special Energy Efficient Items
> block below, and the

IMPROVEMENTS - INSULATION; Energy Efficient Items
> lines.

COST APPROACH - Porches, Patios, etc.
> accounted for here should also appear under:

SALES COMPARISON ANALYSIS - SUBJECT: Porches, Patio, Pools, etc.;
> and

COMMENTS - Additional features
> or elsewhere in the report or its addenda.

COST APPROACH - Garage/Carport
> must be consistent with

SALES COMPARISON ANALYSIS - SUBJECT: Garage/Carport
> and the

AUTOS
> section.

*An exception is when a cost service is used that does not base its square foot calculations on GLA.

Fannie Mae   June 30, 2002   Part XI Chapter 4, Section 407   Cost Approach
Reproduction Cost

- The *reproduction cost estimate* should reflect the cost of construction based on the current prices of producing a replica of the property being appraised—including all of its positive and negative characteristics. Although the construction materials used for the estimate should be as similar as possible to those used for the subject property they do not have to be exactly the same.

COST APPROACH

| Depreciation | Physical - Functional - External |

```
Valuation Section        UNIFORM RESIDENTIAL APPRAISAL REPORT    File No.
ESTIMATED SITE VALUE ................. = $_____    Comments on Cost Approach (such as, source of cost estimate,
ESTIMATED REPRODUCTION COST-NEW-OF IMPROVEMENTS:    site value, square foot calculation and for HUD, VA and FmHA, the
Dwelling _____ Sq. Ft @ $ _____ = $ _____      estimated remaining economic life of the property): _____
                Sq. Ft @ $ _____ = _____
                                 = _____
Garage/Carport _____ Sq. Ft @ $ ____ = _____
Total Estimated Cost New ........... = $
Less        Physical   Functional   External
Depreciation |_____|_____|_____| = $
Depreciated Value of Improvements ......... = $
"As-is" Value of Site Improvements ......... = $
INDICATED VALUE BY COST APPROACH ....... = $
```

The three types of **Depreciation - Physical** deterioration, **Functional** and **External** obsolescence and the items included in each caetory are described in detail in the **COMMENTS** - **Depreciation** section of this Guide. The appraiser should estimate the value lost to each of the three types of depreciation and enter the dollar value in the appropriate column in this space. The total of all three types of depreciation is then entered on the blank line at the right after the **$** sign.

Fannie Mae   June 30, 2002   Part XI Chapter 4, Section 407   **Cost Approach**
Physical Depreciation
- Physical depreciation (which is traditionally referred to as physical deterioration) is a loss in value that is caused by deterioration in the physical condition of the improvements .All appraiser generally classifies physical deterioration as "curable" or "incurable!' Curable physical deterioration refers to items of deferred maintenance—for example, painting or items currently in need of repair (such as broken stair rails). Incurable physical deterioration refers to other items that currently are not practical or feasible to correct—for example, furnaces or roof shingles that have not reached the end of their economic life.

Fannie Mae   June 30, 2002   Part XI Chapter 4, Section 407   **Cost Approach**
Functional Depreciation   *[handwritten: ALSO VERY HIGH CEILINGS - 14 FT. HIGH]*
- *Functional depreciation* (which is traditionally referred to as functional obsolescence) is a loss in value that is caused by defects in the design of the structure-for example, inadequacies in -such items as architecture, floor plan, or sizes and types of rooms. It also can be caused by changes in market preferences that result in some aspect of the improvements being considered obsolete by current standards-for example, the location of a bedroom on a level with no bathroom, or access to a bedroom only through another bedroom.

Fannie Mae   June 30, 2002   Part XI Chapter 4, Section 407   **Cost Approach**
External Depreciation
- *External depreciation* (which is traditionally referred to as economic obsolescence) is a loss in value that is caused by negative influences that are outside of the site, such as economic factors or environmental changes—for example, shopping centers, expressways, or factories that are adjacent to the subject property.

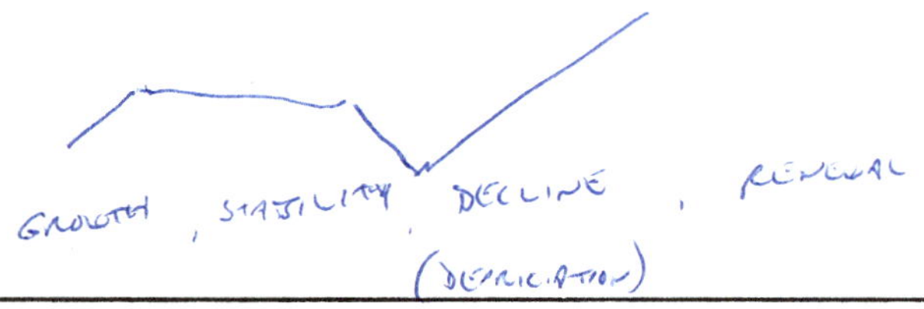

[handwritten: GROWTH, STABILITY, DECLINE, RENEWAL (DETERIORATION)]

[handwritten: IT IS ALSO IN THE DECLINE PHASE OF IT'S CYCLE]

CONSISTENCY CHECK: Information in this section of the URAR relates to another section of the form as indicated below. The appraiser should check to make sure data in both places is consistent!

COST APPROACH - Depreciation:

All deductions for items of depreciation should be explained somewhere on the URAR: Under

COMMENTS - Depreciation

or in extra space in the

COST APPROACH - BUILDING SKETCH

block; or in an addendum. Conversely, any items of depreciation listed in the above areas require an appropriate deduction here. These items should also be considered when rating

SALES COMPARISON ANALYSIS - SUBJECT: Functional Utility,

so appropriate adjustments are made to the comparables.

COST APPROACH

Depreciated Value of Improvements

Valuation Section — UNIFORM RESIDENTIAL APPRAISAL REPORT — File No.

- ESTIMATED SITE VALUE .... = $ _____
- ESTIMATED REPRODUCTION COST-NEW-OF IMPROVEMENTS:
- Dwelling _____ Sq. Ft @ $ _____ = $ _____
- _____ Sq. Ft @ $ _____ = _____
- = _____
- Garage/Carport _____ Sq. Ft @ $ _____ = _____
- Total Estimated Cost New .... = $ _____
- Less   Physical   Functional   External
- Depreciation   = $ _____
- Depreciated Value of Improvements .... = $ _____
- "As-is" Value of Site Improvements .... = $ _____
- INDICATED VALUE BY COST APPROACH .... = $ _____

Comments on Cost Approach (such as, source of cost estimate, site value, square foot calculation and for HUD, VA and FmHA, the estimated remaining economic life of the property): _____

On the URAR, unlike old versions of the form, site improvements are not included in the total **Depreciated Value of Improvements**. They are shown as a separate item on the next line.

The **Depreciated Value of Improvements** is their reproduction cost (or replacement cost) less all forms of depreciation.

Subtract the total **Depreciation: Physical**, **Functional** and **External** from the **Total Estimated Cost New** to obtain the **Depreciated Value of Improvements**.

COST APPROACH

"As is" Value of Site Improvements

Valuation Section	UNIFORM RESIDENTIAL APPRAISAL REPORT	File No.
ESTIMATED SITE VALUE .... = $ _____		Comments on Cost Approach (such as, source of cost estimate, site value, square foot calculation and for HUD, VA and FmHA, the estimated remaining economic life of the property): _____
ESTIMATED REPRODUCTION COST-NEW-OF IMPROVEMENTS:		
Dwelling _____ Sq. Ft @ $ _____ = $ _____		
_____ Sq. Ft @ $ _____ = _____		
Garage/Carport _____ Sq. Ft @ $ _____ = _____		
Total Estimated Cost New .... = $ _____		
Less Physical Functional External		
Depreciation _____	_____	_____ = $ _____		
Depreciated Value of Improvements .... = $ _____		
"As-is" Value of Site Improvements......... = $ _____		

There is no universal agreement among appraisers as to which improvements are classified as site improvements and which are part of the site value. Based on the **SITE** section of the Property Description side of the URAR, it appears the following items should be included in the **"As-is" Value of Site Improvements** value. If these are included as site improvements, do not also include them as part of the **ESTIMATED SITE VALUE**.

1. Clearing, grading or other landscaping
2. Drainage systems
3. Installation of public utilities
4. Access driveways, streets and alleys
5. Outside lighting and poles
6. Sidewalks and curbs
7. Fences and walls

The appraiser must also decide whether to include the following items as site improvements or as part of the house. The custom of the area where the subject house is located should be considered.

1. Septic systems and cesspools
2. Utility connections
3. Wells and well pumps
4. Patios, pools and tennis courts

The best way to avoid confusion is to list on an addendum sheet those items which are included as part of the site, site improvement, and improvement value estimates.

NOTE: "**As is**" means that the items are reported at their contributory or depreciated value. This eliminates the need to estimate the reproduction cost of large trees and other site improvements.

COST APPROACH

INDICATED VALUE BY COST APPROACH

```
Valuation Section          UNIFORM RESIDENTIAL APPRAISAL REPORT   File No.
ESTIMATED SITE VALUE .................. = $____        Comments on Cost Approach (such as, source of cost estimate,
ESTIMATED REPRODUCTION COST-NEW-OF IMPROVEMENTS:       site value, square foot calculation and for HUD, VA and FmHA, the
Dwelling _____ Sq. Ft @ $ _____ = $ _____         estimated remaining economic life of the property): _____
                 Sq. Ft @ $ _____ = _____
                                   = _____
Garage/Carport _____ Sq. Ft @ $ ____ = _____
Total Estimated Cost New ............. = $ _____
Less         Physical    Functional   External
Depreciation _____|_____|_____ = $
Depreciated Value of Improvements .......... = $
INDICATED VALUE BY COST APPROACH ........ = $
```

The **INDICATED VALUE BY COST APPROACH** is calculated by adding the **"As-is" Value of Site Improvements** value and the **ESTIMATED SITE VALUE** to the **Depreciated Value of Improvements**.

If the final value estimated by the appraiser is the **INDICATED VALUE BY COST APPROACH**, the appraiser should state the source of cost factor data and list comparable land sales on an attachment.

<u>Fannie Mae   June 30, 2002   Part XI Chapter 4, Section 407   Cost Approach - Indicated Value</u>
The appraiser arrives at the indicated value of a property by estimating the reproduction cost of new improvements, subtracting the amount of depreciation from all causes, and adding his or her opinion of value for the site if it were vacant and available to be developed to its highest and best use.

COST APPROACH

Comments	source of cost estimate

```
Valuation Section      UNIFORM RESIDENTIAL APPRAISAL REPORT    File No.
    ESTIMATED SITE VALUE ..................... = $_____      Comments on Cost Approach (such as, source of cost estimate,
    ESTIMATED REPRODUCTION COST-NEW-OF IMPROVEMENTS:           site value, square foot calculation and for HUD, VA and FmHA, the
    Dwelling_____ Sq. Ft @ $_____ = $_____                  estimated remaining economic life of the property): _____
                   Sq. Ft @ $_____ = _____
                                    = _____
    Garage/Carport___ Sq. Ft @ $_____ = _____
    Total Estimated Cost New ............. = $_____
    Less         Physical    Functional   External
    Depreciation_____|_____|_____ = $_____
    Depreciated Value of Improvements............. = $_____
    "As-is" Value of Site Improvements............. = $_____
    INDICATED VALUE BY COST APPROACH........... = $_____
```

The **Cost Approach** section was modified to include a new area for comments on the cost approach (by eliminating the space dedicated to the building sketch on the previous version of the form).

The appraiser should indicate the **source of cost estimate.** Many appraisers attached to the addenda section of the report to the computer printout sheet or their worksheets that show how the Reproduction Cost was calculated.

Fannie Mae   June 30, 2002   Part XI Chapter 4, Section 407   Cost Approach
Comments

In reviewing the appraisal report, the lender should make sure that the appraiser's analysis -and comments for the cost approach to value are consistent with comments and adjustments mentioned elsewhere in the appraisal report. For example, if the neighborhood or site description reveals that the property backs up to a shopping center, the lender should expect to see an adjustment for external depreciation in the cost approach. Similarly, if the improvement analysis indicates that It is necessary to go through one bedroom to get to another bedroom, the lender should expect to see an adjustment for functional depredation.

COST APPROACH

| Comments | site value |

```
Valuation Section        UNIFORM RESIDENTIAL APPRAISAL REPORT    File No.
ESTIMATED SITE VALUE ..................... = $_____      Comments on Cost Approach (such as, source of cost estimate,
ESTIMATED REPRODUCTION COST-NEW-OF IMPROVEMENTS:           site value, square foot calculation and for HUD, VA and FmHA, the
Dwelling _____ Sq. Ft @ $ _____ = $ _____             estimated remaining economic life of the property): _____
                  Sq. Ft @ $ _____ = _____
                                   = _____
Garage/Carport ____ Sq. Ft @ $ ____ = _____
Total Estimated Cost New .......... = $ _____
Less         Physical    Functional   External
Depreciation _____|_____|_____ = $ _____
Depreciated Value of Improvements .......... = $ _____
"As-is" Value of Site Improvements .......... = $ _____
INDICATED VALUE BY COST APPROACH ........ = $
```

The basis of the **ESTIMATED SITE VALUE** should be explained in a comments section or on an addendum sheet. Included in the site value should be all costs to develop the site not included on the **"As-is" Value of Site Improvements** line. Be careful not to duplicate items. For example, wells and septic systems are significant items that often (by mistake) are included in both the site value and the site improvement value. For a further list of these items, see the previous **"As-is" Value of Site Improvements** page of this Guide.

When a house is on leased land and the land rent being paid is the same as the current economic (market) rent, there is no leasehold value. "0" is entered for the **ESTIMATED SITE VALUE**. If the rent being paid is less than the economic (market) rent, the discounted value of the difference is the value of the leasehold and this figure is entered for estimated site value. For properties involving a leasehold, an addendum sheet should be attached with details of the lease and how leasehold value (if any) is calculated.

Site value can be estimated in built-up areas by estimating what percentage of a total property value (in the same neighborhood) the typical site is. The percentage can then be used to estimate the value of the site being appraised, by multiplying the estimated total value of the property by the typical site/property ratio. Care should be exercised in using this technique as it may be subject to substantial error.

<u>Fannie Mae June 30, 1993 Announcement - Cost Approach</u>
<u>Comments Section</u>

"The "cost approach" section was modified to include a new area for comments on the cost approach (by eliminating the space dedicated to the building sketch on the current version of the form)."

Fannie Mae   June 30, 1993 Announcement   - Cost Approach
Exterior Building Sketch

"Appraisers may continue to show the square foot (size) calculation for the property in this area or they may indicate it on the exterior building sketch of the improvements that we require as an exhibit to each appraisal report."

MODEL COMMENTS: The following are examples of explanatory remarks reviewers find useful. They are especially important when data on the subject property falls outside the normal range. Usually these comments require customization to reflect the special characteristics of the specific property being appraised.

HIGH ESTIMATED SITE VALUE:

     The high demand for sites in _____ [city, town or market] coupled with a diminishing supply of vacant land has resulted in site values exceeding ____ [%] percent of the total property value. This is typical of properties in _____ [area] in general and _____ [county or city] specifically. There is ____ (no, a) resulting adverse effect on marketability.

WHEN ESTIMATED SITE VALUE EXCEEDS 30% OF THE PROPERTY VALUE:

     The value of the site is greater than _____ [30% or more] of the total property value. This is _____ (common, uncommon) in this area and is due to _____ (water influence, exceptional view, small improvements, large site size).

CONSISTENCY CHECK: Information in this section of the URAR relates to another section of the form as indicated below. The appraiser should check to make sure data in both places is consistent!

   Make sure that the accounting in the

COST APPROACH - **ESTIMATED SITE VALUE, Site Improvements**
   and

COST APPROACH - **ESTIMATED REPRODUCTION COST - NEW - OF IMPROVEMENTS:**
   are separate and no items are included in more than one section.

   Any "adverse easements, encroachments, special assessments, slide areas, etc." listed in the

SITE - **COMMENTS**
   section that have a negative effect on property value need to have a corresponding deduction in value made in either:

COST APPROACH - **Functional** or **External: Depreciation;**
   or

COST APPROACH - **ESTIMATED SITE VALUE.**
   Care must be taken to make the proper deduction in <u>one and only one</u> place.

COST APPROACH

| Comments | square foot calculation |

```
Valuation Section        UNIFORM RESIDENTIAL APPRAISAL REPORT    File No.

  ESTIMATED SITE VALUE ................... , ..... = $ _____   Comments on Cost Approach (such as, source of cost estimate,
  ESTIMATED REPRODUCTION COST-NEW-OF IMPROVEMENTS:                site value, square foot calculation and for HUD, VA and FmHA, the
C  Dwelling _____ Sq. Ft @ $ _____ = $ _____                estimated remaining economic life of the property): _____
O
S              _____ Sq. Ft @ $ _____ = _____
T
A                             =
P  Garage/Carport _____ Sq. Ft @ $ _____ = _____
P  Total Estimated Cost New ............. = $ _____
R
O  Less        Physical    Functional    External
A  Depreciation _____|_____|_____ = $ _____
C  Depreciated Value of Improvements ................ = $ _____
H  "As-is" Value of Site Improvements ................ = $ _____
   INDICATED VALUE BY COST APPROACH ............ = $ _____
```

Appraisers may continue to show the **square foot** (size) **calculation** for the property in this area or they may indicate it on the exterior building sketch of the improvements which Fannie Mae requires as an exhibit in the Addenda section of each appraisal report.

Measurements		No. Stories		Sq. Ft.
30' x 30'	x	1	=	900
6' x 26'	x	1	=	156
26' x 32'	x	1	=	832
Total Gross Living Area				1,888

The above is an example of the correct way to enter the measurements of the house shown in the case study.

NOTE: Freddie Mac and Fannie Mae require that this space show only square foot Gross Living Area calculations and cost approach comments. The sketch of the building should be attached on a separate sheet.

<u>Veterans Benefits Administration   Circular 26-93-25   1993</u>
<u>Exhibit Attachment - Square Foot Size Calculations</u>

This section was modified to include a new area for comments on the cost approach (by eliminating the space dedicated to the building sketch). For VA purposes, the required economic life estimate is to be provided in this section. The entry for the appraiser's estimate of the site value is now located above the estimated reproduction cost-of-new improvements. As a new VA requirement, VA fee appraisers must now show their square foot (size) calculation for the property in this area or may indicate it on the perimeter building sketch (footprint) of the improvements which now must be provided as an exhibit to the appraisal report.

COST APPROACH

| Comments | for HUD, VA, and FmHA, the estimated remaining economic life of the property |

Valuation Section — UNIFORM RESIDENTIAL APPRAISAL REPORT   File No.

```
ESTIMATED SITE VALUE ....................... = $_____
ESTIMATED REPRODUCTION COST-NEW-OF IMPROVEMENTS:
Dwelling _____ Sq. Ft @ $ _____ = $_____
                 Sq. Ft @ $ _____ = _____
                                    = _____
Garage/Carport _____ Sq. Ft @ $ _____ = _____
Total Estimated Cost New ............... = $_____
Less          Physical   Functional   External
Depreciation _____|_____|_____ = $_____
Depreciated Value of Improvements ............ = $_____
"As-is" Value of Site Improvements ............. = $_____
INDICATED VALUE BY COST APPROACH .......... = $
```

Comments on Cost Approach (such as, source of cost estimate, site value, square foot calculation and for HUD, VA and FmHA, the estimated remaining economic life of the property): _____

This space may also be used for miscellaneous **COST APPROACH** comments. All items of physical deterioration, functional obsolescence and external obsolescence should be explained either here, on the Property Description side of the report or in the addenda. The appraiser may also choose to use this space for comments on any of the following items he or she feels are appropriate. It is not expected that every appraisal will have comments on each item.

1. How site value was estimated: comparable site sales, assessor's ratios or subdivision lot sales.

2. How reproduction cost is estimated: cost service, local builder's figures;or other sources.

3. Physical deterioration curable: Items that should be repaired and how costs were estimated.

4. Physical deterioration: Deferred maintenance of items not ready to be replaced now,but which will have to be replaced within the term of the proposed loan, such as painting and decorating, roofing, mechanical systems, structural items, andsite improvements.

5. Physical deterioration, incurable and how was it estimated: age/life method; abstraction from the market or other method.

Construction Warranty programs are gaining popularity with home buyers and sellers in many areas. These warranties provide protection against structural and mechanical defects for purchasers of new and used residences, but often vary substantially from each other with respect to the defects covered and the term of the coverage. The URAR no longer provides space to indicate whether or not the residence is covered by a construction warranty. When such a policy is in effect the name of the warranty program and when the warranty program expires can be reported here or in the addenda. The appraiser should report their judgment as to what effect (if any) the warranty insurance policy has on the value of the property.

The National Association of Home Builders and the National Association of Realtors have both endorsed specific construction warranty programs. Endorsement by either organization indicates that the program meets minimum standards which they have established.

As a general rule, those programs which require prior inspection provide broader coverage than those that do not.

The appraiser should determine if, in the market of the house being appraised, there is any difference in value between houses covered by home warranty insurance policies and houses that are not. When there is a value difference, the appraiser must be consistent as to how this factor is treated in the three approaches to value.

CONSISTENCY CHECK: Information in this section of the URAR relates to another section of the form as indicated below. The appraiser should check to make sure data in both places is consistent!

<u>COST APPROACH</u> - BUILDING SKETCH; Gross Living Area Above Grade
    as either building sketch dimensions (HUD) or GLA calculations (FNMA and FHLMC) is found in three other places on the URAR:

<u>ROOM LIST</u> - Square Feet of Gross Living Area
    on the "Finished area **above** grade contains:" line;

<u>SALES COMPARISON ANALYSIS</u> - SUBJECT: Above Grade Room Count Gross Living Area; Sq. Ft.;
    and

<u>COST APPROACH</u> - Dwelling _____ Sq. Ft.
    line.*

*An exception is when a cost service is used that does not base its square foot calculations on GLA.

The **estimated remaining economic life** is the appraiser's forecast of the number of years that the improvements will contribute to the value of the property. Often the site itself has substantial value at the end of this period.

The URAR provides space for an estimate of remaining economic life. Appraisers must take great care in making this estimate, as some lenders limit the term of the mortgage based on it.

Many appraisers believe it is impossible to estimate remaining economic life, unless a property is nearing the end of that life. However, most feel the estimate can be made, provided it is qualified by projecting no substantial future changes in the four great forces (Governmental, Physical, Economic and Social) that affect value in a particular neighborhood. The problem is that the probability of these forces remaining unchanged for long periods of time is remote. Therefore an estimate of long remaining economic life based on this assumption serves little purpose.

It is no longer considered good appraisal practice to estimate the remaining economic life by projecting an historic rate of depreciation into the future.

When forecasting remaining economic life, the appraiser must consider the quality of both design and construction of the house, along with its condition, in relation to the projected effects of the four great forces on its value and economic life. When a residence is remodeled, subjected to excessive wear and tear, or affected by forces different from those projected, the remaining economic life may also change.

Fannie Mae and Freddie Mac do <u>not</u> require the appraiser to fill in the **Estimated Remaining Physical Life** blank, but VA and FHA do.

Caution must be exercised in the use of tables that purport to estimate the total physical life of different types of houses. They are of limited use to the appraiser. They are even less useful in estimating the Remaining Economic Life.

<u>**Fannie Mae   June 30, 2002   Part XI Chapter 4, Section 405.10   Remaining Economic Life**</u>
Because our appraisal report forms that are used for manually underwritten mortgages are designed to meet the needs of several different user groups, they address the remaining economic life for the property being appraised. However, the appraiser does not need to report the remaining economic life for a mortgage that will be delivered to us. Even if the appraiser does report this information, the lender does not need to consider it because any related property deficiencies will be discussed in the sections of the appraisal report that address the improvements analysis and comments on the condition of the property. We have no requirement -that the mortgage term have any correlation to the remaining economic life of the property.

<u>**Veterans Benefits Administration   Circular 26-93-2   1993**</u>
<u>**Description of Improvements Section - Remaining Economic Life**</u>

Other modifications included moving the requirement to report the estimated remaining economic life to the cost approach section;

MODEL COMMENTS: The following are examples of explanatory remarks reviewers find useful. They are especially important when data on the subject property falls outside the normal range. Usually these comments require customization to reflect the special characteristics of the specific property being appraised.

ESTIMATED REMAINING PHYSICAL LIFE:

   This appraisal report has been prepared within FNMA and FHLMC guidelines, which do not require an estimate of remaining physical life. Physical life is the time period during which the house may be expected to remain physically in existence if it receives normal maintenance. Since over 90% of the houses ever built in the United States are still in existence and since houses in Europe have lasted hundreds of years, it is almost impossible to forecast the Estimated Remaining Physical Life of a house.

Notes

Notes

SALES COMPARISON ANALYSIS

Introduction

ITEM	SUBJECT	COMPARABLE NO. 1		COMPARABLE NO. 2		COMPARABLE NO. 3	
Address							
Proximity to Subject							
Sales Price	$		$		$		$
Price/Gross Liv. Area	$	$		$		$	
Data and/or Verification Source							
VALUE ADJUSTMENTS	DESCRIPTION	DESCRIPTION	+ (-) $ Adjustment	DESCRIPTION	+ (-) $ Adjustment	DESCRIPTION	+ (-) $ Adjustment
Sales or Financing Concessions							
Date of Sale/Time							
Location							
Leasehold/Fee Simple							
Site							
View							
Design and Appeal							
Quality of Construction							
Age							
Condition							
Above Grade Room Count	Total | Bdrms | Baths	Total | Bdrms | Baths		Total | Bdrms | Baths		Total | Bdrms | Baths	
Gross Living Area	Sq. Ft.	Sq. Ft.		Sq. Ft.		Sq. Ft.	
Basement & Finished Rooms Below Grade							
Functional Utility							
Heating/Cooling							
Energy Efficient Items							
Garage/Carport							
Porch, Patio, Deck, Fireplace(s), etc.							
Fence, Pool, etc.							
Net Adj. (total)		☐ + ☐ -	$	☐ + ☐ -	$	☐ + ☐ -	$
Adjusted Sales Price of Comparable			$		$		$

Comments on Sales Comparison (including the subject property's compatability to the neighborhood, etc.): _____

ITEM	SUBJECT	COMPARABLE NO. 1	COMPARABLE NO. 2	COMPARABLE NO. 3
Date, Price and Data Source, for prior sales within year of appraisal				

Analysis of any current agreement of sale, option, or listing of the subject property and analysis of any prior sales of subject and comparables within one year of the date of appraisal:

INDICATED VALUE BY SALES COMPARISON APPROACH . . . . $ _____

In applying the **SALES COMPARISON ANALYSIS**, the appraiser:

1. Studies the market and selects the sales and listings of properties most comparable to the residence being appraised, generally, the most current and similar comparable sales. Often, more sales and listings are considered than are finally used.
2. Collects and verifies data on each selected property's selling and listing prices, dates of transaction, physical and locational characteristics and any special conditions.

3. Analyzes and compares each property with the subject as to time of sale, location, physical characteristics and conditions of sale.
4. Adjusts the sale or listing price of each comparable for dissimilarities between it and the subject, using *matched pairs*, (as described under **Location**), regression analysis and other adjustment techniques.
5. Reconciles the adjusted prices of the comparable properties into an indicated market value of the appraised residence.

The following are subsections of the **SALES COMPARISON ANALYSIS:**

Address
Proximity to Subject
Sales Price
Price/Gross Liv. Area
Data and/or Verification Source
VALUE ADJUSTMENTS
Sales or Financing Concessions
Date of Sale/Time
Location
Leasehold/Fee Simple
Site
View
Design and Appeal
Quality of Construction
Age
Condition
Above Grade Room Count Gross Living Area
Basement & Finished Rooms Below Grade
Functional Utility
Heating/Cooling
Energy Efficient Items
Garage/Carport
Porch, Patio, Deck, Fireplace(s), etc.
Fence, Pool, etc.
Net Adj. (total)
Adjusted Sales Price of Comparable
Comment on Sales Comparison
Date, Price and Data Source, for prior sales within year of appraisal.
Analysis of any current argreement of sale, option, or listing of the subject property and analysis of any prior sales of subject and comparables within one year of the date of appraisal
INDICATED VALUE BY SALES COMPARISON APPROACH

Veterans Benefits Administration   Circular 26-93-25   1993
Sales Comparison Section - Location of Comparable Sale and Subject
VA will now require that a location map be provided with every appraisal report indicating the location of each comparable sale and the subject.

SALES COMPARISON ANALYSIS

Grid

ITEM	SUBJECT	COMPARABLE NO. 1		COMPARABLE NO. 2		COMPARABLE NO. 3	
Address							
Proximity to Subject							
Sales Price	$		$		$		$
Price/Gross Liv. Area	$ ☐	$	☐	$	☐	$	☐
Data and/or Verification Source							
VALUE ADJUSTMENTS	DESCRIPTION	DESCRIPTION	+ (-) $ Adjustment	DESCRIPTION	+ (-) $ Adjustment	DESCRIPTION	+ (-) $ Adjustment
Sales or Financing Concessions							
Date of Sale/Time							
Location							
Leasehold/Fee Simple							
Site							
View							
Design and Appeal							
Quality of Construction							
Age							
Condition							
Above Grade Room Count	Total ¦ Bdrms ¦ Baths	Total ¦ Bdrms ¦ Baths		Total ¦ Bdrms ¦ Baths		Total ¦ Bdrms ¦ Baths	
Gross Living Area	Sq. Ft.	Sq. Ft.		Sq. Ft.		Sq. Ft.	
Basement & Finished Rooms Below Grade							
Functional Utility							
Heating/Cooling							
Energy Efficient Items							
Garage/Carport							
Porch, Patio, Deck, Fireplace(s), etc.							
Fence, Pool, etc.							
Net Adj. (total)		☐ + ☐ -	$	☐ + ☐ -	$	☐ + ☐ -	$
Adjusted Sales Price of Comparable			$		$		$

Comments on Sales Comparison (including the subject property's compatability to the neighborhood, etc.): _____

ITEM	SUBJECT	COMPARABLE NO. 1	COMPARABLE NO. 2	COMPARABLE NO. 3
Date, Price and Data Source, for prior sales within year of appraisal				

Analysis of any current agreement of sale, option, or listing of the subject property and analysis of any prior sales of subject and comparables within one year of the date of appraisal:

INDICATED VALUE BY SALES COMPARISON APPROACH . . . . $_____

The grid used for the **SALES COMPARISON ANALYSIS** on the URAR has been redesigned to make it easier for the appraiser to use and the reviewer to read. Figures which are intended to be added line up in a column and other numbers are positioned to avoid confusion. Space for **Sales or Financing Concessions** is located at the top of the grid below **Value Adjustments** to emphasize its importance.

SALES COMPARISON ANALYSIS

General Instructions

The following Fannie Mae and HUD/FHA instructions apply to the **Sales Comparison Analysis**

Always select the comparable sales with the fewest dissimilarities. Use older sales only if more recent ones are not available and be sure to explain the reason for their use in the **Comments on Sales Comparison** section.

Fannie Mae   June 30, 2002   Part XI Chapter 4, Section 406   Sales Comparison Approach to Value

The sales comparison approach to value—traditionally referred to as the market data approach—is an analysis of comparable sales, contract offerings, and current listings of properties that are the most comparable to the subject property. The appraiser's analysis of a property must take into consideration all factors that have an effect on value, recognizing that a well-informed or -well-advised purchaser will pay no more for a property than the price he or she would pay for a similar property of equal desirability and utility if it were purchased without undue delay. To accomplish this, the appraiser must analyze the closed or settled sales, the contract sales, and the current listings of properties that are the most comparable to the subject property in order to identify any significant differences (or elements of comparison) that could affect' his or her opinion of value for the subject property. This is particularly important in soft or declining markets because the competing current listings and contracts probably reflect the upper-end of value for the subject property as of the effective date of the appraisal (and we expect the appraiser to accurately report and reflect market conditions as of that date). The comparable market data must be verified, analyzed, and adjusted for differences between the comparable properties and the subject property. On most appraisal forms, the appraiser -will identify these adjustments by assigning a dollar value to reflect the market's reaction to any features of the comparable properties that differ from those of the subject property.

Fannie Mae   June 30, 2002   Part XI Chapter 4, Section 406.01   Sales Comparison Approach to Value
Verification Source

The appraiser's opinion of market value is no better than the reliability of the comparable data that is used, therefore, the appraiser must exercise due diligence to ensure the reliability of the comparable sales data that he or she uses. The appraiser must report his or her data and/or verification source(s) for each comparable-sale on the appraisal report' form. An appraiser may use a single source for the data and verifications or multiple sources if they are needed to adequately verify the comparable sales. The quality of the data available varies from source to source and from one locality to another. In view of this, a single data source may be adequate if the appraiser uses a source that provides quality sales data that is confirmed or verified by closed or settled transactions. On the other hand, if the appraiser's basic data source does not confirm or verify the sales data, the appraiser will need to use additional sources. When comparable sales data is provided by a party that has a financial interest in either the sale or financing of the subject property, the appraiser must reverify the data with a party that does not have a financial interest in the subject transaction.

Fannie Mae   June 30, 2002   Part XI Chapter 4, Section 406.02   Sales Comparison Approach to Value
Selection of Comparable Sales

We require an appraiser to research, analyze, and consider influences that may affect value based on market evidence (such as closed sales, contract sales, and properties for sale in the market area; market studies; etc.). For example, if a property Is located in a neighborhood that includes (or is close to) an airport or hazardous waste site or that has relatively high property taxes or vacant or boarded-up properties, we expect the appraiser to research, analyze and use comparable sales from the same neighborhood or affected area (whenever possible) in his or her analysis. This will assure that any effect of these value-influencing characteristics is taken into consideration in the development of the opinion of value for the property.

If a property is located in an area in which there is a shortage of truly comparable sales—either because of the nature of the property improvements or the relatively low number of sales transactions in the neighborhood— the appraiser might need to use as comparable sales properties that are not truly comparable to the subject property or properties that are located in competing neighborhoods. In some situations, sales of properties that are not truly comparable or sales of properties that are located in competing neighborhoods may simply be the best comparables available and the most appropriate for the appraiser's analysis. The use of such comparables is acceptable as long as the appraiser adequately documents his or her analysis and explains why these comparable sales were used (including a discussion of how a competing neighborhood is comparable to the subject neighborhood).

The appraiser must report a minimum of three comparable sales as part of the sales comparison approach to value. The appraiser may submit more than three comparable sales to support his or her opinion of market value, as long as at least three are actual settled or closed sales. Generally, the appraiser should use comparable sales that have been settled or closed within the last 12 months. However, the appraiser may use older comparable sales if he or she believes that it is appropriate, and selects comparable sales that are the best indicators of value for the subject property The appraiser must comment on the reasons for using any comparable sales that are more than six months old. For example, if the subject property is located in a rural area that has minimal sales activity, the appraiser may not be able to locate three truly comparable sales that sold in the last 12 months. In this case, the appraiser may use older comparable sales as long as he or she explains why they are being used.

The appraiser may use the subject property as a fourth comparable sale or as supporting data if the property previously was sold (and closed or settled). If the appraiser believes that it is appropriate, he or she also may use contract offerings and current listings as supporting data. However, in no instance may the appraiser create comparable sales by combining vacant land sales with the contract purchase price of a home (although this type of information may be included as additional supporting documentation).

For properties that are in established subdivisions or for units in established condominium or PUD projects that have resale activity, the appraiser should use comparable sales from within the same subdivision or project as the subject -property if there are any available. Resale activity from within the subdivision or project should be the best indicator of value for properties in that subdivision or project. If the appraiser uses sales of comparable properties that are located outside of the subject neighborhood, he or she must include an explanation with the analysis.

For properties in new subdivisions or for units in new (or recently converted) condominium or PUD projects, the appraiser must compare the subject property to other properties in its general market area as well as to properties within the subject subdivision or project. This comparison should help demonstrate market acceptance of new developments and the properties within them. Generally, the appraiser should select one comparable sale from the subject subdivision or project and one comparable sale from outside the subject subdivision or project. The third comparable sale can be from inside or outside of the subject subdivision or project, as long as the appraiser considers it to be a good indicator of value for the subject property. In selecting the comparables, the appraiser should keep in mind that sales or resales from within the subject subdivision or project are preferable to sales from outside the subdivision or project as long as the developer or builder of the subject property is not involved in the transactions.

Because **rural properties** often have large lot sizes and rural locations can be relatively undeveloped, there may be a shortage (or absence) of recent truly comparable sales 'in the immediate vicinity of a subject property that is in a rural location. **This means that the appraiser will often need to select comparable sales that are located a considerable distance from the subject property.** In such cases, the appraiser must use his or her knowledge of the area and apply good judgment in selecting comparable sales that are the best indicators of value for the subject property. The appraiser should include an explanation of why the particular comparables were selected in his or her analysis.

Fannie Mae   June 30, 2002   Part XI Chapter 4, Section 406.03   Adjustments to comparable Sales

Each comparable sale that is used in the sales comparison approach to value must be analyzed for differences and similarities between it and the property that Is being appraised. The appraiser must base his or her analysis and any adjustments to the comparable sales on the market data for the particular neighborhood and for competing locations—not on predetermined or assumed dollar adjustments. If an appraiser's adjustments to comparable sales (or the reconciliation of the comparable sales) are based on unsupported assumptions or personal opinion that cannot be supported by market data, poor quality appraisals that could have a discriminatory effect may result.

Comparable sales must be adjusted to the subject property—except for sales and financing concessions, which are adjusted to the market at the time of sale. The appraiser must make appropriate adjustments for location, terms and conditions of sale, date of sale, and the physical characteristics of the properties. "Time" adjustments must be representative of the market and should be supported by the comparable sales whenever possible. The adjustments must reflect the time that elapsed between the contract date (or the date of the "meeting of the minds") for the comparable sale and the effective date of the appraisal for the subject property.

The subject property is the standard against which the comparable sales are evaluated and adjusted. Thus, if an item in the comparable property is superior to that in the subject property, a negative adjustment is required to make that item equal to that in the subject property. Conversely, if an item in the comparable property is inferior to that in the subject property, a positive adjustment is required to make that item equal to that in the subject property. If an item in a comparable property is equal to that in the subject property no adjustment is required.

A. Quantitative sales comparison analysis. Most appraisal forms require the appraiser to use a quantitative sales comparison analysis in which he or she assigns a dollar value to reflect the market's reaction to any features of the -comparable sales that differ from those of the subject property. The proper selection of comparable properties minimizes both the need for, and the size of, any dollar adjustments. However, when there are no similar or truly comparable sales for a particular property—because of the uniqueness of the property or other conditions—the appraiser must select comparable sales that represent the best indicators of value for the subject property and make adjustments to reflect the actions of typical purchasers in that market. Dollar adjustments must reflect the market's reaction to the difference in the properties, not necessarily the cost of the difference. Swimming pools, electronic air filters, intercom systems, elaborately finished basements, carpets, and other special features generally do not affect value to the extent of their cost.

We have established guidelines for the net and-gross percentage adjustments that underwriters may rely on as a general indicator of whether a property should be used as a comparable sale. Generally, the dollar amount of the net adjustments for each comparable sale should not exceed 15% of the sales price of the comparable. When the adjustments exceed 15%, the appraiser must comment on the reasons for not using a more similar comparable. Further, the dollar amount of the gross adjustments for each comparable sale should not exceed 25% of the sales price of the comparable. The amount of the gross adjustment is determined by adding all individual adjustments without regard to the positive or negative adjustments. When the adjustments exceed 25%, the appraiser must comment on the reasons for not using a more similar comparable.

Individual adjustments that are excessively high should be explained by the appraiser and reviewed carefully by the lender's underwriter. In some circumstances, the use of comparables with higher-than-normal adjustments may be warranted, but the appraiser must satisfactorily justify his or her use of them.

The appraiser must research the market and select the most comparable sales that are available for the subject property and then adjust them to reflect the reaction of the market to the differences (except for sales and financing concessions) between the comparable sales and the subject property, without regard for the 'percentage or amount of the dollar adjustments. If the appraiser's adjustments do not fall within our net and gross percentage adjustment guidelines, but the appraiser believes that the comparable sales used in the analysis are the best available, as well as the best indicators of value for the subject property the appraiser simply has to provide an appropriate explanation. If the extent of the appraiser's adjustments to the comparable sales is great enough to indicate that the property may not conform to the general market area, the lender's underwriter must review the property carefully.

The value factors of **Location**, **Site**, **View**, **Design and Appeal**, **Quality of Construction**, **Age**, **Condition**, and **Functional Utility** are all subjective factors that require subjective adjustments. Be careful that your adjustments are reasonable--not excessive.

MODEL COMMENTS: The following are examples of explanatory remarks reviewers find useful. They are especially important when data on the subject property falls outside the normal range. Usually these comments require customization to reflect the special characteristics of the specific property being appraised.

WHEN COMPS DO NOT MEET FNMA GUIDELINES:

In this appraiser's judgment, the _____ (rapid appreciation of house values, unique price structure of the subject neighborhood, distinct price structure of _____ {ranches, etc.}, effect of GLA on value in this market) makes it most important to use comparables that are _____ (the most recent similar sales, within the subject neighborhood, similar in style, similar in size). In order to do this, it is necessary to use comparables _____ (over 1 mile away, over 6 months old, with different styles, with large GLA differences, requiring large adjustments, etc.). These comparable sales are the best indicators of the subject's market value available at the time of this appraisal.

WHEN COMPS DO NOT MEET FNMA GUIDELINES DUE TO THE UNIQUENESS OF THE SUBJECT:

Due to the subject's _____ (large acreage, excess GLA, small GLA, uncommon style, unique appeal, etc.), the comparables used_____ (are smaller, are larger, etc.). This results in large _____ (net adjustments, gross adjustments, differences in GLA). Despite their differences, this appraiser feels these comparables are the best available to accurately indicate the subject's market value at the time of this appraisal.

SALES COMPARISON ANALYSIS

Address

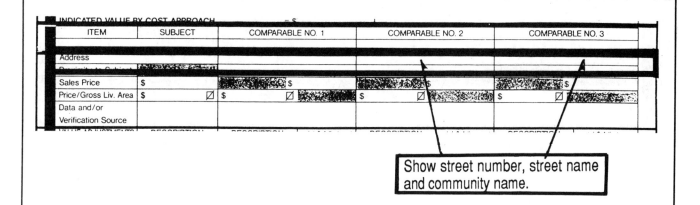

Under **Address**, identify the location of the subject and all comparables by exact street number, street name and community name.

CONSISTENCY CHECK: Information in this section of the URAR relates to another section of the form as indicated below. The appraiser should check to make sure data in both places is consistent!

<u>SALES COMPARISON ANALYSIS</u> - SUBJECT: **Address**
    also appears as
<u>SUBJECT</u> - **Property Address.**

SALES COMPARISON ANALYSIS

Proximity to Subject

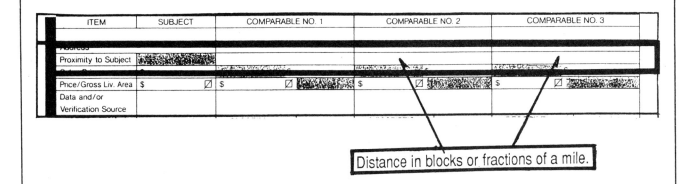

The **Proximity to Subject** is the distance and direction <u>from</u> the <u>subject</u> property <u>to</u> each <u>comparable</u> in terms of blocks, fractions of a mile or miles as the case may be.

<u>**Fannie Mae**   **June 30, 2002**   **Part XI Chapter 4, Section 406.05**   **Sales Comparison Approach**</u>
Proximity to Subject Property and Location
The description of the proximity of the comparable sale to the subject property must be specific (e.g., two blocks south). Whenever possible, the appraiser should use comparable sales in the same neighborhood as the subject property because the sales prices of comparable properties in the neighborhood should reflect the same positive and negative locational characteristics.

SALES COMPARISON ANALYSIS

Sales Price

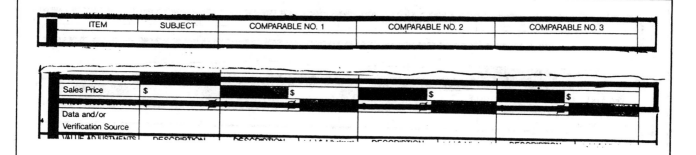

The **Sales Price** shown for the subject property is the pending contract price when the appraisal is made for lending purposes. It is <u>not the last recorded sale price</u> of the subject property.

<u>Fannie Mae   June 30, 2002   Part XI Chapter 4, Section 406.05   Sales Comparison Approach</u>
<u>Sales Price</u>
The sales price of each comparable sale should be within the general range of the appraiser's opinion of market value for the subject property. A $100,000 comparable sale for a $75,000 subject property would raise questions about the validity of the comparable.

MODEL COMMENTS: The following are examples of explanatory remarks reviewers find useful. They are especially important when data on the subject property falls outside the normal range. Usually these comments require customization to reflect the special characteristics of the specific property being appraised..

<u>WHEN NO PERSONAL PROPERTY WAS INCLUDED IN COMPS</u>:

   The comparable sales were verified and no personal property was included in their sales prices.

<u>WHEN COMPS DO NOT BRACKET THE SUBJECT'S VALUE ESTIMATE</u>:

   A thorough search for comparable sales was made in an attempt to find sales which bracket the final value estimated for the subject property. After consideration of locations, dates of sale, physical differences and special conditions, in the appraiser's judgment, the comparables used are the best indicators of the subject's value although they are all _____ (higher, lower) in price than the final value estimated for the subject.

CONSISTENCY CHECK: Information in this section of the URAR relates to another section of the form as indicated below. The appraiser should check to make sure data in both places is consistent!

<u>SALES COMPARISON ANALYSIS</u> - SUBJECT: **Sales Price**
      also appears as
<u>SUBJECT</u> - Sale Price **$**.

SALES COMPARISON ANALYSIS

Price/Gross Liv. Area

ITEM	SUBJECT	COMPARABLE NO. 1	COMPARABLE NO. 2	COMPARABLE NO. 3
Proximity to Subject				
Price/Gross Liv. Area	$ ☐	$ ☐	$ ☐	$ ☐
Verification Source				

Calculate the **Price/Gross Liv. Area** (total sale price per square foot of gross above-grade living area [GLA]) for the subject and each of the comparable sales by dividing each **Sales Price** (above) by total GLA.

When measurements provided by another source are used, there is a substantial possibility that the Gross Living Area will be incorrect, either because the reported measurements are inaccurate or the area reported is not Gross Living Area as described in the **ROOMS** section on the Property Description side of the form.

MODEL COMMENTS: The following are examples of explanatory remarks reviewers find useful. They are especially important when data on the subject property falls outside the normal range. Usually these comments require customization to reflect the special characteristics of the specific property being appraised.

COMPS' PRICES/GLA DIFFER BY MORE THAN 10%:
```
    The price per gross living area is a package price incorp-
orating all items which contribute to the sale.  In this instance
it was not possible to find 3 comparables with prices per gross
living area within 10% of each other.  This was due to
_____ [reason for difference, i.e. comps have
dissimilar lot sizes].
```

CONSISTENCY CHECK: Information in this section of the URAR relates to another section of the form as indicated below. The appraiser should check to make sure data in both places is consistent!

SALES COMPARISON ANALYSIS - SUBJECT: Price/Gross Liv. Area
    is calculated by dividing the
SUBJECT - Sales Price $
    by the total
ROOMS - Square Feet of Gross Living Area
    from the "Finished area above grade contains:"

SALES COMPARISON ANALYSIS

Data and/or Verification Source

ITEM	SUBJECT	COMPARABLE NO. 1	COMPARABLE NO. 2	COMPARABLE NO. 3
Proximity to Subject				
Sales Price	$	$	$	$
Price/Gross Liv. Area	$	$	$	$
Data and/or Verification Source				

The <u>Sales Comparison Analysis</u> adjustment grid was modified to include an entry in which the appraiser reports the **Data and/or Verification Source** for the comparable sales (to assure compliance with the USPAP requirement that the appraiser verify comparable market data). An appraiser may use a single source for his or her data and verifications or may use multiple sources if they are needed to adequately verify the comparable sales. The quality of the data available for single-family residential properties varies from source to source and from one locality to another. In view of this, a single data source may be adequate if the appraiser uses a source that provides quality sales data that is confirmed or verified by closed or settled transactions. On the other hand, if the appraiser's basic data source does not confirm or verify the sales data, the appraiser will need to use additional sources.

Give the data source from which the information pertaining to each comparable was obtained (e.g., deed records, recordation tax stamps, brokers, multiple listings, data bank, buyer or seller, etc.).

For the subject property, indicate the source of data about the pending sale for which the mortgage loan has been applied. It is assumed that other information about the subject property comes from the appraiser's personal inspection.

The following is a list of some good sources of market data:

1. Appraiser's own files
2. Multiple listing services
3. Deed records
4. Title companies
5. Assessment records
6. Mortgage loan records
7. Real estate brokers' files
8. Government and private mortgage insurers
9. Atlases and survey maps

10. Other appraisers
11. Real estate newspapers
12. Special publications
13. General circulation newspapers
14. SREA Market Data Center
15. Miscellaneous sources

<u>**Fannie Mae   June 30, 2002   Part XI Chapter 4, Section 406.01   Sales Comparison Approach to Value**</u>
Verification Source
The appraiser's opinion of market value is no better than the reliability of the comparable data that is used; therefore, the appraiser must exercise due diligence to ensure the reliability of the comparable sales data that he or she uses. The appraiser must report his or her data and/or verification source(s) for each comparable-sale on the appraisal report' form. An appraiser may use a single source for the data and verifications or multiple sources if they are needed to adequately verify the comparable sales. The quality of the data available varies from source to source and from one locality to another. In view of this, a single data source may be adequate if the appraiser uses a source that provides quality sales data that is confirmed or verified by closed or settled transactions. On the other hand, if the appraiser's basic data source does not confirm or verify the sales data, the appraiser will need to use additional sources. When comparable sales data is provided by a party that has a financial interest in either the sale or financing of the subject property, the appraiser must reverify the data with a party that does not have a financial interest in the subject transaction.

Veterans Benefits Administration   Circular 26-93-25   1993
Sales Comparison Section - Data and/or Verification Sources

The sales comparison analysis adjustment grid was modified to include an entry in which the appraiser reports the data and/or verification sources for the comparable sales (to assure compliance with the Uniform Standards requirement that the appraiser verify comparable market data). An appraiser may use a single source for the data and verifications or may use multiple sources if they are needed to adequately verify the comparable sales. The quality of the data available for single-family residential properties varies from source to source and from one locality to another. In view of this, a single data source may be adequate if the appraiser uses a source that provides quality sales data that are confirmed or verified by closed or settled transactions. On the other hand, if the appraiser's basic data source does not confirm or verify the sales data, the appraiser will need to use additional sources.

MODEL COMMENTS: The following are examples of explanatory remarks reviewers find useful. They are especially important when data on the subject property falls outside the normal range. Usually these comments require customization to reflect the special characteristics of the specific property being appraised.

COMPS ARE ALL CLOSED SALES:

    All comparable sales are closed sales.

COMMENT ON WHERE COMPS WERE SEARCHED FOR:

    In order to locate comparable sales, the following sources were used: _____ (office data file, public records, MLS, SREA Data Center, Commercial Record, appraiser's own files, etc.).

SALES COMPARISON ANALYSIS

| VALUE ADJUSTMENTS | | Sales or Financing Concessions |

ITEM	SUBJECT	COMPARABLE NO. 1	COMPARABLE NO. 2	COMPARABLE NO. 3
Sales or Financing Concessions				
Location				
Leasehold/Fee Simple				

Sales or Financing Concessions adjustments are different from all of the other adjustments in the **SALES COMPARISON ANALYSIS** grid in that there is no **DESCRIPTION** in the **SUBJECT** column. Concessions that are involved in the comparables but not the subject are described and adjusted for in the appropriate **COMPARABLE** column. Fannie Mae requires that these adjustments be negative. Any properties requiring positive adjustments cannot be considered as comparables. All adjustments should reflect the difference between the comparable's actual **Sales Price** and what the property would have sold for without any concessions.

The following examples show how to make minus adjustments when the buyer of **COMPARABLE NO. 1** is able to assume or obtain a VA mortgage in a market where this type of financing is atypical. A minus adjustment is also made when the seller of **COMPARABLE NO. 2** pays an FHA or other financing fee.

VALUE ADJUSTMENTS	DESCRIPTION	DESCRIPTION	+ (-) $ Adjustment	DESCRIPTION	+ (-) $ Adjustment
Sales or Financing Concessions		Buyer assumed V.A. mortgage	-2,500	Seller paid FHA fee	-1,600.
Date of Sale/Time					

Below are examples of plus adjustments (<u>not allowed by FNMA</u>, but acceptable under FHA/VA regulations) made to reflect the fact that the seller received consideration in addition to the reported sale price.

VALUE ADJUSTMENTS	DESCRIPTION	DESCRIPTION	+ (-) $ Adjustment	DESCRIPTION	+ (-) $ Adjustment
Sales or Financing Concessions		Seller given 6 Mo Occup.	+3,200.	Buyer gave Seller boat	+6,000
Date of Sale/Time					

Sales or Financing Concessions

The dollar amount of sales or financing concessions paid by the seller must be reported for the comparable sides if the information is reasonably available. Examples of sales or financing concessions include interest rate buydowns or other below-market rate financing; loan discount points; loan origination fees; closing costs customarily paid by the buyer; payment of condominium, PUD, or cooperative fees or assessment charges; refunds of (or credit for) the borrower's expenses; absorption of monthly payments; assignment of rent payments; and the inclusion of non-realty items in the transaction.

Generally, sales or financing data for comparable sales—such as the mortgage amount, loan type, interest rate, term, and any fees or concessions the seller paid—is available. The appraiser should obtain this information from an individual who was a party to the comparable transaction (the broker, buyer, or seller) or from a data source that the appraiser considers to be reliable. We recognize that there may be some situations in which sales or financing information is not available because of legal restrictions or other disclosure-related problems. In such cases, the appraiser must explain why the information is not available—however, we will not accept an explanation that indicates that the appraiser did not make an effort to verify the information. <u>In all other cases, the appraiser must provide the sales and financing concession information that was available (and verified) for the comparable sales.</u> If the appraisal report form does not provide enough space to discuss this information, the appraiser should make an adjustment (or a relative relationship assessment) for the concessions on the form and include an explanation in an addendum to the appraisal report.

When a quantitative sales comparison analysis is used, the amount of the negative dollar adjustment for each comparable with sales or financing concessions should be equal to any increase in the purchase price of the comparable that the appraiser determines to be attributable to the concessions. The need to make negative dollar adjustments for sales and financing concessions and the amount of the adjustments to the comparable sales are not based on how typical the, concessions might be for a segment of the market area—large sales concessions can be relatively typical in a particular segment of the market and still result in sale prices that reflect more than the value of the real estate. Adjustments based on mechanical, dollar-for-dollar deductions that are equal to the cost of the concessions to the seller (as a strict cash equivalency approach would dictate) are not appropriate. We recognize that the effect of the sales concessions on sales prices can vary with the amount of the concessions and differences in various markets. The adjustments must reflect the difference between what the comparables actually sold for with the sales concessions and what they would have sold for without the concessions so that the dollar amount of the adjustments will approximate the reaction of the market to the concessions.

Positive adjustments (or relative relationship assessments) for sales or financing concessions are not acceptable. For example, if local tradition or law results in virtually all of the property sellers in the market area paying a 1% loan origination fee for the purchaser, and a property seller in that market did not pay any loan fees or concessions for the purchaser, the sale would be considered as a cash equivalent sale in that market. The appraiser should recognize comparable sales that sold for all cash or with cash equivalent financing and use them as comparable sales if they are the best indicators of value for the subject property. Such sales can also be useful to the appraiser in determining those costs that are normally paid by sellers as the result of tradition or law in the market area.

MODEL COMMENTS: The following are examples of explanatory remarks reviewers find useful. They are especially important when data on the subject property falls outside the normal range. Usually these comments require customization to reflect the special characteristics of the specific property being appraised.

COMMENT ON VERIFICATION OF SALES OR FINANCING CONCESSIONS:

    The comparable sales _____ (were, were not) verified and the appraiser was _____ (able, unable) to ascertain that there were _____ (no, significant) sales concessions, special financing or other special considerations.

CONSISTENCY CHECK: Information in this section of the URAR relates to another section of the form as indicated below. The appraiser should check to make sure data in both places is consistent!

SALES COMPARISON ANALYSIS - SUBJECT: Sales or Financing Concessions
    should consider
COMMENTS - General market conditions.

SALES COMPARISON ANALYSIS

| VALUE ADJUSTMENTS | | Date of Sale/Time | |

ITEM	SUBJECT	COMPARABLE NO. 1	COMPARABLE NO. 2	COMPARABLE NO. 3
VALUE ADJUSTMENTS	DESCRIPTION	DESCRIPTION　+ (-) $ Adjustment	DESCRIPTION　+ (-) $ Adjustment	DESCRIPTION　+ (-) $ Adjustment
Sales or Financing				
Date of Sale/Time				
Leasehold/Fee Simple				

The appraiser is now required by FNMA to report both a contract date and a closing date for the comparables in the **Date of Sale/Time** space. If one of the dates is unavailable, the sale date reported must be identified as either the contract date or the closing date. Also, if only the contract date is reported, a comment must be added stating that the sales have, in fact, closed.

Fannie Mae   June 30, 2002   Part XI Chapter 4, Section 406.05   Sales Comparison Approach
Date of sale/time adjustment
We will accept more than three comparable sales as part of the appraisal report, but at least three of them must be actual settled or closed sales. The appraiser should provide the date of the sales contract and the settlement or closing date for each comparable sale. Unless the appraiser believes that the exact date is necessary to understand the adjustments, only the month and year of the sale need to be reported. If the appraiser does not report both the contract date and the settlement or closing date, he or she must identify the reported sale date as either the "contract date" or the "settlement or closing date." If the appraiser reports the contract date only, he or she must state whether the contract resulted in a settlement or a closing.

Fannie Mae   June 30, 2002   Part XI Chapter 4, Section 406.02   Sales Comparison Approach
Selection of Comparable Sales
The appraiser must report a minimum of three comparable sales as part of the sales comparison approach to value. The appraiser may submit more than three comparable sales to support his or her opinion of market value, as long as at least three are actual settled or closed sales. Generally, the appraiser should use comparable sales that have been settled or closed within the last 12 months. However, the appraiser may use older comparable sales if he or she believes that it is appropriate, and selects comparable sales that are the best indicators of value for the subject property The appraiser must comment on the reasons for using any comparable sales that are more than six months old. For example, if the subject property is located in a rural area that has minimal sales activity, the appraiser may not be able to locate three truly comparable sales that sold in the last 12 months. In this case, the appraiser may use older comparable sales as long as he or she explains why they are being used.

MODEL COMMENTS: The following are examples of explanatory remarks reviewers find useful. They are especially important when data on the subject property falls outside the normal range. Usually these comments require customization to reflect the special characteristics of the specific property being appraised.

WHEN COMPS OVER SIX MONTHS OLD ARE USED:

    A thorough search for comparable sales was made in this market area. Comparables that sold within 6 months of the date of the appraisal were significantly different in _____ (location, size, age, condition, special conditions, style, etc.). In the appraiser's judgment, the comparables selected are a better indication of the subject's value than more recent sales. Market studies serve as the basis for making the required time adjustment.

WHEN ONLY CLOSING DATE(S) ARE REPORTED:

    The _____ (date, dates) of sale reported for _____ (the subject property, Comparable #1, Comparable #2, etc.) _____ (is, are) the closing _____ (date, dates).

WHEN ONLY CONTRACT DATE(S) ARE REPORTED:

    The _____ (date, dates) of sale reported for _____ (the subject property, Comparable #1, Comparable #2, etc.) _____ (is, are) the contract _____ (date, dates). All of the sales have closed as of the date of this appraisal.

CONSISTENCY CHECK: Information in this section of the URAR relates to another section of the form as indicated below. The appraiser should check to make sure data in both places is consistent!

SALES COMPARISON ANALYSIS - SUBJECT: Date of Sale/Time
    contains the
SUBJECT - Date of Sale.

SALES COMPARISON ANALYSIS

VALUE ADJUSTMENTS — Location

ITEM	SUBJECT	COMPARABLE NO. 1		COMPARABLE NO. 2		COMPARABLE NO. 3	
VALUE ADJUSTMENTS	DESCRIPTION	DESCRIPTION	+ (-) $ Adjustment	DESCRIPTION	+ (-) $ Adjustment	DESCRIPTION	+ (-) $ Adjustment
Sales or Financing Concessions							
Location							

Give an overall quality rating (good, average, fair, etc.) for the **Location** of the subject and a comparison rating (superior, equal or inferior) for the comparables. Then make the adjustment indicated by the market for any differences between the comparables and the subject property.

The best way to obtain a location adjustment is to use *matched pairs.* This technique involves finding a pair of houses in the area which are similar except that one is in the neighborhood for which a location adjustment is sought, while the other is in the neighborhood of the house being appraised. After adjusting the prices for any other discrepancies between the sales, the remaining price difference are attributable to their difference in location. This price difference then can be used as a location adjustment.

Below is an example of how the location adjustment is made when the value of the property being appraised is greater than that of the comparable sales. **COMPARABLE NO.1** and **COMPARABLE NO. 2** are both less valuable because properties which are near their location sold for less than similar properties which sold and are located nearer to the location of the property being appraised.

Date of Sale/Time							
Location	Average	Inferior	+3,000.	Inferior	+3,000.		
Site/View							

The next example shows how adjustments are made when the value of the comparable sales is greater than the value of the property being appraised. In this example, **COMPARABLE NO.1** and **COMPARABLE NO. 2** are each more valuable because properties near their location sold for more than similar properties near the location of the house being appraised.

Date of Sale/Time					
Location	Average	Superior	-800.	Superior	-1,300
Site/View					

MODEL COMMENTS: The following are examples of explanatory remarks reviewers find useful. They are especially important when data on the subject property falls outside the normal range. Usually these comments require customization to reflect the special characteristics of the specific property being appraised.

COMPS OVER ONE MILE AWAY USED:

    Comparable sales over one mile away were used because they are the best available in this _____ (small community, rural area, neighborhood). Expanding the search to a radius greater than 1 mile developed sales that are still within the same market. These sales are the best comparables to the subject property and are therefore used in this report.

WHEN COMPS FROM A DIFFERENT NEIGHBORHOOD OR SCHOOL DISTRICT ARE USED:

    A thorough search for comparable sales was made in this _____ (neighborhood, school district). These comparable sales have significantly different _____ (dates of sale, sizes, ages, conditions, special conditions, styles, etc.). In the appraiser's judgment the comparables selected are the best indication of the value of the subject. Studies using _____ [technique, i.e. matched pairs] serve as the basis for making the required location adjustment.

CONSISTENCY CHECK: Information in this section of the URAR relates to another section of the form as indicated below. The appraiser should check to make sure data in both places is consistent!

SALES COMPARISON ANALYSIS - SUBJECT: Location
    rating must be consistent with the
NEIGHBORHOOD - Marketing conditions analysis

SALES COMPARISON ANALYSIS

| VALUE ADJUSTMENTS | | Leasehold/Fee Simple | | | | | |

ITEM	SUBJECT	COMPARABLE NO. 1		COMPARABLE NO. 2		COMPARABLE NO. 3	
VALUE ADJUSTMENTS	DESCRIPTION	DESCRIPTION	+ (-) $ Adjustment	DESCRIPTION	+ (-) $ Adjustment	DESCRIPTION	+ (-) $ Adjustment
Sales or Financing Concessions							
Date of Sale/Time							
Leasehold/Fee Simple							

When the subject property is in "fee simple" form of ownership, it is preferable to use comparable sales that are also in "fee simple" ownership. If it is necessary to use a comparable sale that is a "leasehold," a significant adjustment may be required to reflect that the site value is not part of a "leasehold" sale price. •

When the subject property is a "leasehold" form of ownership, it is preferable to use comparable sales that are also in "leasehold" ownership. If it is necessary to use a comparable sale that is in "fee simple" ownership, a significant adjustment may be required to reflect that the value of the site is not included in the appraised value of the subject property.

SALES COMPARISON ANALYSIS

VALUE ADJUSTMENTS | **Site**

ITEM	SUBJECT	COMPARABLE NO. 1	COMPARABLE NO. 2	COMPARABLE NO. 3
Site				
Design and Appeal				
Quality of Construction				

An overall quality rating of good, average, fair or poor is to be given for the subject property and a comparison rating, as indicated under **Location** above, should be provided for the **Site** for each comparable. Factors to be considered by the appraiser under **Site** include size, shape, topography, drainage, encroachments, easements or any detrimental site conditions.

Again, the best way to estimate any adjustment for the physical characteristics of the site is to use matched pairs. Find properties that have physical characteristics similar to that for which the adjustment is being sought, and which have sold. Compare these sales with other properties without these characteristics which are otherwise very similar. After adjustments are made for any other differences, the remainder can be attributed to the difference in physical characteristics.

Below is an example of how the **Site** adjustment is made when the value of the property being appraised is greater than that of the comparables. Each comparable is less valuable than the subject because properties with similar physical characteristics (a stream) sold for less than those without a stream.

Leasehold/Fee Simple						
Site	Good (stream)	Avg. (no strm)	+3,000	Avg. (no strm)	+3,000	
View						

The example below shows how adjustments are made when the site of the comparable sale is better than that of the property being appraised. In this example, **COMPARABLE NO.1** and **COMPARABLE NO. 2** were each more valuable when they sold than a similar property without their special attribute of bigger size.

Leasehold/Fee Simple					
Site	Average (½Ac)	Good (1 Ac.)	−5,000	Excl. (2Ac.)	−10,000
View					

SALES COMPARISON ANALYSIS

VALUE ADJUSTMENTS — View

ITEM	SUBJECT	COMPARABLE NO. 1	COMPARABLE NO. 2	COMPARABLE NO. 3
View				
Quality of Construction				

An overall quality rating of good, average, fair or poor is to be given for the subject property and a comparison rating, as indicated under **Location** above, should be provided for the **View** for each comparable.

Again, the best way to estimate any adjustment for the view of the site is to use matched pairs. Find properties that have a view similar to that for which the adjustment is being sought, and which have sold. Compare these sales with other properties without these characteristics which are otherwise very similar. After adjustments are made for any other differences, the remainder can be attributed to the difference in view.

Below is an example of how the **View** adjustment is made when the value of the property being appraised is greater than that of the comparables. Each comparable is less valuable than the subject because properties with similar view sold for less than those without them.

Site				
View	Excl.(water)	Good(no wtr.) +7,000	Good(no wtr.) +7,000	
Design and Appeal				

The example below shows how adjustments are made when the view of the comparable sale is better than that of the property being appraised. In this example, **COMPARABLE NO.1** and **COMPARABLE NO. 2** were each more valuable when they sold than a similar property without their special attribute of better view.

Site				
View	Avg. (no water)	Good (Part water) −2,000	V.Good(water) −5,000	
Design and Appeal				

8-24

SALES COMPARISON ANALYSIS

VALUE ADJUSTMENTS	Design and Appeal

ITEM	SUBJECT	COMPARABLE NO. 1	COMPARABLE NO. 2	COMPARABLE NO. 3
Leasehold/Fee Simple				
Site				
Design and Appeal				

The **Design and Appeal** category considers such aspects of the property as appeal of exterior design, interior attractiveness and special features. Also included are any other characteristics which would change the property's attractiveness to purchasers in general or otherwise alter its marketability. The appraiser is to give comparison ratings, as indicated for the preceding items above, for each of the comparables. The appropriate adjustments may then be made.

Appraisers must be careful when making the **Design and Appeal** adjustment to reflect the standards of the market rather than their own personal standards.

The exterior design of the residence will often affect the value. This is especially true when the design is different from the majority of houses in the market. This does not mean that the style and type must conform exactly with the rest of the neighborhood. In many areas, the public's taste has changed and the old principle of uniformity no longer applies as it did in the past. Now, in both old and new neighborhoods, Colonial, European and Contemporary styles and even commercial and industrial uses all coexist in harmony.

More important is the public's increasing awareness of good design and the rejection of poor design. The Post World War II badly designed tract house, for example, may have suffered little or no functional obsolescence in the market when it was new, but now, may be heavily penalized for inferior design. As a general rule, a well designed house will have more value and depreciate slower than a poorly designed house in the same neighborhood, in similar condition.

Below is an example of how the **Design and Appeal** adjustment is made when the value of the property being appraised is greater than that of the comparable sales. **COMPARABLE NO. 1** and **COMPARABLE NO. 2** are each less valuable because their design and appeal is inferior to that of the property being appraised.

Site/View						
Design and Appeal	Average	Fair/Inf.	+1,800.	Fair/Inf.	+1,600.	
Quality of Construction						

Next is an example that first shows how an adjustment is made when the value of the comparable sale is greater than the property being appraised. In the example, **COMPARABLE NO. 1** is more valuable because its design and appeal is superior to the house being appraised. In the second example, design and appeal of **COMPARABLE NO. 2** is the same as the house being appraised. Therefore, no adjustment is needed.

Site/View					
Design and Appeal	Average	Good/Sup	-2,000.	Average/Same	-0-
Quality of Construction					

CONSISTENCY CHECK: Information in this section of the URAR relates to another section of the form as indicated below. The appraiser should check to make sure data in both places is consistent!

<u>**SALES COMPARISON ANALYSIS**</u> - **SUBJECT: Design and Appeal**
    rating should consider

<u>**IMPROVEMENTS**</u> - **GENERAL DESCRIPTION: Design (Style)**

SALES COMPARISON ANALYSIS

VALUE ADJUSTMENTS		Quality of Constuction		

ITEM	SUBJECT	COMPARABLE NO. 1	COMPARABLE NO. 2	COMPARABLE NO. 3
Site				
View				
Quality of Construction				

The **Quality of Construction** adjustment covers quality of materials and workmanship including exterior walls, roof covering, framing, finish flooring, interior walls, trim, doors, hardware, plumbing and electrical systems, baths, kitchen and mechanical equipment. The appraiser should indicate an overall quality rating for the subject property and give comparison ratings for each of the comparables. Any adjustments should reflect the market's monetary reaction based on these comparisons.

When the house being appraised is constructed either better or poorer than the standard found in the market an adjustment may be needed. Like other adjustments, the best way to obtain it is to find matched pairs of sales. When this is impossible, a judgment should be made as to the impact of the difference in quality on value. If the subject's quality of construction is substantially different, the adjustment may not actually reflect the market's reaction.

Below is an example of how a **Quality of Construction** adjustment is made when value of the property being appraised is greater than the comparable sales. **COMPARABLE NO. 1** and **COMPARABLE NO. 2** are each less valuable because their quality of construction is inferior to that of the property being appraised.

Design and Appeal						
Quality of Construction	Average	Fair/Inf.	+1,200	Fair/Inf	+1,000	
Age						

The following example shows how adjustments are made when the values of **COMPARABLE NO. 1** and **COMPARABLE NO. 2** are both greater than that of the property being appraised. The quality of construction is above average and superior, respectively.

Design and Appeal					
Quality of Construction	Average	Good/Sup.	-1,500	Good/Sup.	-3,000.
Age					

CONSISTENCY CHECK: Information in this section of the URAR relates to another section of the form as indicated below. The appraiser should check to make sure data in both places is consistent!

<u>SALES COMPARISON ANALYSIS</u> - **SUBJECT: Quality of Construction**
     rating also appears as
<u>COMMENTS</u> - **Quality of Construction**

SALES COMPARISON ANALYSIS

| VALUE ADJUSTMENTS | | | Age | |

ITEM	SUBJECT	COMPARABLE NO. 1	COMPARABLE NO. 2	COMPARABLE NO. 3
Age				
Above Grade Room Count	Total | Bdrms | Baths	Total | Bdrms | Baths	Total | Bdrms | Baths	Total | Bdrms | Baths
Gross Living Area	Sq. Ft.	Sq. Ft.	Sq. Ft.	Sq. Ft.
Basement & Finished Rooms Below Grade				

Indicate "Effective", "Actual" or "Eff../Act." Age

[Handwritten: EFF AGE. IS YOUR ESTIMATE OF A PROPERTY AGE BASED ON AMT OF WEAR & TEAR IT HAS SUSTAINED.]

The **Age** line may be used to adjust for either the actual age, effective age or both. Differences in age (either actual or effective) between the subject property and the comparable sales may require adjustment. To avoid confusion, the appraiser should indicate which age is being adjusted for by writing "Actual", "Effective" or "Act./Eff" as appropriate after the word **Age**.

The following shows the way to make adjustments for differences in effective age when **COMPARABLE NO. 1** and **COMPARABLE NO. 2** have effective ages (18 and 16 Yrs. respectively) greater than that of the subject property (14 Yrs).

Quality of Construction						
Age Effective	14 Yrs	18 Yrs/Inf	+800.	16 Yrs/Inf	+600.	
Condition						

The below example shows how adjustments are made when the value of the comparable sales is greater than the property being appraised. In this example, **COMPARABLE NO. 1** and **COMPARABLE NO. 2** are each more valuable based on their age because their actual ages of 12 and 10 years are both less than the house being appraised.

Quality of Construction						
Age Actual	14 Years	12 Yrs/Sup	-800	10 Yrs/Sup	-1,600.	
Condition						

This example shows how adjustments are made when the value of the comparable sales is greater and less than the property being appraised. **COMPARABLE NO. 1** is inferior because its effective and actual is greater than the subject and **COMPARABLE NO. 2** is superior because its effective age and actual age are less than the house being appraised.. In this example both the effective age and the actual age is reported. The adjustment is based on the effective age.

Quality of Construction						
Age Act/Eff	14Yrs/14Yrs	20/15 Inf.	+2,000	10/10 Sup.	-1,500	
Condition						

Notes

SALES COMPARISON ANALYSIS

| VALUE ADJUSTMENTS | Condition |

ITEM	SUBJECT	COMPARABLE NO. 1	COMPARABLE NO. 2	COMPARABLE NO. 3
Condition				
Room Count				
Gross Living Area	Sq. Ft.	Sq. Ft.	Sq. Ft.	Sq. Ft.
Basement & Finished Rooms Below Grade				

The **Condition** line includes the appraiser's opinion of the subject property's condition (whether good, average, fair or poor), comparison ratings (superior, equal or inferior) for the comparables, and adjustments made as indicated by the market.

The **Condition** adjustment should be limited to items that have not already been included in the **Age** adjustment. It would be a mistake to increase the effective age of a residence because of its condition, and also make adjustment here for the same condition factors.

One way to prevent duplication is to restrict the **Condition** adjustment to items of physical deterioration-<u>curable</u>. The items of physical deterioration-<u>incurable</u>, then, are included in the **Age** adjustment. The cost-to-cure acts as a guide to the amount of depreciation here. The reason such items are classified as curable is that they will, when taken care of, add value equal to or greater than the cost to cure them.

Below is an example of how the **Condition** adjustment is made when value of the subject property is greater than both **COMPARABLE NO. 1** and **COMPARABLE NO. 2**, because they are in poorer condition.

Age							
Condition	Average	Fair/Inf.	+2,000.	Poor/ Inf.	+6,000.		
Above Grade	Total | Bdrms | Baths	Total | Bdrms | Baths		Total | Bdrms | Baths			

The following example shows how adjustments are made when the value of the comparable sales is greater than the property being appraised. In this example, **COMPARABLE NO. 1** and **COMPARABLE NO. 2** are each more valuable because they are both in better condition.

Age					
Condition	Average	Good/Sup.	−2,000.	Good/Sup.	−3,000.
Above Grade	Total | Bdrms | Baths	Total | Bdrms | Baths		Total | Bdrms | Baths	

CONSISTENCY CHECK: Information in this section of the URAR relates to another section of the form as indicated below. The appraiser should check to make sure data in both places is consistent!

SALES COMPARISON ANALYSIS - SUBJECT: Condition
    also appears as the
INTERIOR - Material/Condition
    rating. Both ratings will also be affected if there is a significant difference between
IMPROVEMENTS - GENERAL DESCRIPTION: Age (Yrs.) and Effective Age (Yrs.).

SALES COMPARISON ANALYSIS

| VALUE ADJUSTMENTS | Above Grade Room Count, Gross Living Area |

ITEM	SUBJECT	COMPARABLE NO. 1	COMPARABLE NO. 2	COMPARABLE NO. 3
Age				
Above Grade Room Count	Total / Bdrms / Baths	Total / Bdrms / Baths	Total / Bdrms / Baths	Total / Bdrms / Baths
Gross Living Area	Sq. Ft.	Sq. Ft.	Sq. Ft.	Sq. Ft.
Rooms Below Grade				

The appraiser is to report the total **Above Grade Room Count** including the number of bedrooms and baths. Adjustments reflective of the market maybe needed for any differences between the room count of the subject property and the comparable sale. The appraiser may elect to make a separate adjustment for differences in room count or combine it with the GLA adjustment.

Adjusting for the number of rooms must be done very carefully. More than likely, most of the difference in value has already been adjusted for when the **Gross Living Area** adjustment is made. In contrast, the adjustment of an extra bath or a deficiency in baths is often greater than just the square foot adjustment involved.

Also, make sure that all adjustments made here are for <u>above</u> grade rooms. Any below grade or partially below grade rooms should <u>not</u> be included in GLA and are adjusted for under **Basement & Finished Rooms Below Grade**.

Below is an example of how the **Above Grade Room Count** adjustment is made when value of the property being appraised is greater than the comparable sales. In this case, **COMPARABLE NO. 1** and **COMPARABLE NO. 2** are each less valuable than the subject. **COMPARABLE NO. 1** has only 1 1/2 baths as compared with the 2 baths in the house being appraised while **COMPARABLE NO. 2** has one less room and only one bath.

Condition						
Above Grade Room Count	Total / Bdrms / Baths 8 / 3 / 2	Total / Bdrms / Baths 8 / 3 / 1.5	+ 3,000	Total / Bdrms / Baths 7 / 2 / 1	+ 12,000
Gross Living Area	2,000 Sq. Ft.	2,000 Sq. Ft.		1,900 Sq. Ft.	

Fannie Mae   June 30, 2002   Part XI Chapter 4, Section 406.05   Sales Comparison Approach
Above-grade room count and gross living area

Only finished above-grade areas should be included in the calculation of the gross living area for a one-family property or a unit in a condominium or PUD project. The appraiser should consider the basement and other partially below-grade areas separately and adjust for them accordingly. The room count and gross living area should be similar for the subject property and all comparable sales. For example, a four bedroom comparable sale generally is not acceptable to support the value of a two bedroom subject property. The appraiser must address large differences between the subject property and the comparable sales since they raise doubts about the validity of the comparable sales as good indicators of value.

MODEL COMMENTS: The following are examples of explanatory remarks reviewers find useful. They are especially important when data on the subject property falls outside the normal range. Usually these comments require customization to reflect the special characteristics of the specific property being appraised.

WHEN THE NUMBER OF ROOMS IS TYPICAL:

The number of rooms, bedrooms, baths and lavatories is typical of houses in this neighborhood. Foyers, laundry rooms and all rooms below grade are excluded from the total room count.

TOO FEW BEDROOMS:

The number of bedrooms is less than what is typical in this market. This has _____ (no, a) negative effect on the value of the property.

DISSIMILAR NUMBER OF BATHROOMS OR BEDROOMS:

The number of _____ (baths, bedrooms) is _____ (less, more) than what is typical in this market. A deduction for value _____ (is, is not) being made since there is _____ (a negative, no) effect on marketability.

EXTRA BEDROOMS:

The comparable sale has more bedrooms than the subject property. In this market, houses with extra bedrooms sell for more than houses with the standard _____ three bedrooms. Part of this difference is reflected in the additional square footage of the extra bedroom(s). The extra bedroom room adjustment reflects the extra addition to value caused by the extra bedroom in excess of the value increase caused by the increase in GLA.

EXTRA BATHROOMS

The comparable sale has _____(number) more bathrooms than the subject property. For this type of property in this market the number of bathrooms that is standard is ____(number). In this market houses with more bathrooms sell for more than houses with fewer bathrooms. Part of this difference is reflected in the additional square footage of the extra bathroom(s). The extra bathroom room adjustment reflects the extra addition to value caused by the extra bathroom in excess of the value increase caused by the increase in GLA

CONSISTENCY CHECK: Information in this section of the URAR relates to another section of the form as indicated below. The appraiser should check to make sure data in both places is consistent!

SALES COMPARISON ANALYSIS - SUBJECT: Above Grade Room Count Gross Living Area; Total, Bdrms, Baths and Sq. Ft.
are all filled with data from the

ROOM LIST -
"Finished area **above** grade contains:" line.

The appraiser is to report the total sq. ft. **Gross Living Area** (GLA) for the subject property and for each comparable. Adjustments reflective of the market are to be made for each foot of differnce.

Some appraisers make an adjustment whenever there is a difference between the GLA of the subject property and a comparable sale. Others feel that in some markets it not necessary to make an adjustment for small differences in GLA.

Multiple Regression Analysis of house sales done by computer has shown repeatedly that the single most important variable affecting the value of a residence is its size. All but very small GLA differences usually require adjustment. Small adjustments for size differences can often be based on the selling price per square foot. However, when size adjustments are made for houses that have not actually been measured by the appraiser, the possibility of an error is substantial.

One of the major ongoing problems encountered by appraisers is inaccurate measurements, especially for comparable sales. Part of the problem is that many people taking measurements are unfamiliar with the standard system used to obtain Gross Living Area. Those unfamiliar with the system will often include finished attic and basement space in their measurements or use some inside measurements. Another problem is that some appraisers, even those familiar with the system, measure inaccurately.

Adjusting for GLA differences must be done very carefully. More than likely, most of the difference in value has already been adjusted for when the **Room Count** adjustment is made.

Below is an example of how the total **Gross Living Area** adjustment is made when value of the property being appraised is greater than the comparable sales. In this case, **COMPARABLE NO. 1** and **COMPARABLE NO. 2** are each less valuable than the subject. **COMPARABLE NO. 1** is smaller as compared with the house being appraised and **COMPARABLE NO. 2** is also smaller. The adjustment for differences in GLA in this example is $75.00 per sq. ft. GLA.

Condition										
Above Grade	Total	Bdrms	Baths	Total	Bdrms	Baths		Total	Bdrms	Baths
Room Count	8	3	2	8	3	2	+3,750	8	3	2
Gross Living Area	1,900	Sq. Ft.		1,850	Sq. Ft.			1,775	Sq. Ft.	+9,375
Basement & Finished										

The following guidelines will help you correctly calculate the/ **Gross Living Area** of the comparable sales:

1. Measure around the outside of the house above the foundation.
2. In multi-floor houses count each floor above grade.
3. Include all of the above grade habitable living area.
4. Do not include the basement (even when it is finished and heated).
5. Garages are never included in the GLA.
6. Porches are included only when they are heated and finished in a way similar in quality to the rest of the house.
7. Upper stories are divided into two areas.
    a. Attic is the unfinished part or that part with low ceilings (below 5ft.).
    b. Habitable area finished and heated substantially like the rest of the house with normal ceiling heights (5ft. is the most common height used by appraisers as normal ceiling height in attics).

Note : (See Description of Improvements section for more details on how to determine the GLA).

SALES COMPARISON ANALYSIS" adjustment grid. To assure consistency in the sales comparison analysis, the appraiser generally should compare above-grade areas to above-grade areas and below-grade areas to below-grade areas. The appraiser may deviate from this approach if the style of the subject property or of any of the comparables does not lend itself to such comparisons. However, in such instances, he or she must explain the reason for the deviation and clearly describe the comparisons that were made.

CONSISTENCY CHECK: Information in this section of the URAR relates to another section of the form as indicated below. The appraiser should check to make sure data in both places is consistent!

Room Count & Gross Living Area:

The Gross Living Area and Room Count appear in many places on the URAR and in the addenda. All the figures should be consistent. When a different measuring system is used in the Cost Approach this should be clearly noted in the report.

SALES COMPARISON ANALYSIS

| VALUE ADJUSTMENTS | Basement & Finished Rooms Below Grade |

ITEM	SUBJECT	COMPARABLE NO. 1	COMPARABLE NO. 2	COMPARABLE NO. 3
Address				
Age				
Condition				
Above Grade Room Count	Total | Bdrms | Baths	Total | Bdrms | Baths	Total | Bdrms | Baths	Total | Bdrms | Baths
Gross Living Area	Sq. Ft.	Sq. Ft.	Sq. Ft.	Sq. Ft.
Basement & Finished Rooms Below Grade				

The **Basement & Finished Rooms Below Grade** adjustment should include any basement or other fully or partially below grade improvements found in the subject property and the comparables. If there is no basement (in a house with a slab or crawl space) or only a partial basement, this should also be indicated. Appropriate adjustments must then be made to reflect differences between the comparables and the subject property.

When the measurement system is the Gross Living Area system as required for this appraisal form, special care is needed to correctly adjust for all differences between the subject and comparables in <u>one</u> and <u>only one place</u>. Make sure that the comparables have been measured using the GLA system and that any adjustments made in the **Above Grade Room Count Gross Living Area** and **Other** sections are not duplicated here. At the same time, check to make sure all differences between the subject and comparables are adjusted for somewhere in an appropriate section.

The **Basement & Finished Rooms Below Grade** adjustment is really two separate adjustments combined into one. First, there is the adjustment for full basement versus partial basement versus crawl space versus slab. In many markets, there are significant value differences between similar houses with these various foundations. In areas where basements are expected by the typical buyer, houses without basements often sell for substantially less than similar houses with basements. Conversely, in markets where most houses are built on a slab or over a crawl space, there may be little or no premium paid for houses with basements.

The second adjustment is for that portion of the basement that is finished. Prior to the adoption of the Gross Living Area measurement system, many appraisals included finished, heated basement in the overall square footage of living area. When using the GLA system, the finished basement is <u>not</u> included, so any adjustment must be made here. Note that using cost figures, rather than value contribution estimated from the market, will often lead to errors in the indicated value.

Below is an example of how the **Basement and Finished Rooms Below Grade** adjustment should be made when the basement of the property being appraised is more valuable than the comparable sales. **COMPARABLE NO. 1** and **COMPARABLE NO. 2** are both less valuable because **NO. 1** has no recreation room and **NO. 2** is on a slab.

Room Count					
Gross Living Area	Sq. Ft.	Sq. Ft.		Sq. Ft.	
Basement & Finished Rooms Below Grade	Half basement Recreation Rm	Half basement No Rec. Rm.	+2,000.	Slab No Rec. Rm.	+5,000.
Functional Utility					

The below example shows how adjustments are made when the basement value of each comparable is greater than that of the property being appraised. In this example **COMPARABLE NO. 1** and **COMPARABLE NO. 2** are more valuable, because **NO. 1** has a full basement and recreation room as does **NO. 2**, which also has a dark room.

Room Count					
Gross Living Area	Sq. Ft.	Sq. Ft.		Sq. Ft.	
Basement & Finished Rooms Below Grade	Crawl Space	Full Basement Recreation Rm.	-3,000.	Full basement Rec. Rm&Drk Rm	-4,500.
Functional Utility					

CONSISTENCY CHECK: Information in this section of the URAR relates to another section of the form as indicated below. The appraiser should check to make sure data in both places is consistent!

<u>SALES COMPARISON ANALYSIS</u> - **SUBJECT: Basement & Finished Rooms Below Grade**
    may contain
<u>IMPROVEMENTS</u> - **BASEMENT: Area Sq. Ft. or % Finished,**
    when the comparables need to be adjusted for these factors.

SALES COMPARISON ANALYSIS

VALUE ADJUSTMENTS		Functional Utility		

ITEM	SUBJECT	COMPARABLE NO. 1	COMPARABLE NO. 2	COMPARABLE NO. 3
Functional Utility				
Energy Efficient Items				
Garage/Carport				

Functional Utility refers to, among other things, room sizes, layout and overall livability. A rating should be given for the subject property which will summarize the ratings for these factors found on the Property Description side of the URAR. Comparison ratings such as those indicated previously for **Location** are to be given for the comparables and appropriate adjustments made to represent the market's reaction to any differences.

The **Functional Utility** adjustment should take into account the size of the rooms in both the subject and comparable sales. Each room should be at least the FHA minimum required size and many markets require rooms be larger than the FHA minimum standards.

Also, any items of functional obsolescence listed under **Depreciation** in the **COMMENTS** section need to be considered in making this adjustment. These include both deficiencies and superadequacies or over-improvements.

Below is an example of how to make **Functional Utility** adjustments. **COMPARABLE NO. 1** has fair functional utility, which is inferior to the appraisal property, and requires a positive adjustment. **COMPARABLE NO. 2**, on the other hand has functional utility superior to the subject and needs a negative adjustment.

Basement & Finished Rooms Below Grade				
Functional Utility	Average	Fair/Inferior +4,500.	Good/Superior −3,200	
Heating/Cooling				

CONSISTENCY CHECK: Information in this section of the URAR relates to another section of the form as indicated below. The appraiser should check to make sure data in both places is consistent!

SALES COMPARISON ANALYSIS - SUBJECT: Functional Utility
    should be consistent with the
COMMENTS - Depreciation
    section, the
COST APPROACH - Functional: Depreciation
    section, or anywhere else in the report should be considered in making this rating.

SALES COMPARISON ANALYSIS

VALUE ADJUSTMENTS	Heating/Cooling

ITEM	SUBJECT	COMPARABLE NO. 1	COMPARABLE NO. 2	COMPARABLE NO. 3
Heating/Cooling				
Garage/Carport				

In most parts of the country, an "Average" Heating system is a standard quality central system fueled by gas, oil or electricity. In some areas one fuel so dominates the market that the appraiser must consider whether a system using another fuel causes functional obsolescence.

Quality heat pump systems and central air conditioning add extra value in most areas. Appropriate adjustments for central air can range from the cost of installation in markets where central air is standard to almost no adjustment when it is considered to be a superadequacy.

Window units provide Cooling in many homes. Appraisers must know whether or not window units are legally classified as real estate in their area. When window units are **not** considered real estate, they should be treated like any other item of personal property included in a sale; their value should **not** be included in the market value estimate.

Again, the matched pairs technique is useful in estimating the amount of **Heating/Cooling** adjustment required.

Below is an example adjustments made for a house with a standard central air conditioning system and a house with a good quality heat pump system which are both superior to the subject in this market.

Functional Utility						
Heating/Cooling	Heat Ave/NoAC	CentAir/Sup.	-4,000	Heat Pump/Sup	-5,000	
Garage/Carport						

CONSISTENCY CHECK: Information in this section of the URAR relates to another section of the form as indicated below. The appraiser should check to make sure data in both places is consistent!

SALES COMPARISON ANALYSIS - SUBJECT: Heating/Cooling

should contain the

INTERIOR - HEATING: Type or Fuel

(if different than standard for the market). This is followed by the

INTERIOR - COOLING: Central

air conditioning) or an abbreviated description of the system (like "2 Wndw", if

INTERIOR - COOLING: Other

is filled). Regardless, information must be consistent on both sides of the form.

SALES COMPARISON ANALYSIS

VALUE ADJUSTMENTS	Energy Efficient Items

ITEM	SUBJECT	COMPARABLE NO. 1	COMPARABLE NO. 2	COMPARABLE NO. 3
Functional Utility				
Heating/Cooling				
Energy Efficient Items				

Energy Efficient Items often are installed at a cost exceeding their contribution to the value of the residence. Any difference the appraiser estimates to exist between the cost of these items and the value on the date of the appraisal should be divided between physical deterioration and functional obsolescence.

Here is a list of some of the items that are considered to be **Energy Efficient Items**:

1. Solar heating
2. Solar domestic hot water system
3. Extra insulation
4. Special insulated window glass
5. Automatic thermostat controls
6. Automatic flue opening and closing devices
7. Electric use monitors
8. Special furnace controls with outdoor temperature monitors
9. Any wind or hydroelectric power device

Fannie Mae June 30, 2002 part XI Chapter 4, Section 405.03 Insulation and Energy Efficiency
Some of our appraisal report forms provide an area for the appraiser to state the "R" value for insulation (if he or she is aware of it) and to comment on the adequacy of the insulation. The appraiser should list the additional energy-efficient features in the "comments" area. The appraiser should also compare the energy-efficient features of the subject property to those of the comparable properties in the "sales comparison analysis" grid to assure that the overall contribution of these items is reflected in his or her opinion of the market value of the subject property. An energy-efficient property is one that uses cost-effective design, materials, equipment, and site orientation to conserve nonrenewable fuels. Special energy saving items should be recognized in the appraisal process The nature of these items and their contribution to value will vary throughout the country because of climactic conditions and differences in utility costs.

CONSISTENCY CHECK: Information in this section of the URAR relates to another section of the form *as* indicated below. The appraiser should check to make sure data in both places is consistent!

SALES COMPARISON ANALYSIS - SUBJECT: Energy Efficient items
    should consider information from the
COMMENTS - Additional features (special energy efficient Items)
    space.

SALES COMPARISON ANALYSIS

VALUE ADJUSTMENTS		Garage/Carport	

ITEM	SUBJECT	COMPARABLE NO. 1	COMPARABLE NO. 2	COMPARABLE NO. 3
Functional Utility				
Heating/Cooling				
Energy Efficient Items				
Garage/Carport				

Garage/Carport adjustments are based on whether the subject property and the comparables have garages or carports and, if so, their car storage capacity. The increase or decrease in value should not necessarily represent the cost of construction but should rather be based on the market's response.

In many areas the market is very sensitive to the influence that garages and carports have on the value of a property. Often there is a market standard or price range within a neighborhood and properties which do not conform to the standard suffer substantial depreciation. For example, the market may expect a two-car attached garage. The construction cost differential between a two-car attached garage and a one-car attached garage may be about $3,000, yet matched pairs of sales will indicate a $5,000 sales price differential. In the same market, a property with a three-car attached garage may sell for only $1,000 more than one with a two-car attached garage. The use of cost as a value indication would therefore result in a substantial error.

Below is an example of how a **Garage/Carport** adjustment should be made in the market described above.

Heating/Cooling						
Garage/Carport	2 car att.gar	1car att gar	+5,000	3car att gar	-1,000
Porches, Patio, Pools, etc.					

CONSISTENCY CHECK: Information in this section of the URAR relates to another section of the form as indicated below. The appraiser should check to make sure data in both places is consistent!

SALES COMPARISON ANALYSIS - SUBJECT: Garage/Carport
   line should be consistent with

CAR STORAGE - None, Garage, # of cars, Attached, Detached, Built-In, Carport, Driveway
   as well as data in the

COST APPROACH - Garage/Carport _____ Sq. Ft.
   blank.

SALES COMPARISON ANALYSIS

| VALUE ADJUSTMENTS | Porch, Patio, Deck, Fireplace(s) - Fence, Pool, etc. |

ITEM	SUBJECT	COMPARABLE NO. 1	COMPARABLE NO. 2	COMPARABLE NO. 3
Porch, Patio, Deck, Fireplace(s), etc.				
Fence, Pool, etc.				

The appraiser should indicate the presence or absence of a **Porch, Patio, Pools, Fireplace(s), Fence, Pool, etc.** or similar exterior building or site improvements and make the necessary adjustments indicated by the market. Cost data may, at times, serve as a guide but is not necessarily indicative since improvements such as pools may not return their entire cost upon resale as added value.

Swimming pools have become a major appraisal problem in many parts of the country. They range from simple above-ground, semi-portable pools to elaborate in-ground pools with pumping and filtering systems. Some even have pool houses with wet bars and cooking facilities (and sometimes sleeping quarters), lighting and heating systems and occasionally, year 'round covers or tops. Regardless, the appraiser must first decide if the pool is part of the real estate to be included in the appraised value. The status of the pool should then be clearly indicated on the report.

As with other adjustments, the best way to estimate the value various kinds of pools add is to use matched pairs. First find houses with pools similar to the pool of the house being appraised, that have sold and other sales of properties that are without pools. After adjusting for other differences, the remaining difference can be attributed to the value of the pool.

In some parts of the country, porches and patios add little or no value to properties; in other areas, they add value greater than their cost. Again, matched pairs of sales are the best indication of the value of such features. When the adjustment is very small, some portion of the porch or patio cost may be used. However, it should be recognized that an adjustment made on this basis is nothing but an educated guess.

Fannie Mae   June 30, 2002   Part XI Chapter 4, Section 406.05   Sales Comparison Approach

Over-Improvements

In some instances, the improvements can represent an over-improvement for the neighborhood, but still be within the neighborhood price range—such as a property with an in-ground swimming pool, a large addition, or an oversized garage in a market that does not demand these kinds of improvements. The appraiser must comment on such over-improvements and indicate their contributory value in the—"sales comparison analysis" adjustment grid.

Because an over-improved property may not be acceptable to the typical purchaser, the lender's underwriter must review appraisals on this type of property carefully to ensure that the appraiser has reflected only the contributory value of the over-improvement in his or her analysis.

CONSISTENCY CHECK: Information in this section of the URAR relates to another section of the form as indicated below. The appraiser should check to make sure data in both places is consistent!

SALES COMPARISON ANALYSIS - SUBJECT: Porch, Patio, Deck, Fireplace(s) etc.:
When a pool, porch or patio, etc. is reported under

COMMENTS - Additional features,
it must also be entered into the space. This should also be consistent with

COST APPROACH - ESTIMATED REPRODUCTION COST: Extras or **Porches, Patios, etc.**

CONSISTENCY CHECK: Information in this section of the URAR relates to another section of the form as indicated below. The appraiser should check to make sure data in both places is consistent!

SALES COMPARISON ANALYSIS - SUBJECT: Fireplace(s)
contains the

INTERIOR - # Fireplace(s).

SALES COMPARISON ANALYSIS

	VALUE ADJUSTMENTS			Other	
ITEM	SUBJECT	COMPARABLE NO. 1	COMPARABLE NO. 2	COMPARABLE NO. 3	
Address					
Porch, Patio, Deck, Fireplace(s), etc.					

The following is a list of some of the items that may be adjusted for in the **Other** section:

    Kitchen: Counters, Cabinets & Built-In equipment and appliances
    Plumbing systems: Special features & fixtures, Deficiencies &
        Special bathroom features
    Domestic hot water system
    Electric: Service (size and age) & Wiring (type and condition)
    Water supply
    Waste disposal system
    Other special purpose rooms
    Attic finish
    Insulation
    Fire & burglar alarm systems
    Rehabilitation, Modernization & Remodeling
    Any additional items which require adjustments, but did not fall
        under any other category

It is important to remember that a comparable sales condition and its special features at the time of its sale may differ from what they are at inspection on the date of the appraisal. For example, a comparable may have needed painting and a new roof when it was sold and these items have been repaired since. Changes in condition and features can often be determined by interviewing the current owner, seller, broker or closing attorney. Information on the MLS card may also be helpful.

CONSISTENCY CHECK: Information in this section of the URAR relates to another section of the form as indicated below. The appraiser should check to make sure data in both places is consistent!

<u>SALES COMPARISON ANALYSIS</u> - SUBJECT: Other
    Any item for which an adjustment is made must be explained elsewhere on the form (for example, under
<u>INTERIOR</u> - KITCHEN EQUIP.
    in the
<u>COMMENTS</u> - Additional features
    section, or of course in an addendum). Also make sure that all items in the above sections (and elsewhere on the form) that require adjustments are included somewhere in the
<u>SALES COMPARISON ANALYSIS</u>.
    If such an item does not fit any previous category, include it here.

SALES COMPARISON ANALYSIS

	VALUE ADJUSTMENTS			Net Adj. (total)	

ITEM	SUBJECT	COMPARABLE NO. 1	COMPARABLE NO. 2	COMPARABLE NO. 3
Net Adj. (total)		☐ + ☐ - $	☐ + ☐ - $	☐ + ☐ - $
of Comparable		$	$	$

The **Net Adj. (total)** space is used to report the net total of all **VALUE ADJUSTMENTS** made in the + (-) $ Adjustment column above. The appraiser must also indicate whether, on balance, the total is positive or negative by checking the appropriate box. If the total adjustments appear excessive in relation to the sale price as outlined in the box above, the appraiser would be well advised to reexamine the comparability of that sale.

Fannie Mae   June 30, 2002   Part XI Chapter 4, Section 406.03   Sales Comparison Approach
Adjustments to comparable Sales

We have established guidelines for the net and-gross percentage adjustments that underwriters may rely on as a general indicator of whether a property should be used as a comparable sale.

• Generally, the dollar amount of the net adjustments for each comparable sale should not exceed 15% of the sales price of the comparable. When the adjustments exceed 15%, the appraiser must comment on the reasons for not using a more similar comparable.

• Further, the dollar amount of the gross adjustments for each comparable sale should not exceed 25% of the sales price of the comparable. The amount of the gross adjustment is determined by adding all individual adjustments without regard to the positive or negative adjustments. When the adjustments exceed 25%, the appraiser must comment on the reasons for not using a more similar comparable.

• Individual adjustments that are excessively high should be explained by the appraiser and reviewed carefully by the lender's underwriter. In some circumstances, the use of comparables with higher-than-normal adjustments may be warranted, but the appraiser must satisfactorily justify his or her use of them.

The appraiser must research the market and select the most comparable sales that are available for the subject property and then adjust them to reflect the reaction of the market to the differences (except for sales and financing concessions) between the comparable sales and the subject property, without regard for the 'percentage or amount of the dollar adjustments. If the appraiser's adjustments do not fall within our net and gross percentage adjustment guidelines, but the appraiser believes that the comparable sales used in the analysis are the best available, as well as the best indicators of value for the subject property the appraiser simply has to provide an appropriate explanation. If the extent of the appraiser's adjustments to the comparable sales is great enough to indicate that the property may not conform to the general market area, the lender's underwriter must review the property carefully.

MODEL COMMENTS: The following are examples of explanatory remarks reviewers find useful. They are especially important when data on the subject property falls outside the normal range. Usually these comments require customization to reflect the special characteristics of the specific property being appraised.

WHEN A COMP'S NET ADJUSTMENT EXCEEDS 15%:

A thorough search for comparable sales was made in an attempt to find ones with net adjustments of less than 15% of their sale price. After considering locations, dates of sale, physical differences and special conditions, in the appraiser's judgment, the sales selected are better indicators of the value of the subject property than those with smaller net adjustments.

WHEN A COMP'S GROSS ADJUSTMENT EXCEEDS 25%:

A thorough search for comparable sales was made in an at-tempt to find ones with gross adjustments of less than 25% of their sale price. After considering locations, dates of sale, physical differences and special conditions, in the appraiser's judgment, the sales selected are better indicators of the value of the subject property than those with smaller gross adjustments.

SALES COMPARISON ANALYSIS

| VALUE ADJUSTMENTS | Adjusted Sales Price of Comparable |

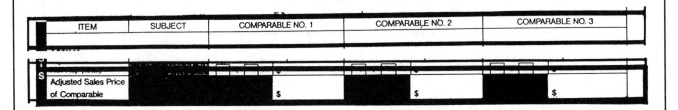

The Adjusted Sales Price of Comparable is calculated for each comparable by adding (or subtracting if appropriate) its **Net Adj. (total)** to (or from) its **Sales Price.**

It is good appraisal practice to round the **Adjusted Sales Price of Comparable** to reflect the appraiser's opinion of the accuracy of the adjusted value. When the market data is so good that the appraiser feels the estimate is within one hundred dollars, the estimate should be rounded to the nearest hundred dollars. More often the appraiser will feel that the estimate is accurate to the nearest thousand and on more expensive homes to the nearest five thousand dollars.

MODEL COMMENTS: The following are examples of explanatory remarks reviewers find useful. They are especially important when data on the subject property falls outside the normal range. Usually these comments require customization to reflect the special characteristics of the specific property being appraised.

SUMMARY OF SALES COMPARISON ANALYSIS:
```
The subject is a _____ [age] year old _____ [style] that has been
_____ (adequately, well, poorly, fairly) maintained. It is similar
to most properties in this _____ _____(good, moderate, low) income
neighborhood, so good comparable sales are available. The
estimated value of the subject property by the Sales Comparison
Analysis approach is _____ [$$] It would likely take _____
[estimate marketing time].to sell at this price.
```

SALES COMPARISON ANALYSIS

VALUE ADJUSTMENTS		Comments on Sales Comparison		
ITEM	SUBJECT	COMPARABLE NO. 1	COMPARABLE NO. 2	COMPARABLE NO. 3

Comments on Sales Comparison (including the subject property's compatability to the neighborhood, etc.):

The **Comments on Sales Comparison** section has two major uses.

The first is to explain how the **SALES COMPARISON ANALYSIS** is reconciled. This should not be an averaging technique but rather a reasoning process. Explain which comparable sales are given most weight, which adjustments seem most reliable and how the final sales comparison estimate of value is selected.

The second use is to explain the basis for the adjustments, especially those which are significant in size. Adjustments can be based on the following:

1. Market studies made by the appraiser or made available to the appraiser.

2. Matched pairs of sales where other differences are eliminated.

3. Cost data from which the appraiser deducts appropriate estimated depreciation. (This is a good technique for small differences in physical characteristics).

4. Estimates based on the appraiser's training, experience and knowledge of the market. (All too often, this is the only method available to make a particular adjustment).

5. Regression and other computer studies that in the appraiser's judgment, apply to the subject market and property.

NOTE: It is a rare appraisal where all of the above will fit in the **Comments on Sales Comparison**. Therefore, an addendum page is usually necessary.

MODEL COMMENTS: The following are examples of explanatory remarks reviewers find useful. They are especially important when data on the subject property falls outside the normal range. Usually these comments require customization to reflect the special characteristics of the specific property being appraised.

WHICH COMP WAS GIVEN THE MOST WEIGHT:

Many comparable closed sales were considered in making this appraisal. The _____ [#] closed sales displayed are considered to be the most comparable and the best indications of value for the subject property. Most weight is given to Comparable # _____ [#] because it _____ (requires the fewest adjustments, is most similar to the subject, has the most reliable adjustments, is located nearest to the subject, etc.).

WHEN COMP GIVEN THE MOST WEIGHT DOES NOT HAVE THE SMALLEST NET ADJUSTMENT:

The closed sales displayed were carefully selected and are considered to be the most comparable and the best indications of value for the subject property. Most weight is given to Comparable # _____ [#] in spite of the fact it has a greater net adjustment than Comparable # _____ [#]. This is due to the belief of this appraiser that the adjustments to _____ [comparable given most weight] are the most reliable.

SALES COMPARISON ANALYSIS

SALES HISTORY	Subject and Comparables

ITEM	SUBJECT	COMPARABLE NO. 1	COMPARABLE NO. 2	COMPARABLE NO. 3
Date, Price and Data Source, for prior sales within year of appraisal				

Analysis of any current agreement of sale, option, or listing of the subject property and analysis of any prior sales of subject and comparables within one year of the date of appraisal.

INDICATED VALUE BY SALES COMPARISON APPROACH . . . . $
INDICATED VALUE BY INCOME APPROACH (If Applicable) Estimated Market Rent $_____ /Mo. x Gross Rent Multiplier ____ = $

Space was added after the adjustment grid to report the date, price, and data source for prior sales of the subject property and comparable sales within 1 year of the effective date of the appraisal.

The data source for the prior sales of the subject and the comparables does not have to be the same as the appraiser's data and/or verification source that was reported at the top of the adjustment grid.

USPAP STANDARDS RULE 1-5: This rule effective 01/01/03 requires an appraiser to report and analyze all prior sales of the subject property within the past three (3) years, if such information available in the normal course of business.
For all types of property (including Single Family Residence) you are required to report a **three year sales history** if the information is available.

SALES COMPARISON ANALYSIS

	SALES HISTORY		Analysis of current agreement of sale, option, or listing of subject property & prior sales	
ITEM	SUBJECT	COMPARABLE NO. 1	COMPARABLE NO. 2	COMPARABLE NO. 3
Date, Price and Data Source, for prior sales				

Analysis of any current agreement of sale, option, or listing of the subject property and analysis of any prior sales of subject and comparables within one year of the date of appraisal:

INDICATED VALUE BY SALES COMPARISON APPROACH: $
INDICATED VALUE BY INCOME APPROACH (If Applicable) Estimated Market Rent $ _____ /Mo. x Gross Rent Multiplier _____ = $

The space used for providing **narrative comments** related to the sales comparison analysis was also significantly expanded for the appraiser's analysis of any prior sales of the subject property and the comparables, as well as of any current agreement of sale, option, or listing of the subject property (to assure compliance with the Uniform Standards).

Fannie Mae June 30, 1993 Announcement - Sales Comparison Analysis
Narrative Comments - Prior Sales of Subject and Comparables Analysis

"A new area for narrative comments was created for the appraiser's analysis of any prior sales of the subject property and the comparables, as well as of any current agreement of sale, option, or listing of the subject property (to assure compliance with the Uniform Standards). The space used for providing narrative comments related to the sales comparison analysis was also significantly expanded."

Veterans Benefits Administration Circular 26-93-25 1993 Sales Comparison Section - Comments Prior Sales of Comparables/Subject

A new area for narrative comments was created for the appraiser's analysis of any prior sales of the subject property and the comparables, as well as any current agreement of sale, option, or listing of the subject property (to assure consistency with the Uniform Standards). The space used for providing narrative comments related to the sales comparison analysis was also significantly expanded.

Fannie Mae June 30, 2002 Part XI Chapter 4, Section 406.06 Appraiser's Comments and Indicated Value

The appraiser's analysis for a property should include narrative comments about any prior sales of the subject property and the comparable sales, as well as about any current agreement of sale, option, or listing of the subject property. The appraiser's comments should also reflect his or her reconciliation of the adjusted (or indicated) values for the comparable sales and identify the sales that were given the most weight in arriving at the indicated value for the subject property For two- to four-family properties, the appraiser should also provide an evaluation of the typical purchaser's motivation-for purchasing the property and an analysis of any current agreement of sale option or listing for the subject property.

Veterans Benefits Administration   Circular 26-93-25   1993
Sales Comparison Section - Competitive Listings and Contract offerings

As discussed in paragraph 4c of this extract and in the comments under the neighborhood section, VA considers the research, review and analysis of competitive listings and contract offerings to be a necessity and a significant consideration in the appraisal process. This information assists appraisers in reconciling or rationalizing the closed sale data with current market conditions. To assist VA in evaluating competing market conditions and the trends affecting the subject property, in those instances in which a time adjustment is made to any of the comparables in the adjustment grid, the appraiser must provide an addendum citing three relevant competitive listings or contract offerings. Contract offerings are considered more desirable than listings. The format of the addendum will be consistent with that required for liquidation appraisal assignments. Original pictures of the listings/contract offerings are not required (if listing service sheets are used, the picture must be provided, if available) nor is the appraiser required to provide the information on a sales comparison analysis grid with adjustments made.

SALES COMPARISON ANALYSIS

INDICATED VALUE BY SALES COMPARISON APPROACH

ITEM	SUBJECT	COMPARABLE NO. 1	COMPARABLE NO. 2	COMPARABLE NO. 3
Date, Price and Data Source, for prior sales within year of appraisal				

Analysis of any current agreement of sale, option, or listing of the subject property and analysis of any prior sales of subject and comparables within one year of the date of appraisal:

INDICATED VALUE BY SALES COMPARISON APPROACH .... $ _____

INDICATED VALUE BY INCOME APPROACH (If Applicable) Estimated Market Rent $ _____ /Mo. x Gross Rent Multiplier _____ = $ _____

Notes

INDICATED VALUE BY INCOME APPROACH

INDICATED VALUE BY INCOME APPROACH (If Applicable) Estimated Market Rent $ _____ /Mo. x Gross Rent Multiplier _____ = $ _____
This appraisal is made ☐ as is ☐ subject to the repairs, alterations, inspections or conditions listed below ☐ subject to completion per plans and specifications.
Conditions of Appraisal: _____

To determine the **INDICATED VALUE BY INCOME APPROACH**:

1. Find comparable rental properties in the same or a similar neighborhood to the property being appraised. Compare their monthly rent with that of the property being appraised (if it is rented) to confirm that the subject's rent is typical of the market. If the subject property is rented and the price is typical, enter the monthly rent in the **Estimated Market Rent $** space. Otherwise, adjust each comparable's rent for significant differences between the comparable and the subject property. Consider the adjusted monthly rents and reconcile the data into the **Estimated Market Rent $** for the appraisal property assuming it is vacant and available to let on the date of the appraisal.

2. Find residences in the same or a similar neighborhood to the property being appraised that recently sold and were rented at the time of sale. The residences themselves should also be reasonably similar to the subject. Divide the sale price of each property by its <u>monthly</u> rental (unfurnished & without utilities) to obtain a multiplier as below.

Comparable	Sale Price	Rent on Sale Date	Multiplier
1	$79,800	$720.	111
2	$82,400	$750.	110
3	$85,000	$760.	112
4	$85,900	$770.	112
5	$88,000	$800.	110

Reconcile the multipliers developed above to derive a **Gross Rent Multiplier** (GRM) applicable to the subject. This should not be an average, but rather a judgment of comparability and applicability.

3. Multiply the **Estimated Market Rent $** by the **Gross Rent Multiplier** to obtain an **INDICATED VALUE BY INCOME APPROACH** for the residence being appraised.

The **INCOME APPROACH** is used by very few appraisers for single family houses. This is unfortunate because when used correctly, it can be a valuable tool. There are ample rentals to develop the needed **Gross Rent Multiplier** and **Estimated Market Rent** in far more markets than most appraisers realize. The **INCOME APPROACH** works best when a large number of comparable rental/sales are used to develop the market rent and multiplier. A good source of these comparables is Realtors who are active in the market where the subject property is located.

NOTE: *The Uniform Standards of Professional Appraisal Practice* require that all approaches to value be used unless there is a valid reason for the omission of one. If an approach is not used, the reason should be explained under **Comments and Conditions of Appraisal**.

Fannie Mae   June 30, 2002 Part XI Chapter 4, Section 408   Income Approach to Value
Introduction
The income approach to value is based on the assumption that market value is related to the market rent or income that a property can be expected to earn. Its use generally is appropriate in- neighborhoods that consist of one-family properties when there is a substantial rental market, and it can be an important approach in the valuation of two- to four-family properties. However, it generally is not appropriate in areas that consist mostly of owner-occupied properties since adequate rental data generally does not exist for those areas. We will not accept an appraisal -if the appraiser relies solely on the income approach to value as an indicator of market value.

Fannie Mae   June 30, 2002   Part XI Chapter 4, Section 408   Income Approach to Value
Steps
To arrive at the indicated value by the income approach to value, the appraiser multiplies the total gross estimated monthly market rent for the subject property by a reconciled gross monthly rent multiplier. (Because of the way the appraiser's opinion of value is derived under this approach, the income approach to value provides a reliable indication of value only when the comparable sales are truly comparable.)

Fannie Mae   June 30, 2002   Part XI Chapter 4, Section 408   Income Approach to Value
Market Rent
Estimated market rent Is based on an analysis of comparable rentals in the neighborhood. After appropriate adjustments are made to the comparable properties, their adjusted (or indicated) values are reconciled to develop an estimated monthly market rent for the subject property.

Fannie Mae   June 30, 2002   Part XI Chapter 4, Section 408   Income Approach to Value
Rent Multiplier
• The *gross rent multiplier* is determined by dividing the sales prices of comparable properties that were rented at the time of sale by their monthly market rent, which is then reconciled to create a single gross rent multiplier (or a range of multipliers) for the subject property.

Fannie Mae   June 30, 2002   Part XI Chapter 4, Section 408   Income Approach to Value
Applicability
The appraiser must use his or her best judgment regarding the applicability of the income approach to value. An instance in which the income approach may not be an appropriate indicator of value involves the appraisal of a two-family rental property in a neighborhood that is dominated by two-family properties that are owner-occupied. In such cases,- the appraiser does not need to develop a gross monthly rent multiplier, but must report the estimated market rent for the subject property. In such cases, the appraiser should provide an appropriate explanation of why he or she chose to report in this manner.

Fannie Mae June 30, 2002 Part XI Chapter 4, Section 408   Income Approach to Value-Investment Property

Single-Family Comparable Rent Schedule (Form 1007)

When the property being appraised is a one-family property that will be used as an investment property, the appraiser must prepare a *Single-Family Comparable Rent Schedule* (Form 1007) in addition to the appropriate appraisal report form. [This form is not required for a two- to four-family property since the *Small Residential Income Property Appraisal Report* (Form 1025) provides substantially the same information, nor is it required for a Community Living group home mortgage,] when the appraiser is relying on the income approach to value, be or she should attach the supporting comparable rental and sales data, and the calculations used to determine the gross rent multiplier, as an addendum to the appraisal report form.

MODEL COMMENTS: The following are examples of explanatory remarks reviewers find useful. They are especially important when data on the subject property falls outside the normal range. Usually these comments require customization to reflect the special characteristics of the specific property being appraised.

<u>WHEN THE APPRAISER ELECTS NOT TO USE THE INCOME APPROACH:</u>

```
     The income approach was considered inapplicable, because in
this market few single family houses are rented and there is
insufficient data available to develop either an Estimated Market
Rent or a GRM.
```

9-3

Notes

RECONCILIATION

Introduction

```
This appraisal is made ☐ "as is"  ☐ subject to the repairs, alterations, inspections or conditions listed below  ☐ subject to completion per plans and specifications.
Conditions of Appraisal: _____
Final Reconciliation: _____

The purpose of this appraisal is to estimate the market value of the real property that is the subject of this report, based on the above conditions and the certification, contingent
and limiting conditions, and market value definition that are stated in the attached Freddie Mac Form 439/Fannie Mae Form 1004B (Revised _____).
I (WE) ESTIMATE THE MARKET VALUE, AS DEFINED, OF THE REAL PROPERTY THAT IS THE SUBJECT OF THIS REPORT, AS OF _____
(WHICH IS THE DATE OF INSPECTION AND THE EFFECTIVE DATE OF THIS REPORT) TO BE $ _____
APPRAISER:                                               SUPERVISORY APPRAISER (ONLY IF REQUIRED):
Signature                                                Signature                                          ☐ Did  ☐ Did Not
Name                                                     Name                                               Inspect Property
Date Report Signed                                       Date Report Signed
State Certification #                      State         State Certification #                      State
Or License #                               State         Or License #                               State
```

Fannie Mae has clarified that the purpose of the appraisal is to estimate the market value of the "real property" which is the subject of the report. This means that the appraiser would need to perform a separate analysis if significant personal property is included. Therefore, when a property is sold including kitchen appliances, washer and dryer, and other items of personal property, it is quite common for the appraised value to be less than the sale price, which includes these non-realty items.

The line **Date Report Signed** below the name of the appraiser and supervisory appraiser is the date they actually signed the report. It may be many days or even weeks after the date the property was inspected. It is not usually the effective date of the report, but rather it indicates the date when the report was completed.

Space was also included for the appraiser to note their **State Certification # Or License #** and to acknowledge the roles of assistants in the appraisal process and co-signers of the appraisal report. This change (and the accompanying certification in the revised Certification and Limiting Conditions) allows an appraiser who has relied on significant professional assistance from any individual(s) in the performance of the appraisal or the preparation of the report to name the individual(s) and the specific tasks performed in the "Reconciliation" section of the report and to certify that the named individual(s) are qualified to perform the tasks. These modifications also acknowledge that, in some states, the appraisal report will still be viewed as complying with the intent of the Real Estate Appraisal Reform Amendments (Title XI) of FIRREA if an unlicensed or uncertified appraiser who is working as an employee or subcontractor of a licensed or certified appraiser performs a significant amount of the appraisal (or the entire appraisal if he or she is qualified to do so) — as long as the appraisal report is signed by a licensed or certified "supervisory" appraiser.

The supervisory appraiser must certify that he or she directly supervised the appraiser who prepared the appraisal report, has reviewed the appraisal report, agrees with the statements and conclusions of the appraiser, agrees to be bound by some of the same certifications that the appraiser made, and takes full responsibility for the appraisal report. The supervisory function just described would also apply when the appraisal reports of a state licensed or certified appraiser are co-signed by his or her employer or contractor if the lender or client requests that the supervisory relationship between the appraiser and his or her employer or contractor be acknowledged (or if such an acknowledgment is traditional in the locality).

Fannie Mae   June 30, 2002   Part XI Chapter 4, Section 409   Final Reconciliation

The valuation sections of our appraisal report forms enable an appraiser to develop and report in concise format an adequately supported opinion of market value—based on the cost, sales comparison, and income approaches to value (as applicable), and, in the case of-small residential income properties, on comparable rental data. If the appraiser believes that additional information needs to—be provided because of the uniqueness of the property or some other condition he or she should provide additional supporting data in an addendum to the appraisal report form.

The reconciliation process that leads to the appraiser's opinion of market value is an on-going process throughout the appraiser's analysis. In the final reconciliation, the appraiser must reconcile the reasonableness and reliability of each applicable approach to value and the reasonableness and validity of the indicated values and the available data, and then must select and report the approach or approaches that were given the most weight. The final reconciliation must never be an averaging technique.

If the appraiser has provided a comprehensive and logical analysis of the neighborhood and the property; the lender's underwriter should be able to reach a sound conclusion on the adequacy of the property as security for the mortgage.

Veterans Benefits Administration   Circular 26-93-25   1993
Reconciliation Section - Required Certification/Limiting Conditions/
Definition of Market Value

Several significant modifications were made to the reconciliation section. It clarified the purpose of the appraisal, which is to estimate the market value of the real property that is the subject of the report. Two modifications were made that are designed to assure consistency with the Uniform Standards. One modification relates to requiring the appraiser's certification and statement of limiting conditions and the definition of market value to be attached to each appraisal report (instead of allowing the appraiser to file the certification with the client). The second modification requires the appraiser to report both the date of the appraisal report and the effective date of the report (as opposed to requiring only the effective date of the report, which is the date of the property inspection).

Veterans Benefits Administration   Circular 26-93-25   1993
Reconciliation Section - VA Appraiser - VA Requirements

Under VA's fee panel system, VA is required by statute to maintain a list of appraisers who have been determined by VA to meet its qualification requirements and to assign appraisers on a rotational basis. VA fee appraisers must personally view both the interior and exterior of the subject property, the exterior of all of the comparables, and are responsible for the selection and analysis of the comparables and the final value estimate. The VA fee appraiser cannot delegate these important functions to another, such as an assistant or another individual, even though that person may be licensed or certified. The individual who signs the URAR as the appraiser must be the VA fee panel member who was assigned on the rotational basis by VA. The URAR (and the accompanying Freddie Mac Form 439/Fannie Mae Form 1004B) acknowledges the use of assistants and that, in some States, will still be viewed as complying with the intent of the Real Estate Appraisal Reform Amendments (Title XI) of FIRREA (Financial Institutions Reform, Recovery, and Enforcement Act) if an unlicensed or uncertified appraiser who is working as an employee or subcontractor performs a significant amount of the appraisal (or the entire appraisal if he or she is qualified to do so), as long as the appraisal report is signed by a licensed or certified supervisory appraiser. While the URAR acknowledges this activity, <u>it is not acceptable to VA.</u> Essentially, the activities that an assistant can perform alone without the VA fee appraiser are limited. VA will allow an assistant to sign a report as an assistant in order to document qualifying experience for future licensing and certification purposes. However, the primary signatory on the report must be the authorized fee appraiser. In addition, VA fee appraisers must clearly specify the activities the assistant performed. Failure to comply with VA's requirements in this area will constitute a basis for removal from the fee panel.

RECONCILIATION

This appraisal is made: "as is" — subject to repairs, alterations, inspections, or conditions — subject to completion per plans and specification

> This appraisal is made ☐ "as is" ☐ subject to the repairs, alterations, inspections or conditions listed below ☐ subject to completion per plans and specifications.
>
> Conditions of Appraisal: _____
>
> Final Reconciliation: _____
>
> The purpose of this appraisal is to estimate the market value of the real property that is the subject of this report, based on the above conditions and the certification, contingent and limiting conditions, and market value definition that are stated in the attached Freddie Mac Form 439/Fannie Mae Form 1004B (Revised _____).
> I (WE) ESTIMATE THE MARKET VALUE, AS DEFINED, OF THE REAL PROPERTY THAT IS THE SUBJECT OF THIS REPORT, AS OF _____
> (WHICH IS THE DATE OF INSPECTION AND THE EFFECTIVE DATE OF THIS REPORT) TO BE $ _____
>
> APPRAISER: SUPERVISORY APPRAISER (ONLY IF REQUIRED):
> Signature Signature ☐ Did ☐ Did Not
> Name Name Inspect Property
> Date Report Signed Date Report Signed
> State Certification # State State Certification # State
> Or License # State Or License # State
>
> Freddie Mac Form 70 6-93   10 CH.   PAGE 2 OF 2   Fannie Mae Form 1004 (6-93)

Indicate, by checking the appropriate box, whether **This appraisal is made**:

1) **"as is"**,

2) **subject to the repairs, alterations, inspections or conditions listed below**

3) **subject to completion per plans and specifications.**

Most lenders require that the value estimated be in **"as is"** condition. However, if structural repairs are needed to make the property liveable or saleable, they should be itemized together with an estimate of their cost. Some lenders also require a list (with costs-to-cure) of items of physical curable deterioration.

If the appraisal is made **subject to repairs, alterations or conditions**, the appraiser must carefully and in detail spell out exactly what the repairs, alterations and conditions are. Often a mortgage will be made subject to a requirement that the borrower make the needed repairs or alterations and correct the reported conditions. Unless these items are precisely described by the appraiser, the lender and borrower will have trouble determining exactly what needs to be done.

When the appraisal is made subject to **plans and specifications**, the appraisal should indicate the source, location and exact identity of the plans and specifications.

NOTE: Some appraisers are now checking the "subject to the repairs, alterations, inspections or conditions listed below" box whenever they have not been supplied with a phase 1, 2 or 3 environmental inspection. They indicate in the comments that their value estimate is based on the assumption that the property does not contain any detrimental environmental conditions or hazardous substances which might be revealed by an environmental inspection.

Fannie Mae   June 30, 2002   Part XI Chapter 4, Section 202   Status of Construction (Proposed Construction)

Generally, we require the improvements for the subject property to have been completed when the mortgage is delivered to us. However, we do make some exceptions to this and, in such cases, an appraisal report should be developed in accordance with the following criteria:

- For *new or proposed construction,* an appraisal may be based on either plans and specifications or an existing model home, if the lender obtains a certification of completion before it delivers the mortgage to us. This certification should be completed by the appraiser, state that the improvements were completed in accordance with the requirements and conditions in the original appraisal report, arid be accompanied by photographs of the completed improvements.

Fannie Mae   June 30, 2002   Part XI Chapter 4, Section 202   Status of Construction (Existing Construction)

- For *existing construction*, an appraisal may be based on the "as is" condition of the property if minor conditions that do not affect the livability of the property exist—such as minor deferred maintenance—as long as the appraiser's opinion of value reflects the existence of these conditions. The lender must review carefully the appraisal for a property appraised in an "as is" condition to assure that the property does not have any physical deficiencies or conditions that would affect its livability. If there are none, the lender does not need to require minor repairs to be completed before it delivers the mortgage to us.

When there are incomplete items or conditions that do affect the livability of the property—such as a partially completed addition or renovation—or physical deficiencies that could affect the soundness or structural integrity of the improvements,; the property must be appraised subject to completion of the specific alterations or repairs. In such cases, the lender must obtain a certificate of completion from an appraiser before it delivers the mortgage to us. The certification does not need to include photographs of the property unless those that accompanied the original appraisal report are no longer representative of the completed property

Generally, the original appraiser should complete any required certification of completion; *however, the lender may use a substitute appraiser. In such cases, the substitute appraiser must review the original appraisal and certify that the original appraiser's description of the property was accurate and the opinion of market value was reasonable on the date of the original appraisal report.* The lender should note in its files why the original appraiser was not used.

Note: There are many people, including the author, who believe that the proceedure prescribed in the proceeding paragraph (shown in italics) does not comply with the 2003 USPAP.

Veterans Benefits Administration   Circular 26-93-25   1993
Reconciliation Section - "As Is" and "Subject to Repairs"

VA fee appraisers will check "as is" if the property is considered to meet VA MPRs with no repairs or "subject to repairs" if MPR repairs are considered necessary. If repairs are recommended, the condition of appraisal narrative area of the reconciliation section must be noted with the statement "Subject to the MPR repairs noted in the comments section" (which is on the frontside of the URAR).

MODEL COMMENTS: The following are examples of explanatory remarks reviewers find useful. They are especially important when data on the subject property falls outside the normal range. Usually these comments require customization to reflect the special characteristics of the specific property being appraised.

WHEN THE VALUE ESTIMATED IS NOT THE "AS IS" VALUE:

The value estimated is based on the assumption that additional work will be completed. A schedule of additional work is included in the addenda.

WHEN THE SUBJECT IS PROPOSED OR UNDER CONSTRUCTION:

The subject is a _____ [description: units, stories, design] which is _____ (proposed, under construction). When completed it will be _____ (similar to, unlike) most properties in this _____ (good, moderate, low) income neighborhood. At the estimated value, its marketability is likely _____ [estimate marketing time].

PLANS AND SPECS:

This appraisal is made subject to completion per plans and specifications provided by _____ [buyer, seller, real estate agent, builder, lender, etc.] on _____ [date].

WHEN THE APPRAISER IS CONCERNED THAT THE VALUE OF THE PROPERTY MAY BE ADVERSELY AFFECTED BY DETRIMENTAL ENVIRONMENTAL CONDITIONS OR HAZARDOUS SUBSTANCES:

The value estimated in this report is based on the assumption that the property is not negatively affected by the existence of hazardous substances or detrimental environmental conditions. The appraiser is not an expert in the identification of hazardous substances or detrimental environmental conditions. The appraiser's routine inspection of and inquiries about the subject property _____ (did or did not) develop any information that indicated any apparent significant hazardous substances or detrimental environmental conditions which would affect the property negatively. It is possible that tests and inspections made by a qualified hazardous substance and environmental expert would reveal the existence of hazardous materials and environmental conditions on or around the property that would negatively affect its value.

CONSISTENCY CHECK: Information in this section of the URAR relates to another section of the form as indicated below. The appraiser should check to make sure data in both places are consistent!

RECONCILIATION -
    Be sure that the box checked is consistent with
IMPROVEMENTS - GENERAL DESCRIPTION: Existing, Proposed or **Under Construction.**
    Also, if the appraisal is made "subject to the repairs, alterations,....": 1) The modernization or repairs needed must be detailed under
COMMENTS - Depreciation
    or in an addendum; and 2) The appraiser should ascertain that no deduction from value for the items needing repair or modernization was taken in the
COST APPROACH - Physical or **Functional: Depreciation**
    section.

RECONCILIATION

Conditions of Appraisal

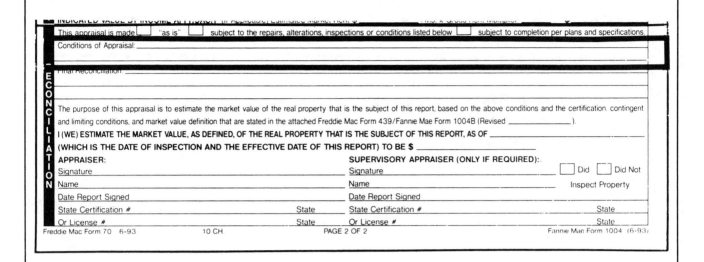

The **Conditions of Appraisal** lines are provided so the appraiser can make any explanations needed to complete the appraisal process. If more space is needed, use an addendum sheet.

Fannie Mae has clarified that the purpose of the appraisal is to estimate the market value of the "real property" which is the subject of the report. This means that the appraiser would need to perform a separate analysis if significant personal property is included. Therefore, when a property is sold including kitchen appliances, washer and dryer, and other items of personal property, it is quite common for the appraised value to be less than the sale price, which includes these non-realty items.

RECONCILIATION

Final Reconciliation

> [Form excerpt: Freddie Mac Form 70 6-93 / Fannie Mae Form 1004 (6-93), Page 2 of 2]
>
> This appraisal is made ☐ "as is" ☐ subject to the repairs, alterations, inspections or conditions listed below ☐ subject to completion per plans and specifications.
> Conditions of Appraisal: _____
>
> Final Reconciliation: _____
>
> The purpose of this appraisal is to estimate the market value of the real property that is the subject of this report, based on the above conditions and the certification, contingent and limiting conditions, and market value definition that are stated in the attached Freddie Mac Form 439/Fannie Mae Form 1004B (Revised _____).
> I (WE) ESTIMATE THE MARKET VALUE, AS DEFINED, OF THE REAL PROPERTY THAT IS THE SUBJECT OF THIS REPORT, AS OF _____
> (WHICH IS THE DATE OF INSPECTION AND THE EFFECTIVE DATE OF THIS REPORT) TO BE $ _____
>
> APPRAISER: / SUPERVISORY APPRAISER (ONLY IF REQUIRED): ☐ Did ☐ Did Not Inspect Property
> Signature / Name / Date Report Signed / State Certification # / Or License #

In this space, the appraiser must indicate any changes made to the Fannie Mae 1004 - Freddie Mac 439 on the **Final Reconciliation** lines. The appraiser should also explain the relevance and validity of each approach to value and present justification for the value selected as the final value estimate. The final reconciliation is not an averaging process.

The reconciliation leading to a value conclusion takes place in each step of the appraisal process. There is also a final reconciliation which leads to the final value estimate. ...The accuracy of an appraisal depends on the appraiser's knowledge, experience, and judgment. Equally important are the quantity and quality of the available data that will be reconciled in the final value conclusion. A judgment is made as to the validity and reliability of each of the value indications derived from the three approaches to value.[1]

Fannie Mae   June 30, 2002   Part XI Chapter 4, Section 409   Final Reconciliation

The reconciliation process that leads to the appraiser's opinion of market value is an on-going process throughout the appraiser's analysis. In the final reconciliation, the appraiser must reconcile the reasonableness and reliability of each applicable approach to value and the reasonableness and validity of the indicated values and the available data, and then must select and report the approach or approaches that were given the most weight. The final reconciliation must never be an averaging technique.

If the appraiser has provided a comprehensive and logical analysis of the neighborhood and the property; the lender's underwriter should be able to reach a sound conclusion on the adequacy of the property as security for the mortgage.

---

[1] George F. Bloom and Henry S. Harrison, *Appraising the Single Family Residence.* Chicago: American Institute of Real Estate Appraisers, 1978, P. 295.

MODEL COMMENTS: The following are examples of explanatory remarks reviewers find useful. They are especially important when data on the subject property falls outside the normal range. Usually these comments require customization to reflect the special characteristics of the specific property being appraised.

FINAL RECONCILIATION:

```
     Most weight was given to the value estimate derived by the
(Cost, Sales Comparison, Income) Approach,, which is well
supported by the _____ (Cost, Sales Comparison, Income) Approach.
```

RECONCILIATION

The purpose of this appraisal . . . conditions and the certification, contingent and limiting conditions, and market value definiton

This appraisal is made ☐ "as is" ☐ subject to the repairs, alterations, inspections or conditions listed below ☐ subject to completion per plans and specifications	
Conditions of Appraisal: _____	
Final Reconciliation: _____	

The purpose of this appraisal is to estimate the market value of the real property that is the subject of this report, based on the above conditions and the certification, contingent and limiting conditions, and market value definition that are stated in the attached Freddie Mac Form 439/Fannie Mae Form 1004B (Revised _____).

I (WE) ESTIMATE THE MARKET VALUE, AS DEFINED, OF THE REAL PROPERTY THAT IS THE SUBJECT OF THIS REPORT, AS OF _____ (WHICH IS THE DATE OF INSPECTION AND THE EFFECTIVE DATE OF THIS REPORT) TO BE $ _____

APPRAISER:	SUPERVISORY APPRAISER (ONLY IF REQUIRED):	
Signature	Signature	☐ Did ☐ Did Not
Name	Name	Inspect Property
Date Report Signed	Date Report Signed	
State Certification # _____ State	State Certification # _____ State	
Or License # _____ State	Or License # _____ State	

Freddie Mac Form 70 6-93   10 CH   PAGE 2 OF 2   Fannie Mae Form 1004 (6-93)

The URAR has been designed for use not only by FHLMC & FNMA, but also for VA, FmHA and FHA use. Other agencies also may permit its use in the future. So far there has been no agreement among the agencies (except between FHLMC & FNMA) on a standard **certification, contingent and limiting conditions and market value definition**. By filling in the date, the appraiser indicates the FHLMC/FNMA **certification, contingent and limiting conditions and market value definition** which apply. If the FHLMC/FNMA standard term does not apply, these lines should be crossed out and in the above comments a statement made that the certification, contingent and limiting conditions, and market value definition that does apply is in the addenda.

Fannie Mae June 30, 2002 Part XI Chapter 4, Section 206 Certifivation and Statements of Limiting Conditions
Each of our appraisal (or property inspection) report forms includes an appraiser's certification (and, if applicable, a supervisory appraiser's certification) and a statement of limiting c6nditions. Some forms include the limiting conditions and certifications as part of the form itself; others require the use of a separate document as an exhibit to the appraisal report.

The *Statement of Limiting Conditions and Appraiser's Certification* (Form 100413) must be included as an exhibit for appraisals prepared on the *Uniform Residential Appraisal Report* (Form 1004), the *Small Residential Income Property Appraisal Report* (Form *1025),* the *Individual Condominium Unit Appraisal Report* (Form 1073), or the *Individual Cooperative Interest Appraisal Report* (Form *1075).* Form 100413 includes ten limiting conditions and nine appraiser's certifications, as well as a supervisory appraiser's certification. To acknowledge that the current version of the Form 100413 was used and to assure the lender that the appraiser is certifying to our current definition of value, the appraiser must insert "06/93" in the blank that references "Freddie Mac Form 439/Fannie Mae Form 1004B (Revised_____)" in the "Reconciliation" section of the applicable appraisal report form.

The appraiser may not make a change or a deletion to the appraiser's certifications, although he or she may make additional certifications on a separate page or form. Acceptable additional certifications might include those required by state law, those related to the appraiser's continuing education or membership in an appraisal organization, or those related to the appraiser's compliance with privacy laws and regulations in the development, reporting, and storage of an appraisal and the information on which it is based. (An appraiser may not add additional limiting conditions.) The lender is responsible for reviewing any additional certifications made by an appraiser to assure that they do not conflict with any of our policies or with the standard certifications on our various appraisal forms or Form 1004B.

Veterans Benefits Administration   Circular 26-93-25   1993
Freddie Mac 439/Fannie Mae 1004B - Additions and deletions

Because VA is modifying its appraisal standards to specifically acknowledge the Uniform Standards of Professional Appraisal Practice as the minimum standard of the appraisal industry, VA will require the Freddie Mac Form 439/Fannie Mae Form 1004B to be signed and submitted by the appraiser as an exhibit to the appraisal report form for each appraisal assignment. Maintaining a copy "on file" is not consistent with USPAP. As noted in paragraph 2, mandatory use of Freddie Mac Form 439/Fannie Mae Form 1004B for VA purposes is effective January 1, 1994. Appraisers will not be permitted to make additions or deletions to the certification and statement of limiting conditions form. (For VA purposes, an exception to this is allowed for those liquidation appraisal reports in which the appraiser was either denied or unable to gain access to the subject property. Certification item 8 may be altered to reflect that fact.) It is believed that the reasons appraisers found it necessary to modify the existing Freddie Mac Form 439/Fannie Mae Form 1004B have been addressed in the revised test form.

Veterans Benefits Administration   Circular 26-93-25   1993
Additional Certifications

However, the appraiser will be permitted to make additional certifications (but not limiting conditions) on a separate form or page. Among other things, acceptable additional certifications include those required by State law or those related to the appraiser's continuing education or membership in an appraisal organization(s). Any additional certifications made by an appraiser must not conflict with the standard certifications on Freddie Mac Form 439/Fannie Mae Form 1004B or with any of VA's policies.

CONSISTENCY CHECK: Information in this section of the URAR relates to another section of the form as indicated below. The appraiser should check to make sure data in both places is consistent!

RECONCILIATION -
   Before signing the URAR, the appraiser should ascertain that all required items are filled in, all data is appropriate and all necessary attachments are included so that the appraisal complies with the appropriate agency guidelines. This is especially true when the appraisal is for HUD, FmHA and/or VA, whose instructions are quite different from FNMA or FHLMC, particularly in the

COST APPROACH
   section.

RECONCILIATION

MARKET VALUE, DEFINITION, DATE OF INSPECTION AND THE EFFECTIVE DATE OF THIS REPORT

INDICATED VALUE BY INCOME APPROACH (If Applicable) Estimated Market Rent $ _____ /Mo. x Gross Rent Multiplier _____ = $ _____
This appraisal is made ☐ "as is" ☐ subject to the repairs, alterations, inspections or conditions listed below ☐ subject to completion per plans and specifications.
Conditions of Appraisal: _____
Final Reconciliation: _____
The purpose of this appraisal is to estimate the market value of the real property that is the subject of this report, based on the above conditions and the certification, contingent and limiting conditions, and market value definition that are stated in the attached Freddie Mac Form 439/Fannie Mae Form 1004B (Revised _____).
I (WE) ESTIMATE THE MARKET VALUE, AS DEFINED, OF THE REAL PROPERTY THAT IS THE SUBJECT OF THIS REPORT, AS OF _____
(WHICH IS THE DATE OF INSPECTION AND THE EFFECTIVE DATE OF THIS REPORT) TO BE $ _____

APPRAISER: SUPERVISORY APPRAISER (ONLY IF REQUIRED):   ☐ Did ☐ Did Not Inspect Property
Signature _____   Signature _____
Name _____   Name _____
Date Report Signed _____   Date Report Signed _____
State Certification # _____ State _____   State Certification # _____ State _____
Or State License # _____ State _____   Or State License # _____ State _____

Freddie Mac Form 70 6-93   10 CH.   PAGE 2 OF 2   Fannie Mae Form 1004 (6-93)
©1993 Forms and Worms® Inc., 315 Whitney Ave., New Haven, CT 06511 1 (800) 243-4545   Item #112660

The URAR has been designed for use by a variety of agencies. FIRREA spells out what an acceptable definition of Market Value for federally related appraisals. The revised Freddie Mac Form 439/Fannie Mae Form 1004B (6/93 Revision) meets the FIRREA requirements. It is acceptable to Fannie Mae, Freddie Mac, HUD/FHA, VA and FmHA.

For non-federally related appraisals or appraisals that are exempt from FIRREA because they are for transactions below the de minimis level, the client may request the use of a different definition of value. When a different value definition is used the line should be crossed out or altered to reflect what value is being estimated. The addenda must always contain a definition of the value being estimated that is acceptable to the client.

Fannie Mae   June 30, 2002   Part XI Chapter 4, Section 205   Definition of Market Value

Our definition of market value is intended to assure that appraisals reflect an opinion of market value after adjustments for any special or creative financing or sales concessions—such as seller contributions, interest rate buydowns, etc.—have been made. The appraiser must certify that he or she used the following definition of market value:

The appraiser must certify that he or she used the following definition of market value (which is stated in the 6/93 version of Form 1004B):

Market value is the most probable price which a property should bring in a competitive and open market under all conditions requisite to a fair sale, the buyer and seller each acting prudently, knowledgeably and assuming the price is not affected by undue stimulus. Implicit in this definition is the consummation of a sale as of a specified date and the passing of title from seller to buyer under conditions whereby: (1) buyer and seller are typically motivated; (2) both parties are well informed or well advised, and each acting in what he considers his own best interest; (3) a reasonable time is allowed for exposure in the open market; (4) payment is made in terms of cash in US dollars or in terms of financial arrangements comparable thereto; and (5) the price represents the normal consideration for the property sold unaffected by special or creative financing or sales concessions granted by anyone associated with the sale.

Adjustments to the comparables must be made for special or creative financing or sales concessions. No adjustments are necessary for those costs which are normally paid by sellers as a result of tradition or law in a market area; these costs are readily identifiable since the seller pays these costs in virtually all sales transactions. Special or creative financing adjustments can be made to the comparable property by comparisons to financing terms offered by a third party institutional lender that is not already involved in the property or transaction. Any adjustment should not be calculated on a mechanical dollar for dollar cost of the financing or concession but the dollar amount of any adjustment should approximate the market's reaction to the financing or concessions based on the appraiser's judgment.

The asterisked section of the definition provides consistent interpretation for the appraiser. Specifically, we want to emphasize that the phrases "...those costs which are normally paid by sellers as a result of tradition or law in a market area; these costs are readily identifiable since the seller pays these costs in virtually all sales transactions..." refer to all of the sellers in a specific market area. No distinction is made between a specific group of sellers, builders, developers, or individuals in the resale market—they are all considered to be individual sellers in the market. To illustrate: When a property seller is paying part of the purchaser's settlement or closing costs—or is paying for an interest-rate buydown or other below-market financing—but virtually all of the other sellers in the market are—not doing the same as a result of law or tradition, the appraiser would need to make an adjustment even if there are other groups of sellers—such as builders—who are also offering concessionary financing.

The appraiser can adjust a comparable property that has special or creative financing or sales concessions by comparing it to other properties that had financing terms offered by a third-party institutional lender—as long as that lender is not already involved in the subject property or transaction. The appraiser should use his or her judgment in establishing the dollar amount for any adjustment to assure that it approximates the market's reaction to the financing or concession at the time of the sale.

Normally the date that the property is last inspected is the effective date of the appraisal. If for some reason this is not true, than an explanation as to why this is so is required.

<u>Veterans Benefits Administration   Circular 26-93-25   1993</u>
<u>Reconciliation Section - Date of Appraisal & Date of Report</u>

The second modification requires the appraiser to report both the date of the appraisal report and the effective date of the report (as opposed to requiring only the effective date of the report, which is the date of the property inspection).

RECONCILIATION

APPRAISER

```
INDICATED VALUE BY INCOME APPROACH (If Applicable) Estimated Market Rent $ _____ /Mo. x Gross Rent Multiplier _____ = $ _____
This appraisal is made ☐ "as is"  ☐ subject to the repairs, alterations, inspections or conditions listed below  ☐ subject to completion per plans and specifications.
Conditions of Appraisal: _____
Final Reconciliation: _____

The purpose of this appraisal is to estimate the market value of the real property that is the subject of this report, based on the above conditions and the certification, contingent and limiting conditions, and market value definition that are stated in the attached Freddie Mac Form 439/Fannie Mae Form 1004B (Revised _____ ).
I (WE) ESTIMATE THE MARKET VALUE, AS DEFINED, OF THE REAL PROPERTY THAT IS THE SUBJECT OF THIS REPORT, AS OF _____
(WHICH IS THE DATE OF INSPECTION AND THE EFFECTIVE DATE OF THIS REPORT) TO BE $ _____

APPRAISER:                                      SUPERVISORY APPRAISER (ONLY IF REQUIRED):
Signature _____                                Signature _____                    ☐ Did  ☐ Did Not
Name _____                                     Name _____                         Inspect Property
Date Report Signed _____                       Date Report Signed _____
State Certification # _____    State _____    State Certification # _____    State _____
Or License # _____             State _____    Or License # _____             State _____

Freddie Mac Form 70  6-93              PAGE 2 OF 2              Fannie Mae Form 1004 (6-93)
```

Both the **APPRAISER(s) Signature** and his/her printed or typed **Name** are filled in here. In addition, many lenders require appraisers to indicate their professional designations after their names.

Because the appraiser certifies that he/she <u>has</u> inspected both the interior and exterior of the subject property, the boxes **Did** and **Did Not Inspect Property** apply only to the **Supervisory Appraiser (if applicable)**. **If the appraiser has <u>not</u> inspected <u>both</u> the interior and exterior of the subject property, the certification must be modified and this fact stated prominently in the reconciliation section of the report.**

The line **Date Report Signed** below the name of the appraiser and supervisory appraiser is the date they actually signed the report. It may be many days or even weeks after the date the property was inspected. It is not usually the effective date of the report, but rather it indicates the date when the report was completed.

Space was also included for the appraiser to note their **State Certification #** or **State License #** and to acknowledge the roles of assistants in the appraisal process and co-signers of the appraisal report. This change (and the accompanying certification in the revised Certification and Limiting Conditions) allows an appraiser who has relied on significant professional assistance from any individual(s) in the performance of the appraisal or the preparation of the report to name the individual(s) and the specific tasks performed in the "Reconciliation" section of the report and to certify that the named individual(s) are qualified to perform the tasks. These modifications also acknowledge that, in some states, the appraisal report will still be viewed as complying with the intent of the Real Estate Appraisal Reform Amendments (Title XI) of FIRREA if an unlicensed or uncertified appraiser who is working as an employee or subcontractor of a licensed or certified appraiser performs a significant amount of the appraisal (or the entire appraisal if he or she is qualified to do so) — as long as the appraisal report is signed by a licensed or certified "supervisory" appraiser.

<u>Fannie Mae</u>   June 30, 2002   Part XI Chapter 4, Section 202   <u>Use of Supervisory Appraisers</u>
<u>Signatures</u>

We allow unlicensed or uncertified appraiser who works as an employee or sub-contractor of a licensed or certified appraiser to perform a significant amount of the appraisal (or the entire appraisal If he or she is qualified to do so)'—**as long as the appraisal report is signed by a licensed or certified—"supervisory" or "review" appraiser and is acceptable under state law**. In some cases, a lender may request that the appraisal reports prepared by a specific state-licensed or -certified appraiser be co-signed by his or her employer or contractor as a "supervisory" appraiser either because that is a tradition in the locality or because it wants to acknowledge the relationship between the appraiser and the employer or contractor. When a "supervisory" appraiser is used, the "supervisory" appraiser must certify that he or she directly supervises the appraiser who prepared the appraisal report, has reviewed the appraisal report, agrees with the statements and conclusions of the appraiser, agrees to be bound by some of the same certifications that the appraiser made, and takes full responsibility for the appraisal report.

The question of who can sign an appraisal report is not nationally uniform. Fannie Mae and Freddie Mac currently have taken the position that unlicensed and/or uncertified appraisers and trainees under so circumstances can sign an appraisal report as long as it is also signed by a Supervisory Appraiser who assumes total responsibility for the report. They both acknowledge that this may not be permitted by the law of some of the states.

HUD/FHA has taken the position that only licensed or certified appraisers may sign an appraisal report.

Veterans Benefits Administration   Circular 26-93-25   1993
Reconciliation Section - Role of Assistants

....and to acknowledge the role of assistants in the appraisal process and co-signers of the appraisal report. VA fee appraisers must continue to comply with VA's policy concerning assistants. An appraiser who has relied on significant professional assistance from any individual in the performance of the appraisal or the preparation of the appraisal report must name the individual and the specific tasks performed in the reconciliation section of the report.

Veterans Benefits Administration   Circular 26-93-25   1993
Reconciliation Section - Appraiser's License/Certification Number

Also included is a space for the appraiser to note his or her State license or certification number and to acknowledge the role of assistants in the appraisal process and co-signers of the appraisal report. VA fee appraisers must continue to comply with VA's policy concerning assistants. An appraiser who has relied on significant professional assistance from any individual in the performance of the appraisal or the preparation of the appraisal report must name the individual and the specific tasks performed in the reconciliation section of the report. Under VA's fee panel system, VA is required by statute to maintain a list of appraisers who have been determined by VA to meet its qualification requirements and to assign appraisers on a rotational basis. VA fee appraisers must personally view both the interior and exterior of the subject property, the exterior of all of the comparables, and are responsible for the selection and analysis of the comparables and the final value estimate. The VA fee appraiser cannot delegate these important functions to another, such as an assistant or another individual, even though that person may be licensed or certified. The individual who signs the URAR as the appraiser must be the VA fee panel member who was assigned on the rotational basis by VA. The URAR (and the accompanying Freddie Mac Form 439/Fannie Mae Form 1004B) acknowledges the use of assistants and that, in some States, will still be viewed as complying with the intent of the Real Estate Appraisal Reform Amendments (Title XI) of FIRREA (Financial Institutions Reform, Recovery, and Enforcement Act) if an unlicensed or uncertified appraiser who is working as an employee or subcontractor performs a significant amount of the appraisal (or the entire appraisal if he or she is qualified to do so), as long as the appraisal report is signed by a licensed or certified supervisory appraiser. While the URAR acknowledges this activity, it is not acceptable to VA. Essentially, the activities that an assistant can perform alone without the VA fee appraiser are limited. VA will allow an assistant to sign a report as an assistant in order to document qualifying experience for future licensing and certification purposes. However, the primary signatory on the report must be the authorized fee appraiser. In addition, VA fee appraisers must clearly specify the activities the assistant performed. Failure to comply with VA's requirements in this area will constitute a basis for removal from the fee panel.

RECONCILIATION

SUPERVISORY APPRAISER (ONLY IF REQUIRED):

```
INDICATED VALUE BY INCOME APPROACH (If Applicable) Estimated Market Rent $ _____ /Mo. x Gross Rent Multiplier _____ = $ _____
This appraisal is made ☐ "as is" ☐ subject to the repairs, alterations, inspections or conditions listed below ☐ subject to completion per plans and specifications.
Conditions of Appraisal: _____
Final Reconciliation: _____

The purpose of this appraisal is to estimate the market value of the real property that is the subject of this report, based on the above conditions and the certification, contingent
and limiting conditions, and market value definition that are stated in the attached Freddie Mac Form 439/Fannie Mae Form 1004B (Revised _____).
I (WE) ESTIMATE THE MARKET VALUE, AS DEFINED, OF THE REAL PROPERTY THAT IS THE SUBJECT OF THIS REPORT, AS OF _____
(WHICH IS THE DATE OF INSPECTION AND THE EFFECTIVE DATE OF THIS REPORT) TO BE $ _____
APPRAISER:                                    SUPERVISORY APPRAISER (ONLY IF REQUIRED):
Signature                                     Signature                         ☐ Did  ☐ Did Not
Name                                          Name                              Inspect Property
Date Report Signed                            Date Report Signed
State Certification #              State      State Certification #              State
Or License #                       State      Or License #                       State
Freddie Mac Form 70  6-93     10 CH.     PAGE
```

Both the **SUPERVISORY APPRAISER(s) Signature** and his/her printed or typed **Name** are filled in here. In addition, many lenders require supervisory appraisers to indicate their professional designations after their names.

Because the appraiser certifies that he/she <u>has</u> inspected both the interior and exterior of the subject property, the boxes **Did** and **Did Not Inspect Property** apply only to the **Supervisory Appraiser** (if applicable).

The line **Date Report Signed** below the name of the appraiser and supervisory appraiser is the date they actually signed the report. It may be many days or even weeks after the date the property was inspected. It is not usually the effective date of the report, but rather it indicates the date when the report was completed.

The supervisory appraiser must certify that:

1. he or she directly supervises the appraiser who prepared the appraisal report,

2. has reviewed the appraisal report,

3. agrees with the statements and conclusions of the appraiser,

4. agrees to be bound by some of the same certifications that the appraiser made,

5. and takes full responsibility for the appraisal report.

The supervisory function just described would also apply when the appraisal reports of a state-licensed or -certified appraiser are co-signed by his or her employer or contractor if the lender or client requests that the supervisory relationship between the appraiser and his or her employer or contractor be acknowledged (or if such an acknowledgment is traditional in the locality).

If an appraiser is performing a "review" function that is different from the relationship(s) described above, he or she must prepare a separate review report and attach it to the appraisal report being reviewed. For instance, this approach would apply when a lender chooses to delegate the appraisal management function to a specific appraiser or an appraisal service and one of the conditions of this delegation is that the specific appraiser or appraisal service will assume responsibility for the appraisal. This approach is consistent with the appraisal review function outlined in Standard 3 of the Uniform Standards of Professional Appraisal Practice and with the Residential Appraisal Review Report (Form 2000), which is FNMA's appraisal review form.

RECONCILIATION

Attachments – Required and Optional

ATTACHMENTS are a vital part of the appraisal report. The following is a list of the most common attachments. The ones marked with an asterisk are required for appraisals submitted to FNMA & FHLMC.

MAPS
    State or County
    Community (city or town)
    *Street Map (showing location of subject and comparables).
    Neighborhood Boundary Map
    Plat or plot plan
    Census tract
    FEMA Flood Insurance Rate Map [FIRM] (if applicable)

SKETCHES
    *Exterior Building Sketch with dimensions
    Interior with room dimensions
    *Approximate Floor Plan (showing location of all finished rooms, walls and doors. NOTE: This is required only when the floor plan is obsolete)

ADDENDUM SHEETS OF ADDITIONAL COMMENTS- as necessary when space on the form is inadequate or to provide additional information needed to justify the estimate of the subject's value.

PHOTOGRAPHS
    *Subject property (from both front and rear)
    Additional exterior photographs of subject property
    Interior photographs of subject property
    *Street scene of subject property
    *Comparables (one picture of the front of each)

LEGAL DESCRIPTION (of location, site dimensions or shape of subject property and/or comparables)

CERTIFICATIONS
    *Definition of Market Value (FHLMC #439 - FNMA #1004B) or some other definition
    *Certification and Statement of Limiting Conditions (FHLMC #439 - FNMA #1004B) or some other certification and statement of limiting conditions
    *Certification of Completion and Value (for proposed construction or appraisals more than 4 months old)

FORMS
    Energy Addendum (FHLMC #70A)
    **Single-Family Comparable Rent Schedule* (FNMA #1007) for single-family investment properties
    **Operating Income Statement* (FNMLA #216) for investment properties

PUD Addenda
    Recommended when URAR is used to appraise a property located in a Planned Unit Development (PUD)

Environmental Addenda
    Optional

Fannie Mae   June 30, 2002   Part XI Chapter 2, Section 204.01   Exhibits to Appraisal Reports

We require certain exhibits to support each appraisal (or property inspection) report. The exhibits may vary depending on the underwriting method, the type of property whether the borrower is purchasing the property as a residence or for investment purposes, or the type of property inspection performed. Unless we specify otherwise, we require the following exhibits for any appraisal report that is used for a manually underwritten mortgage:

- A street map that shows the location of the subject property and of all comparables that the appraiser used;
- An exterior building sketch of the improvements that indicates the dimensions. (For a unit in condominium or cooperative project, the sketch of the unit must indicate interior perimeter unit dimensions rather than exterior building dimensions.) Generally, the appraiser must also include calculations to show how he or she arrived at the estimate for gross living area; however, for a unit in a condominium or cooperative project, the appraiser may rely on the dimensions and estimate for gross living area that are shown on the plat. In such cases, the appraiser does not need to provide a sketch of the unit as long as he or she includes a copy of the plat with the appraisal report. A floor plan sketch that indicates the dimensions is required instead of the exterior building or unit sketch if the floor plan is atypical or functionally obsolete, thus limiting the market appeal for the property in comparison to competitive properties in the neighborhood;
- Clear, descriptive photographs (either in black and white or color) that show the front back, and a street scene of the subject property and that are appropriately identified. (Photographs must be originals that are produced either by photography or electronic imaging.);
- Clear, descriptive photographs (either in black and white or color) that show the fronts of each comparable sale and that are appropriately identified. (We do not require photographs of comparable rentals and listings.) Generally, photographs should be originals that are produced by photography or electronic imaging; however, copies of photographs from a multiple listing service or from the appraiser's files are acceptable if they are clear and descriptive;
- Certification of completion or appraisal update—either as a letter or as a form that provides the necessary information—if applicable;
- An *Operating Income Statement* (Form 216) or a similar cash flow and operating income statement, if the property is an investment property (including a two- to four family property in which the applicant will occupy one unit as a principal residence). Generally, the statement may be prepared by either the applicant or the appraiser (although the applicant for a Community Living mortgage must prepare the statement). (When the applicant prepares a Form 216, the appraiser's comments on the reasonableness of the projected operating income must be included on the form. When the appraiser prepares a Form 216, the lender must make sure the appraiser has operating statements, expense statements related to mortgage insurance premiums, owners association dues, leasehold payments, or subordinate financing payments; and any other pertinent information related to the property);
- A *Single-Family Comparable Rent Schedule* (Form 1007), if the property is a one-family investment property (other than one that secures a Community Living mortgage); and
- Any other data—as an attachment or addendum to the appraisal report form—that are necessary to provide an adequately supported opinion of market value.

Veterans Benefits Administration   Circular 26-93-25   1993
Reconciliation Section - Location of Comparable Sale and Subject

VA will now require that a location map be provided with every appraisal report indicating the location of each comparable sale and the subject.

U.S. Dept of Housing and Urban Development Handbook 4150.1 Revision 1 Chapter 8
Photographs

The appraiser is required to take a picture of the front and rear of the subject property from oblique angles so as to include the sides as well as the front and rear of the property and all buildings on the subject property having contributory value. The appraiser must also take a frontal picture of each comparable used in the report; <u>having someone else take the picture is not acceptable</u>. In addition, the appraiser is required to provide a copy of a local street map showing the subject and each comparable.

Exception: There may be a case in a rural area in which an appraiser wishes to use a comparable that had been used in a previous case but the picture was taken with a Polaroid camera and there is no negative from which to reproduce the picture. In such case, if the comparable is a great distance away, the field office may waive the requirement for a picture of that comparable provided that the appraiser cites the previous case number in which that comparable had been used and a picture provided. This authority is to be used only in rural areas where it is a great distance to the comparable.

RECONCILIATION

DEFINITION OF MARKET VALUE: The most probable price which a property should bring in a competitive and open market under all conditions requisite to a fair sale, the buyer and seller, each acting prudently, knowledgeably and assuming the price is not affected by undue stimulus. Implicit in this definition is the consummation of a sale as of a specified date and the passing of title from seller to buyer under conditions whereby: (1) buyer and seller are typically motivated; (2) both parties are well informed or well advised, and each acting in what he considers his own best interest; (3) a reasonable time is allowed for exposure in the open market; (4) payment is made in terms of cash in U. S. dollars or in terms of financial arrangements comparable thereto; and (5) the price represents the normal consideration for the property sold unaffected by special or creative financing or sales concessions* granted by anyone associated with the sale.

*Adjustments to the comparables must be made for special or creative financing or sales concessions. No adjustments are necessary for those costs which are normally paid by sellers as a result of tradition or law in a market area; these costs are readily identifiable since the seller pays these costs in virtually all sales transactions. Special or creative financing adjustments can be made to the comparable property by comparisons to financing terms offered by a third party institutional lender that is not already involved in the property or transaction. Any adjustment should not be calculated on a mechanical dollar for dollar cost of the financing or concession but the dollar amount of any adjustment should approximate the market's reaction to the financing or concessions based on the appraiser's judgment.

STATEMENT OF LIMITING CONDITIONS AND APPRAISER'S CERTIFICATION

CONTINGENT AND LIMITING CONDITIONS: The appraiser's certification that appears in the appraisal report is subject to the following conditions:

1. The appraiser will not be responsible for matters of a legal nature that affect either the property being appraised or the title to it. The appraiser assumes that the title is good and marketable and, therefore, will not render any opinions about the title. The property is appraised on the basis of it being under responsible ownership.

2. The appraiser has provided a sketch in the appraisal report to show approximate dimensions of the improvements and the sketch is included only to assist the reader of the report in visualizing the property and understanding the appraiser's determination of its size.

3. The appraiser has examined the available flood maps that are provided by the Federal Emergency Management Agency (or other data sources) and has noted in the appraisal report whether the subject site is located in an identified Special Flood Hazard Area. Because the appraiser is not a surveyor, he or she makes no guarantees, express or implied, regarding this determination.

4. The appraiser will not give testimony or appear in court because he or she made an appraisal of the property in question, unless specific arrangements to do so have been made beforehand.

5. The appraiser has estimated the value of the land in the cost approach at its highest and best use and the improvements at their contributory value. These separate valuations of the land and improvements must not be used in conjunction with any other appraisal and are invalid if they are so used.

6. The appraiser has noted in the appraisal report any adverse conditions (such as, needed repairs, depreciation, the presence of hazardous wastes, toxic substances, etc.) observed during the inspection of the subject property or that he or she became aware of during the normal research involved in performing the appraisal. Unless otherwise stated in the appraisal report, the appraiser has no knowledge of any hidden or unapparent conditions of the property or adverse environmental conditions (including the presence of hazardous wastes, toxic substances, etc.) that would make the property more or less valuable, and has assumed that there are no such conditions and makes no guarantees or warranties, express or implied, regarding the condition of the property. The appraiser will not be responsible for any such conditions that do exist or for any engineering or testing that might be required to discover whether such conditions exist. Because the appraiser is not an expert in the field of environmental hazards, the appraisal report must not be considered as an environmental assessment of the property.

7. The appraiser obtained the information, estimates, and opinions that were expressed in the appraisal report from sources that he or she considers to be reliable and believes them to be true and correct. The appraiser does not assume responsibility for the accuracy of such items that were furnished by other parties.

8. The appraiser will not disclose the contents of the appraisal report except as provided for in the Uniform Standards of Professional Appraisal Practice.

9. The appraiser has based his or her appraisal report and valuation conclusion for an appraisal that is subject to satisfactory completion, repairs, or alterations on the assumption that completion of the improvements will be performed in a workmanlike manner.

10. The appraiser must provide his or her prior written consent before the lender/client specified in the appraisal report can distribute the appraisal report (including conclusions about the property value, the appraiser's identity and professional designations, and references to any professional appraisal organizations or the firm with which the appraiser is associated) to anyone other than the borrower; the mortgagee or its successors and assigns; the mortgage insurer; consultants; professional appraisal organizations; any state or federally approved financial institution; or any department, agency, or instrumentality of the United States or any state or the District of Columbia; except that the lender/client may distribute the property description section of the report only to data collection or reporting service(s) without having to obtain the appraiser's prior written consent. The appraiser's written consent and approval must also be obtained before the appraisal can be conveyed by anyone to the public through advertising, public relations, news, sales, or other media.

Freddie Mac Form 439 6-93   Page 1 of 2   Fannie Mae Form 1004B 6-93

RECONCILIATION

APPRAISER'S CERTIFICATION: The Appraiser certifies and agrees that:

1. I have researched the subject market area and have selected a minimum of three recent sales of properties most similar and proximate to the subject property for consideration in the sales comparison analysis and have made a dollar adjustment when appropriate to reflect the market reaction to those items of significant variation. If a significant item in a comparable property is superior to, or more favorable than, the subject property, I have made a negative adjustment to reduce the adjusted sales price of the comparable and, if a significant item in a comparable property is inferior to, or less favorable than the subject property, I have made a positive adjustment to increase the adjusted sales price of the comparable.

2. I have taken into consideration the factors that have an impact on value in my development of the estimate of market value in the appraisal report. I have not knowingly withheld any significant information from the appraisal report and I believe, to the best of my knowledge, that all statements and information in the appraisal report are true and correct.

3. I stated in the appraisal report only my own personal, unbiased, and professional analysis, opinions, and conclusions, which are subject only to the contingent and limiting conditions specified in this form.

4. I have no present or prospective interest in the property that is the subject to this report, and I have no present or prospective personal interest or bias with respect to the participants in the transaction. I did not base, either partially or completely, my analysis and/or the estimate of market value in the appraisal report on the race, color, religion, sex, handicap, familial status, or national origin of either the prospective owners or occupants of the subject property or of the present owners or occupants of the properties in the vicinity of the subject property.

5. I have no present or contemplated future interest in the subject property, and neither my current or future employment nor my compensation for performing this appraisal is contingent on the appraised value of the property.

6. I was not required to report a predetermined value or direction in value that favors the cause of the client or any related party, the amount of the value estimate, the attainment of a specific result, or the occurrence of a subsequent event in order to receive my compensation and/or employment for performing the appraisal. I did not base the appraisal report on a requested minimum valuation, a specific valuation, or the need to approve a specific mortgage loan.

7. I performed this appraisal in conformity with the Uniform Standards of Professional Appraisal Practice that were adopted and promulgated by the Appraisal Standards Board of The Appraisal Foundation and that were in place as of the effective date of this appraisal, with the exception of the departure provision of those Standards, which does not apply. I acknowledge that an estimate of a reasonable time for exposure in the open market is a condition in the definition of market value and the estimate I developed is consistent with the marketing time noted in the neighborhood section of this report, unless I have otherwise stated in the reconciliation section.

8. I have personally inspected the interior and exterior areas of the subject property and the exterior of all properties listed as comparables in the appraisal report. I further certify that I have noted any apparent or known adverse conditions in the subject improvements, on the subject site, or on any site within the immediate vicinity of the subject property of which I am aware and have made adjustments for these adverse conditions in my analysis of the property value to the extent that I had market evidence to support them. I have also commented about the effect of the adverse conditions on the marketability of the subject property.

9. I personally prepared all conclusions and opinions about the real estate that were set forth in the appraisal report. If I relied on significant professional assistance from any individual or individuals in the performance of the appraisal or the preparation of the appraisal report, I have named such individual(s) and disclosed the specific tasks performed by them in the reconciliation section of this appraisal report. I certify that any individual so named is qualified to perform the tasks. I have not authorized anyone to make a change to any item in the report; therefore, if an unauthorized change is made to the appraisal report, I will take no responsibility for it.

SUPERVISORY APPRAISER'S CERTIFICATION: If a supervisory appraiser signed the appraisal report, he or she certifies and agrees that: I directly supervise the appraiser who prepared the appraisal report, have reviewed the appraisal report, agree with the statements and conclusions of the appraiser, agree to be bound by the appraiser's certifications numbered 4 through 7 above, and am taking full responsibility for the appraisal and the appraisal report.

ADDRESS OF PROPERTY APPRAISED: _____

APPRAISER:	**SUPERVISORY APPRAISER** (only if required):
Signature: _____	Signature: _____
Name: _____	Name: _____
Date Signed: _____	Date Signed: _____
State Certification #: _____	State Certification # _____
or State License #: _____	or State License #: _____
State: _____	State: _____
Expiration Date of Certification or License: _____	Expiration Date of Certification or License: _____
	☐ Did ☐ Did Not Inspect Property

Freddie Mac Form 439 6-93   Page 2 of 2   Fannie Mae Form 1004B 6-93

RECONCILIATION

Statement of Limiting Conditions and Appraiser's Certification
(Fannie Mae 1004B-Freddie Mac 439)

In 1993 The Uniform Standards of Professional Appraisal Practice specifically required an appraiser's certification to be included in each individual appraisal report. Freddie Mac Form 439 (6-93) Fannie Mae Form 1004B (6/93) was revised to comply with these requirements. The following are the highlights of the changes that were made in 1993. On 3/31/99 the U.S.P.A.P was revised. The 6/93 form does not appear to comply with all of these revisions. As of May 1999 when this is being written Freddie Mac and Fannie Mae still require the use of the 6/93 form. It is necessary to supplement this certification to comply with the 3/31/99 U.S.P.A.P. revisions. (See the following page 10-26).

- an expanded contingent and limiting condition clarifying that the appraiser is not an expert in the field of environmental hazards and the appraisal report is not to be considered an environmental assessment of the property, and acknowledging that the appraiser is responsible for noting any adverse conditions (such as hazardous wastes, toxic substances, etc.) observed during the inspection of the subject property or that he or she became aware of during the normal research involved in performing the appraisal;

- a new certification stating that the appraiser has examined flood maps provided by the Federal Emergency Management Agency (or other data sources) and has noted whether the subject property is located in a Special Flood Hazard Area. We also clarified that the appraiser makes no guarantees regarding this determination since he or she is not a surveyor;

- an expanded certification clarifying the parties to whom the lender/client specified in the appraisal report can distribute the appraisal report;

- a new certification addressing the appraiser's research and selection of comparable sales and adjustments in the sales comparison approach to value;

- an expanded certification stating that the appraiser has no present or contemplated future interest in the property (or the participants in the transaction) and that neither his or her current or future employment nor compensation for performing the appraisal is contingent on the appraised value of the property;

- an expanded certification stating that the appraiser did not base, either partially or completely, his or her analysis and/or estimate of market value in the appraisal report on the race, color, religion, sex, handicap, familial status, or national origin of either the prospective owners or occupants of the subject property or of the present owners or occupants of the properties in the immediate vicinity of the subject property;

- a new certification stating that the appraiser was not required to report a predetermined value or direction in value that favors the cause of the client or any related party, the amount of the value estimate, the attainment of a specific result, or the occurrence of a subsequent event in order to receive his or her compensation for performing the appraisal. (The appraiser must also certify that he or she did not base the appraisal report on a requested minimum valuation, a specific valuation, or the need to approve a specific mortgage loan.);

- a new certification stating that the appraisal report was performed in compliance with the Uniform Standards of Professional Appraisal Practice (with the exception of the departure provision which does not apply);

- a new certification acknowledging that an estimate of reasonable time for exposure in the open market is a condition of the definition of market value and clarifying that the appraiser's estimate of reasonable exposure time is consistent with the marketing time noted in the "Neighborhood" section (unless otherwise noted in the "Reconciliation" section of the report);

- an expanded certification addressing the appraiser's personal inspection of the interior and exterior of the subject property, the exterior of all properties listed as comparables in the appraisal report, and his or her responsibility to note apparent or known adverse conditions that he or she is aware of in the subject improvements, on the subject site, or on any site within the immediate vicinity of the subject property;

- an expanded certification stating that the appraiser either prepared all conclusions and opinions about the real estate that were set forth in the appraisal report or relied on significant professional assistance from another person in the performance of the appraisal or the preparation of the report. (In the latter instance, the appraiser must name in the appraisal report individuals providing the assistance, disclose the specific tasks performed by such individuals, and certify that the individuals are qualified to perform the tasks they did); and

- a new certification clarifying the role of the "supervisory appraiser" (which we currently refer to as a "review appraiser") who signs an appraisal report prepared by an employee or subcontractor that he or she directly supervises, to assure compliance with the guidance from the Appraisal Standards Board of The Appraisal Foundation and the Appraisal Reform Amendments (Title XI) of FIRREA.

Fannie Mae   **June 30, 2002**   **Part XI Chapter 4, Section 206**

Certification and Statements of Limiting Conditions

Each of our appraisal (or property inspection) report forms includes an appraiser's certification (and, if applicable, a supervisory appraiser's certification) and a statement of limiting conditions. Some forms include the limiting conditions and certifications as part of the form itself; others require the use of a separate document as an exhibit to the appraisal report.

The *Statement of Limiting Conditions and Appraiser's Certification* (Form 1004B) must be included as an exhibit for appraisals prepared on the *Uniform Residential Appraisal Report* (Form 1004), the *Small Residential Income Property Appraisal Report* (Form 1025), the *Individual Condominium Unit Appraisal Report* (Form 1073), or the *Individual Cooperative Interest Appraisal Report* (Form *1075)*. Form 1004B includes ten limiting conditions and nine appraiser's certifications, as well as a supervisory appraiser's certification. To acknowledge that the current version of the Form 1004B was used and to assure the lender that the appraiser is certifying to our current definition of value, the appraiser must insert "06/93" in the blank that references "Freddie Mac Form 439/Fannie Mae Form 1004B (Revised_____)" in the "Reconciliation" section of the applicable appraisal report form.

The appraiser may not make a change or a deletion to the appraiser's certifications, although he or she may make additional certifications on a separate page or form. Acceptable additional certifications might include those required by state law, those related to the appraiser's continuing education or membership in an appraisal

On 3/31/99 the U.S.P.A.P was revised. The Freddie Mac Form 439 (6-93) Fannie Mae Form 1004B (6/93) appears not to comply with all of these revisions. As of May 1999 when this is being written Freddie Mac and Fannie Mae still require the use of their 6/93 form. It is necessary to supplement this certification to comply with the 3/31/99 U.S.P.A.P. revisions. The SUPPLEMENTAL INFORMATION AND APPRAISER'S CERTIFICATION FORM is designed to comply with these new U.S.P.A.P. certification requirements and to provide space for other new information required by the revised U.S.P.A.P.

SUPPLEMENTAL INFORMATION AND APPRAISER'S CERTIFICATION

TYPE OF APPRAISAL AND TYPE OF APPRAISAL REPORT

This is a _____ appraisal. This is a _____ appraisal report.

IDENTIFICATION OF CLIENT(S)

The client(s) for whom this appraisal is made is (are):
_____

INTENDED USES AND USERS OF THE APPRAISAL

The intended use(s) of the appraiser's opinions and conclusions is (are):
_____

The intended user(s) of the appraiser's opinions and conclusions is (are):
_____

REASONABLE EXPOSURE TIME

In my opinion the reasonable exposure time linked to the value opinion is:
_____

SUPPORT FOR HIGHEST AND BEST USE CONCLUSIONS

The following additional information is supplied to support the highest and best use conclusions:
_____
_____
_____

ADDITIONAL CERTIFICATION

<u>Additionally I (we) certify that, to the best of my (our) knowledge and belief:</u>

- the statements of fact contained in this report are true and correct.

- the reported analyses, opinions, and conclusions are limited only by the reported assumptions and limiting conditions, and are my personal, impartial, and unbiased professional analyses, opinions, and conclusions.

- I have no (or the specified) present or prospective interest in the property that is the subject of this report, and no (or the specified) personal interest with respect to the parties involved.

- I have no bias with respect to the property that is the subject of this report or to the parties involved with this assignment.

- my engagement in this assignment was not contingent upon developing or reporting predetermined results.

- my compensation for completing this assignment is not contingent upon the development or reporting of a predetermined value or direction in value that favors the cause of the client, the amount of the value opinion, the attainment of a stipulated result, or the occurrence of a subsequent event directly related to the intended use of this appraisal.

- my analyses, opinions, and conclusions were developed, and this report has been prepared, in conformity with the Uniform Standards of Professional Appraisal Practice.

-The appraiser(s) ____ have ____ have not made a personal inspection of the property that is the subject of this report.

-The supervisory appraiser (s) ____ have ____ have not made a personal inspection of the property that is the subject of this report.

_____   _____
Appraiser   Supervisory Appraiser (only if required)

Date signed_____   Date signed_____

FHLMC 70A ENERGY ADDENDUM

An energy efficient property is one which uses cost effective design, materials, equipment, and site orientation in providing conservation of non-renewable fuels. Implicit in this definition are proper design and installation of materials and equipment consistent with climatic conditions in the area.

Normal insulation is not considered to be a special energy efficient item but super insulation is. For further details see **IMPROVEMENTS - INSULATION: Energy Efficient Items** section of this Guide.

Special energy efficient items include, but are not limited to:

1. Super Insulation (as above)
2. Special caulking and weatherstripping
3. Double or Triple pane window(s)
4. Window shades and blinds used for solar control
5. Window Quilt(s)
6. Landscaping used for solar control
7. Roof overhang designed for solar control
8. Storm fittings
9. Automatic setback thermostat(s)
10. Heating, cooling, lighting systems and built in appliances designed specifically to be energy efficient
11. Solar systems (passive and active) for water heating, space heating and cooling
12. Wood-fired heating systems
13. Other special design features which minimize energy use, such as smaller window areas and earth shelters.

At Seller's option, the Energy Addendum-Residential Appraisal Report (FHLMC Form 70A, Part V, Exhibit X) may be used to identify, rate and evaluate the property's energy-related features. Sellers are encouraged to give special consideration to these items since an energy efficient property could affect credit underwriting guidelines.

EA-1

Property and Appraisal Analysis
Special Appraisal Considerations

Selling

Fannie Mae   **June 30, 2002**   **Part XI Chapter 3, Section 313**
Energy Efficient Properties

A lender may consider a newly constructed dwelling as energy-efficient If it is built in compliance with qualifying energy conservation programs that the National Association of Home Builders (NAHB) classifies as meeting the NAHB Thermal Performance Guidelines or if it is constructed in a manner that meets or exceeds the standards established by the Council of American Building Officials (CABO) 1992 Model Energy Code. New construction—as well as existing homes—may also be qualified as energy-efficient through an appraiser's or an energy consultant's development of an energy-efficient rating using either a rating form from the Energy Rated Homes of America or Part I of our *Energy Addendum* (Form 1004A).

The appraiser must include an evaluation of the energy-efficient characteristics of the property and an overall rating—of "high", "adequate," or "low"—for the energy efficiency of the dwelling in the applicable appraisal report form. The lender may take the energy savings into consideration when evaluating the borrower's debt-to-income ratio, if the property receives an overall rating of "high" (as discussed in Part X, Section 302.08). Generally, a dwelling must include features from each of the following three major categories to receive a "high" rating:

A. "Insulation **and infiltration.** "We require insulation with adequate "R" values and infiltration barriers in the form of the following:

• Insulation in ceilings, roofs, or attic floors that are over conditioned spaces, in exterior walls, under floors that cover unheated areas, around slabs, around heating or cooling ducts or pipes that run through unconditioned spaces, around the sill area, and around the water heater;

• Special fireplace devices or features, such as combustion-air and -flue dampers, and a fire door;

• Sealing of the sole plate and penetrations of the exterior shell; and

• Damper for exhaust fans.

B.   **Windows and doors.** We require either double- or triple-pane windows or storm windows, and either storm doors or insulated doors.
We also require caulking and weather stripping around windows and door areas and at the sill area.

C.   **Heating and cooling systems.** We require the following types of heating and cooling systems:

• New efficient heating and cooling systems, or appropriate modifications to an existing system;

• Zoned heating and/or air conditioning;

• Automatic set-back thermostats; or

• Solar equipment or design.

Fannie Mae　　　　June 30, 2002　　　　Part XI Chapter 3, Section 313
Energy Efficient Properties

Regardless of the method used for qualifying a dwelling as energy-efficient, the appraiser must consider the reaction of the market to the energy-efficient improvements (or proposed alterations) and reflect their contributory value in the "sales comparison analysis" adjustment grid. This adjustment must be based on the appraiser's analysis of comparable sales. When adequate comparable sales are not available, the appraiser may use Part 2 of the *Energy Addendum* (Form 1004A) to develop an opinion about the value of the energy-efficient items, which should be equal to the lesser of the present worth of the estimated savings in utility costs and the installed cost of the energy-efficient items (as adjusted for physical, functional, or external depreciation.

ENERGY ADDENDUM — General

ENERGY ADDENDUM FILE NO.

This energy addendum is a two-part optional report designed to assist lenders in underwriting energy-efficient properties. Each part has a particular use, and the parts are to be treated as separate reports.

Part 1 of this addendum is for rating the energy efficiency of the subject property. It must be completed by an energy consultant or an appraiser. An energy-efficient rating of "high" is required to justify additional consideration in the credit underwriting process.

Part 2 of this addendum is for estimating the value of energy-efficient items <u>only</u> when adequate comparable market data are not available. It must be completed by an appraiser.

Borrower:

Property Address:

Part 1—Energy checklist

In this section, the energy consultant or appraiser should note the energy-efficient characteristics of the subject property and use these characteristics as a basis for rating the property's overall energy efficiency (high, adequate, or low). Generally, a dwelling should contain energy-efficient features for insulation, windows and doors, and heating and cooling to receive a "high" rating.

The comments sections should be used to describe the specific features and the quality and adequacy of the installation of the energy-efficient item(s) or technique(s). For example, if the energy-efficient furnace box is checked in the heating and cooling section below, those features that make the furnace "energy efficient" should be explained. In addition, the <u>estimated monthly savings</u>* from the energy-efficient items should be noted (*not required by Fannie Mae). The estimated monthly savings should be calculated as follows:

- for existing homes: the actual dollar difference between the current energy costs for an existing item and the estimated energy costs for the proposed energy-efficient item <u>or</u> the actual dollar difference between the current energy costs for an existing energy-efficient item and the estimated energy costs for whatever is prevalent for that item in the subject neighborhood ("neighborhood norm").

- for new homes: the actual dollar difference between the energy costs of the builder's base item and the estimated energy costs of the proposed energy-efficient item (if no base exists with which to compare, the base would be the neighborhood norm).

The best way to estimate the value of an energy-saving item is to develop the information directly from the market. Often there may be a substantial difference between what an energy-saving item costs and what it contributes to the value of the property.

For example, when installed a year ago, a solar domestic hot water heater cost $3,000 (its replacement cost now is $3,500). The property owner received a $1,400 tax credit. However, based on sales in this market, there appears to be only a $2,000 to $2,500 difference between the prices of houses with and without similar solar domestic hot water heaters. We correctly conclude from this information that the value of similar one year old domestic solar hot water heaters in this market is $2,000 to $2,500.

Without this market data information, we could estimate the value of the solar domestic hot water heater using the following calculations:

Estimated monthly savings:	$35.00
Expected life:	7 years
Home Improvement Interest rate:	14 %
Present worth of estimated savings:	$1,868

NOTE: This calculation is used primarily when the appraiser wants to justify an increase in value caused by an energy efficient characteristic of the subject property, but insufficient market data is available to support the estimated value increase.

ENERGY ADDENDUM — Insulation

A. Insulation (check if present, state "R" value if known)
- ☐ Attic/roof: R- _____
- ☐ Ceiling: R- _____
- ☐ Exterior walls: R- _____
- ☐ Floors: R- _____
- ☐ Slab/perimeter: R- _____
- ☐ Foundation walls: R- _____
- ☐ Insulated water heater   ☐ Insulation wrap: R- _____
- ☐ Insulated heat/cooling ducts or pipes: R- _____

Comments (describe quality and adequacy): _____
_____
_____
*Estimated monthly savings $ _____

    The standard measurement for the effectiveness of **INSULATION** is its "R" value (resistance to heat flow) and most brand name insulation products are marked with their "R" value. The rate of heat loss through a material is proportional to its "R" value, and the higher the "R" value the better the insulation. Therefore, an insulation with an "R" value of 20 is twice as effective as one with an "R" value of 10.

    Attic/roof: Most products have an "R" value of about 3 per inch of thickness. The standard 6 1/2" fiberglass blanket or batt has an "R" value of 22.

    Walls: Standard 3 1/2" fiberglass or batt in the walls has an "R" value of about 10 or 12. Rigid board insulation has 1 and 1/2 to 2 times the "R" value per inch.

    Floors: Fiberglass and Rockwool blankets or batts are the most popular materials with an "R" value of 3+ per inch of thickness typical.

    Slab/perimeter: Most products used have an "R" value of about 3 per inch of thickness.

    Foundation walls: Commonly used products are blankets and batts with "R" ratings of 3 per inch of thickness and rigid board with "R" ratings of 4 to 6 per inch. Sloppy installation reduces effectiveness.

    Water Heater: Typical 3" of insulation has an "R" value of about 10.

    Heat/cooling ducts and pipes: Typical 1" of insulation has an "R" value of 3 to 4.

ENERGY ADDENDUM — Windows and doors

B. Windows and doors
- ☐ Double (storm)/triple glazed windows
- ☐ Storm doors: On _____ of _____ doors
- ☐ Insulated doors
- ☐ Weatherstripping
- ☐ Caulking
- ☐ Other: _____

Comments (describe quality and adequacy): _____

*Estimated monthly savings $

Double (storm)/triple glazed windows: In northern areas each square foot of single glazed window loses the annual equivalent of about two gallons of heating oil. Combination storm windows cut in half and triple glazed windows by 2/3rds the loss, thereby saving 10% to 20% of the total fuel consumption.

Storm doors: The form has a line to report the number of storm doors. A good set can save up to 5% of the fuel cost, but they are not nearly as cost effective as storm windows.

Weatherstripping: Various products range in cost from the cheapest which is foam rubber with adhesive back (life 1-2 years) to expensive cushion bronze (life 10-20+ years). The more expensive types are well worth the cost and extra time they take to install. Good weatherstripping installation can save up to 5% of fuel cost; however, typical installations save only 2% to 3%.

Caulking: This is the solution for fixed joints. Potential fuel savings in newer homes is around 1% to maybe 3% in older homes. However, caulking is cheap and therefore cost effective.

ENERGY ADDENDUM
PART 1 – ENERGY CHECKLIST

Energy rating

Energy rating
Has an energy audit/rating been performed on the subject property?
☐ Yes (attach, if available) ☐ No ☐ Unknown

Energy efficiency appears:
☐ High ☐ Adequate ☐ Low

Comments: (including sources of above data and specifications) _____

*Total estimated monthly savings of energy-efficient features $ _____

SIGNATURE

COMPANY NAME

NAME

DATE

Freddie Mac Form 70A 6/89

Fannie Mae Form 1004A 6/89

Energy audits and ratings are now available in many communities. They range from simple one page reports to complex lengthy computer assisted reports that go into great detail on energy saving methods, home improvement costs and estimates of potential savings as a result of each action.

The energy efficiency of any home that does not have at least six and one-half inches of mineral wool, glass fiber or cellulose insulation in the attic, either over the ceiling of the top floor or under the roof between the roof rafters or trusses, should be rated as low. This deficiency will increase a home's fuel consumption by over 20%.

The total potential fuel savings between a home of standard construction without insulation, storm windows and doors, good caulking and weatherstripping and one with all these features is up to 50%. Houses with passive or active solar heating and super insulation may further increase the savings. However, improvements needed to increase fuel savings above 50% are rarely cost effective.

ENERGY ADDENDUM PART 2

Estimate of value of energy-efficient items

Part 2—Estimate of value of energy-efficient items

This section can be used to help estimate the value of energy-efficient items only when adequate comparable market data are not available.

In such cases, the value of the energy-efficient items should be the lesser of

(a) the present worth of the estimated savings in utility costs, as determined by capitalizing the savings at an interest rate that is not less than the current interest rate for home mortgages for a period that does not exceed the lesser of the item's expected physical life or seven years, or

(b) the installed cost of the energy-efficient item or construction technique, less any physical, functional, and external depreciation.

For example, if the subject property is an existing house with inadequate insulation and infiltration barriers—such as one without storm windows, caulking, and weatherstripping—and the estimated savings per month is $35 for upgrading the property (based on an energy audit/rating), the appraiser could use the following calculations as a guide.

Installed cost (less depreciation)	$2,500	
Expected life	7 + years	
Expected monthly savings	$35 per month	$420 x 4.789 = $2,011.38
Expected annual savings	$420 per year	
Present value factor (annual compound interest at 10.5% for 7 years)	4.789	

For this example, it would appear reasonable **(only if adequate comparable data were not available)** that a typical purchaser might pay a premium of $2,000 for the property as improved with the suggested energy-related items.

Value calculations (Use additional forms if more than three items)

1. Description of item or construction technique _____

Estimated monthly savings $ _____   Expected life: _____ years
Source(s) of savings estimate: _____
Use this space to show all calculations

a. Present worth of estimated savings . . . . $ _____
b. Installed cost of item or technique (less any depreciation) . . . . $ _____
Estimated value of item (the lesser of a or b) . . . . $ _____ (1)

2. Description of item or construction technique _____

Estimated monthly savings $ _____   Expected life: _____ years
Source(s) of savings estimate: _____
Use this space to show all calculations

a. Present worth of estimated savings . . . . $ _____
b. Installed cost of item or technique (less any depreciation) . . . . $ _____
Estimated value of item (the lesser of a or b) . . . . $ _____ (2)

3. Description of item or construction technique _____

Estimated monthly savings $ _____   Expected life: _____ years
Source(s) of savings estimate: _____
Use this space to show all calculations

a. Present worth of estimated savings . . . . $ _____
b. Installed cost of item or technique (less any depreciation) . . . . $ _____
Estimated value of item (the lesser of a or b) . . . . $ _____ (3)

Estimated total value of item(s) or technique(s) (the sum of (1), (2), and (3) above) . . . . $ _____

I have used acceptable valuation methodology in this analysis to estimate the present worth of the items and techniques contributing to the energy efficiency of the property. The results are subject to variance based on the effective use and maintenance of the items and the lifestyle of the occupants of the property.

Appraiser SIGNATURE   COMPANY NAME

NAME   DATE

Freddie Mac Form 70A 6/89   Fannie Mae Form 1004A 6/89

Notes

Notes

SINGLE FAMILY COMPARABLE RENT SCHEDULE — FNMA 1007

SINGLE FAMILY COMPARABLE RENT SCHEDULE

This form is intended to provide the appraiser with a familiar format to estimate the market rent of the subject property. Adjustments should be made only for items of significant difference between the comparables and the subject property.

ITEM	SUBJECT	COMPARABLE NO. 1		COMPARABLE NO. 2		COMPARABLE NO. 3	
Address							
Proximity to Subject							
Date Lease Begins / Date Lease Expires							
Monthly Rental	If Currently Rented: $	$		$		$	
Less: Utilities / Furniture	$	$		$		$	
Adjusted Monthly Rent	$	$		$		$	
Data Source							
RENT ADJUSTMENTS	DESCRIPTION	DESCRIPTION	+(−) $ Adjustment	DESCRIPTION	+(−) $ Adjustment	DESCRIPTION	+(−) $ Adjustment
Rent Concessions							
Location/View							
Design and Appeal							
Age/Condition							
Above Grade Room Count	Total / Bdrms / Baths	Total / Bdrms / Baths		Total / Bdrms / Baths		Total / Bdrms / Baths	
Gross Living Area	Sq. Ft.	Sq. Ft.		Sq. Ft.		Sq. Ft.	
Other (e.g., basement, etc.)							
Other:							
Net Adj. (total)		☐ + ☐ − $		☐ + ☐ − $		☐ + ☐ − $	
Indicated Monthly Market Rent		$		$		$	

Comments on market data, including the range of rents for single family properties, an estimate of vacancy for single family rental properties, the general trend of rents and vacancy, and support for the above adjustments. (Rent concessions should be adjusted to the market, not to the subject property.)

Final Reconciliation of Market Rent:

I (WE) ESTIMATE THE MONTHLY MARKET RENT OF THE SUBJECT AS OF _____ 19___ TO BE $_____

Appraiser(s) SIGNATURE _____

NAME _____

Review Appraiser SIGNATURE _____ (If applicable)

NAME _____

Freddie Mac Form 1000 (8/88)

1 (800) 243-4545

Item #237080

Fannie Mae Form 1007 (8/88)

SINGLE FAMILY COMPARABLE RENT SCHEDULE   FNMA 1007

The *Single Family Comparable Rent Schedule* is used whenever the appraiser finds the **HIGHEST & BEST USE** of the residence is as a rental unit rather than an owner occupied dwelling (even if it is currently owner occupied or the owner intends to occupy the house).

This form is required under the above circumstances, even if the appraiser elects not to use the **INCOME APPROACH**. It is also used whenever the unit is actually rented or intended to be rented in the near future.

The purpose of the grid is to display the data the appraiser uses to estimate the **Indicated Gross Monthly Market Rental for Subject Property**.

This form now requires dollar adjustments on the grid for items of significant difference between the comparables and the subject property. The adjustments should be the dollars per month that reflect the difference between the comparable rentals and the subject property.

The comparables used for rentals do not have to be the same properties as are used in the Comparable Sales Grid. However, when the same properties are used there should be a relationship between the adjustments made on the Sales Comparison Grid and the adjustments made on the Rent Schedule.

The Comments line now specifically asks the appraiser to "Comment on Market Data". Comments should be made on the range of rents in the market for single family properties. In the "Final Reconciliation of Market Rent" box, the Appraiser should explain which rentals were most comparable and how the line "Market Rent" of the subject property was estimated.

Notes

OPERATING INCOME STATEMENT — Front of Form

Operating Income Statement
One- to Four-Family Investment Property and Two- to Four-Family Owner-Occupied Property

Property Address

Street   City   State   Zip Code

General Instructions: This form is to be prepared jointly by the loan applicant, the appraiser, and the lender's underwriter. The applicant must complete the following schedule indicating each unit's rental status, lease expiration date, current rent, market rent, and the responsibility for utility expenses. Rental figures must be based on the rent for an "unfurnished" unit.

	Currently Rented	Expiration Date	Current Rent Per Month	Market Rent Per Month	Utility Expense	Paid By Owner	Paid By Tenant
Unit No. 1	Yes __ No __		$	$	Electricity	☐	☐
Unit No. 2	Yes __ No __		$	$	Gas	☐	☐
Unit No. 3	Yes __ No __		$	$	Fuel Oil	☐	☐
Unit No. 4	Yes __ No __		$	$	Fuel (Other)	☐	☐
Total			$	$	Water/Sewer	☐	☐
					Trash Removal	☐	☐

The applicant should complete all of the income and expense projections and for existing properties provide actual year-end operating statements for the past two years *(for new properties the applicant's projected income and expenses must be provided)*. This Operating Income Statement and any previous operating statements the applicant provides must then be sent to the appraiser for review, comment, and/or adjustments next to the applicant's figures *(e.g., Applicant/Appraiser 288/300)*. If the appraiser is retained to complete the form instead of the applicant, the lender must provide to the appraiser the aforementioned operating statements, mortgage insurance premium, HOA dues, leasehold payments, subordinate financing, and/or any other relevant information as to the income and expenses of the subject property received from the applicant to substantiate the projections. The underwriter should carefully review the applicant's/appraiser's projections and the appraiser's comments concerning those projections. The underwriter should make any final adjustments that are necessary to more accurately reflect any income or expense items that appear unreasonable for the market. *(Real estate taxes and insurance on these types of properties are included in PITI and not calculated as an annual expense item.)* Income should be based on current rents, but should not exceed market rents. When there are no current rents because the property is proposed, new, or currently vacant, market rents should be used.

Annual Income and Expense Projection for Next 12 months

	By Applicant/Appraiser	Adjustments by Lender's Underwriter
Income *(Do not include income for owner-occupied units)*		
Gross Annual Rental *(from unit(s) to be rented)*	$	$
Other Income *(include sources)*	+	+
Total	$	$
Less Vacancy/Rent Loss	− (%)	− (%)
Effective Gross Income	$	$

Expenses *(Do not include expenses for owner-occupied units)*

- Electricity
- Gas
- Fuel Oil
- Fuel .... (Type - _____)
- Water/Sewer
- Trash Removal
- Pest Control
- Other Taxes or Licenses
- Casual Labor
  This includes the costs for public area cleaning, snow removal, etc., even though the applicant may not elect to contract for such services.
- Interior Paint/Decorating
  This includes the costs of contract labor and materials that are required to maintain the interiors of the living units.
- General Repairs/Maintenance
  This includes the costs of contract labor and materials that are required to maintain the public corridors, stairways, roofs, mechanical systems, grounds, etc.
- Management Expenses
  These are the customary expenses that a professional management company would charge to manage the property.
- Supplies
  This includes the costs of items like light bulbs, janitorial supplies, etc.
- Total Replacement Reserves - See Schedule on Pg. 2
- Miscellaneous

Total Operating Expenses $ $

Freddie Mac Form 998 Aug 88   Item # 114700   Fannie Mae Form 216 Aug 88

[Handwritten notes: "FIRST THING" and "ESTIMATE GROSS INCOME OPERATING"]

OPERATING INCOME STATEMENT — Back of Form

Replacement Reserve Schedule

Adequate replacement reserves must be calculated regardless of whether actual reserves are provided for on the owner's operating statements or are customary in the local market. This represents the total average yearly reserves. Generally, all equipment and components that have a remaining life of more than one year—such as refrigerators, stoves, clothes washers/dryers, trash compactors, furnaces, roofs, and carpeting, etc.—should be expensed on a replacement cost basis.

Equipment	Replacement Cost	Remaining Life		By Applicant/Appraiser	Lender Adjustments
Stoves/Ranges	@ $ _____	ea. + ____ Yrs. x	_____ Units	= $ _____	$ _____
Refrigerators	@ $ _____	ea. + ____ Yrs. x	_____ Units	= $ _____	$ _____
Dishwashers	@ $ _____	ea. + ____ Yrs. x	_____ Units	= $ _____	$ _____
A/C Units	@ $ _____	ea. + ____ Yrs. x	_____ Units	= $ _____	$ _____
C. Washer/Dryers	@ $ _____	ea. + ____ Yrs. x	_____ Units	= $ _____	$ _____
HW Heaters	@ $ _____	ea. + ____ Yrs. x	_____ Units	= $ _____	$ _____
Furnace(s)	@ $ _____	ea. + ____ Yrs. x	_____ Units	= $ _____	$ _____
(Other)	@ $ _____	ea. + ____ Yrs. x	_____ Units	= $ _____	$ _____

Roof .... @ $ _____ + ____ Yrs. x One Bldg. = $ _____ $ _____

Carpeting (Wall to Wall)   Remaining Life

(Units) _____ Total Sq. Yds. @ $ ____ Per Sq. Yd. + ____ Yrs. = $ _____ $ _____

(Public Areas) _____ Total Sq. Yds. @ $ ____ Per Sq. Yd. + ____ Yrs. = $ _____ $ _____

Total Replacement Reserves. (Enter on Pg. 1) $ _____ $ _____

Operating Income Reconciliation

$ _____ − $ _____ = $ _____ ÷ 12 = $ _____
Effective Gross Income   Total Operating Expenses   Operating Income   Monthly Operating Income

$ _____ − $ _____ = $ _____
Monthly Operating Income   Monthly Housing Expense   Net Cash Flow

(Note: Monthly Housing Expense includes principal and interest on the mortgage, hazard insurance premiums, real estate taxes, mortgage insurance premiums, HOA dues, leasehold payments, and subordinate financing payments.)

Underwriter's instructions for 2-4 Family Owner-Occupied Properties

- If Monthly Operating Income is a positive number, enter as "Net Rental Income" in the "Gross Monthly Income" section of Freddie Mac Form 65/Fannie Mae Form 1003. If Monthly Operating Income is a negative number, it must be included as a liability for qualification purposes.

- The borrower's monthly housing expense-to-income ratio must be calculated by comparing the total Monthly Housing Expense for the subject property to the borrower's stable monthly income.

Underwriter's instructions for 1-4 Family Investment Properties

- If Net Cash Flow is a positive number, enter as "Net Rental Income" in the "Gross Monthly Income" section of Freddie Mac Form 65/Fannie Mae Form 1003. If Net Cash Flow is a negative number, it must be included as a liability for qualification purposes.

- The borrower's monthly housing expense-to-income ratio must be calculated by comparing the total monthly housing expense for the borrower's primary residence to the borrower's stable monthly income.

Appraiser's Comments *(Including sources for data and rationale for the projections)*

_____

Appraiser Name   Appraiser Signature   Date

Underwriter's Comments and Rationale for Adjustments

_____

Underwriter Name   Underwriter Signature   Date

Freddie Mac Form 998 Aug 88   Fannie Mae Form 216 Aug 88

1 (800) 243-4545

OPERATING INCOME STATEMENT
Property Identification
Rent Schedule - Utility Expense

Operating Income Statement
One- to Four-Family Investment Property and Two- to Four-Family Owner-Occupied Property

Property Address

_____
Street   City   State   Zip Code

General Instructions: This form is to be prepared jointly by the loan applicant, the appraiser, and the lender's underwriter. The applicant must complete the following schedule indicating each unit's rental status, lease expiration date, current rent, market rent, and the responsibility for utility expenses. Rental figures must be based on the rent for an "unfurnished" unit.

	Currently Rented	Expiration Date	Current Rent Per Month	Market Rent Per Month	Utility Expense	Paid By Owner	Paid By Tenant
Unit No. 1	Yes ___ No ___	_____	$_____	$_____	Electricity...........	☐	☐
Unit No. 2	Yes ___ No ___	_____	$_____	$_____	Gas...................	☐	☐
Unit No. 3	Yes ___ No ___	_____	$_____	$_____	Fuel Oil	☐	☐
Unit No. 4	Yes ___ No ___	_____	$_____	$_____	Fuel (Other)	☐	☐
Total			$_____	$_____	Water/Sewer	☐	☐
					Trash Removal	☐	☐

The top of this section provides room for the **Date** and **Property Address**.

The **Rent Schedule** provides a line for each unit. It asks for the number of rooms, bedrooms and baths as well as the actual rent being charged (or asked if vacant) on the date of the appraisal. (If forecasted rents are greater than current rents and leases expire less than three months from appraisal date, forecasted rents may be used. Otherwise, current rents should be used.)

When rent control is in effect, an addendum should be attached with the appraiser's opinion of the effect of rent control on the value of the property.

Below is space to indicate whether each unit is currently rented (check **Yes** box) or vacant (check **No** box). If the unit is owner occupied check **No**. When there is a lease, indicate the date it expires in the appropriate space.

The **Utility Expense** section has boxes to check showing who pays for various utilities, the owner or the tenant. When it is correct to check both boxes (i.e., owner pays for hall and outdoor electricity and tenant pays for electricity inside unit), explain the breakdown on an addendum sheet.

OPERATING INCOME STATEMENT — Instructions

> The applicant should complete all of the income and expense projections and for existing properties provide actual year-end operating statements for the past two years *(for new properties the applicant's projected income and expenses must be provided)*. This Operating Income Statement and any previous operating statements the applicant provides must then be sent to the appraiser for review, comment, and/or adjustments next to the applicant's figures *(e.g., Applicant/Appraiser 288/300)*. If the appraiser is retained to complete the form instead of the applicant, the lender must provide to the appraiser the aforementioned operating statements, mortgage insurance premium, HOA dues, leasehold payments, subordinate financing, and/or any other relevant information as to the income and expenses of the subject property received from the applicant to substantiate the projections. The underwriter should carefully review the applicant's/appraiser's projections and the appraiser's comments concerning those projections. The underwriter should make any final adjustments that are necessary to more accurately reflect any income or expense items that appear unreasonable for the market. *(Real estate taxes and insurance on these types of properties are included in PITI and not calculated as an annual expense item.)* Income should be based on current rents, but should not exceed market rents. When there are no current rents because the property is proposed, new, or currently vacant, market rents should be used.
>
> **Annual Income and Expense Projection for Next 12 months**

The instructions make it clear that the applicant should complete all of the income and expense projections and provide actual year-end operating statement for the past two years for existing properties. The applicant's projected income and expenses must be provided for new properties.

"This Operating Income Statement and any previous operating statements the applicant provides must then be sent to the appraiser for review."

"If the appraiser is retained to complete the form instead of the applicant, the lender must provide to the appraiser the aforementioned operating statements, mortgage insurance premium, HOA dues, leasehold payments, subordinate financing, and/or any other relevant information as to the income and expenses of the subject property received from the applicant to substantiate the projections."

<u>Without this information, it is impossible for the **appraiser to complete this form.**</u>

OPERATING INCOME STATEMENT
Annual Income and Expense Projection for Next 12 months

[Form image: Freddie Mac Form 998 Aug 88 / Fannie Mae Form 216 Aug 88, Page 1 of 2, Item # 114700 — "Annual Income and Expense Projection for Next 12 months" containing fields for Income (Gross Annual Rental, Other Income, Total, Less Vacancy/Rent Loss, Effective Gross Income) and Expenses (Electricity, Gas, Fuel Oil, Fuel (Type), Water/Sewer, Trash Removal, Pest Control, Other Taxes or Licenses, Casual Labor, Interior Paint/Decorating, General Repairs/Maintenance, Management Expenses, Supplies, Total Replacement Reserves, Miscellaneous, Total Operating Expenses), with columns "By Applicant/Appraiser" and "Adjustments by Lender's Underwriter".]

As part of the loan application procedure, the lender is supposed to obtain, from the applicant, the following information:

1. Actual Rents being collected at the time of the application and the dates any existing leases expire.

2. A projection of the next twelve months rental income and expenses.

If this information is not provided, the lender may instruct the appraiser to obtain it. In such a situation, the appraiser should obtain the information from the owner and transcribe it onto the form in the column indicating it was supplied by the applicant. If the information is obtained by the appraiser, this should be noted on the form.

The projected **Income** includes an estimated rent for any owner occupied unit (this should be comparable to the rents for similar units in the market).

Expenses include only expenses paid by the owner, including any expenses for an owner occupied unit. **Equipment Replacement** and **Carpeting Replacement** are calculated in the **Replacement Reserve Schedule** on the back of the form and transferred to the front.

OPERATING INCOME STATEMENT — Replacement Reserve Schedule

Replacement Reserve Schedule

Adequate replacement reserves must be calculated regardless of whether actual reserves are provided for on the owner's operating statements or are customary in the local market. This represents the total average yearly reserves. Generally, all equipment and components that have a remaining life of more than one year—such as refrigerators, stoves, clothes washers/dryers, trash compactors, furnaces, roofs, and carpeting, etc.—should be expensed on a replacement cost basis.

Equipment	Replacement Cost	Remaining Life		By Applicant/Appraiser	Lender Adjustments
Stoves/Ranges	@ $ _____ ea.	+ ____ Yrs. x	_____ Units	= $ _____	$ _____
Refrigerators	@ $ _____ ea.	+ ____ Yrs. x	_____ Units	= $ _____	$ _____
Dishwashers	@ $ _____ ea.	+ ____ Yrs. x	_____ Units	= $ _____	$ _____
A/C Units	@ $ _____ ea.	+ ____ Yrs. x	_____ Units	= $ _____	$ _____
C. Washer/Dryers	@ $ _____ ea.	+ ____ Yrs. x	_____ Units	= $ _____	$ _____
HW Heaters	@ $ _____ ea.	+ ____ Yrs. x	_____ Units	= $ _____	$ _____
Furnace(s)	@ $ _____ ea.	+ ____ Yrs. x	_____ Units	= $ _____	$ _____
(Other)	@ $ _____ ea.	+ ____ Yrs. x	_____ Units	= $ _____	$ _____
Roof	@ $ _____	+ ____ Yrs. x One Bldg. =		$ _____	$ _____

Carpeting (Wall to Wall) — Remaining Life

(Units)	____ Total Sq. Yds. @ $ ____ Per Sq. Yd.	+ ____ Yrs. =		$ _____	$ _____
(Public Areas)	____ Total Sq. Yds. @ $ ____ Per Sq. Yd.	+ ____ Yrs. =		$ _____	$ _____

* Total Replacement Reserves. (Enter on Pg. 1) $ _____ $ _____

The **Replacement Reserve Schedule** is used to support the **Equipment Replacement**, **Roof** and **Carpeting (wall to wall) Replacement** estimates required on the front of the form.

The number of years used for the life of the item should not be taken from a tax or depreciation table. Instead, it should reflect the appraiser's judgment of the remaining life of each item based on its quality, present condition, present age and projected use.

OPERATING INCOME STATEMENT — Operating Income Reconciliation

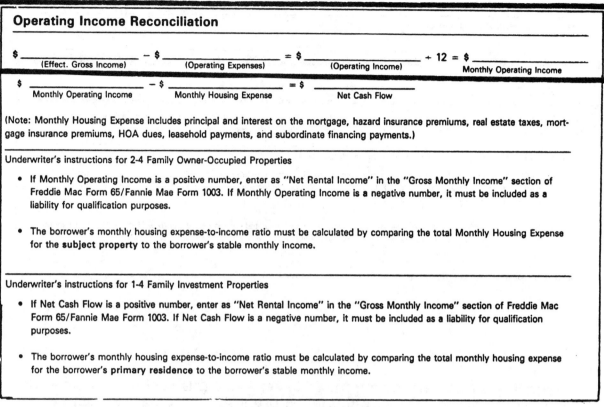

The **Operating Income Reconciliation** section is supposed to be completed by the lender. However, many lenders ask appraisers to complete it for them.

Effect. Gross Income: Copy this figure from the **Adjustment by Lender's Underwriter** column on the front of the form.

Operating Expenses: Copy this figure from the **Adjustment by Lender's Underwriter** column on the front of the form.

Operating Income: This is calculated by subtracting **Operating Expenses** from **Effect. Gross Income**.

Monthly Operating Income: Convert the **Operating Income** to a monthly figure by dividing by 12.

OPERATING INCOME STATEMENT — Operating Income Reconciliation

```
Operating Income Reconciliation

$ _____  - $ _____  = $ _____  ÷ 12 = $ _____
  Effective Gross Income   Total Operating Expenses   Operating Income              Monthly Operating Income

$ _____  - $ _____  = $ _____
  Monthly Operating Income   Monthly Housing Expense    Net Cash Flow
```

(Note: Monthly Housing Expense includes principal and interest on the mortgage, hazard insurance premiums, real estate taxes, mortgage insurance premiums, HOA dues, leasehold payments, and subordinate financing payments.)

Underwriter's instructions for 2-4 Family Owner-Occupied Properties

- If Monthly Operating Income is a positive number, enter as "Net Rental Income" in the "Gross Monthly Income" section of Freddie Mac Form 65/Fannie Mae Form 1003. If Monthly Operating Income is a negative number, it must be included as a liability for qualification purposes.

- The borrower's monthly housing expense-to-income ratio must be calculated by comparing the total Monthly Housing Expense for the **subject property** to the borrower's stable monthly income.

Monthly Operating Income: Copied from line above.

Monthly PITI: For the appraiser to complete this section, the lender must supply information about the proposed mortgage (**P**rincipal and **I**nterest), **T**axes and **I**nsurance costs (**PITI**). The sum of the mortgage principal and interest payments, the estimated property taxes and Homeowners insurance payments is the **Monthly PITI**. The appraiser should make sure that each payment is converted to a monthly payment if it is not already in that form.

The appraiser should verify the taxes as being those for the current year. Often the figure supplied by the owner or lender is for the previous year.

The insurance cost should pay for a Homeowners policy in which the residence is valued equal to or more than the proposed mortgage. Often the insurance cost supplied to the appraiser is for a policy that is insufficient.

An exception to this rule is when the site value is a high percentage of the total property value. The amount of insurance the lender should require is the replacement cost of the improvements. There is no point in forcing the homeowner to carry an amount of insurance greater than this, because, in the event of a loss, the amount the insurance company will pay is limited to the cost to rebuild the improvements.

Net Cash Flow: This is calculated by subtracting the **Monthly PITI** from the **Monthly Operating Income.**

OPERATING INCOME STATEMENT — Appraiser's Comments

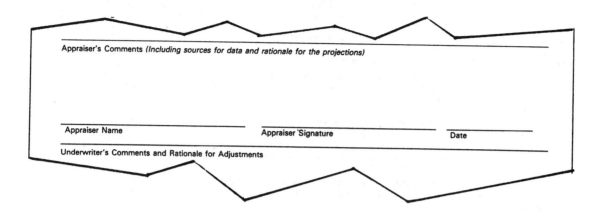

In the **Appraiser's Comments** section, the appraiser should comment on the reasonableness of the projected income and expenses.

It is very helpful if the owner supplies an operating statement for the previous two years. If these statements are not attached, note from whom they were requested and why they were not provided.

MODEL COMMENTS: The following are examples of explanatory remarks reviewers find useful. They are especially important when data on the subject property falls outside the normal range. Usually these comments require customization to reflect the special characteristics of the specific property being appraised.

WHEN THE VACANCY/RENT LOSS EXCEEDS 5%:

The Vacancy/Rent loss is estimated to be ____ [%, greater than 5%]. This is due to _____ [explanation].

WHEN THE DEBT SERVICE COVERAGE RATIO IS LESS THAN 90% IN AN OWNER OCCUPIED (OR 75% FOR NON-OWNER OCCUPIED) PROPERTY:

The Debt Service Coverage Ratio is ____ [% estimated]. This is lower then usual, because _____ [explanation].

OPERATING INCOME STATEMENT — Underwriter's instructions / Underwriter's Comments

Underwriter's instructions for 2-4 Family Owner-Occupied Properties

- If Monthly Operating Income is a positive number, enter as "Net Rental Income" in the "Gross Monthly Income" section of Freddie Mac Form 65/Fannie Mae Form 1003. If Monthly Operating Income is a negative number, it must be included as a liability for qualification purposes.
- The borrower's monthly housing expense-to-income ratio must be calculated by comparing the total Monthly Housing Expense for the **subject property** to the borrower's stable monthly income.

Underwriter's instructions for 1-4 Family Investment Properties

- If Net Cash Flow is a positive number, enter as "Net Rental Income" in the "Gross Monthly Income" section of Freddie Mac Form 65/Fannie Mae Form 1003. If Net Cash Flow is a negative number, it must be included as a liability for qualification purposes.
- The borrower's monthly housing expense-to-income ratio must be calculated by comparing the total monthly housing expense for the borrower's **primary residence** to the borrower's stable monthly income.

Appraiser's Comments *(Including sources for data and rationale for the projections)*

_____ _____ _____
Appraiser Name   Appraiser Signature   Date

Underwriter's Comments and Rationale for Adjustments

_____ _____ _____
Underwriter Name   Underwriter Signature Date

Freddie Mac Form 998 Aug 88   Page 2 of 2   Fannie Mae Form 216 Aug 88

Forms and Worms® Inc. 315 Whitney Ave. New Haven, Ct. 06511 All Rights Reserved 1 (800) 243-4545

The form ends with **Underwriters Instructions** for 2-4 Family Owner-Occupied Properties and 1-4 Family Investment Properties.

The appraiser *should not* complete these sections. It is no longer permissible for the same person to act as the appraiser and the underwriter.

Notes

Notes

APPRAISAL CASE STUDY
SINGLE FAMILY HOUSE

HOW TO FILL OUT A
RESIDENTIAL APPRAISAL REPORT

by Henry S. Harrison, MAI, SRPA, RM, ASA, IFAS, CSA, DREI
315 Whitney Avenue, New Haven, Connecticut 06511

About twenty years ago, the late Dr. George Bloom and I developed a case study to be used in our seminar in training appraisers how to fill out the Single Family Residential Appraisal Report.

Since then, many thousands of appraisers have attended the seminars given by George and myself using this case study. Many students have asked that we publish the case study together with a suggested solution.

On the following pages is the latest version followed by a suggested solution. It is important to remember that there is no one "correct solution" to any appraisal problem. Equally well qualified appraisers using the same data will typically produce different acceptable solutions to the same problem.

This case study contains information about a subject property to be appraised, this community, neighborhood and site. There is a location map showing the location of the subject and the comparable sales. Also included is a complete description of information needed to do a Cost Approach, such as site values, reproduction costs of houses like the subject and estimates of depreciation. Finally, there is information about three comparable sales.

I also wish to acknowledge the help of Barbara Kaye, Judith Fowler, Leonard D'Agostino and his staff at ABC America's Homebuying Consultants, Stephen Watts and Maura Gianakos who typed this case study.

Subject Property

Note: The Lender is the only intended user of this appraisal. It will be used to determine the suitablility of the property for mortgage loan security.

Address:	420 Gladville Avenue Bloomville, Lake County Illinois 60611
Census Map:	SMSA 8480
Map Reference:	628
Assessors Parcel No.:	7163
Borrower:	Will N. Buyer
Date of sale:	March 1, this year (date of appraisal March 1, this year)
Seller (occupant):	Mae B. Zeller
Sales contract:	$85,000. (There were no loan charges paid by the seller or any other sales concession)
Financing:	Buyer has applied for an 80%, 20 year 11% fixed rate mortgage with a point fee
Corner lot:	Yes
Type:	One-Story
Style:	Ranch
Age:	About 30 years old
Lender:	Easy Money Institution
Directions to the property:	Two blocks east of Bloomville Railroad Station
Property rights to be appraised:	Fee simple
Taxes:	$2,660.
Instructions to appraiser:	Make an appointment first
Supervisory appraiser:	A. Hawkeye (did not physically inspect subject property)
Loan term:	20 years
Neighborhood:	Wrightville
Sales history:	Purchased 8 years ago

Regional Data

Greater metropolitan Chicago is the nation's third largest metropolitan area. It consists of eight counties located at the western foot of Lake Michigan.

Basic economic support is very diversified. Manufacturing companies employ over one million workers and produce a variety of durable goods, electrical and non-electrical machinery, fabricated and primary metals together with printing, publishing and food products. It is a major center for trade, commerce, services, finance and Federal Government offices.

Chicago is the railroad center of the nation. It is served by 15 of the major railroads that operate one-half of the nation's railroad mileage. Over 12,000 trucks provide extensive services with daily schedules to 54,000 communities. Airlines handle about 40 million passengers annually and 15 percent of the nation's air cargo. Being the connecting link between the St. Lawrence Seaway and the Mississippi River, it has become a major seaport.

The area population has grown from about 4.5 million people in 1940 to about 8 million people today. The growth rate is close to the national average. The City of Chicago's population has decreased while the growth has been in the suburbs.

The strong economic base, good transportation facilities and continued growth of the suburban population all are indications of a continuation of a strong demand for housing in the suburbs. This could have a positive affect upon house values in Bloomville and the property being appraised.

Community Data

Bloomville, Illinois, is a suburb located 20 miles northwest of Chicago, Illinois. It is the fifteenth stop along the northwest finger of communities paralleling the Chicago and Northwestern Railroad's right of way.

The Post-World War II expansion of Chicago northwestwards as well as in several other directions has had a direct affect on the growth of Bloomville.

The population was 4,000 in 1960, 10,000 in 1970, 20,000 in 1980 and is estimated to be 25,000 now. Housing starts, including multi-family dwellings, averaged 250 per year until recently. They have increased about 300 units this year.

The post office and local financial institutions are located near the village hall and across the street from local shopping.

The central business district has adequate public parking and is about one mile to the east. The commuter railroad station is on the east boundary of the neighborhood.

The Town is divided into six neighborhoods. The downtown neighborhood which was developed primarily between World War I and World War II has several medium-size department stores and a variety of specialty shops and other commercial buildings.

So far, retail sales have remained at a high enough level to prevent any flight of merchants to the two community shopping centers. The Sears Center is located on the east side of town and the West Mall is on the west side of town. The two major employers and most of the other commercial activity also are located on the east side of town.

The fire department operates on a volunteer basis. Its equipment and service are considered average.

The Town consists of 17.5 square miles of land which is used as follows:

Roads and sidewalks:	3 sq. miles
Parks, schools and other public uses:	3 sq. miles
One-family houses:	4 sq. miles
Two to four-family houses:	1 sq. mile
Apartment houses	1 sq. mile
Condominiums:	1/2 sq. mile
Commercial uses:	2 sq. miles
Industrial uses:	1 sq. mile
*Vacant land:	2 sq. miles

*One-half zoned Commercial and one-half zoned Residential

Utilities in the town are provided by a municipal water company, public gas company, a Bell Telephone subsidiary and a public electric company. Municipal water is drawn from the nearby lake. Water quality and supply are excellent. Their rates are typical of the region. All of the existing residences and the commercial and industrial buildings are served by sanitary sewers. However, the pipes have not been extended to the undeveloped tracts. The treatment plant is now operating close to capacity.

Bloomville's economy is tied to metropolitan Chicago's economy because over 2,000 commuters work in the City. The local economic base industries consist of the national fraternal organization. Other base industries are two food processing plants, a large printing plant and a variety of other small manufacturing companies. There is a ratio of two workers in base employment to one worker in non-base employment.

The school system has an average rating and physically is reported adequate to serve the present and foreseeable needs of the community. The Bloomville Elementary School is one-quarter mile from the house being appraised and the high school is one-half mile away.

The public school system is about average for the region. Municipal government is stable. The police department is typical for this type of community but like many others, is unable to stop the steadily increasing crime rate.

There is a variety of local and regional recreational facilities. There are eight houses of worship within the Town's borders and many others in surrounding communities.

The local government operates in the village hall. The administration is sensitive to the growing resistance of the local residents to any major residential construction which will overtax the capacity of the sewer treatment plant. There is little room left for much new commercial or industrial expansion. The two major employers seem to have stopped growing, at least temporarily.

Demand for housing in Bloomville should remain steady for the foreseeable future. The Chicago area continues to grow. Other competing suburban communities will have to be farther away. Bloomville's appeal to commuters is expected to continue.

Neighborhood Data

There are three residential neighborhoods. Southville was the first developed and some of the housing stock is now substandard. Many of the homes are now being extensively renovated from going into a state of decline. Wrightville is in the vicinity of the community railroad station. It was developed starting in the 1920's but primarily in the 1960's. Most of the houses are between 30 to 60 years old.

Hoppiville is to the north and was developed after World War II. Most of the houses are well maintained. About 75 percent of its inhabitants live in single family, detached dwellings and the rest in condominiums, rental apartment units and town houses. This neighborhood still has several large tracts of land available for future development.

The house being appraised is located in the Wrightville neighborhood. This neighborhood is about 95% percent built-up with single family and multi-family residences. It is bordered on the north by the railroad tracks; on the south by Mapleton Street; on the east by Halsted Avenue and on the west by Stevenson Road.

In Wrightville about 50% of the houses are single family, 6% two to four family and 6% apartments. About 5% of the land along the railroad right of way is industrial. Houses near the railroad station and industrial area are selling for 5% less than houses in the other part of the neighborhood. A few of the houses have medical and other offices in them. There also are a variety of other commercial uses together using 13% of the land in the neighborhood.

There are about 10 acres of useable vacant land zoned for single family use with a minimum lot size of 20,000 sq. ft. The remainder of the vacant land is about 15 percent. Recently a developer filed a five-acre subdivision plan. No hearing has been set by the Planning and Zoning Commission yet.

In the late 1960's a subdivision known as Stuart Acres was developed. The developer also bought some nearby vacant lots at the same time nearby in the developed part of Stuart Acres. He built 254 single family residences and many are similar to the house being appraised. They have seven rooms and two bathrooms and contain a living room, dining room, kitchen, three bedrooms, recreation room and a two-car attached garage.

The range of typical incomes in Wrightville is between $20,000 and $30,000. The typical resident of the neighborhood is a young family occupying their first home. It is a stepping stone neighborhood and many families remain only a few years and then move up to large, more expensive homes. Most of the houses are well maintained.

In the 1960's the average sale price of a single family house was $20,000 to $25,000. By 1970, the average had increased to $35,000 to $40,000. In 1980 it was between $50,000 and $60,000. Today a typical house sells for about $65,000. The range is from $55,000 to $75,000.

There are now, as there has been for the past year, about a dozen houses for sale in the Wrightville neighborhood ranging in asking price from $69,000 to $145,000. Houses are selling at the rate of about 4 per month with a typical marketing time of 3 months.

When owners try to sell their houses themselves, it usually takes about six months. Some agents average about the same. However, a recent study done by the local Multiple Listing Service system showed that houses which were listed within 10 percent of the ultimate selling price usually sold within three months.

About 90 percent of the homes in Wrightville are owner-occupied.

Site Data

Lot size:	100-foot frontage on Gladville Avenue; 115-foot frontage on Cedar Street. Corner lot. Total area: 11,500 sq. ft. Lot size is typical of those in this neighborhood.
Zoning:	Single family. House conforms to zoning with reference to size, setback requirements, yard lines, etc.
Street improvements:	Street is paved with asphalt. There are no curbs, or gutters. The sidewalks are concrete. The streets are maintained by the town.
Utilities:	Municipal gas - good Municipal water - good Public electricity - good (overhead wires) Public storm sewers - good Bell Telephone Co. - good (overhead wires) Street lights - good (overhead wires) Municipal sanitary sewers - good
Driveway:	Paved with asphalt.
Easements, encroachments or other adverse influences:	None that detract from value.
Other data:	Site is level with good drainage. Site has good bearing qualities. View from site is average.
Legal description:	North 100 feet by Gladville Avenue; West 115 feet by Cedar Street; South 100 feet by land owned by others and East 115 feet by land owned by others.
Flood area:	The property is not in a flood area. It is in a "C" zone Flood Map 095060 0003 B 11-10-9__.
Easements:	Typical utility easements for electricity, sewer and telephone do not effect value.

Site Valuation

A recent study made by the Bloomville assessor showed that in Bloomville the average ratio between the value of the site to the value of the improvements when the property is improved with a single family dwelling is 30 percent site and 70 percent improvements.

Recently there was a lot sold on Jefferson Street, corner of McKinley Street. This is about 3/4 miles south of the subject property. It was 100 feet by 120 feet. It was the last lot on the street. Most of the houses around it were about 30 years old. It sold for $25,000.

Last year a 10-acre tract of land on the corner of Elm Street and Seventh Avenue was sold to a developer. It was subdivided into 33 lots. Most of the lots were .25 acre. The developer built houses that sold for an average price of $75,000. Some individual lots were sold for $16,000 to $18,000.

In making your site value estimate you should consider the following:

1. The Assessor's typical ratio is for the whole community.

2. "Last" lots in an improved neighborhood usually sell for a premium which disappears when the lot is improved.

3. Jefferson Street is about 1 mile south of the Railroad station.

4. The lots in the subdivision the builder sold off had no landscaping.

House Plan Sketch

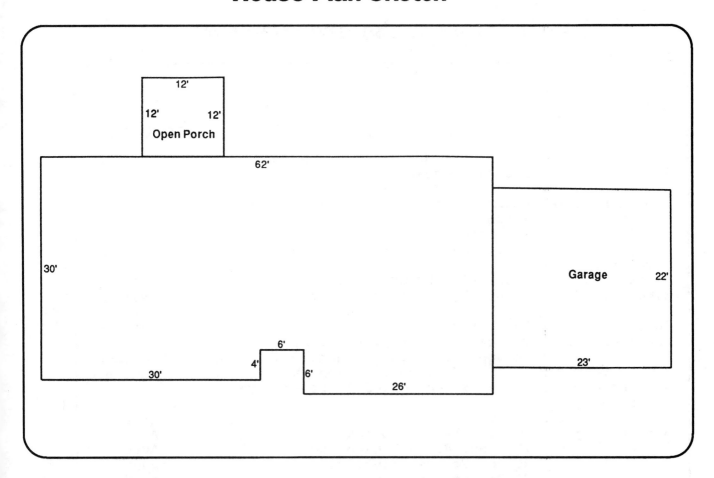

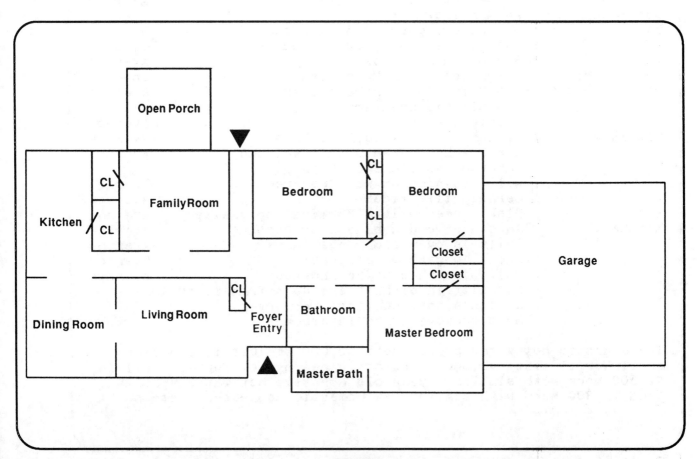

CS-11

Description of the Improvements

	Description/Material	Condition
Type:	One story, detached, crawl space	Average
Age:	Actual 30 years	
	Effective 30 years	
Remaining Life:	Economic 45 yrs, Physical 70 yrs	
Style:	Ranch	
Foundation:	Concrete, no sump pump, no sign of settlement, dampness or infestation	Average
Type of Construction:	Frame with brick veneer	Average
Windows:	Double-hung wood sash, combination aluminum storm windows & screens	Average
Roof:	Asphalt shingles	Average
Car Storage:	Two car attached garage, no entry to house, electric overhead doors, open ceiling and no interior partitioning	Average/ Adequate
Gutters/ Downspouts:	Aluminum. Connected to storm sewers	
Walls/Ceilings:	Plaster	Average
Subflooring:	Diagonally laid plank subflooring	Average
Floors:	1722 Sq. Ft. oak hardwood	Average
	96 Sq. Ft. resilient tile	Average
	70 Sq. Ft. ceramic tile	Average
Doors:	Wood-Hollow core	Average
Heat:	Hot water, gas-fired furnace	Average
	Adequacy average, condition is:	Good
	Baseboard radiators	Average
Hot Water:*	50-gallon solar HW system	Good
Electric System:	220 Volt, 100 ampere system	Average
	16 circuit breakers, B.X. cable wiring	Average
Bathrooms:	Syphon jet toilets, 5 ft cast iron tubs, ceramic tile wainscot around tub and shower area.	Average Average
	Walls painted or wall papered	Average
	Ceramic tile floor	Average
	Sink recessed into Formica top vanity	Average
Kitchen:	Adequate wood cabinets & counters	Average
	Built-in oven and range (gas)	Average
	Built in garbage disposal	Average
	Built in exhaust fan and hood	Average
	No built in dishwasher, no refrigerator	
	No compactor, no washer or dryer,	
	No microwave or no Intercom	

The domestic hot water system cost $3,000 to install one year ago. Now it costs $3,500. Houses in nearby development sell for $2,500 more with similar 1 year old domestic hot water systems and $2,800 more with similar new domestic hot water systems.

	Description/Material	Condition
Living room:	Atractive. Masonry Fireplace	Average
Attic:	None	
Trim/finish	Average quality wood mouldings	Average
Plumbing:	Copper water, cast iron waste	Average
Air conditioning:	Two window units (MBR & Liv R) Considered real estate. Typical for this market.	Average
Insulation:	Batts over ceilings and in walls. None under floors. Adequacy under-determined.	Average
Layout:		
Foyer:	4' x 6'	Average
Living room:	15' x 12' (one closet)	Average
Dining room:	12' x 12'	Average
Kitchen:	8' x 12' (one closet); no room for table	Average
Bedroom:	10' x 14' (two closets)	Average
Bedroom:	11' x 11' (one double closet)	Average
Bedroom:	11' x 12' (one double closet)	Average
Recreation Rm:	15' x 10' (one closet)	Average
Bathroom:	5' x 7'	Average
Bathroom:	5' x 7'	Average
Porch (rear):	12' x 12' (open with steps, roof and ceiling)	Average

Quality of Construction: Average for this market
Layout analyzed: The layout is average.
   Lack of general storage space
   No kitchen eating area
   No basement

Overall Condition: Average
Construction warranty: None

OWNERS PROJECTION OF INCOME AND EXPENSES FOR THE NEXT 12 MONTHS:

Annual Rental: $6,700; one year lease; no rent loss; tenant pays for electricity, heating, cooking, hot water (solar), water and sewer charges. Landlord estimated casual labor will be $100, interior painting/decorating $200, general repairs/maintenance $500, management expense none (owner will manage), supplies $75.

Equipment reserves are estimated by the owner as follows:

1 oven range cost $600 life expectancy 10 years
No refrigerator
No dishwasher
2 window air conditioning cost each $400, life expectancy 10 years
No clothes washer or dryer
1 domestic hot water heater cost $3,000 15 yr. life expectancy
1 garbage disposal cost $350, 5 yr. life expectancy
1 exhaust fan and hood cost $250, 15 yr. life expectancy
No carpets

Location Map

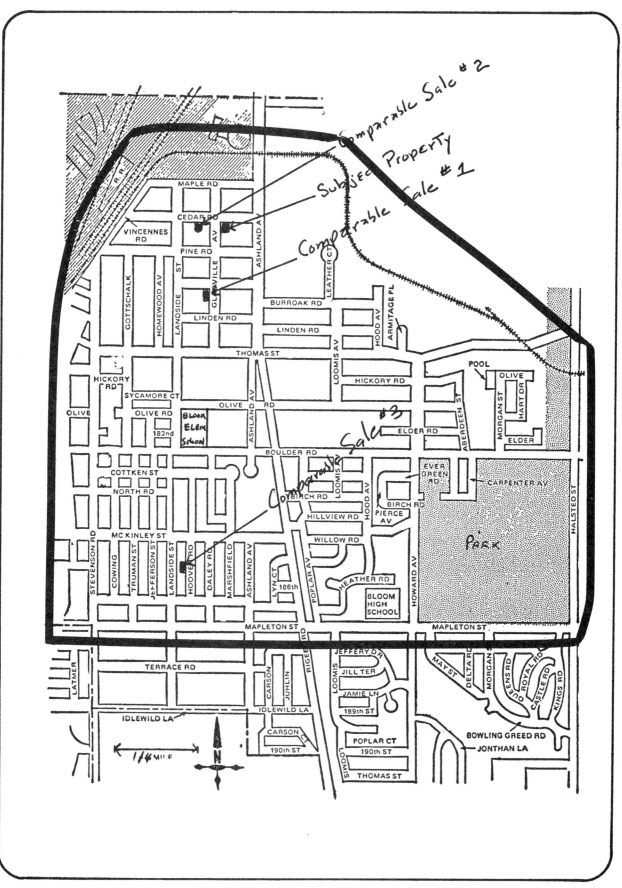

CS-14

Map

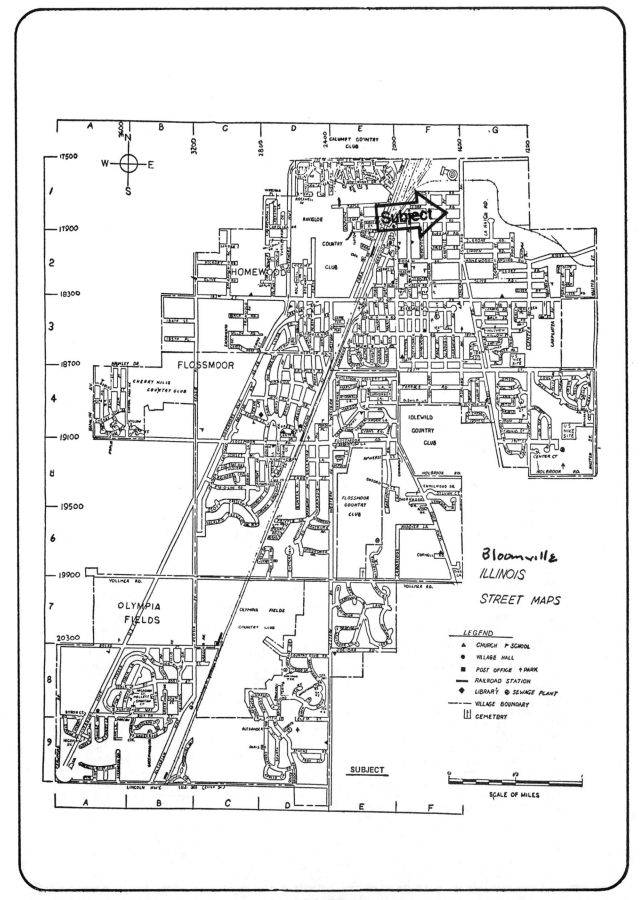

CS-15

Cost Approach

REPRODUCTION COST

The reproduction cost of the house was obtained by using the Marshall and Swift cost service. Information about the suject house was inputed into an office computer using the Marshall and Swift software. The cost calculations were printed on our printer as shown below:

```
City, State, ZIP: Bloomville, IL, 60611
Surveyed by     : Henry S. Harrison
Date of Survey  : March 12,

Single Family Residence            Floor Area: 1,888 square feet
Effective Age: 30 years            Quality: Average
                                   Condition: Average

              Style:  One Story
  Heating & Cooling:  Baseboard, Hot Water
      Exterior Wall:  Face Brick
            Roofing:  Composition Shingle
    Floor Structure:  Wood Subfloor
        Floor Cover:  Standard Allowance
           Plumbing:  Standard Allowance
         Appliances:  Standard Allowance
     Other Features:  Single Fireplace
```

	Units	Cost	Total
Basic Structure Cost............	1,888	53.35	100,721
Garage:			
Attached Garage................	506	16.15	8,170
Extras:			
Roofed Porch w/Steps...........	144	13.44	1,935
Domestic Solar Hot Water Unit.			3,500
Subtotal......................			5,435
Replacement Cost New...........	1,888	60.55	114,326
Less Depreciation:			
Physical Depreciation.........	<40.0%>		<45,730>
Functional Depreciation.......	<7.9%>		<9,000>
Locational Depreciation.......	<5.0%>		<5,716>
Subtotal......................	<52.9%>		<60,446>
Depreciated Cost...............	1,888	28.54	53,880
Miscellaneous:			
Land...........................			20,000
Site Improvements..............			3,000
Subtotal......................			23,000
Total.........................	1,888	40.72	76,880

Cost data by MARSHALL and SWIFT

The dwelling cost per square foot is obtained from the Marshall and Swift cost report as follows:

	Units	Cost	Total
Basic Structure Cost	1,888	$53.35	$100,721.

The lump sum costs for the solar domestic hot water heater are taken directly from the cost report:

    Solar domestic hot water heater: $3,500 lump sum

The square foot costs for the open porch and garage is taken directly from the cost report.

    Open Porch: $13.44 per sq. ft. porch area

    Garage: $16.15 per sq. ft. garage area

It is impossible, except for some new homes to estimate the reproduction cost of site improvements (driveway, landscaping, etc.). The figure in the cost report represents the appraiser's estimate of the site improvements contribution to the value of the property. It therefore should not be any further depreciated.

    Site Improvements: $3,000 lump sum

DEPRECIATION

Physical Incurable (Based on the age life method):

    Typical Economic Life: 75 years $\frac{30}{75}$ = 40 depreciated

    Effective age: 30 years

Physical-Curable: None

Functional-Curable: None

Functional-Incurable:
    Crawl space: $4,000
    Lack of storage: $2,000
    No eating in kitchen: $2,000
    Solar hot water heater: $1,000

Economic Obsolescence: $5,716 (5%)

Remarks: Fireplace and porches add approximately their depreciated (physical deterioration) value to properties in this neighborhood.

Note: The estimated Remaining Economic Life is 45+ years.

Market Data Approach — Comparable Sale No.1

Address:	341 Pine Road Bloomville, Illinois
Date of sale:	Contract 1/6/this year Closed 2/3/this year
Effective age:	30 years
Condition:	Similar to subject
Size:	1,820 sq. ft.
Sale price:	$70,000
Garage:	2-car, attached
Air conditioning:	2 window units
Type and style:	One-story, ranch
General description:	Frame construction, brick veneer exterior walls, plaster interior walls, no porch. Shortage of storage space, no basement (crawl space), no attic.
Electric service:	100 amp. with circuit breakers, B.X. cable
Heat:	Gas, hot water furnace, 50-gallon gas domestic hot water tank
General layout:	Living room (no fireplace), dining room, kitchen (no eating area), rec. room, three bedrooms, two baths
Location:	One block south of subject. Same external obsolescence as subject from Railroad Station and Industrial area.
Financing:	80% conventional mortgage
Rental:	$575 per month, no lease, unfurnished, no utilities included
Sale obtained from:	SREA Market Data Center
Site:	Level, good drainange. Size 100' x 115'
View:	Typical of neighborhood.
Previous sale (MLS):	$69,000 6 months ago

Market Data Approach — Comparable Sale No. 2

Address:	413 Cedar Street Bloomville, Illinois
Date of sale:	Contract 11/31/last year Closed 1/3/this year
Effective age:	30 years
Condition:	Similar to subject
Size:	1,875 sq. ft.
Sale price:	$73,000
Garage:	2-car, attached
Air conditioning:	2 window units
Type and style:	Ranch, one-story
General description:	Frame construction, brick veneer exterior walls, plaster interior walls, no porch, shortage of storage space, no basement (crawl space), no attic
Electric service:	100 amp., circuit breakers, B.X. cable
Heat:	Gas, hot water furnace, 50-gallon gas-fired domestic hot water tank
General layout:	Entry hall, living room with fireplace, dining room, kitchen (no eating area), rec. room, three bedrooms, two baths
Location:	Half block west of subject. Same external obsolescence as subject caused by nearby Railroad Station and Industrial area.
Financing:	80% conventional mortgage
Rental:	$600. per month at time of sale. No lease, unfurnished, no utilities included
Sale obtained from:	Multiple Listing Service
Site:	Level, good drainage. Size 11,250 sq. ft.
View:	Typical for neighborhood
Previous sales:	None in past year

Market Data Approach — Comparable Sale No. 3

Address:	210 Hover Road Bloomville, Illinois
Date of sale:	Contract 12/4/last year Closed 1/10/this year
Effective age:	30 years
Condition:	Similar to subject
Size:	1,900 sq. ft.
Sale price:	$82,000
Garage:	2-car, attached
Air conditioning:	2 window units
Type and style:	One-story, ranch
General description:	Frame construction, brick veneer exterior walls, plaster interior walls, 144 sq. ft. open porch, shortage of storage space, no basement (crawl space), no attic
Electric service:	100 amp., circuit breakers, B.X. cable
Heat:	Gas, hot water furnace
Domestic hot water:	50-gallon solar domestic hot water system
General layout:	Entry hall, living room with fireplace, dining room, kitchen (no eating area), rec. room, three bedrooms and two baths
Location:	3/4 mile south of the subject in the same neighborhood. No external obsolescence
Financing:	80% conventional mortgage
Rental:	$670. per month at time of sale, no lease, unfurnished, no utilities included
Sale obtained from:	Seller
Site:	Level, good drainage. Size 95' x 120'
View:	Typical for neighborhood
Previous sales:	None in past year

CS-21

Income Approach — GMRM

Rentals of other houses in the neighborhood similar to the house being appraised except as noted:

Rental No. 1: Rented one year ago on a two-year lease for $575. per month.

Rental No. 2: Recently rented for $500. per month for two months. Tenant cared for owners' cats while they were on a trip around the world.

Rental No. 3: Recently rented for $700. per month for two years. Tenant has an option to purchase the house at the end of this time.

Four other houses in the neighborhood recently sold which were rented at the time of the sale. They were similar to the house being appraised and there were no special conditions affecting the rentals.

Rental/Sale No. 1: Recently was rented and then sold. Rent was $555. per month. Selling price was $78,000.

Rental/Sale No. 2: Was rented for $725. per month on a two-year lease begun two years ago, with an option. At the end of the lease, two months ago, the tenant purchased the house for $75,000.

Rental/Sale No. 3: Was rented two years ago for $625. per month on a three-year lease. Recently it was sold (not to the tenant) for $80,000.

Rental/Sale No. 4: Was rented three months ago on a month-to-month basis for $560. per month. The house sold one month ago for $75,000.

SUGGESTED SOLUTION

SUBJECT - NEIGHBORHOOD PUD - SITE

COMPLETE APPRAISAL - SUMMARY APPRAISAL REPORT
UNIFORM RESIDENTIAL APPRAISAL REPORT   File No.

Property Description

Property Address	420 Gladville Avenue
City	Bloomville
State	IL
Zip Code	60611
Legal Description	(See attached addenda sheet)
County	Lake County
Assessor's Parcel No.	7163
Tax Year	200_
Taxes $	2,660
Special Assessments $	None
Borrower	Will N. Buyer
Current Owner	Mae B. Zeller
Occupant	[X] Owner
Property rights appraised	[X] Fee Simple
Project Type	PUD
HOA$	None /Mo.
Neighborhood or Project Name	Wrightville
Map Reference	628
Census Tract	8403 1462
Sale Price $	85,000
Date of Sale	3/1/
Loan charges/concessions paid by seller	None
Lender/Client/User	Easy Money Institution
Address	Center City, USA
Appraiser	Your Name
Address	Your Address

Neighborhood

Location	[X] Suburban
Built up	[X] Over 75%
Growth rate	[X] Stable
Property values	[X] Stable
Demand/supply	[X] In balance
Marketing time	[X] 3-6 mos.
Predominant occupancy	[X] Owner, [X] Vacant (0-5%)

Single family housing: PRICE $(000) Low 30, High 60, Predominant 35; AGE (yrs) Low 30, High 60, Predominant 35

Present land use %: One family 50, 2-4 family 6, Multi-family 6, Commercial 13, See below 25

Land use change: [X] Likely — To: Park to condo

Note: Race and the racial composition of the neighborhood are not appraisal factors.

Neighborhood boundaries and characteristics: *Present land use 5% industrial, 5% parks and 15% vacant. Wrightville neighborhood boundries shown on neighborhood map in addenda. (Additional comments in add.)

Factors that affect the marketability of the properties in the neighborhood: Center City offers a wide range of employment opportunities. Grammar and High School within walking distance. House is like many others in this neighborhood. A typical resident is a young family occupying their first house (See addenda)

Market conditions in the subject neighborhood: There are now as there has been for the past year about a dozen houses for sale in the Wrightville neighborhood. Their asking prices range form $69,000 to $145,000. Sales average about 4 per month. Typical marketing time is three months when listed within 10% of ultimate selling price. Ample conventional financing is available from local savings and loans and mortgage brokers. Loan discounts, interest buydowns and concessions are not common. (See addenda)

PUD

Project Information for PUDs (If applicable) -- Is the developer/builder in control of the Home Owners' Association (HOA)? [ ] Yes [ ] No

Approximate total number of units in the subject project _____   Approximate total number of units for sale in the subject project _____

Describe common elements and recreational facilities:

Site

Dimensions	100' x 115'
Site area	11,500 Sq. Ft.
Corner Lot	[X] Yes
Specific zoning classification and description	Single Family Residential
Zoning compliance	[X] Legal
Highest & best use as improved	[X] Present use
Topography	Level/Typical
Size	About ¼ Acre/Typical
Shape	Rec./Typical
Drainage	Good/Typical
View	Average/Typical
Landscaping	Average/Typical
Driveway Surface	Asphalt/Typical
Apparent easements	Typical Utility Ease.
FEMA Special Flood Hazard Area	[X] No
FEMA Zone	C
Map Date	11/10/9_
FEMA Map No.	095060 0003 B

Utilities (Public): Electricity [X], Gas [X], Water [X], Sanitary sewer [X], Storm sewer [X]

Off-site Improvements: Street Asphalt [Public X], Curb/gutter None [Public X], Sidewalk Cement [Public X], Street lights Good [Public X], Alley None

Comments: Typical utility easements for electricity, sewer and telephone do not effect value. No apparent adverse easements, encroachments, special assessments, slide areas, etc. (See addenda)

SUGGESTED SOLUTION

DESCRIPTION OF IMPROVEMENTS COMMENTS

DESCRIPTION OF IMPROVEMENTS

GENERAL DESCRIPTION
- No. of Units: 1
- No. of Stories: 1
- Type (Det./Att.): Det.
- Design (Style): Ranch
- Existing/Proposed: Existing
- Age (Yrs.): 30
- Effective Age (Yrs.): 30

EXTERIOR DESCRIPTION
- Foundation: Concrete
- Exterior Walls: Brick Ven.
- Roof Surface: Asph. Shin.
- Gutters & Dwnspts.: Aluminum
- Window Type: Wood/DH
- Storm/Screens: Comb. Alum.
- Manufactured House: --

FOUNDATION
- Slab: --
- Crawl Space: Yes
- Basement: None
- Sump Pump: None
- Dampness: None Evid.
- Settlement: None Evid.
- Infestation: None Evid.

BASEMENT
- Area Sq. Ft.: N/A
- % Finished: N/A
- Ceiling: N/A
- Walls: N/A
- Floor: N/A
- Outside Entry: N/A

INSULATION
- Roof:
- Ceiling: Unkn [X]
- Walls: Unkn [X]
- Floor:
- None:
- Unknown:
- Adequacy unknown

ROOMS	Foyer	Living	Dining	Kitchen	Den	Family Rm.	Rec. Rm.	Bedrooms	# Baths	Laundry	Other	Area Sq. Ft.
Basement												
Level 1	1	1	1	1			1	3	2		UH Porch	1,888
Level 2												

Finished area **above** grade contains: 7 Rooms; 3 Bedroom(s); 2 Bath(s); 1,888 Square Feet of Gross Living Area

INTERIOR — Materials/Condition
- Floors: Hardwood/Ave.
- Walls: Plaster/Ave.
- Trim/Finish: Wood/Ave.
- Bath Floor: Cer.tile/Ave.
- Bath Wainscot: Cer.tile/Ave.
- Doors: Wood/Ave.

HEATING
- Type: HW
- Fuel: Gas
- Condition: Good

COOLING
- Central: None
- Other: 2 Window
- Condition: Ave.

KITCHEN EQUIP.
- Refrigerator:
- Range/Oven: [X]
- Disposal: [X]
- Dishwasher:
- Fan/Hood: [X]
- Microwave:
- Washer/Dryer:

ATTIC
- None: [X]
- Stairs:
- Drop Stair:
- Scuttle:
- Floor:
- Heated:
- Finished:

AMENITIES
- Fireplace(s) #: 1 [X]
- Patio:
- Deck:
- Porch:
- Fence:
- Pool:

CAR STORAGE:
- None:
- Garage: 2 # of cars
- Attached: X
- Detached:
- Built-In:
- Carport:
- Driveway:

COMMENTS

Additional features (special energy efficient items, etc.): Domestic solar hot water system (50 gal.) adds $2,500 value based on matched pairs of sales. They cost $3,500 new. (Continued in addenda)

Condition of the improvements, depreciation (physical, functional, and external), repairs needed, quality of construction, remodeling/additions, etc.: There are no significant repairs needed now. There is a general lack of storage space. No eating area in kitchen and no basement. The market recognized these deficiencies. Nearby railroad and industrial area estimated to cause 5% external obsolescense. (Continued in addenda)

Adverse environmental conditions (such as, but not limited to, hazardous wastes, toxic substances, etc.) present in the improvements, on the site, or in the immediate vicinity of the subject property.: (See attached Environmental Addenda)

Freddie Mac Form 70 6-93 10 CH. PAGE 1 OF 2 Fannie Mae Form 1004 (6-93) Item #112660

SUGGESTED SOLUTION — COST APPROACH

Valuation Section — UNIFORM RESIDENTIAL APPRAISAL REPORT — File No.

ESTIMATED SITE VALUE	= $ 20,000
ESTIMATED REPRODUCTION COST-NEW-OF IMPROVEMENTS:	
Dwelling 1,888 Sq. Ft @ $ 53.35	= $ 100,725
144 Sq. Ft @ $ 13.44	= 1,935
Solar domestic hot water	= 3,500
Garage/Carport 506 Sq. Ft @ $ 16.15	= 8,172
Total Estimated Cost New	= $ 114,332
Less Physical $45,733	Functional $9,000	External $5,716	= $ 60,449
Depreciated Value of Improvements	= $ 53,886
"As-is" Value of Site Improvements	= $ 3,000
INDICATED VALUE BY COST APPROACH	= $ 77,000 RD

Comments on Cost Approach (such as, source of cost estimate, site value, square foot calculation and for HUD, VA and FmHA, the estimated remaining economic life of the property):

Measurements	No. Stories	Sq. Ft.
30' x 30'	1	= 900
6' x 26'	1	= 156
26' x 32'	1	= 832
Total Gross Living Area		1,888 Sq. Ft.

Cost from Marshall & Swift (See Addenda)
Explanation of depreciation (See Addenda)
Estimated remaining economic life 45+ yrs.

SUGGESTED SOLUTION — SALES COMPARISON ANALYSIS

ITEM	SUBJECT	COMPARABLE NO. 1		COMPARABLE NO. 2		COMPARABLE NO. 3	
Address	420 Gladville Avenue, Bloomville, IL	341 Pine Road Bloomville, IL		413 Cedar Street Bloomville, IL		210 Hoover Road Bloomville, IL	
Proximity to Subject		1 Block South		½ Block West		7 Blocks South	
Sales Price	$85,000	$70,000		$73,000		$82,000	
Price/Gross Liv. Area	$45.02	$38.46		$38.93		$43.16	
Data and/or Verification Source	Lender	SREA Mkt. Data Center		MLS Service		Appraiser's File	
VALUE ADJUSTMENTS	DESCRIPTION	DESCRIPTION	+(-) $ Adjustment	DESCRIPTION	+(-) $ Adjustment	DESCRIPTION	+(-) $ Adjustment
Sales or Financing Concessions		None reported Equal		None Reported Equal		None Reported Equal	
Date of Sale/Time		1/6/ 2/		11/3/ 1/		12/4/ 1/	
Location	Average	Avg./Equal		Avg./Equal		Good/Sup.	-5,000
Leasehold/Fee Simple	Fee Simple	Fee Simple		Fee Simple		Fee Simple	
Site	11,500 Sq Ft	About Equal		About Equal		About Equal	
View	Avg./Typical	Equal		Equal		Equal	
Design and Appeal	Ranch/Avg.	Equal		Equal		Equal	
Quality of Construction	Average	Avg./Equal		Avg./Equal		Avg./Equal	
Age Act./Eff.	30A/30E	30A/30E Equal		30A/30E Equal		30A/30E Equal	
Condition	Average	Avg./Equal		Avg./Equal		Avg./Equal	
Above Grade Room Count	Total 7 / Bdrms 3 / Baths 2	7 / 3 / 2		7 / 3 / 2		7 / 3 / 2	
Gross Living Area	1,888 Sq. Ft.	1,820 Sq. Ft.	+1,700	1,875 Sq. Ft.	+325	1,900 Sq. Ft.	-300
Basement & Finished Rooms Below Grade	Crawl Space	Crawl Space Equal		Crawl Space Equal		Crawl Space Equal	
Functional Utility	Avg./Poor Stor	Equal/Poor Stor.		Equal/Poor Stor.		Equal/Poor Stor.	
Heating/Cooling	HW/2 Window	Equal/Equal		Equal/Equal		Equal/Equal	
Energy Efficient Items	Dom Solar HW	None	+2,500	None	+2,500	Dom Solar HW	
Garage/Carport	2 Car Att.Gar	2 Car Att./Eq		2 Car Att.Eq		2 Car Att./Eq	
Porch, Patio, Deck,	144 Sq Ft Por	No Porch	+1,000	No Porch	+1,000	Open Por/Eq.	
Fireplace(s), etc.	1 Fireplace	No Fireplace	+2,000	1 Fireplace		1 Fireplace/Eq	
Fence, Pool, etc.	Fence	Equal		Equal		Equal	
Kit Eating Area	None	None/Equal		None/Equal		None/Equal	
Net Adj. (total)		[X] + [ ] -	$7,200	[X] + [ ] -	$3,825	[ ] + [X] -	$5,300
Adjusted Sales Price of Comparable			$77,200		$76,825		$76,700

Comments on Sales Comparison (including the subject property's compatibility to the neighborhood, etc.): Subject Property is typical of many houses in the neighborhood as are all the comparable sales. Size adjustment was based on $25 per sq. ft. of GLA difference which is the approximate value of the comparable improvements (after deducting their site value). Fireplaces estimated to add $2,000 value. Porches add value approximately equal to their depreciated cost. $2,500 Domestic Hot Water Heating System adjustment taken from the market by matched pairs. (See addenda)

ITEM	SUBJECT	COMPARABLE NO. 1	COMPARABLE NO. 2	COMPARABLE NO. 3
Date, Price and Data Source, for prior sales within year of appraisal	Purchased by Present owner 8 years ago	$69,000 six months ago. MLS Service	None in past year	None in past year.

Analysis of any current agreement of sale, option, or listing of the subject property and analysis of any prior sales of subject and comparables within one year of the date of appraisal: Copy of the ratified sales contract attached to this report.

INDICATED VALUE BY SALES COMPARISON APPROACH $77,000
INDICATED VALUE BY INCOME APPROACH (If Applicable) Estimated Market Rent $640 /Mo. x Gross Rent Multiplier 122 = $78,080

SUGGESTED SOLUTION — RECONCILIATION

This appraisal is made ☐ "as is" ☒ subject to the repairs, alterations, inspections or conditions listed below ☐ subject to completion per plans and specifications.

Conditions of Appraisal: Recommend a termite inspection

This appraisal is to be used only by the lender client for mortgage loan security purposes.

Final Reconciliation: This is a one story brick veener, 30 year old ranch home (7,3,2). It is typical of many houses in this area. Good data was available for all three approaches to value. $77,000 was selected as the final value estimate. (See addenda). Report includes 16 addenda pages.

The purpose of this appraisal is to estimate the market value of the real property that is the subject of this report, based on the above conditions and the certification, contingent and limiting conditions, and market value definition that are stated in the attached Freddie Mac Form 439/Fannie Mae Form 1004B (Revised 6/30/93).

I (WE) ESTIMATE THE MARKET VALUE, AS DEFINED, OF THE REAL PROPERTY THAT IS THE SUBJECT OF THIS REPORT, AS OF 3/1/ (WHICH IS THE DATE OF INSPECTION AND THE EFFECTIVE DATE OF THIS REPORT) TO BE $ 77,000

APPRAISER:
- Signature: Appraiser's Signature
- Name: Appraiser's printed or typed name
- Date Report Signed: March 20,
- State Certification #: Appraiser's number State: State
- Or State License #: Appraiser's number State: State

SUPERVISORY APPRAISER (ONLY IF REQUIRED):
- Signature: Supervisor's Signature ☐ Did ☒ Did Not Inspect Property
- Name: Supervisor's printed or typed name
- Date Report Signed: March 20
- State Certification #: Supervisor's number State: State
- Or State License #: Supervisor's number State: State

SUGGESTED SOLUTION — Sales Contract

Approved Standard Agreement Form

AGREEMENT

This Agreement to buy and to sell real property is made between

1. SELLER (S): Mae B. Zeller
   ADDRESS: 420 Gladville Avenue, Bloomville, IL
2. BUYER (S): Will N. Buyer
   ADDRESS: 23 Oak Park Rd., Oakville, IL 60611
3. PURCHASE PRICE: $ 85,000
   Payable as follows:
   a. By Initial Deposit submitted herewith .... $ 1,000
   b. By Additional Deposit due upon Seller's acceptance .... $ 4,000
   c. By Additional Deposit due upon satisfaction of financing contingency ... $ 5,000
   d. By Proceeds of Third Party Financing .... $ 75,000
   e. By Proceeds of Seller Financing .... $
   f. Balance due at closing .... $
   TOTAL (MUST EQUAL PURCHASE PRICE) .... $ 85,000
4. REAL PROPERTY:
   a. Street address: 420 Gladville Ave.
   b. Town: Bloomville, IL , Connecticut
   c. Approximate land size: ¼ Acre
5. PERSONAL PROPERTY, IF ANY, TO BE INCLUDED: None

6. THIRD PARTY FINANCING CONTINGENCY:
   a. Amount: $ 75,000
   b. Initial Interest Rate: 7 % per annum Fixed
   c. Term: 20 years
   d. Time limit for commitment: 30 days
   (If 6a, 6b, 6c and 6d are completed, item #G on the reverse side is automatically made a part of this Agreement.)
7. SELLER FINANCING:
   a. Amount: $ —
   b. Interest Rate: % per annum
   c. Term: years
   d. Demand Date:
   e. SELLER to approve BUYER's credit within .... days
   (If 7a, 7b, 7c, 7d and 7e are completed, item #H on the reverse side is automatically made a part of this Agreement.)
8. PHYSICAL INSPECTION CONTINGENCY:
   a. Inspection period after contract 10 days
   b. Notification period after inspection period 10 days
   (If 8a and 8b are completed, item #I on the reverse side is automatically made a part of this Agreement.)
9. CLOSING DATE: 5 / 25 /
   (month) (day) (year)
10. TITLE SEARCH: The expense of the examination of title and Certificate of Title shall be the expense of the BUYER.
11. TAX ADJUSTMENT: We both agree to pro rate the taxes at the time of closing. This adjustment will be based upon "the uniform fiscal year method."
12. UNLESS DELETED, THE FOLLOWING PARAGRAPHS ON THE REVERSE SIDE ARE HEREBY MADE A PART OF THIS AGREEMENT: A, B, C, D, E, F, J, K, L, M, N, O, P
13. LISTING BROKER: Bloomville Real Estate Co.
14. COOPERATING BROKER, IF ANY: Oak Park Realtors
15. TIME TO ACCEPT: The SELLER shall have 5 days following the date set forth in #16 to accept this Agreement.
16. BUYER'S SIGNATURE (S): Will N. Buyer   Date: 2-25-
17. SELLER'S SIGNATURE (S): Mae B. Seller   Date: 2-29-

Revision 2-92 (5th Printing)

SUGGESTED SOLUTION

Photographs of Subject & Street / Photographs of Comparable Sales

PHOTOGRAPH ADDENDUM

Borrower/Client: Will N. Buyer
Property Address: 420 Gladville Avenue
City: Bloomville   County: Lake   State: IL   Zip Code: 60611
Lender: Easy Money Institution

FRONT OF SUBJECT PROPERTY

The photograph of the front of the subject should also include one side of the subject property.

REAR OF SUBJECT PROPERTY

The photograph of the rear of the subject should also include the side of the subject property not shown in the photograph of the front of the subject property.

STREET SCENE

The photograph of the street should show the subject property in the foreground.

☐ ADDITIONAL PHOTOGRAPHS ON REVERSE SIDE

PHOTOGRAPH ADDENDUM

Borrower/Client: Will N. Buyer
Property Address: 420 Gladville Avenue
City: Bloomville   County: Lake   State: IL   Zip Code: 60611
Lender: Easy Money Institution

COMPARABLE SALE #1

A photograph of each comparable sale is now required by the FHLMC and the FNMA.

COMPARABLE SALE #2

A photograph of each comparable sale is now required by the FHLMC and the FNMA.

COMPARABLE SALE #3

A photograph of each comparable sale is now required by the FHLMC and the FNMA.

☐ ADDITIONAL PHOTOGRAPHS ON REVERSE SIDE

SUGGESTED SOLUTION — Building Sketch

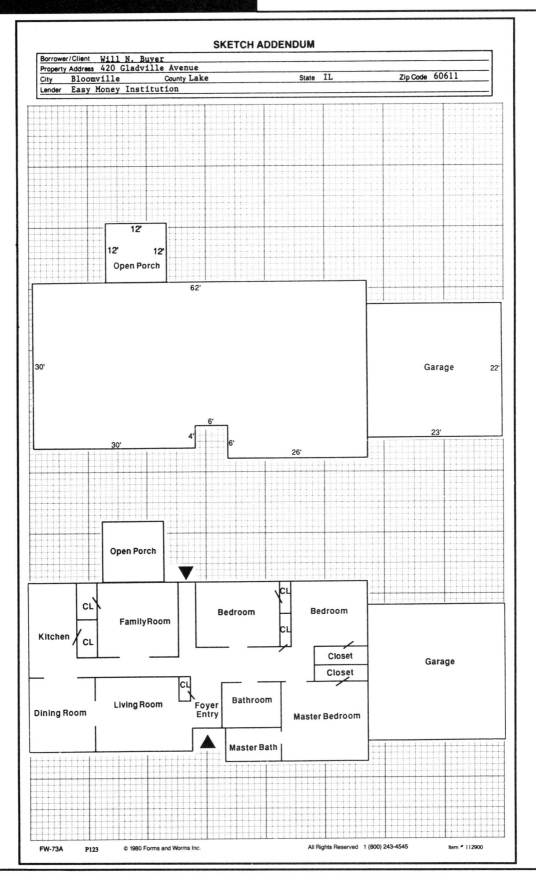

SUGGESTED SOLUTION

Neighborhood Map

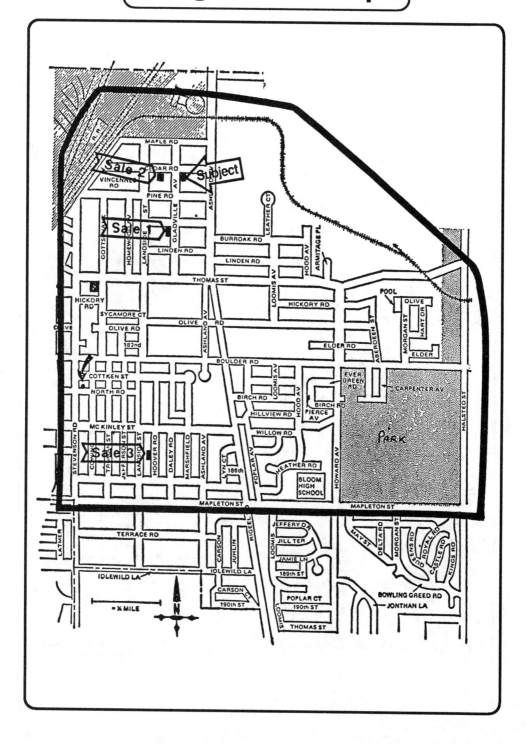

SUGGESTED SOLUTION — Community Map

Community Map

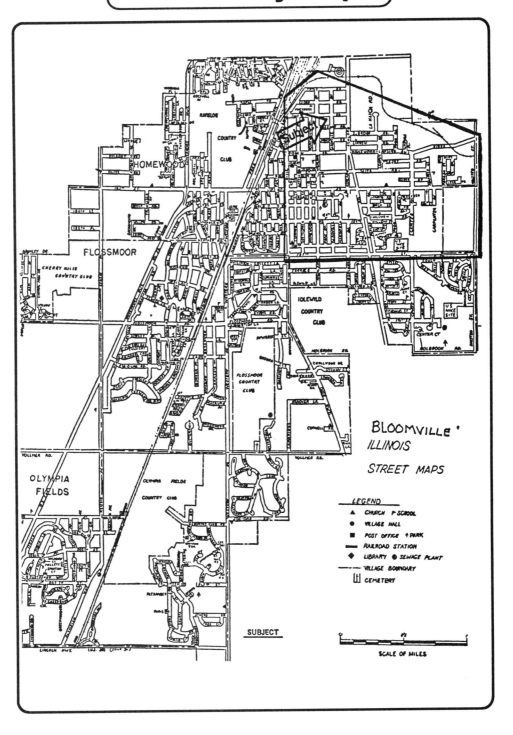

SUGGESTED SOLUTION — Regional Map

Regional Map

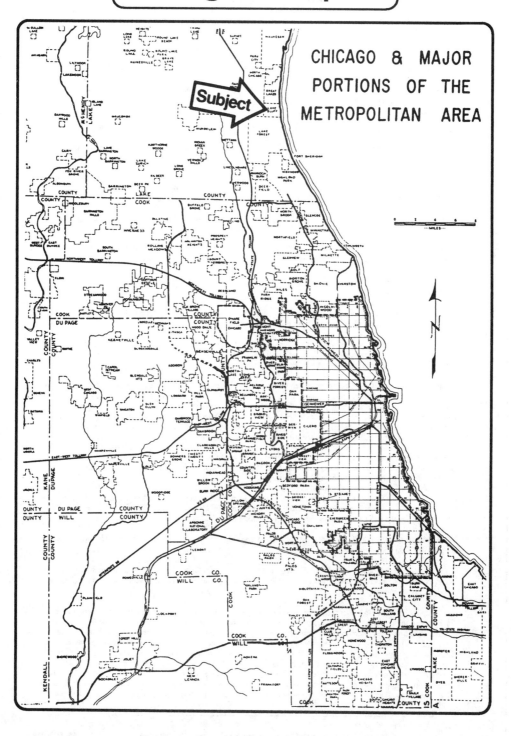

CHICAGO & MAJOR PORTIONS OF THE METROPOLITAN AREA

SUGGESTED SOLUTION

DEFINITION OF MARKET VALUE CONTINGENT AND LIMITING CONDITIONS

DEFINITION OF MARKET VALUE: The most probable price which a property should bring in a competitive and open market under all conditions requisite to a fair sale, the buyer and seller, each acting prudently, knowledgeably and assuming the price is not affected by undue stimulus. Implicit in this definition is the consummation of a sale as of a specified date and the passing of title from seller to buyer under conditions whereby: (1) buyer and seller are typically motivated; (2) both parties are well informed or well advised, and each acting in what he considers his own best interest; (3) a reasonable time is allowed for exposure in the open market; (4) payment is made in terms of cash in U. S. dollars or in terms of financial arrangements comparable thereto; and (5) the price represents the normal consideration for the property sold unaffected by special or creative financing or sales concessions* granted by anyone associated with the sale.

*Adjustments to the comparables must be made for special or creative financing or sales concessions. No adjustments are necessary for those costs which are normally paid by sellers as a result of tradition or law in a market area; these costs are readily identifiable since the seller pays these costs in virtually all sales transactions. Special or creative financing adjustments can be made to the comparable property by comparisons to financing terms offered by a third party institutional lender that is not already involved in the property or transaction. Any adjustment should not be calculated on a mechanical dollar for dollar cost of the financing or concession but the dollar amount of any adjustment should approximate the market's reaction to the financing or concessions based on the appraiser's judgment.

STATEMENT OF LIMITING CONDITIONS AND APPRAISER'S CERTIFICATION

CONTINGENT AND LIMITING CONDITIONS: The appraiser's certification that appears in the appraisal report is subject to the following conditions:

1. The appraiser will not be responsible for matters of a legal nature that affect either the property being appraised or the title to it. The appraiser assumes that the title is good and marketable and, therefore, will not render any opinions about the title. The property is appraised on the basis of it being under responsible ownership.

2. The appraiser has provided a sketch in the appraisal report to show approximate dimensions of the improvements and the sketch is included only to assist the reader of the report in visualizing the property and understanding the appraiser's determination of its size.

3. The appraiser has examined the available flood maps that are provided by the Federal Emergency Management Agency (or other data sources) and has noted in the appraisal report whether the subject site is located in an identified Special Flood Hazard Area. Because the appraiser is not a surveyor, he or she makes no guarantees, express or implied, regarding this determination.

4. The appraiser will not give testimony or appear in court because he or she made an appraisal of the property in question, unless specific arrangements to do so have been made beforehand.

5. The appraiser has estimated the value of the land in the cost approach at its highest and best use and the improvements at their contributory value. These separate valuations of the land and improvements must not be used in conjunction with any other appraisal and are invalid if they are so used.

6. The appraiser has noted in the appraisal report any adverse conditions (such as, needed repairs, depreciation, the presence of hazardous wastes, toxic substances, etc.) observed during the inspection of the subject property or that he or she became aware of during the normal research involved in performing the appraisal. Unless otherwise stated in the appraisal report, the appraiser has no knowledge of any hidden or unapparent conditions of the property or adverse environmental conditions (including the presence of hazardous wastes, toxic substances, etc.) that would make the property more or less valuable, and has assumed that there are no such conditions and makes no guarantees or warranties, express or implied, regarding the condition of the property. The appraiser will not be responsible for any such conditions that do exist or for any engineering or testing that might be required to discover whether such conditions exist. Because the appraiser is not an expert in the field of environmental hazards, the appraisal report must not be considered as an environmental assessment of the property.

7. The appraiser obtained the information, estimates, and opinions that were expressed in the appraisal report from sources that he or she considers to be reliable and believes them to be true and correct. The appraiser does not assume responsibility for the accuracy of such items that were furnished by other parties.

8. The appraiser will not disclose the contents of the appraisal report except as provided for in the Uniform Standards of Professional Appraisal Practice.

9. The appraiser has based his or her appraisal report and valuation conclusion for an appraisal that is subject to satisfactory completion, repairs, or alterations on the assumption that completion of the improvements will be performed in a workmanlike manner.

10. The appraiser must provide his or her prior written consent before the lender/client specified in the appraisal report can distribute the appraisal report (including conclusions about the property value, the appraiser's identity and professional designations, and references to any professional appraisal organizations or the firm with which the appraiser is associated) to anyone other than the borrower; the mortgagee or its successors and assigns; the mortgage insurer; consultants; professional appraisal organizations; any state or federally approved financial institution; or any department, agency, or instrumentality of the United States or any state or the District of Columbia; except that the lender/client may distribute the property description section of the report only to data collection or reporting service(s) without having to obtain the appraiser's prior written consent. The appraiser's written consent and approval must also be obtained before the appraisal can be conveyed by anyone to the public through advertising, public relations, news, sales, or other media.

Freddie Mac Form 439 6-93   Fannie Mae Form 1004B 6-93

SUGGESTED SOLUTION

Appraiser's Certification
Supervisory Appraiser's Certification

APPRAISER'S CERTIFICATION: The Appraiser certifies and agrees that:

1. I have researched the subject market area and have selected a minimum of three recent sales of properties most similar and proximate to the subject property for consideration in the sales comparison analysis and have made a dollar adjustment when appropriate to reflect the market reaction to those items of significant variation. If a significant item in a comparable property is superior to, or more favorable than, the subject property, I have made a negative adjustment to reduce the adjusted sales price of the comparable and, if a significant item in a comparable property is inferior to, or less favorable than the subject property, I have made a positive adjustment to increase the adjusted sales price of the comparable.

2. I have taken into consideration the factors that have an impact on value in my development of the estimate of market value in the appraisal report. I have not knowingly withheld any significant information from the appraisal report and I believe, to the best of my knowledge, that all statements and information in the appraisal report are true and correct.

3. I stated in the appraisal report only my own personal, unbiased, and professional analysis, opinions, and conclusions, which are subject only to the contingent and limiting conditions specified in this form.

4. I have no present or prospective interest in the property that is the subject to this report, and I have no present or prospective personal interest or bias with respect to the participants in the transaction. I did not base, either partially or completely, my analysis and/or the estimate of market value in the appraisal report on the race, color, religion, sex, handicap, familial status, or national origin of either the prospective owners or occupants of the subject property or of the present owners or occupants of the properties in the vicinity of the subject property.

5. I have no present or contemplated future interest in the subject property, and neither my current or future employment nor my compensation for performing this appraisal is contingent on the appraised value of the property.

6. I was not required to report a predetermined value or direction in value that favors the cause of the client or any related party, the amount of the value estimate, the attainment of a specific result, or the occurrence of a subsequent event in order to receive my compensation and/or employment for performing the appraisal. I did not base the appraisal report on a requested minimum valuation, a specific valuation, or the need to approve a specific mortgage loan.

7. I performed this appraisal in conformity with the Uniform Standards of Professional Appraisal Practice that were adopted and promulgated by the Appraisal Standards Board of The Appraisal Foundation and that were in place as of the effective date of this appraisal, with the exception of the departure provision of those Standards, which does not apply. I acknowledge that an estimate of a reasonable time for exposure in the open market is a condition in the definition of market value and the estimate I developed is consistent with the marketing time noted in the neighborhood section of this report, unless I have otherwise stated in the reconciliation section.

8. I have personally inspected the interior and exterior areas of the subject property and the exterior of all properties listed as comparables in the appraisal report. I further certify that I have noted any apparent or known adverse conditions in the subject improvements, on the subject site, or on any site within the immediate vicinity of the subject property of which I am aware and have made adjustments for these adverse conditions in my analysis of the property value to the extent that I had market evidence to support them. I have also commented about the effect of the adverse conditions on the marketability of the subject property.

9. I personally prepared all conclusions and opinions about the real estate that were set forth in the appraisal report. If I relied on significant professional assistance from any individual or individuals in the performance of the appraisal or the preparation of the appraisal report, I have named such individual(s) and disclosed the specific tasks performed by them in the reconciliation section of this appraisal report. I certify that any individual so named is qualified to perform the tasks. I have not authorized anyone to make a change to any item in the report; therefore, if an unauthorized change is made to the appraisal report, I will take no responsibility for it.

SUPERVISORY APPRAISER'S CERTIFICATION: If a supervisory appraiser signed the appraisal report, he or she certifies and agrees that: I directly supervise the appraiser who prepared the appraisal report, have reviewed the appraisal report, agree with the statements and conclusions of the appraiser, agree to be bound by the appraiser's certifications numbered 4 through 7 above, and am taking full responsibility for the appraisal and the appraisal report.

ADDRESS OF PROPERTY APPRAISED: 420 Gladville Avenue, Bloomville, IL

APPRAISER:
Signature: Appraiser's Signature
Name: Appraiser's printed or typed name
Date Signed: March 20,
State Certification #: Appraiser's number
or State License #: Appraiser's number
State: IL
Expiration Date of Certification or License: Date

SUPERVISORY APPRAISER (only if required):
Signature: Supervisor's Signature
Name: Supervisor's printed or typed name
Date Signed: March 20,
State Certification #: Supervisor's number
or State License #: Supervisor's number
State: IL
Expiration Date of Certification or License: Date

[ ] Did [XX] Did Not Inspect Property

Freddie Mac Form 439 6-93   Fannie Mae Form 1004B 6-93

SUGGESTED SOLUTION

SINGLE FAMILY COMPARABLE RENT SCHEDULE

This form is intended to provide the appraiser with a familiar format to estimate the market rent of the subject property. Adjustments should be made only for items of significant difference between the comparables and the subject property.

ITEM	SUBJECT	COMPARABLE NO. 1		COMPARABLE NO. 2		COMPARABLE NO. 3	
Address	420 Gladville Bloomville, IL	341 Pine Road Bloomville, IL 60611		413 Cedar Street Bloomville, IL 60611		210 Hover Road Bloomville, IL 60611	
Proximity to Subject		3 blocks south		5 blocks south		1 block east	
Date Lease Begins / Date Lease Expires	No Lease	No Lease		No Lease		No Lease	
Monthly Rental	If Currently Not Rented: $ rented	$575		$600		$670	
Less: Utilities Furniture	$ unfurnished	$ unfurnished		$ unfurnished		$ unfurnished	
Adjusted Monthly Rent	$ not rented	$575		$600		$670	
Data Source	owner	owner		owner		owner	
RENT ADJUSTMENTS	DESCRIPTION	DESCRIPTION	+(−) $ Adjustment	DESCRIPTION	+(−) $ Adjustment	DESCRIPTION	+(−) $ Adjustment
Rent Concessions		None	0	None	0	None	0
Location/View	Ave/Ave	Ave/Ave	0	Ave/Ave	0	Good/Ave	−25
Design and Appeal	Ave	Ave	0	Ave	0	Ave	0
Age/Condition	30yrs/Ave	30yrs/Ave	0	30yrs/Ave	0	30yrs/Ave	0
Above Grade Room Count	Total 7 / Bdrms 3 / Baths 2	Total 7 / Bdrms 3 / Baths 2	+30	Total 7 / Bdrms 3 / Baths 2	+15	Total 7 / Bdrms 3 / Baths 2	−5
Gross Living Area	1,888 Sq. Ft.	1,820 Sq. Ft.		1,875 Sq. Ft.		1,900 Sq. Ft.	
Other (e.g., basement, etc.) Fireplace	1 Masonry	None	+10	1 Masonry	0	1 Masonry	0
Other: Solar H.W.	Solar H.W.	No Solar H.W.	+25	No Solar H.W.	+25	Solar H.W.	0
Net Adj. (total)		[x] + [ ] − $ 65		[x] + [ ] − $ 40		[ ] + [x] − $ 30	
Indicated Monthly Market Rent		$ 640		$ 640		$ 640	

Comments on market data, including the range of rents for single family properties, an estimate of vacancy for single family rental properties, the general trend of rents and vacancy, and support for the above adjustments. (Rent concessions should be adjusted to the market, not to the subject property.)

Comparable No. 1: Locaton is inferior to subject's. No domestic hot water system, no fireplace, no porch.

Comparable No. 2: Locaton is inferior to subject's. No domestic hot water system, no porch.

Comparable No. 3: Very similar to subject.

Final Reconciliation of Market Rent:
Equal weight as given to all three comparable rentals which were good indications of the rental value of the subject property.

I (WE) ESTIMATE THE MONTHLY MARKET RENT OF THE SUBJECT AS OF __March 1__ TO BE $ __640__

Appraiser(s) SIGNATURE __Your signature__   Review Appraiser SIGNATURE __Review Appraiser's signature__ (If applicable)

NAME __Your name printed or typed__   NAME __Review Appraiser's Printed or Typed__

Freddie Mac Form 1000 (8/88)   Fannie Mae Form 1007 (8/88)

SUGGESTED SOLUTION — **Operating Income Statement (front)**

Operating Income Statement
One- to Four-Family Investment Property and Two- to Four-Family Owner-Occupied Property

Property Address
420 Gladville Avenue, Bloomville, IL 60611
Street / City / State / Zip Code

General Instructions: This form is to be prepared jointly by the loan applicant, the appraiser, and the lender's underwriter. The applicant must complete the following schedule indicating each unit's rental status, lease expiration date, current rent, market rent, and the responsibility for utility expenses. Rental figures must be based on the rent for an "unfurnished" unit.

	Currently Rented	Expiration Date	Current Rent Per Month	Market Rent Per Month	Utility Expense	Paid By Owner	Paid By Tenant
Unit No. 1	Yes X No	No lease	Not rental	640.	Electricity	☐	☒
Unit No. 2	Yes __ No __		$	$	Gas	☐	☒
Unit No. 3	Yes __ No __		$	$	Fuel Oil	☐	☐
Unit No. 4	Yes __ No __		$	$	Fuel (Other)	☐	☐
Total			$	$	Water/Sewer	☐	☒
					Trash Removal	☐	☒

The applicant should complete all of the income and expense projections and for existing properties provide actual year-end operating statements for the past two years (for new properties the applicant's projected income and expenses must be provided). This Operating Income Statement and any previous operating statements the applicant provides must then be sent to the appraiser for review, comment, and/or adjustments next to the applicant's figures (e.g., Applicant/Appraiser 288/300). If the appraiser is retained to complete the form instead of the applicant, the lender must provide to the appraiser the aforementioned operating statements, mortgage insurance premium, HOA dues, leasehold payments, subordinate financing, and/or any other relevant information as to the income and expenses of the subject property received from the applicant to substantiate the projections. The underwriter should carefully review the applicant's/appraiser's projections and the appraiser's comments concerning those projections. The underwriter should make any final adjustments that are necessary to more accurately reflect any income or expense items that appear unreasonable for the market. (Real estate taxes and insurance on these types of properties are included in PITI and not calculated as an annual expense item.) Income should be based on current rents, but should not exceed market rents. When there are no current rents because the property is proposed, new, or currently vacant, market rents should be used.

Annual Income and Expense Projection for Next 12 months

Income (Do not include income for owner-occupied units)	By Applicant/Appraiser	Adjustments by Lender's Underwriter
Gross Annual Rental (from unit(s) to be rented)	$ 7,680	$
Other Income (include sources)	+ 0	+
Total	$ 7,680	$
Less Vacancy/Rent Loss	− 384 (5 %)	− (%)
Effective Gross Income	$ 7,296	$

Expenses (Do not include expenses for owner-occupied units)		
Electricity	0	
Gas	0	
Fuel Oil	−	
Fuel (Type - ___)	0	
Water/Sewer	0	
Trash Removal	0	
Pest Control	0	
Other Taxes or Licenses	0	
Casual Labor	0	

This includes the costs for public area cleaning, snow removal, etc., even though the applicant may not elect to contract for such services.

Interior Paint/Decorating	200	

This includes the costs of contract labor and materials that are required to maintain the interiors of the living units.

General Repairs/Maintenance	300	

This includes the costs of contract labor and materials that are required to maintain the public corridors, stairways, roofs, mechanical systems, grounds, etc.

Management Expenses	384 (5%)	

These are the customary expenses that a professional management company would charge to manage the property.

Supplies	50	

This includes the costs of items like light bulbs, janitorial supplies, etc.

Total Replacement Reserves - See Schedule on Pg. 2	493	
Miscellaneous		
Total Operating Expenses	$ 1427	$

Freddie Mac Form 998 Aug 88 — Item # 114700 — Fannie Mae Form 216 Aug 88

Forms and Worms® Inc. 315 Whitney Ave. New Haven, Ct. 06511 All Rights Reserved 1 (800) 243-4545

SUGGESTED SOLUTION — Operating Income Statement (back)

Replacement Reserve Schedule

Adequate replacement reserves must be calculated regardless of whether actual reserves are provided for on the owner's operating statements or are customary in the local market. This represents the total average yearly reserves. Generally, all equipment and components that have a remaining life of more than one year—such as refrigerators, stoves, clothes washers/dryers, trash compactors, furnaces, roofs, and carpeting, etc.—should be expensed on a replacement cost basis.

Equipment	Replacement Cost	Remaining Life			By Applicant/Appraiser	Lender Adjustments
Stoves/Ranges	@ $ 600	ea. + 10 Yrs. x	1	Units = $	60	$
Refrigerators	@ $ N/A	ea. + ___ Yrs. x		Units = $		$
Dishwashers	@ $ N/A	ea. + ___ Yrs. x		Units = $		$
A/C Units	@ $ 500	ea. + 10 Yrs. x	1	Units = $	50	$
C. Washer/Dryers	@ $ N/A	ea. + ___ Yrs. x		Units = $		$
HW Heaters	@ $	ea. + ___ Yrs. x		Units = $		$
Furnace(s)	@ $	ea. + ___ Yrs. x		Units = $		$
(Other) Solar Hot water	@ $ 3,500	ea. + 15 Yrs. x		Units = $	233	$
Roof	@ $ 3,000	___ + 20 Yrs. x One Bldg. =			$ 150	$

Carpeting (Wall to Wall) — Remaining Life

(Units) N/A Total Sq. Yds. @ $___ Per Sq. Yd. + ___ Yrs. = $ _____ $ _____
(Public Areas) N/A Total Sq. Yds. @ $___ Per Sq. Yd. + ___ Yrs. = $ _____ $ _____

Total Replacement Reserves. (Enter on Pg. 1) $ 493 $ _____

Operating Income Reconciliation

$ 7,296 (Effective Gross Income) − $ 1,427 (Total Operating Expenses) = $ 5,869 (Operating Income) ÷ 12 = $ 489 (Monthly Operating Income)

$ 489 (Monthly Operating Income) − $ 530.80 (Monthly Housing Expense) = $ (41.80) (Net Cash Flow)

(Note: Monthly Housing Expense includes principal and interest on the mortgage, hazard insurance premiums, real estate taxes, mortgage insurance premiums, HOA dues, leasehold payments, and subordinate financing payments.)

Underwriter's Instructions for 2-4 Family Owner-Occupied Properties

- If Monthly Operating Income is a positive number, enter as "Net Rental Income" in the "Gross Monthly Income" section of Freddie Mac Form 65/Fannie Mae Form 1003. If Monthly Operating Income is a negative number, it must be included as a liability for qualification purposes.

- The borrower's monthly housing expense-to-income ratio must be calculated by comparing the total Monthly Housing Expense for the subject property to the borrower's stable monthly income.

Underwriter's Instructions for 1-4 Family Investment Properties

- If Net Cash Flow is a positive number, enter as "Net Rental Income" in the "Gross Monthly Income" section of Freddie Mac Form 65/Fannie Mae Form 1003. If Net Cash Flow is a negative number, it must be included as a liability for qualification purposes.

- The borrower's monthly housing expense-to-income ratio must be calculated by comparing the total monthly housing expense for the borrower's primary residence to the borrower's stable monthly income.

Appraiser's Comments (including sources for data and rationale for the projections)

The estimate of projected income and expenses supplied by the owner seem reasonable based on the rentals and expenses known to the appraiser of similar properties in this market.

Appraiser's name typed | Appraiser's signature | March 1,

Underwriter's Comments and Rationale for Adjustments

Buyer has applied for a $68,000., 20 year, 11% fixed rate mortgage with a $312.47 monthly payment. Monthly taxes are $188.33 ($2,660/12). Hazard Insurance is $30 monthly ($360/12).

Underwriter's name typed | Underwriter's signature | March 1,

Freddie Mac Form 998 Aug 88 — Fannie Mae Form 216 Aug 88

SUGGESTED SOLUTION — Additional Comments

Borrower/Client: Will N. Buyer   **Lender:** Easy Money Institution

ADDITIONAL COMMENTS

SUBJECT:

Information about the pending sale was obtained from the Lender and verified by the Seller Mae B. Seller. A copy of the ratified sales contract is included as part of the addenda.

Information about any special conditions and/or loan charges ,to be paid by the Seller was obtained from the lender who said there were none.

The subject property has not sold within the past year. It was purchased by the present owner about 8 years ago.

NEIGHBORHOOD:

In this neighborhood there is little direct relationship between the age of houses and their value. Older houses that have been modernized sell for prices per sq. ft. of gross living area similar to newer houses.

The house being appraised is newer than the typical house in this neighborhood It conforms sufficiently in size and value with the older houses in the neighborhood. Therefore it does not suffer any additional functional obsolescence.

This house is within walking distance of the grammar and high schools. There is good public transportation available near the subject property including frequent train service to Center City. However, this ,has little effect on the value of the property because may properties in the market have similar transportation available.

There are few recreational facilities available near the subject property. They consist of a swimming pool, tennis courts and a golf course. This has little effect on the value of the property because the available facilities are similar to many house in the same market.

This market provides an average environmental for the house being appraised. There are not observed factor in the neighborhood that effect negatively the marketability of the house. All the items in the rating grid are rated good or average. The public schools. parks, view and noise levels are typical for this type of neighborhood

The subject property is on the north side of the Wrightville neighborhood near the railroad station and industrial area and is effected negatively by them.

This market is stable. The community continues to grow at a steady rate.

SITE:

The improvement on the property appear to conform to the current zoning regulations. In the event of a major loss by fire it could be rebuilt without obtaining a zoning variance.

The improvements are substantially the Highest and Best Use except for those items of depreciation which are described in the appraisal as items of functional obsolescence.

The landscaping on this site is average which is typical of other sites in this neighborhood.

The size, shape and landscaping of this site is typical of many sites in this neighborhood. There are no apparent adverse easements, encroachments, special assessments, slide areas, etc. that will have a negative effect on the value of the property.

DESCRIPTION OF IMPROVEMENTS.

This house is in average condition for a house of this age in this neighborhood. Its actual age and effective age are the same (30 years).

There is no evidence of termite or other infestation. However, because of its age and the prevalence of termites in this area a termite inspection is recommended.

The number of rooms, bedrooms and baths is typical of many houses In this neighborhood. The foyer has been excluded from the room count.

COMMENTS:

The interior and equipment are typical of houses in this neighborhood. The appraised value includes only those items of equipment that are considered to be part of the real estate. The house is well maintained. No significant repairs are currently needed. See Environmental Addenda for additional information on environmental hazards.

COST APPROACH:

This house is 30 years old. It does not need any modernization. The bathrooms, kitchen, mechanical equipment and other features of the house meet the current standards for houses of this age in this market.

Included in the value of the site improvements are the walks, driveways, fences, utility connections and landscaping.

The house has a general lack of storage space. $2,000 of functional obsolescence was estimated for this deficiency

There is no eating area in the kitchen which is expected in this market.. $2,000 of functional obsolescence was estimated for this deficiency

There is only a crawl space under the house in a market that prefers. $4,000 of functional obsolescence was estimated for this deficiency. In addition the reproduction cost does not include the cost of a basement so the difference for a house with and without a basement would be greater than $4,000.

The domestic solar hot water heater (which is less than a year old cost $3,500. It adds only $2,500 in value therefore it suffers $1,000 functional obsolescence.

SALES COMPARISON ANALYSIS:

The comparable sales were verified and no personal property was included in their sale price.

All comparable sales are closed sales.

In order to locate these comparable sales we checked the appraisals we previously made in the area, the SREA Market Data Center, MLS Service and our own files..

The comparable sale were verified by the sources shown in the report and the appraiser was able to ascertain that there were no significant sales concessions, special financing or other special considerations.

The dates of sales reported are the closing dates. Many comparable closed sales were considered in making this appraisal. The three closed sales displayed are considered to be the most comparable and the best indicators of value for the subject property. Most weight is given to Comparable #2 because it required the fewest adjustments, is in a similar location to the subject and has the most reliable adjustments.

INCOME APPROACH:

Good rental data and information about houses that were rented when they were sold was available in this neighborhood to develop an Estimated Market Rent and Gross Rent Multiplier.

RECONCILIATION

Most weight was given to the value estimate derived by the Sales Comparison Approach, which is well supported by the Cost and Income Approaches.

COMPETENCY

All signers of this report believe they are competent to make this appraisal based on their experience and educational background.

Supplemental Certification: In addition to the signed certification attached to this appraisal report the signers of the certification further certify that to the best of my (our) knowledge and belief:

- the statements of fact contained in this report are true and correct.
- the reported analyses, opinions, and conclusions are limited only by the reported assumptions and limiting conditions, and are my personal, impartial and unbiased professional analyses, opinions, and conclusions.
- I have no (or the specified) present or prospective interest in the property that is the subject of this report, and no (or the specified) personal interest with respect to the parties involved.
- I have no bias with respect to the property that is the subject of this report or to the parties involved with this assignment.
- my engagement in this assignment was not contingent upon developing or reporting predetermined results.
- my compensation for completing this assignment is not contingent upon the development or reporting of a predetermined value or direction in value that favors the cause of the client, the amount of the value opinion, the attainment of a stipulated result, or the occurrence of a subsequent event directly related to the intended use of this appraisal.
- my analyses, opinions, and conclusions were developed, and this report has been prepared, in conformity with the Uniform Standards of Professional Appraisal Practice.
- I have (or have not) made a personal inspection of the property that is the subject of this report. (If more than one person signs the report, this certification must clearly specify which individuals did and which individuals did not make a personal inspection of the appraisal property.)
- no one provided significant professional assistance to the person signing this report. (If there are exceptions, the name of each individual providing significant professional assistance must be stated.)

SUGGESTED SOLUTION

Front: ENVIRONMENTAL ADDENDUM

ENVIRONMENTAL ADDENDUM
APPARENT* HAZARDOUS SUBSTANCES AND/OR DETRIMENTAL ENVIRONMENTAL CONDITIONS

Borrower/Client	Will N. Buyer				
Address	420 Gladville Avenue				
City	Bloomville	County Lake	State IL	Zip code	60611
Lender	Easy Money Institution				

*Apparent is defined as that which is visible, obvious, evident or manifest to the appraiser.

This universal Environmental Addendum is for use with any real estate appraisal. Only the statements which have been checked by the appraiser apply to the property being appraised.

This addendum reports the results of the appraiser's routine inspection of and inquiries about the subject property and its surrounding area. It also states what assumptions were made about the existence (or nonexistence) of any hazardous substances and/or detrimental environmental conditions. **The appraiser is not an expert environmental inspector** and therefore might be unaware of existing hazardous substances and/or detrimental environmental conditions which may have a negative effect on the safety and value of the property. It is possible that tests and inspections made by a qualified environmental inspector would reveal the existence of hazardous materials and/or detrimental environmental conditions on or around the property that would negatively affect its safety and value.

DRINKING WATER

__X__ Drinking Water is supplied to the subject from a municipal water supply which is considered safe. However the only way to be absolutely certain that the water meets published standards is to have it tested at all discharge points.

____ Drinking Water is supplied by a well or other non-municipal source. It is recommended that tests be made to be certain that the property is supplied with adequate pure water.

__X__ Lead can get into drinking water from its source, the pipes, at all discharge points, plumbing fixtures and/or appliances. The only way to be certain that water does not contain an unacceptable lead level is to have it tested at all discharge points.

__X__ **The value estimated in this appraisal is based on the assumption that there is an adequate supply of safe, lead-free Drinking Water.**

Comments _Because water comes from the lake there is an ample supply year round._

SANITARY WASTE DISPOSAL

__X__ Sanitary Waste is removed from the property by a municipal sewer system.

____ Sanitary Waste is disposed of by a septic system or other sanitary on site waste disposal system. The only way to determine that the disposal system is adequate and in good working condition is to have it inspected by a qualified inspector.

__X__ **The value estimated in this appraisal is based on the assumption that the Sanitary Waste is disposed of by a municipal sewer or an adequate properly permitted alternate treatment system in good condition.**

Comments ____

SOIL CONTAMINANTS

__X__ There are no *apparent* signs of Soil Contaminants on or near the subject property (except as reported in Comments below). It is possible that research, inspection and testing by a qualified environmental inspector would reveal existing and/or potential hazardous substances and/or detrimental environmental conditions on or around the property that would negatively affect its safety and value.

__X__ **The value estimated in this appraisal is based on the assumption that the subject property is free of Soil Contaminants.**

Comments ____

ASBESTOS

__X__ All or part of the improvements were constructed before 1979 when Asbestos was a common building material. The only way to be certain that the property is free of friable and non-friable Asbestos is to have it inspected and tested by a qualified asbestos inspector.

____ The improvements were constructed after 1979. No *apparent* friable Asbestos was observed (except as reported in Comments below).

__X__ **The value estimated in this appraisal is based on the assumption that there is no uncontained friable Asbestos or other hazardous Asbestos material on the property.**

Comments ____

PCBs (POLYCHLORINATED BIPHENYLS)

__X__ There were no *apparent* leaking flourescent light ballasts, capacitors or transformers anywhere on or nearby the property (except as reported in Comments below).

__X__ There was no *apparent* visible or documented evidence known to the appraiser of soil or groundwater contamination from PCBs anywhere on the property (except as reported in Comments below).

__X__ **The value estimated in this appraisal is based on the assumption that there are no uncontained PCBs on or nearby the property.**

Comments ____

RADON

__X__ The appraiser is not aware of any Radon tests made on the subject property within the past 12 months (except as reported in Comments below).

__X__ The appraiser is not aware of any indication that the local water supplies have been found to have elevated levels of Radon or Radium.

__X__ The appraiser is not aware of any nearby properties (except as reported in Comments below) that were or currently are used for uranium, thorium or radium extraction or phosphate processing.

____ **The value estimated in this appraisal is based on the assumption that the Radon level is at or below EPA recommended levels.**

Comments ____

Test Version 2c FW-70EZ JANUARY 1991 © Forms & Worms, Inc. 315 Whitney Avenue New Haven, CT 06511 1-800-243-4545 Item #115050
National Association Environmental Risk Auditors

SUGGESTED SOLUTION — Back: ENVIRONMENTAL ADDENDUM

USTs (UNDERGROUND STORAGE TANKS)

[X] There is no *apparent* visible or documented evidence known to the appraiser of any USTs on the property nor any known historical use of the property that would likely have had USTs.

[X] There are no *apparent* petroleum storage and/or delivery facilities (including gasoline stations or chemical manufacturing plants) located on adjacent properties (except as reported in Comments below).

[ ] There are *apparent* signs of USTs existing now or in the past on the subject property. It is recommended that an inspection by a qualified UST inspector be obtained to determine the location of any USTs together with their condition and proper registration if they are active; and if they are inactive, to determine whether they were deactivated in accordance with sound industry practices.

[X] **The value estimated in this appraisal is based on the assumption that any functioning USTs are not leaking and are properly registered and that any abandoned USTs are free from contamination and were properly drained, filled and sealed.**

Comments _____

NEARBY HAZARDOUS WASTE SITES

[X] There are no *apparent* Hazardous Waste Sites on the subject property or nearby the subject property (except as reported in Comments below). Hazardous Waste Site search by a trained environmental engineer may determine that there is one or more Hazardous Waste Sites on or in the area of the subject property.

[X] **The value estimated in this appraisal is based on the assumption that there are no Hazardous Waste Sites on or nearby the subject property that negatively affect the value or safety of the property.**

Comments _____

UREA FORMALDEHYDE (UFFI) INSULATION

[X] All or part of the improvements were constructed before 1982 when UREA foam insulation was a common building material. The only way to be certain that the property is free of UREA formaldehyde is to have it inspected by a qualified UREA formaldehyde inspector.

[ ] The improvements were constructed after 1982. No *apparent* UREA formaldehyde materials were observed (except as reported in Comments below).

[X] **The value estimated in this appraisal is based on the assumption that there is no significant UFFI insulation or other UREA formaldehyde material on the property.**

Comments _____

LEAD PAINT

[X] All or part of the improvements were constructed before 1980 when Lead Paint was a common building material. There is no *apparent* visible or known documented evidence of peeling or flaking Lead Paint on the floors, walls or ceilings (except as reported in Comments below). The only way to be certain that the property is free of surface or subsurface Lead Paint is to have it inspected by a qualified inspector.

[ ] The improvements were constructed after 1980. No *apparent* Lead Paint was observed (except as reported in Comments below).

[X] **The value estimated in this appraisal is based on the assumption that there is no flaking or peeling Lead Paint on the property.**

Comments _____

AIR POLLUTION

[X] There are no *apparent* signs of Air Pollution at the time of the inspection nor were any reported (except as reported in Comments below). The only way to be certain that the air is free of pollution is to have it tested.

[X] **The value estimated in this appraisal is based on the assumption that the property is free of Air Pollution.**

Comments _____

WETLANDS/FLOOD PLAINS

[X] The site does not contain any *apparent* Wetlands/Flood Plains (except as reported in Comments below). The only way to be certain that the site is free of Wetlands/Flood Plains is to have it inspected by a qualified environmental professional.

[X] **The value estimated in this appraisal is based on the assumption that there are no Wetlands/Flood Plains on the property (except as reported in Comments below).**

Comments _____

MISCELLANEOUS ENVIRONMENTAL HAZARDS

[X] There are no other *apparent* miscellaneous hazardous substances and/or detrimental environmental conditions on or in the area of the site except as indicated below:

- [ ] Excess Noise _____
- [ ] Radiation + Electromagnetic Radiation _____
- [ ] Light Pollution _____
- [ ] Waste Heat _____
- [ ] Acid Mine Drainage _____
- [ ] Agricultural Pollution _____
- [ ] Geological Hazards _____
- [ ] Nearby Hazardous Property _____
- [ ] Infectious Medical Wastes _____
- [ ] Pesticides _____
- [ ] Others (Chemical Storage + Storage Drums, Pipelines, etc.) _____

[X] **The value estimated in this appraisal is based on the assumption that there are no Miscellaneous environmental Hazards (except those reported above) that would negatively affect the value of the property.**

When any of the environmental assumptions made in this addendum are not correct, the estimated value in this appraisal may not be valid.

Test Version 2c FW-70EZ JANUARY 1991   © Forms & Worms, Inc. 315 Whitney Avenue New Haven, CT 06511 1-800-243-4545   Item #115050
National Association Environmental Risk Auditors

Notes

FREDDIE MAC - CHAPTER 44: APPRAISALS

Chapter 44: Appraisals (09/15/95)

44.1: General Requirements (01/31/98)

The Seller must retain with each Mortgage file a written appraisal report on the Mortgaged Premises. The report must be on the applicable Freddie Mac form (see Section 44.5), including exhibits (see Section 44.6) and any required addenda (see Section 44.7). The report must comply with all the requirements in this chapter. Freddie Mac's determination whether a report complies with its requirements will be conclusive.

Regulatory agencies may require an appraisal in some cases when Freddie Mac does not. A Seller must comply with any relevant requirements of such agencies.

With respect to each appraisal report, the Seller represents and warrants that

1. It has reviewed the appraisal report and has concluded that the Mortgaged Premises are adequate security for the Mortgage, in accordance with the requirements of Section 22.2

2. The report complies with the applicable appraisal requirements in this chapter

3. The report is of professional quality and supports all of the appraiser's assumptions, data, analyses, rationale and conclusions that were relied on in estimating the value and marketability of the Mortgaged Premises

4. The information in the report is accurate, internally consistent, written in clearly understandable language, fully supported and sufficiently documented [Page 44-2 09/15/95]

5. All information known to the Seller that may affect the estimate of value or marketability has been provided to the appraiser in conjunction with the appraisal request

Appraisals found to be deficient will be considered a breach of the Seller's warranty as to the investment quality of the Mortgage. Deficient reports will subject the Seller to the remedies available to Freddie Mac. In addition to reviewing the appraisal report submitted by the Seller, Freddie Mac may make property inspections and/or other investigations to assure property eligibility and proper underwriting of the Mortgages offered for sale to Freddie Mac.

(a) Origin of appraisal request

The appraisal report must be signed by an appraiser approved by the Seller. A Seller may not sell a Mortgage to Freddie Mac if its appraisal report is made for anyone other than the Seller or Mortgage originator. The appraiser must reasonably be perceived as impartial. Therefore, the appraiser may not have any present or contemplated future interest in the subject property, and neither current or future employment or compensation for performing the appraisal is contingent on the appraised value of the property.

(b) Date of appraisal report

The appraisal report must be dated within 120 days before the Origination Date with the following exceptions:

FREDDIE MAC - CHAPTER 44: APPRAISALS

- If the appraisal report was prepared more than 120 days but less than 12 months before the Origination Date, the original appraiser, if available, or a qualified appraiser approved by the Seller must certify that the subject property has not declined in value since the date of the original appraisal.

- If construction of the Mortgaged Premises is completed after Mortgage application, the appraisal report may be dated within 180 days before the Origination Date. [Page 44-3 08/15/94]

Under no circumstances may an appraisal report be dated more than 12 months before the Origination Date.

(c) Market value definition

The appraisal report must be based on the following definition of market value:

> The most probable price which a property should bring in a competitive and open market under all conditions requisite to a fair sale, the buyer and seller, each acting prudently, knowledgeably and assuming the price is not affected by undue stimulus. Implicit in this definition is the consummation of a sale as of a specified date and the passing of title from seller to buyer under conditions whereby: (1) buyer and seller are typically motivated; (2) both parties are well informed or well advised, and each acting in what he considers his own best interest; (3) a reasonable time is allowed for exposure in the open market; (4) payment is made in terms of cash in U.S. dollars or in terms of financial arrangements comparable thereto; and (5) the price represents the normal consideration for the property sold unaffected by special or creative financing or sales concessions* granted by anyone associated with the sale.

---

[*] Adjustments to the comparables must be made for special or creative financing or sales concessions. No adjustments are necessary for those costs which are normally paid by sellers as a result of tradition or law in a market area; these costs are readily identifiable since the seller pays these costs in virtually all sales transactions. Special or creative financing adjustments can be made to the comparable property by comparisons to financing terms offered by a third-party institutional lender that is not already involved in the property or transaction. Any adjustment should not be calculated on a mechanical dollar-for-dollar cost of the financing or concession but the dollar amount of any adjustment should approximate the market's reaction to the financing or concessions based on the appraiser's judgment.

The market value estimate of the subject property must not include value assigned to furniture or any other personal property.

(d) Residential requirements

The Mortgaged Premises must be residential, Freddie Mac does not purchase Mortgages secured by vacant land or property used primarily for agriculture, farming or commercial enterprise. [Page 44-4 08/15/94] Factors for the Seller and appraiser to consider in determining whether a property is residential include, but are not limited to,

1. The type of improvements on the subject property and neighboring properties

2. The current use of the subject property and neighboring properties

FREDDIE MAC - CHAPTER 44: APPRAISALS

3. The degree, amount and type of development occurring in the area

4. Pending zoning changes or changes in the use of properties in the area

5. Whether the subject property and neighboring properties are residential and marketable. The location of retail and office property in the neighborhood does not make the subject property ineligible.

6. Whether the land size and land-value-to-total-value ratio are typical

Example 1: A mixed-use property consisting of a one-unit residence with a small storefront. If the property is located in a residential neighborhood, on a street/block that is mostly residences, and is used as the primary residence of the owner who also runs the business, then the Seller may reasonably conclude the property is primarily residential. If that same property were to contain more than one residential unit, were located in a commercial area or on a street/block that is mostly commercial (even with similar storefronts), or if the owner did not reside in the property or leased the storefront to a business operator, then the Seller should reasonably view the property as business or commercial.

Example 2: A residential property in which the owner operates a small business, such as a child day care service or an accounting practice. If the property is located in a residential neighborhood, on a street/block that is mostly residences, and is used as the primary residence of the owner who also runs the business and the building has not been modified in a manner that has an adverse impact on its marketability as a residence, then the Seller may reasonably conclude the property is primarily residential. [Page 44-5 01/31/98]

If that same property were located in a commercial area, or on a street/block that is mostly commercial, or the owner did not reside in the property or leased part of the dwelling to a business operator, or the property had been permanently modified in a manner that had an adverse effect on its marketability as a residence, then the Seller should reasonably view the property as business or commercial.

(e) **Detrimental conditions**

The appraiser must note the presence of detrimental conditions, such as expansive soils, underground mines or subsidence in the immediate area of the subject property. In addition, the appraiser must note any evidence of dampness, infestation or abnormal settlement observed in the subject property and call for correction of the observed condition or professional inspections to determine the seriousness of the condition. The appraiser must also consider the effect of such conditions in estimating the subject property's market value and any effect on marketability.

For any appraisal report that is made subject to inspections or conditions due to detrimental conditions, the Seller must include in the Mortgage file evidence of corrective action as called for by the inspector or appraiser (such as an exterminator's certificate, engineer's report or satisfactory completion certificate) dated before the Delivery Date of the related Mortgage to Freddie Mac. (See also Section 44.8 for satisfactory completion certificate requirements.)

(f) **Limiting conditions and certification**

The Seller must have a Form 439, Statement of Limiting Conditions and Appraiser's Certification, attached to each appraisal report in each Mortgage file. Form 439 must be the version approved for use by Freddie Mac as

FREDDIE MAC - CHAPTER 44: APPRAISALS

of the date of the appraisal report and must be signed and dated by the appraiser. Form 439 reiterates the definition of market value set forth in Section 44.1(c).

(g) Maximum financing

The Seller must consider the appraiser's assessment of the trend of property values in the area in which the subject property is located and apply the requirements of Section 23.5 with respect to offering financing to the maximum loan-to-value (LTV) ratio. [Page 44-6 10/31/97]

44.2: Appraisers (10/31/97)

Freddie Mac does not select or approve individual appraisers or appraisal services. An appraiser is selected and approved by the Mortgage originator and confirmed by the Seller by warranty. The Seller warrants that the appraisal services provided, whether by fee or staff appraisers, comply with the requirements of this chapter and applicable law.

(a) Appraiser qualifications

The Seller represents and warrants that each appraisal was prepared in a professional manner. To ensure the professional preparation of an appraisal, the appraiser must

1. Be certified in a State whose criteria for certification as a real estate appraiser currently meet the minimum criteria for certification issued by the Appraiser Qualifications Board of the Appraisal Foundation, or be licensed in a State whose licensing procedures comply with the requirements of Title XI of the Financial Institutions Reform, Recovery and Enforcement Act (FIRREA), and with respect to which the Appraisal Subcommittee has not issued a finding that the policies, practices or procedures of the State are inconsistent with Title XI. (The certification and licensing requirements of the several States may become effective on different dates. Accordingly, an appraiser must comply with the certification or licensing requirements of a particular State on the effective date of those requirements in that State.)

2. Be experienced in the appraisal of properties similar to the type being appraised

3. Be actively engaged in appraisal work

4. Have successfully completed courses in real estate appraisal [Page 44-7 05/05/95]

5. Have a knowledge of current real estate market conditions and financing trends in the subject area

Note:

The Seller should be particularly attentive to selecting an appraiser who is knowledgeable of the subject area when ordering appraisal reports in central city neighborhoods and rural areas. Appraisers are more likely to use nontraditional data bases in these areas, which may be subject to complex factors influencing the value and marketability of individual properties. Appraisers who are knowledgeable in these areas should be encourage to make extensive use of comment areas to explain market factors and the status of the market.

6. Have a working knowledge of construction costs, materials, methods and standards in the area

7. Maintain a file on real estate sale transactions, including the financing involved

The Seller should maintain a file on each appraiser which documents that the appraiser has the requisite experience, education and facilities to competently perform the required assignments.

(b) Representations to third parties by appraisers or appraisal services

Appraisers and appraisal services must not make any representation to third parties as being approved by Freddie Mac.

(c) Unacceptability of appraiser

Freddie Mac, in its sole discretion, may at any time refuse to accept appraisal reports made by a particular appraiser. Once notified by Freddie Mac of the unacceptability of an appraiser, the Seller may not use that appraiser for any Mortgage submitted to Freddie Mac. [Page 44-8 05/05/95]

44.3: Information Supplied by Mortgage Originators (05/05/95)

The Seller warrants that the Mortgage originator provided the following information on the subject property, as applicable, to the appraiser in conjunction with an appraisal request:

1. The complete legal description (See Section 40.1 for legal description requirements.)

2. Current condominium association budgets

3. The complete sales contract (A sales contract on a new home should state the base price of the house and itemize each option.)

4. Income and expense statements, property leases and a list of nonrealty items that are included in the transaction

5. Any other information that the Mortgage originator knows that may affect the value or marketability of the property. This information includes an affiliation between the property seller and purchaser, proposed changes to the use of the property, and the presence of any Contaminated Site or Hazardous Substance affecting the property or the neighborhood in which the property is located.

44.4: Unacceptable Appraisal Practices (03/31/97)

The following appraisal practices are unacceptable. Any evidence in an appraisal report of any of these practices will be a breach of the Seller's warranty of the professional quality of the appraisal report:

1. The inclusion of inaccurate or incomplete data about the subject property, the neighborhood or any comparable sale used in the appraisal report

2. The failure to report and consider any apparent factor that has an adverse effect on the value and marketability

of the subject property

3. Consideration of the age or location of a dwelling or the age of the neighborhood or census tract where the dwelling is located in a manner that has a discriminatory effect

4. The reliance in the valuation analysis on comparable sales that were not personally inspected by the appraiser (A personal inspection requires at least a visual inspection of the exterior of the comparable property.) [Page 44-9 03/31/97]

5. The reliance in any valuation analyses on inappropriate comparable sales or the failure to use comparable sales that are more physically and locationally similar, without adequate explanation

6. The use of comparable sales data provided by interested parties to the transaction, without verification by a disinterested party

7. The use of inordinate adjustments for differences between the subject property and the comparable sales that do not reflect the market's reaction to such differences or the failure to make proper adjustments for adjustments when they are clearly necessary

8. Consideration of the race, color, religion, sex, handicap, familial status or national origin of the prospective owners or occupants of the subject property or of the present owners or occupants of the properties in the vicinity of the subject property (See also Section 6.2 for equal opportunity compliance requirements and Section 44.9(b) for prohibition against discrimination in appraising.)

9. The development of value and marketability conclusions that are not supported by available market data

10. The appraiser's breach of a certification on Form 439

44.5: Appraisal Forms (03/31/97)

Each appraisal report must be completed using the appraisal form approved by Freddie Mac as of the date of the appraisal. The appraiser must comply with the instructions and guidelines set forth in the appraisal forms as they apply to Mortgages eligible to be sold to Freddie Mac. Names, addresses or logos may be added to any of the following forms, and they may be printed in any color of ink. Forms generated by software programs that have expandability features to allow additional space in any of the "comments" areas are acceptable. However, the page sequence, format and content of a form may not be altered in any way. [Page 44-10 05/05/95]

(a) **Appraisal forms**

The following appraisal forms must be used for the type of property indicated:

FREDDIE MAC - CHAPTER 44: APPRAISALS

Property type	Appraisal report required
One-unit properties	Form 70, Uniform Residential Appraisal Report
Planned Unit Development (PUD) units	Form 70
Condominium Units	Form 465, Appraisal Report -- Individual Condominium or PUD Unit (Addenda A and B to Form 465 are only required on Class I Condominium Projects in accordance with the requirements in Chapter 42.)
Site condominiums (see Section 42.9)	Form 465 or Form 70 with description of project, owners association fees and project maintenance
2-4 unit properties	Form 72, Small Residential Income Property Appraisal Report

(b) Incidental second units

Form 70 is also used for properties that have a second unit that is incidental to the overall value and appearance of the subject property, provided that rental income is not being considered in Borrower qualification. Examples of such properties include a house with a unit above a detached garage and a house with a guest apartment or basement unit. The appraisal report must describe the second unit and analyze any effect on the value or marketability of the subject property.

(c) Form 1032, Residential Appraisal Field Review Report

Form 1032 is available for the review by the Seller of appraisals of 1-4 unit properties. Use of the form is not required. However, the form will help Sellers to underwrite and determine whether an [Page 44-11 03/31/97] appraisal accurately reflects market value. Form 1032 will also help Sellers to conduct quality control reviews of appraisals as required by Section 48.5(d) of the Guide.

44.6: Exhibits Required for all Appraisal Reports (03/31/97)

Each appraisal report must include as attachments the exhibits listed in this section.

(a) Photographs of the subject property

At least three clear color photographs of the subject property are required. The photographs must be originals (produced by photography or electronic imaging), must be appropriately identified and must clearly show the completed improvements. The three photographs must include

- A front view of the property

- A street scene identifying the location of the property and showing neighboring improvements

FREDDIE MAC - CHAPTER 44: APPRAISALS

- A rear view of the property

The appraiser must include additional photographs, if necessary to show clearly the improvements, amenities or external influences that have a material impact on value or marketability.

(b) Building sketch

The exterior sketch of the improvements must include the dimensions and calculations that the appraiser used to determine the size of the subject property.

While an exterior building sketch is used for detached one-unit properties and end PUD units, an interior perimeter sketch is acceptable for Condominium Units and interior PUD units. The dimensions and estimate for gross living area that are shown on the plat or exhibits to the condominium or PUD documents may be relied on to develop the sketch. Legible photocopies of floor plans or individual unit plats are acceptable alternatives to a sketch; however, the dimensions and calculations must be shown. [Page 44-12 03/31/97]

For 2-4 unit properties, the sketch must also include each unit's layout and entries and indicate the square feet of living area per unit and the gross building area (GBA) as defined on Form 72.

(c) Location map

The location map must locate the subject property and all comparable properties (including sale, rental and listing comparables, as applicable). This map may be a photocopy of a printed street map showing the location of the subject property and comparable properties in relation to major streets and influences such as parks and schools.

(d) Photographs of comparable sales

One clear color photograph of the front of each comparable sale is required. Each photograph must be an original (produced by photography or electronic imaging), must be appropriately identified and must be illustrative of the comparable sale. If an original photograph of a comparable sale cannot be obtained, a clear copy of the photograph of the comparable from a multiple listing service (MLS) brochure is acceptable. The appraisal report must reasonably justify using an MLS brochure.

44.7: Addenda Required For Certain Appraisal Reports (03/31/97)

The appraiser may determine that the appraisal report must be supplemented by addenda. In addition, Freddie Mac requires addenda for certain circumstances. When Freddie Mac requires an addendum, it must be the form approved by Freddie Mac as of the date of the appraisal report. All addenda must be attached to the appraisal report and incorporated into the report by reference.

(a) Energy addendum for energy-efficient properties

At the Seller's option, the following may be used to identify, rate and evaluate the subject property's energy-efficient features:

FREDDIE MAC - CHAPTER 44: APPRAISALS

- Evidence of compliance with the Council of American Building Officials (CABO) 1992 Model Energy Code (MEC), or

- Form 70A, Energy Addendum (Residential Appraisal Report) (Exhibit 70A), or [Page 44-13 09/15/95]

- A report from an established Home Energy Rating System (HERS) sponsored by a local utility, home builder association, or a state or local government

See Section 44.11 for guidance on energy-efficient properties.

(b) Operating income statement

For 2-4 unit owner-occupied properties, Freddie Mac requires Form 998, Operating Income Statement, to verify the income attributed to the property. This form should be completed by the Borrower, analyzed and adjusted by the appraiser and further reviewed and adjusted (if necessary) by the Mortgage originator. (This form is not required for a two-unit property that is totally occupied by the Borrowers.)

(c) Earthquake Insurance Analysis Addendum

For a Mortgage secured by a Condominium Unit in a California moderate-risk zip code, Freddie Mac requires Form 465S, Earthquake Insurance Analysis Addendum, to evaluate the subject property's structure for earthquake insurance needs. This form must be completed by the appraiser.

44.8: Satisfactory Completion Certificate (09/15/95)

For appraisal reports made subject to repairs, alterations or conditions or subject to completion in accordance with plans and specifications, the Seller must include a satisfactory completion certificate in the Mortgage file. The certificate must be dated before the Delivery Date of the Mortgage to Freddie Mac unless an Escrow account has been established in accordance with the requirements of Section 22.17 or 23.8. See Form 442, Satisfactory Completion Certificate, for a suggested format for a completion certificate. The certification must

- Be made after completion of the repairs, improvements, alterations, conditions or construction

- Clearly state that all conditions or requirements set forth in the original appraisal report of the Mortgaged Premises have been fulfilled

- Be prepared and signed by the original appraiser, if available, or by another qualified appraiser approved by the Seller

See also Section 44.1(e) for documentation requirements for detrimental conditions. [Page 44-14 09/15/95]

44.9: Property Description and Analysis on the Appraisal Report (01/31/98)

The appraisal report must be completed in a manner that correctly depicts or describes the neighborhood, site and improvements. The Seller should encourage the appraiser to make extensive use of the "comments" areas of the appraisal forms and/or to attach addenda as necessary to ensure the completeness of the report and the presentation

FREDDIE MAC - CHAPTER 44: APPRAISALS

of those factors which influence value and marketability of homes in the area. The appraiser should be encouraged to provide specific information on market conditions and developing trends in the neighborhood whenever possible. While the following sections correspond primarily to Form 70, all of the requirements and guidelines also apply to the other appraisal forms unless otherwise stated in this chapter.

(a) Subject section

This section must clearly identify the subject property. Clarity is accomplished by providing a complete property address and legal description. If a legal description is lengthy, it should be attached to the report.

The "property rights appraised" must be identified as either a fee simple or leasehold. The sales price, contract date and loan charges paid by, or financing and sales concessions made by, the property seller must be set forth as stated in the sales contract.

(b) Neighborhood section

The neighborhood analysis must contain an accurate description of the subject neighborhood and the factors that influence market value and marketability in the neighborhood. The information presented in the neighborhood analysis must be complete and must be consistent with, and support, the conclusions reached by the appraiser throughout the appraisal report. For example, if the subject property is a residential mixed-use property, such as a storefront, then neighborhood analysis must demonstrate that the neighborhood is primarily residential and that storefront/mixed-use properties are acceptable residences in the neighborhood.

Unfavorable factors revealed in the neighborhood analysis require the appraiser to address the impact of those factors on value and marketability. If the appraisal report demonstrates that there is a viable market for housing in the neighborhood or that the [Page 44-15 05/05/95] neighborhood is undergoing revitalization, the unfavorable factors do not necessarily make the Mortgage ineligible for sale to Freddie Mac. An appraiser may use a block-by-block analysis in neighborhoods that have undergone significant deterioration or abandonment in the past, but are now undergoing an evident revitalization effort, to demonstrate that there is a viable market for housing. In this analysis, the appraiser should describe the extent of revitalization efforts under way, the demand evidenced for renovated housing and the boundaries of the revitalized area being used as the subject neighborhood. This analysis must be consistent with the data presented and support the conclusions reached by the appraiser throughout the report.

If the appraiser has selected comparables from a competing neighborhood, the appraiser must identify the competing neighborhood in this section and describe why it is comparable to the subject neighborhood. The appraiser should focus on those factors that establish the similarities in the markets served and why the competing neighborhood is a more relevant source of comparables at this time than the subject neighborhood.

The appraiser must certify that the estimate of market value in the appraisal report is not based on the race, color, sex, handicap, familial status, religion or national origin of

- The prospective owners or occupants of the subject property, or

- The present owners or occupants of the properties in the vicinity of the subject property

In addition, the appraisal must not improperly take into consideration the property modifications made to accommodate handicapped persons, or the age or location of a dwelling, or the age of the neighborhood or

FREDDIE MAC - CHAPTER 44: APPRAISALS

census tract where the dwelling is located.

As a matter of corporate policy, Freddie Mac will not accept any Mortgage supported by an appraisal report that makes reference to the race, color, religion or national origin of any person, or the age or racial composition of the neighborhood. (See Section 44.4 for unacceptable appraisal practices.) [Page 44-16 05/05/95]

(c) Site section

This section must accurately describe the physical characteristics of the site, site improvements and available utilities and must fully analyze any locational factors affecting the site.

- **Zoning classification and compliance:** The appraisal report must accurately state the zoning classification and whether the use of the subject property complies with the reported classification. The use of the Mortgaged Premises must conform to applicable zoning and use restrictions and enable the Mortgage to qualify as a Home Mortgage. Freddie Mac may, however, purchase a Home Mortgage secured by property that does not conform to applicable zoning and use restrictions, provided that the property is a legal use (commonly referred to as legal nonconforming use). The appraiser must comment on any adverse effect of any nonconforming use when estimating the market value and marketability of the property.

  Freddie Mac's policy on legal nonconforming Condominium Projects is found in Section 42.1.

  Zoning requirements cannot be the basis for classifying a project as a PUD.

- **Utilities:** The utilities serving the subject property must meet community standards. In addition, the comparable sales should have utilities similar to the subject property. When differences in utilities exist between the subject property and the comparable sales, any adjustments made to the comparable sales, or lack of adjustments, for significant differences must be explained in the comments area. In addition, the appraisal report must evaluate the effect these differences have on the subject property's value or marketability. [Page 44-17 10/15/96]

- **Streets:** The subject property must have legally appropriate ingress and egress. The streets serving the subject property must be maintained in a manner that generally meets community standards. In addition, the comparable sales should have street maintenance similar to the subject property. When differences exist between the ownership or maintenance of the subject property's streets and the comparable sale's streets, adjustments made to the comparable sale, or lack of adjustments, for the differences must be explained in the comments area. In addition, the appraisal report must evaluate the effect these differences have on the subject property's value or marketability.

- **Flood hazard:** The appraisal report must indicate whether the dwelling on the subject property lies within a "Special Flood Hazard Area" (SFHA) as identified by the Federal Emergency Management Agency (FEMA) through the National Flood Insurance Program (NFIP). The flood zone, flood map number and map date must also be stated.(See Section 58.3 for flood insurance requirements.)

  The appraiser need not complete this section if the flood zone is determined by another party, such as a nonappraiser on the staff of the Seller, a surveyor or a specialized flood zone determination company. If the flood zone determination is not made by an appraiser, the resulting flood zone documentation must contain at least the flood hazard information required in the appraisal report and must be attached to the appraisal report. The Seller warrants that any flood zone determination made on or after June 1, 1995, by a party other than the Seller is guaranteed by the flood zone determination maker to be accurate, in accordance with federal law. The Seller, however, remains responsible to Freddie Mac for the accuracy of any flood zone determination made by the Seller or a party other than the Seller.

Any flood zone determination made by any party on or after January 2, 1996, must be documented by a completed FEMA Standard Flood Hazard Determination, FEMA Form 81-93, dated June 1995, (Standard Flood Hazard Determination Form (SFHDF), Exhibit 13) in accordance with federal law. The SFHDF may be used in printed, computerized or electronic format. If an electronic format is used, the exact format and layout of the SFHDF are not required, but all the fields and elements not identified as optional on the SFHDF are required. At the option of the flood zone determination maker, the SFHDF may be used before January 2, 1996. [Page 44-18 10/15/96]

- **Additional parcels:** When the subject property includes two or more adjoining parcels of real estate, the site description must accurately describe the land and any improvements included in each of the parcels. In addition, the comparable sales should have adjoining parcels similar to the subject property. When differences in sites exist between the subject property and the comparable sales, any adjustments made to the comparable sales, or lack of adjustments, for significant differences must be explained in the comments area. In addition, the appraisal report must evaluate the effect these differences have on the subject property's value or marketability (see also Section 44.1(d)).

(d) Description of improvements

The appraisal report must contain an accurate description of the improvements and any factors that may affect the market value or marketability of the subject property. Freddie Mac does not provide minimum specifications for materials and construction. An unusual floor plan, such as a home with tandem bedrooms or a bathroom off the kitchen, does not make a property ineligible for financing. The appraiser should address whether the floor plan or similar obsolescence is also found in other properties in the neighborhood.

When the subject property does not conform to its neighborhood in terms of type, design, age, and the materials and techniques used in its construction, the appraisal must evaluate the effect the nonconformance has on the property's value and marketability. The appraisal must not improperly take into consideration the age of the dwelling. (See Section 44.4 for unacceptable appraisal practices.)

Other requirements and conditions relating to the improvements are the following:

- The property must be habitable as a year-round residence. The improvement analysis must indicate how the subject property compares to competing properties in the subject neighborhood.

- Freddie Mac does not require an estimate of remaining economic life. [Page 44-19 01/31/98]

(e) Impact of Contaminated Sites, Hazardous Substances and other adverse conditions

The appraiser must consider any known Contaminated Sites or Hazardous Substances that affect the property or the neighborhood in which the property is located. The appraiser must also note the presence of Contaminated Sites or Hazardous Substances in the appraisal report, make any appropriate adjustments to market value to reflect them, and comment on the effect they have on the marketability or value of the subject property.

Examples of matters about which the appraiser must note and comment include, but are not limited to,

FREDDIE MAC - CHAPTER 44: APPRAISALS

- Any presence of asbestos, urea-formaldehyde or any similar insulation in the dwelling

- Proximity of the property and/or its neighborhood to a Contaminated Site

- Proximity of the property to ground water contamination, chemical or petroleum spills or other Hazardous Substances that are expected to impact the area for more than one year

The appraiser must also comment on, and consider the impact on the value of the property of, the proximity of the property to areas that may affect the value or marketability of the property, including, but not limited to, the following:

1. Industrial sites

2. Waste or water treatment facilities

3. Commercial establishments (other than retail establishments that serve the residential neighborhood)

4. Airport approach paths

5. Floodplains

6. Landslide areas

(f) **Comments section**

Any additional features; necessary repairs or modernization; or physical, functional or external inadequacies must be reported in the "comments" sections of the form. Repairs that are not cosmetic must be completed prior to delivery of the Mortgage to Freddie Mac. Cosmetic repairs, defined as those not affecting the safety, structural integrity, mechanical [Page 44-20 10/31/97] systems or habitability of the improvements, need not be repaired as long as the appraisal is not made subject to repairs and as long as the appraiser has addressed whether the condition affects the value or marketability of the property and made any necessary adjustments to the comparables. Examples of cosmetic repairs include: worn floor coverings, minor cracks in windows, minor holes in interior walls or interior doors, etc. If the appraiser notes that additions or alterations were made without required permits, the comments section should also contain comments on the quality and appearance of the work. In addition, a comments section is provided for the appraiser to note special energy-efficient items and adverse environmental conditions.

If the property has been modified to accommodate mixed use, the appraiser should address whether the modifications affect the property's marketability as a residence and whether the cost to restore the property to solely residential use will affect its value.

44.10: Property Valuation on the Appraisal Report (Page 2 of Form 70) (12/15/97)

The appraisal report must support the appraiser's estimate of market value using three approaches to value, unless this chapter specifies that a particular approach is not required. The approaches used in the report, or explanations for nonuse, must be consistent with other information presented in the report and included in the Mortgage file.

FREDDIE MAC - CHAPTER 44: APPRAISALS

(a) **Cost approach**

The cost approach is required only for new properties, for properties that are unique because of their styles or construction methods, or for properties that have functional obsolescence. The cost approach is not required for appraisals of Condominium Units or attached PUD units. Whether or not the cost approach is used, the estimated site value must be included for all detached properties. The cost approach must include proper adjustments for any items detrimental to stability or marketability, such as physical, functional and external depreciation.

Appraisal reports that rely solely on the cost approach for the market value estimate are unacceptable. [Page 44-21 12/15/97]

(b) **Sales comparison analysis section**

Freddie Mac considers the sales comparison approach to be the most reliable approach to value; therefore, a Seller must place primary emphasis on this approach when reviewing and judging the acceptability of each appraisal report.

At least three verified, closed (settled) sales of comparable properties must be analyzed on the appraisal report, with adjustments made for significant differences between the comparable sales and the subject property. Additional comparables, in the form of closed or under contract sales or current listings, may be used to support the appraiser's adjustments and conclusions, address changes in the market, support the use of older comparables in stable neighborhoods or support the use of distant or less similar comparables in rural areas. Additional comparables are not always needed, but may contribute significantly to understanding unusual situations, such as limited markets, neighborhoods with little turnover of property and areas with a variety of distinct property types. For example, if the subject property is mixed-use, such as a storefront residence, then additional comparables may be needed to support the appraiser's conclusion that the property is primarily residential, the value is based on residential use and there is a ready acceptance of such properties as residences.

At least three of the comparable sales listed in the report must be

- Similar to and located near the subject property

- Recently sold (If the sale of a comparable property occurred more than 12 months before the date of the appraisal, the appraiser must justify in the appraisal report the use of the comparable property.)

- One whose closing (settlement) occurred before the date of the appraisal for the subject property

Each comparable sale must be analyzed for similarities and differences between it and the subject property. The appraiser must make appropriate adjustments for differences and indicate the dollar amount of the adjustments. Comparable sales must be adjusted to the subject property (except for sales and financing concessions, which are adjusted to the market at the time of sale). [Page 44-22 12/15/97]

Comparables may be taken from a competing neighborhood as long as the appraiser has established that the neighborhoods are comparable and compete for the same buyers and that comparables taken from this neighborhood are better indicators of current market trends in the subject neighborhood than the existing comparables available in the subject neighborhood.

FREDDIE MAC - CHAPTER 44: APPRAISALS

For properties located in established subdivisions or for units in established condominium or PUD projects (those that have resale activity), the appraisal report may use three comparable sales from within that subject project or subdivision. However, if the subject property is in a controlled market (such as a new subdivision or project, a newly converted project or an area where the property seller owns a substantial number of units), at least one comparable sale must be outside the influence of the developer, builder or property seller. Resales from within the subject project or subdivision may be used to meet this requirement. When comparable sales from outside the subject project or subdivision are used, they must also be outside the influence of the subject property's developer, builder or property seller.

(c) **Income approach**

The income approach is seldom applicable for sales of owner-occupied, one-unit properties.

(d) **Reconciliation**

The reconciliation must contain any conditions of the appraisal on which the final estimate of value is based. The rationale in the final reconciliation must be consistent with the comments, conclusions and assumptions stated throughout the appraisal report. The report must state that the current Form 439 is attached and must contain

- The date of the value estimate

- The estimate of market value

- The appraiser's name, signature and State certification or license number [Page 44-23 12/15/97]

44.11: Energy-Efficient Properties (12/15/97)

An energy-efficient property uses cost-effective design, construction, materials, equipment and site orientation to conserve energy, consistent with the climate of the area in which the property is located. Items that contribute to the energy efficiency of a property include, but are not limited to, the following:

1. Insulation with adequate R-values installed in ceilings, exterior walls and roofs; around hot water heaters; under floors that cover unheated areas; and surrounding ducts and pipes that are not air-conditioned

2. Caulking and weatherstripping

3. Double- or triple-paned windows

4. Window shading or landscaping for solar control

5. Storm doors and windows

6. Automatic setback thermostats

7. Heating, cooling and lighting systems and appliances designed to be energy-efficient

FREDDIE MAC - CHAPTER 44: APPRAISALS

8. Solar systems for water heating, space heating and cooling

9. Wood-fired heating systems (using outside combustion air)

10. Building designs that minimize energy use, such as reduced window areas and earth sheltering

The appraisal report must list the energy-efficient items in the subject property and note their contribution to the value for the Mortgage to receive the special underwriting consideration allowed under Section 37.16. (See Section 44.7(a) for addendum requirements.)

44.12: PUD Units (12/15/97)

The appraisal form (Form 70) must describe the subject project and any common property. It must also identify and analyze any differences between the amenities and monthly unit charge of the subject property and the comparable properties, if the comparable properties are from competing projects. The appraisal form must include the project name for the subject project. (See the definition of PUD Unit in Section 43.1.) **[Page 44-24 12/15/97]**

44.13: Condominium Units (12/15/97)

The appraisal report for Condominium Units (Form 465) requires the appraiser to analyze project information and individual unit data in estimating the condominium's marketability and market value. The appraiser must also report the project name, amenities, unit charge and the property rights for each comparable sale and must compare them to the subject property in the market data analysis. (See the definition of condominium in Chapter 42.)

44.14: 2-4 Unit Properties (Form 72) (12/15/97)

In addition to the requirements and guidelines set forth in Sections 44.9-44.13, the following requirements and guidelines are applicable to completing Form 72 for 2-4 unit properties.

(a) Comparable rent data

At least three rental comparables must be analyzed in the "comparable rental data" section. These rental comparables must

- Have current rental information

- Be units similar to and located near the subject property

The rental comparables are usually not the same comparable properties used in the market data approach. The appraisal report should state that the units and properties selected as rental comparables are comparable to the subject property (both the units and the overall property) and should accurately represent the rental market for the subject property unless otherwise stated in the report.

(b) Subject's rent schedule

This section contains the subject property's current actual rents and the estimated rents. The estimated rents for the subject property must be supported in the appraisal report and be consistent with the data presented throughout the report.

(c) Sales comparison analysis

In addition to the requirements in Section 44.10(b) of the Guide, the appraisal must contain the unadjusted units of comparison for the comparable sales. If the appraisal is prepared in conjunction with a sales transaction, the units of comparison must be provided [Page 44-25 12/15/97] for the subject property as well. These units of comparison are the sales price per GBA, per unit and per room and the gross rent multiplier (GRM). The comment area of the sales comparison analysis must reconcile the adjusted sales prices of the comparable sales and the unadjusted units of comparison, as appropriate, according to the manner in which such properties sell in the defined market area.

The appraiser must indicate in the comments area what factors are deemed most consistent and what factors typical investors or purchasers in that market consider when purchasing a similar property. [Page 44-26 12/15/97]

{Page 44-26 is blank.}

Notes

Proven Appraisal Teaching Packages
Henry S. Harrison's
Pre License & Certification Courses - Seminars

Harrison's Appraisal Books: the BEST value for your students!

America's favorite appraisal author provides everything you need to present his successful courses and seminars!

Course Texts • Seminar Modules • Instructors Manuals • Course Outlines

PLUS Free Overheads, Exams and Answers

PRE LICENSE & CERTIFICATION COURSES 30 ~ 60 hrs	CONTINUING ED SEMINARS 6 ~ 8 hours

Residential Appraising
(30-60 hours)

Basic Income Property Appraising
(30 hours)

Advanced Income Property Appraising
(30 hrs)

FHA License Preparation
(15 hours)

Instructors: Review Copies available upon request.

How to Fill Out the URAR Report
How to Fill Out the Small Income Report
How to Fill Out the Condominium Report
Yield Capitalization
Internal Rate of Return
Environmental Hazards
Narrative Report Writing
Valuation of Partial Interests
Testifying as an Expert Witness
Basic House Construction
Screening for Environmental Hazards (16-30 hrs)

1-800-243-4545

1-800-275-1075

forms & worms
7644 West 78th Street
Minneapolis, MN 55439

www.formsandworms.com
info@formsandworms.com
Order Online 24/7

The MOST POPULAR line-by-line appraisal guides in America...

by Henry S. Harrison

Harrison's Illustrated Guide
How to make a Single Family Appraisal on the **Uniform Residential URAR Appraisal Report**
FHLMC Form 70-FNMA Form 1004 Revised 6/93

Super Line-by-Line Guide

This line-by-line *Illustrated Guide* includes:
- Full Case Study and Model Appraisal
- Current Guidelines from Fannie Mae, Freddie Mac, HUD/FHA, VA
- Model Comments and Consistency Checks
- 400 Pages
- 230 Illustrations

Over 200,000 sold

Henry S. Harrison, MAI, SRPA, ... DREI

Single Family Appraisal
ITEM #300280 $34.95
PLUS SHIPPING

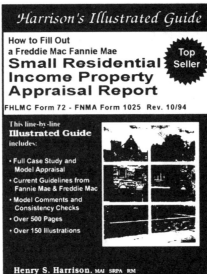

Harrison's Illustrated Guide
How to Fill Out a Freddie Mac Fannie Mae **Small Residential Income Property Appraisal Report**
FHLMC Form 72 - FNMA Form 1025 Rev. 10/94

Top Seller

This line-by-line *Illustrated Guide* includes:
- Full Case Study and Model Appraisal
- Current Guidelines from Fannie Mae & Freddie Mac
- Model Comments and Consistency Checks
- Over 500 Pages
- Over 150 Illustrations

Henry S. Harrison, MAI SRPA RM

Never be at a loss for what to write again!

* Every line is completed with sample answers, for total clarity
* Sample appraisals are included with concrete examples
* You'll know *exactly* what is required to complete each form properly!

Harrisons Illustrated Dictionary of Real Estate & Appraisal
top rated
Spanish – English
Español – Inglés

Henry S. Harrison & Julie Harrison
MAI, SRPA, RM, IFAS, CSA, DREI   Attorney at Law

Over 300 pages with 500 illustrations and 2,500 terms defined in English and Spanish. The perfect reference book for everyone in the real estate field. Takes you from A to Z in the most important two languages in America today!! A superior reference book!

Spanish/English Dictionary
Item #300310 $34.95
PLUS SHIPPING

ENGLISH ONLY DICTIONARY
ITEM #300300 $24.95
PLUS SHIPPING

A hit for over 25 years !!
HOUSES: The Illustrated Guide Construction, Design & System

The number one guide to sing family homes in the country, th classic book covers it all: desig construction details, architectur styles and the latest in hom improvement, as well as comm environmental hazards.

HOUSES
ITEM #300150 $35.00
PLUS SHIPPING

Avoid COSTLY liability errors with proper environmental screening know-how...

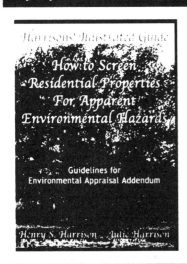

Harrisons' Illustrated Guide
How to Screen Residential Properties For Apparent Environmental Hazards
Guidelines for Environmental Appraisal Addendum
Henry S. Harrison Julie Harrison

Harrison's Illustrated Guide is a comprehensive guide to state-of-the-art screening for environmental hazards. This resource can help you and your staff take appropriate precautions when appraising any residential property.

Shows how to complete a custom environmental addendum which you can use to protect your business.

ENVIRONMENTAL SCREENING GUIDE
ITEM #300120 $34.95
PLUS SHIPPING

You can become an FHA Appraiser
25,000 appraisers have passed. *You can t*

HARRISON'S ILLUSTRATED GUIDE
How to Pass the HUD/FHA Appraiser Qualification Examination

INCLUDES ALL 200 QUESTIONS
with Explanat...
4 Practice Exams with Answer Sheets
Complete HUD/FHA Handbook 4150.2

HENRY S. HARRISON
MAI, SRPA, RM, ASA, IFAS, CSA, DREI

HUD/FHA EXAM PREP
ITEM #300380 $34.95
PLUS SHIPPING

HARRISON'S ILLUSTRATED GUIDE
HOW TO MAKE AN FHA SINGLE FAMILY APPRAIS...

1st edition
-line TED GUIDE includes:
Full Case Study and Model Appraisal
Current Guidelines from HUD/FHA Handbook 4150.2
Model Comments and Consistency Checks
450 Pages
230 Illustrations

HENRY S. HARRISON

FHA APPRAISAL GUID
ITEM #300420 $34.9
PLUS SHIPPING

Forms & Worms • 7644 West 78th Street • Minneapolis, MN 55439
Phone 1-800-243-4545 • Fax 1-800-275-1075 • www.formsandworms.com

Textbooks ~ Illustrated Guides ~ Seminars
by Henry S. Harrison ... America's Favorite Appraisal Author

The proven way to help your students
pass their appraisal licensing and certification exams.

TEXTBOOK WITH FREE CD
ITEM #300800
$ 34.95 PLUS SHIPPING

Q & A WITH 4 PRACTICE EXAMS
ITEM # 300410
$ 34.95 PLUS SHIPPING

STUDENT WORKBOOK
ITEM #300850
$ 19.95 PLUS SHIPPING

APPRAISING RESIDENCES & INCOME PROPERTIES WITH FREE CD-ROM

- Leading Appraisal Textbook
- 60-90 hours of course material
- FREE interactive CD
  includes Student Workbook
- Covers residential & income
- Down-to-earth & readable
- Indexed and comprehensive
- Excellent reference book

1001 Q & A: HOW TO PASS ANY GENERAL OR RESIDENTIAL APPRAISAL EXAM

- Over 500 pages of exam prep!
- 4 practice exams
  (2 General & 2 Residential)
- 1001 sample test questions
- Exam answers keyed to text for easy review
- Fully illustrated glossary
- Proven test-taking techniques

APPRAISING RESIDENCES & INCOME PROPERTIES: STUDENT WORKBOOK

- Companion Workbook
- Outlines for each chapter
- How to Read a House Plan
- Case studies
- Drill problems included
- Review questions
- Ideal student enrichment

INSTRUCTORS: Everything you need to teach the most popular and successful appraisal pre-licensing and certification courses in the country. The basic text, ***Appraising Residences and Income Properties*** has ample material for 60-90 hours of basic appraisal education (except USPAP). It comes with a FREE CD-Rom with the complete text *plus* the companion **Student Workbook**, which is also available in a print edition. Many students also purchase our acclaimed license review book, ***How to Pass any General or Residential Appraisal Examination (1001 Questions & Answers)***. We provide everything you need to get started: free course outlines for state approvals, instructors guides, a set of 130 overheads and practice exams with answers for the instructors.

1-800-243-4545

1-800-275-1075

forms & worms
7644 West 78th Street
Minneapolis, MN 55439

www.formsandworms.com
info@formsandworms.com
Order Online 24/7

Instructor's Materials — Order Form — Appraisal Books

Pre License & Certifications Courses

Pre-License & Certification Courses (30-90 hours)

Quan	Item#	Description	Price	Amount
	300800	Appraising Residence & Income Prop. + CD-Rom	$ 34.95	
	300850	Appraising Residence & Income Prop. Workbook	19.95	
	320050	ARIP Instructor's Manual (looseleaf w/tabs) ❶	50.00	
	320051	Residential Course Outline ❶	Free	
	320052	Basic & Advanced Income Course Outline ❶	Free	
	320053	Examination "Residential" w/answers ❶	Free	
	320054	Examination "Income" w/answers ❶	Free	
	320121	ARIP: Overheads Only ❶	90.00	

Continuing Education Seminars

Fannie Mae URAR & Small Income Property Seminars • 8-16 hours

Quan	Item#	Description	Price	Amount
	300280	How to Fill out the URAR	$ 34.95	
	320075	URAR Instructors Manual ❶	50.00	
	300070	Small Residential Income Property	34.95	

Advanced Appraisal Continuing Ed Seminars • 6-8 Hours

Quan	Item#	Description	Price	Amount
	320100	Instructor's Manual (all 6 modules) ❶	$ 50.00	
	388100	Yield Capitalization ❖	19.95	
	388110	Internal Rate of Return ❖	19.95	
	388120	Valuation of Partial Interest ❖	19.95	
	388130	Narrative Report Writing ❖	19.95	
	388140	Testifying in Court ❖	19.95	
	388150	Environmental Hazards ❖	19.95	

How to Screen for Environmental Hazards • 6-30 Hours

Quan	Item#	Description	Price	Amount
	320090	Environmental Instructor's Manual & Exams ❶	$ 50.00	
	300120	How to Screen for Environmental Hazards	34.95	

Exam Preparation & Reference Books

Quan	Item#	Description	Price	Amount
	300410	1001 Q&A: Pass License/Certification Exams	$ 34.95	
	300300	Illustrated Dictionary of R.E. & Appraisal	24.95	
	300310	Dictionary of R.E. Appraisal Spanish/English	34.95	
	300380	How to Pass the HUD/FHA Exam	34.95	
	300420	How to make an FHA Single Family Appraisal	34.95	
	300822	Advanced Appraisal Methods	34.95	

❶ See "Instructors Materials" for details   ❖ Not subject to discount

Discounts

Available on orders of 5 books or more of the same title

20% Discount: 30 days net; 90-day return privileges; Shipping billed
30% Discount: Prepaid; Non-returnable; Shipping billed

❖ Not Subject to Discount   ❶ See *Instructors' Materials* below

Shipping Chart

ORDER TOTAL	SHIPPING
$ .01 - 45.00	$ 6.00
$ 45.01 - 75.00	$ 8.00
$ 75.01 - 100.00	$ 10.00
$ 100.01 - 150.00	$ 16.00
$ 150.01 - 200.00	$ 18.00
$ 200.01 - 300.00	$ 24.00
$ 300.01 - 500.00	$ 39.00
$ 500.01 - more	$ 59.00

Review Copy Policy: 60 days *free* review. After 60 days, if not adopted or returned, an invoice is issued for the full price of the book (no S&H charged).

❶ **Instructors' Materials:** If the book is adopted, the Instructor's Manual is free. Overheads are available for 90 days *free* use, or purchase at our cost of $50 per set. Instructors who do not adopt our books will be charged $50 per Instructor's Manual and $ 90 for overheads.

Books for Appraisers by Henry S. Harrison

Harrison's Illustrated Line-by-Line Guides

Quan	Item#	Description	Price	Amount
	300280	How to Fill Out the URAR Single Family Form	$ 34.95	
	300070	How to Fill Out Small Res. Income Prop. Form	34.95	
	300420	How to Make an FHA Single Family Appraisal	34.95	

Appraisal Textbooks

Quan	Item#	Description	Price	Amount
	300800	Appraising Residences & Income Prop.+ CD-Rom	$ 34.95	
	300850	Appraising Residences & Income Prop. Workbook	19.95	
	300822	Advanced Appraisal Methods	34.95	

Exam Preparation

Quan	Item#	Description	Price	Amount
	300410	1001 Q&A: Pass License/Certification Exams	$ 34.95	
	300380	How to Pass the HUD/FHA Exam	34.95	

Real Estate Books & Dictionaries

Quan	Item#	Description	Price	Amount
	300150	HOUSES: Illustrated Guide to Construction	$ 35.00	
	300300	Illustrated Dictionary of R.E. & Appraisal	24.95	
	300310	Dictionary of R.E. Appraisal Spanish/English	34.95	

Environmental Guide

Quan	Item#	Description	Price	Amount
	300120	How to Screen for Apparent Env. Hazards	$ 34.95	

Total purchases	
Less discount or credit (see *Discounts*)	—
Shipping (see *Shipping Chart*)	
Subtotal	
State Sales Tax: MN add 6.5% & MA add 5.0%	
GRAND TOTAL	

Order Form

Name _____ Cust. # _____
Address: _____
Address: _____
City: _____ State: _____ Zip: _____
Phone #: _____
Fax #: _____ PO #: _____
Email address: _____
Special instructions: _____

Instructor's Supplemental Information

School: _____
Date classes begin: _____
☐ Please send me _____ free Student Kits
☐ Ask Henry S. Harrison to contact me.
Special instructions: _____

PAYMENT OPTIONS

☐ *Please Charge My Credit Card:*
☐ Visa ☐ MasterCard ☐ Amex ☐ Discover
Acct # _____ Exp: ___/___
Cardholder's Name (please print) _____
Signature _____
☐ Check Enclosed ☐ Please bill me. ☐ C.O.D. (add **extra** $ 7.00

forms & worms
7644 West 78th Street
Minneapolis, MN 55439

www.formsandworms.com
info@formsandworms.com
Order Online 24/7

1-800-243-4545

1-800-275-1075